# Pillsbury Christmas 2011

published by

Taste of Home Books
Reiman Media Group, LLC
5400 S. 60th St., Greendale WI 53129

Taste of Home® is a registered trademark of Reiman Media Group, LLC

Bake-Off® is a registered trademark of General Mills.

All recipes were previously published in a slightly different form.

Front Cover Photograph:
Almond Holly Wreaths p. 200,
Polvorones Cookies p. 213,
Dipped Cream Cheese Strawberries p. 242,
Peppermint Mousse Cups p. 248,
Chocolate Swirl Almond Toffee p. 294.

Title Page Photograph:
Marshmallow Santas p. 271.

Back Cover Photographs:
Herb-Stuffed Flank Steak p. 111,
Honeyed Pumpkin Pie with Broiled Praline Topping p. 251,
Cranberry-Orange Biscotti p. 299,
White Chocolate Gingerbread Bears p. 285,
Chicken Crescent Pot Stickers p. 16.

GENERAL MILLS, INC.
EDITORIAL DIRECTOR: Jeff Nowak
PUBLISHING MANAGER: Christine Gray
COOKBOOK EDITOR: Grace Wells
EDITORIAL ASSISTANT: Kelly Gross
DIGITAL ASSETS MANAGER: Carrie Jacobson
RECIPE DEVELOPMENT AND TESTING: Pillsbury Test Kitchens
PHOTOGRAPHY: General Mills Photography Studio

REIMAN MEDIA GROUP, LLC
EDITOR-IN-CHIEF: Catherine Cassidy
VICE PRESIDENT, EXECUTIVE EDITOR/BOOKS: Heidi Reuter Lloyd
CREATIVE DIRECTOR: Howard Greenberg
SENIOR EDITOR/BOOKS: Mark Hagen
EDITOR: Krista Lanphier
ASSOCIATE CREATIVE DIRECTOR: Edwin Robles Jr.
ART DIRECTOR: Jessie Sharon
CONTENT PRODUCTION MANAGER: Julie Wagner
LAYOUT DESIGNER: Kathy Crawford
COPY CHIEF: Deb Warlaumont Mulvey
COPY EDITOR: Susan Uphill
COVER PHOTOGRAPHY: Reiman Media Group Photo Studio
    PHOTOGRAPHER: Jim Wieland
    FOOD STYLIST: Sarah Thompson
    SET STYLIST: Dee Dee Jacq

NORTH AMERICAN CHIEF MARKETING OFFICER: Lisa Karpinski
VICE PRESIDENT, BOOK MARKETING: Dan Fink
CREATIVE DIRECTOR/CREATIVE MARKETING: Jim Palmen

READER'S DIGEST ASSOCIATION
PRESIDENT AND CHIEF EXECUTIVE OFFICER: Tom Williams
EXECUTIVE VICE PRESIDENT, RDA, AND PRESIDENT,
NORTH AMERICA: Dan Lagani

International Standard Book Number (10): 0-89821-908-6
International Standard Book Number (13): 978-0-89821-908-1
International Standard Serial Number: 1930-1685
Printed in U.S.A.

For additional holiday recipes and other delicious dishes, visit
*Pillsbury.com*.

# contents

Merry Snacks & Beverages    6

Christmas Breads & Baked Goods    38

Seasonal Soups, Sides & Salads    62

Yuletide Entrees    92

Holiday Open House    136

Cozy Christmas Breakfast    174

Festive Cookies & Bars    198

Wintry Desserts    234

Jolly Kitchen Creations    268

Gifts of Good Taste    290

# Come Celebrate the Spirit of Christmas!

*Revel in the holiday* season with your loved ones and tables full of hearty, mouthwatering food. All the recipes you need are right here in *Pillsbury Christmas 2011!*

p. 66

p. 273

p. 274

p. 168

p. 8

*It's that magical time of year* when family and friends gather around the table with platters full of fabulous food and goodies. Here's a way for you to commemorate special occasions this holiday season with hundreds of sensational recipes that guarantee your get-togethers will be bright and cheery!

Whether you host elegant dinners meant to impress, cozy get-togethers featuring comforting favorites or casual parties with appetizer buffets, Pillsbury Christmas 2011 promises to be your go-to recipe source. Take a look inside at the *300+ crowd-pleasing recipes* that will make both casual and elegant dinner parties easier than ever.

p. 109

*For over 100 years*, family cooks have turned to Pillsbury to make mealtime memorable, especially when the holiday season rolls around. The fifth edition of this cookbook, Pillsbury Christmas, offers all of the savory dishes and scrumptious delights to make your Christmas menu sparkle, including savory entrees, fantastic side dishes, crowd-pleasing hors d'oeuvres, show-stopping desserts and much, much more.

With a total of 10 chapters, this keepsake collection offers everything a busy cook needs to make the holidays special! From snappy appetizers and stunning entrees to buttery cookies and luscious desserts, plus everything in between, each recipe includes easy-to-follow instructions so your holiday menus come together smoothly.

For those who enjoy adding a personal touch to their gifts, browse through the "Jolly Kitchen Creations" and "Gifts of Good Taste" chapters. You'll discover how festive cookies, breads, treats and more make perfect Christmas presents for the ones you love.

*You can take comfort* in knowing that each recipe was tested in the Pillsbury Kitchen, so it meets our standards of easy preparation, reliability and great taste. And for additional insurance, we've included many of our Bake-Off® Contest winners…so you know you're preparing the best of the best!

We've also included *cook's notes* with many of the recipes. These bite-sized pieces of information suggest ways to trim prep time, substitute ingredients and more. Similarly, *kitchen tips* offer advice on everything from streamlining cleanup to selecting the ripest produce. We even share a side bar, titled *special touch,* that is scattered throughout the book, which explains how to dress up buffet tables and make meals particularly memorable.

We hope that Pillsbury Christmas 2011 will fill your home with heartwarming memories of Christmas past, present and future. *Merry Christmas!*

p. 209

# Merry Snacks & Beverages

*Spread good cheer* at every holiday event with the delightful bites in this chapter. From casual munchies to elegant appetizers, they always get seasonal parties started.

p. 16

p. 10

p. 17

p. 13

p. 33

spicy chicken
mini burritos p. 12

# bacon-cheeseburger calzones

PREP TIME: 30 Minutes ✳ READY IN: 50 Minutes ✳ SERVINGS: 4

2 slices bacon, cut into 1/4-inch pieces

1/2 lb. lean (at least 80%) ground beef

2 tablespoons dried instant minced onion

2 tablespoons chopped hamburger pickle slices

2 tablespoons ranch dressing

1 can (8 oz.) Pillsbury® refrigerated crescent dinner rolls

1 Italian plum tomato, thinly sliced, if desired

2 slices (3/4 oz. each) American or Cheddar cheese, each cut in half

1 egg, beaten

1 Heat oven to 375°F. In 10-inch nonstick skillet, cook bacon over medium heat 2 minutes. Add ground beef and onion; cook, stirring occasionally, until beef is thoroughly cooked; drain if necessary. Stir in pickles and ranch dressing.

2 Unroll dough and separate into 4 rectangles; place on ungreased cookie sheet. Press each into 7 x 4-inch rectangle, firmly pressing perforations to seal.

3 Spoon about 1/3 cup ground beef mixture onto one end of each rectangle. Top each with tomato slices and 1 piece of cheese. Fold dough over filling; press edges with fork to seal (sandwiches will be full). Brush tops with egg.

4 Bake 15 to 20 minutes or until deep golden brown. Immediately remove calzones from cookie sheet. Serve warm.

NUTRITION INFORMATION PER SERVING: Calories 430 • Total Fat 26g • Saturated Fat 9g • Cholesterol 100mg • Sodium 1060mg • Total Carbohydrate 30g • Dietary Fiber 1g • Protein 20g. DIETARY EXCHANGES: 2 Starch • 2 Medium-Fat Meat • 3 Fat • 2 Carb Choices.

# easy crescent dogs™

PREP TIME: 10 Minutes ✳ READY IN: 25 Minutes ✳ SERVINGS: 8

8  hot dogs

4  slices (3/4 oz. each) American cheese, each cut into 6 strips

1  can (8 oz.) Pillsbury® refrigerated crescent dinner rolls

1  Heat oven to 375°F. Cut lengthwise slit in each hot dog to within 1/2 inch of ends. Insert 3 strips of cheese into each slit.

2  Unroll dough; separate into 8 triangles. Place hot dog on shortest side of each triangle. Roll up each, starting at shortest side of triangle and rolling to opposite point; place cheese side up on ungreased cookie sheet.

3  Bake 12 to 15 minutes or until golden brown. Immediately remove crescent dogs from cookie sheet. Serve warm.

NUTRITION INFORMATION PER SERVING: Calories 280 • Total Fat 20g • Saturated Fat 8g • Cholesterol 35mg • Sodium 1020mg • Total Carbohydrate 15g • Dietary Fiber 0g • Protein 9g. DIETARY EXCHANGES: 1 Starch • 1 High-Fat Meat • 2 Fat • 1 Carb Choice.

# chili con crescent snacks

PREP TIME: 10 Minutes ✳ READY IN: 35 Minutes ✳ SERVINGS: 12

1  can (8 oz.) Pillsbury® refrigerated crescent dinner rolls

1  can (15 oz.) or 1 box (14.3 oz.) chili without beans

1  cup crushed corn chips (3 oz.)

1/4  cup grated Parmesan cheese

1  Heat oven to 425°F. Unroll dough into ungreased 15 x 10 x 1-inch pan; press in bottom to form crust, pressing perforations to seal.

2  Bake 8 minutes or until golden brown. Spread chili evenly over crust; sprinkle with crushed chips and cheese. Bake 8 to 10 minutes longer or until crust is deep golden brown and chili is hot. Cut into squares to serve.

**HIGH ALTITUDE (3500-6500 FT):** In Step 2, bake 12 to 14 minutes.

NUTRITION INFORMATION PER SERVING: Calories 150 • Total Fat 9g • Saturated Fat 2.5g • Cholesterol 5mg • Sodium 370mg • Total Carbohydrate 13g • Dietary Fiber 0g • Protein 5g DIETARY EXCHANGES: 1 Starch • 1-1/2 Fat • 1 Carb Choice.

AGATHA ROTH
Jacksonville, Florida
Bake-Off® Contest 24, 1973

*cook's notes*

To easily crush the corn chips, place them in a food-storage plastic bag and crush with a rolling pin.

*special touch*

To make a tomato rose,

using a paring knife, peel

a 1/2-inch-wide strip of

tomato peel (3 to 4 inches

long) and roll to shape into

a rose.

# individual beef wellingtons with madeira sauce

PREP TIME: 1 Hour 15 Minutes ✱ READY IN: 1 Hour 15 Minutes ✱ SERVINGS: 4

### SAUCE

| | |
|---|---|
| 1/4 | cup chopped onion |
| 2 | tablespoons finely chopped celery |
| 2 | tablespoons finely chopped carrot |
| 1 | tablespoon all-purpose flour |
| 1 | cup beef broth |
| 1/4 | cup chopped seeded tomato |
| 1/4 | cup Madeira wine |

### BEEF

| | |
|---|---|
| 4 | (4 oz.) beef tenderloin steaks (1 inch thick) |
| 1/2 | cup finely chopped onion |

| | |
|---|---|
| 1 | garlic clove, minced |
| 1 | (8 oz.) package fresh mushrooms, finely chopped |
| 1/2 | cup chopped fresh parsley |
| 1 | tablespoon Dijon mustard |
| 1/4 | teaspoon dried thyme leaves, crushed |
| 1/4 | teaspoon salt |
| 1/4 | teaspoon pepper |
| 6 | (17 x 12-inch) sheets frozen phyllo (filo) pastry, thawed |
| | Nonstick cooking spray |

1 Heat small nonstick saucepan over medium-high heat until hot. Add 1/4 cup onion, celery and carrot; cover and cook 5 to 8 minutes or until vegetables begin to brown, stirring occasionally.

2 Add flour; mix well. With wire whisk, slowly stir broth into vegetables. Bring to a boil, stirring constantly. Add tomatoes; cook until sauce begins to thicken.

3 Place sauce in blender container or food processor bowl with metal blade; blend on low speed until smooth. Return sauce to same saucepan. Add wine; cook over medium-low heat until slightly thickened, stirring occasionally. Keep warm.

4 Meanwhile, heat oven to 425°F. Spray large nonstick skillet with nonstick cooking spray. Heat over high heat until hot. Add beef steaks; cook 2 to 3 minutes on each side or until browned. Remove beef from skillet; set aside.

5 Reduce heat to medium. In same skillet, combine 1/2 cup onion and garlic; cover and cook 2 to 3 minutes or until crisp-tender, stirring occasionally. Add mushrooms and parsley; cook uncovered for 8 to 10 minutes or until vegetables are tender. Stir in mustard, thyme, salt and pepper; mix well. Remove skillet from heat.

6 Spray cookie sheet with cooking spray. Unroll phyllo sheets; cover with plastic wrap or towel. Place 1 phyllo sheet on cutting board; spray lightly with cooking spray to coat evenly. Top with second phyllo sheet; spray with cooking spray. Repeat until all phyllo sheets have been used. Cut stacked layers lengthwise in half, then crosswise to make 4 equal portions.

7 Working quickly, spoon 1/4 of mushroom mixture onto center of each phyllo portion; spread mixture until same size as beef steak. Place beef over mushroom mixture. Bring together all 4 corners of phyllo; crimp tightly to seal. Lightly spray each bundle with cooking spray. Place on sprayed cookie sheet.

8 Bake beef wellingtons at 425°F. for 9 to 12 minutes or until golden brown. Serve with the warm Madeira sauce.

NUTRITION INFORMATION PER SERVING: Calories 290 • Total Fat 11g • Saturated Fat 3g • Cholesterol 50mg • Sodium 530mg • Total Carbohydrate 23g • Dietary Fiber 2g • Protein 22g. DIETARY EXCHANGES: 1-1/2 Starch • 1-1/2 Other Carbohydrate • 2-1/2 Lean Meat • 1/2 Fat Carb Choices.

individual beef wellingtons with madeira sauce

# spicy chicken mini burritos

PREP TIME: 45 Minutes ✹ READY IN: 45 Minutes ✹ SERVINGS: 16

| | |
|---|---|
| 1 teaspoon vegetable oil | 3/4 cup salsa verde or green salsa |
| 1 tablespoon finely chopped onion | 16 flour tortillas (6 inch) |
| 1 clove garlic, finely chopped | 1 cup shredded Mexican-style Cheddar Jack cheese with jalapeño peppers (4 oz.) |
| 2 cups shredded cooked chicken | |
| 2 to 3 tablespoons chopped jalapeño chiles | 1 medium plum (Roma) tomato, chopped (about 1/2 cup) |
| 1/2 teaspoon ground cumin | 1/3 cup chopped fresh cilantro |

1 In 10-inch nonstick skillet, heat oil over medium heat. Add onion and garlic; cook 2 to 3 minutes, stirring occasionally, until crisp-tender. Stir in chicken, jalapeño chiles, cumin and salsa verde; cook 4 to 6 minutes or until hot. Keep warm.

2 Heat tortillas as directed on package. Spoon 2 level tablespoons chicken mixture and 1 tablespoon shredded cheese in center of each tortilla. Top with tomato and cilantro. Fold 1/3 of tortilla down over filling; fold sides toward center. Fold remaining side up, and turn over. Serve immediately.

NUTRITION INFORMATION PER SERVING: Calories 140 • Total Fat 6g • Saturated Fat 2g • Cholesterol 20mg • Sodium 290mg • Total Carbohydrate 14g • Dietary Fiber 0g • Protein 9g. DIETARY EXCHANGES: 1/2 Starch • 1/2 Other Carbohydrate • 1 Medium-Fat Meat • 1 Carb Choice.

# buffalo chicken pinwheels

PREP TIME: 20 Minutes ✳ READY IN: 35 Minutes ✳ SERVINGS: 24

1 can (8 oz.) Pillsbury® refrigerated crescent dinner rolls

1/2 cup finely chopped cooked chicken

3/4 teaspoon hot pepper sauce

1 package (2 oz.) cream cheese, softened

1/4 cup crumbled blue cheese (1 oz.)

2 tablespoons chopped fresh chives

1 Heat oven to 350°F. Spray the cookie sheet with cooking spray. Unroll dough and separate into 4 rectangles; firmly press perforations to seal.

2 In small bowl, mix chicken and hot pepper sauce until well coated. Spread 1 tablespoon cream cheese over each rectangle to within 1/4 inch of edges. Sprinkle evenly with chicken, blue cheese and chives.

3 Starting with one short side, roll up each rectangle; press edges to seal. With serrated knife, cut each roll into 6 slices; place cut side down on cookie sheet. Bake 13 to 17 minutes or until edges are golden brown. Serve warm.

NUTRITION INFORMATION PER SERVING: Calories 50 • Total Fat 3.5g • Saturated Fat 1.5g • Cholesterol 5mg • Sodium 100mg • Total Carbohydrate 4g • Dietary Fiber 0g • Protein 2g. DIETARY EXCHANGES: 1/2 High-Fat Meat.

*cook's notes*

*Prepare and bake these appetizers up to 24 hours ahead of time, then cover and refrigerate. Before serving, place the appetizers in a shallow pan and cover with foil. Heat at 350°F for 10 to 15 minutes.*

# stuffed cucumber snacks

PREP TIME: 20 Minutes ✳ READY IN: 20 Minutes ✳ 12 servings

1 large English (seedless) cucumber, about 12 inches long

1/2 cup deli ham salad or garlic-and-herb cream cheese spread

Thin orange or lemon slices, cut into small wedges, if desired

1 Using vegetable peeler, cut lengthwise strips of peel down 4 sides of the cucumber, making a square shape (some peel will remain). Cut cucumber into 1-inch slices.

2 Make indentation in center of each slice by scooping with small melon baller or spoon. Fill each indentation with about 1 teaspoon deli salad. Top each with orange or lemon wedge.

NUTRITION INFORMATION PER SERVING: Calories 15 • Total Fat 1g • Saturated Fat 0g • Cholesterol 0mg • Sodium 30mg • Total Carbohydrate 0g • Dietary Fiber 0g • Protein 0g. DIETARY EXCHANGES: Free.

# blueberry-pomegranate smoothies

PREP TIME: 5 Minutes ✳ READY IN: 5 Minutes ✳ SERVINGS: 2

    1   cup frozen blueberries
  1/2   cup pomegranate juice
  1/2   cup soy milk

1 In blender, place ingredients. Cover; blend on high speed about 1 minute or until smooth. Pour into 2 glasses. Serve immediately.

NUTRITIONAL INFORMATION PER SERVING: Calories 140 • Total Fat 2g • Saturated Fat 0g • Cholesterol 0mg • Sodium 40mg • Total Carbohydrate 28g • Dietary Fiber 4g • Protein 3g DIETARY EXCHANGES: 1 Starch • 1 Fruit • 2 Carb Choices.

*kitchen tip*

*Let the kids put all of the yummy ingredients in the blender. Then show them how to cover and blend—a great kitchen lesson!*

# chicken crescent pot stickers

**PREP TIME:** 35 Minutes ✳ **READY IN:** 55 Minutes ✳ **SERVINGS:** 16

| | |
|---|---|
| 2 cups shredded cooked chicken | 2 teaspoons sesame oil |
| 1/4 cup shredded carrots | 2 teaspoons finely chopped garlic |
| 4 medium green onions, chopped (1/4 cup chopped) | 2 cans (8 oz. each) Pillsbury® Place 'n Bake™ refrigerated crescent rounds |
| 1/3 cup hoisin sauce | 1 egg, beaten |
| 2 tablespoons thick barbecue sauce | 2 tablespoons sesame seed |
| 1 tablespoon grated fresh gingerroot | |

1. Heat oven to 375°F. Grease or spray a large cookie sheet. In medium bowl, mix the cooked chicken, shredded carrots and onions. Stir in the hoisin sauce, barbecue sauce, grated gingerroot, sesame oil and garlic.

2. Unroll dough from both cans on work surface, but do not separate. Firmly press perforations to seal. Roll or press each into 12 x 8-inch rectangle. Cut each rectangle into 8 squares.

3. Spoon about 2 tablespoons chicken mixture in center of each square. Bring edges up, pinching together and twisting to form bundle.

4. Place the pot stickers on a cookie sheet; brush with the beaten egg and sprinkle with sesame seeds. Bake 4 to 18 minutes or until golden brown. Serve warm.

NUTRITION INFORMATION PER SERVING: Calories 170 • Total Fat 9g • Saturated Fat 2.5g • Cholesterol 30mg • Sodium 350mg • Total Carbohydrate 15g • Dietary Fiber 0g • Protein 8g. DIETARY EXCHANGES: 1/2 Starch • 1/2 Other Carbohydrate • 1 Lean Meat • 1 Fat • 1 Carb Choice.

# ranch deviled eggs

PREP TIME: 30 Minutes ✳ READY IN: 1 Hour ✳ SERVINGS: 24

12 eggs
3 teaspoons dry ranch dressing mix
(from 1-oz. envelope)

1/3 cup mayonnaise or salad dressing
1 teaspoon Dijon mustard
1 tablespoon chopped chives

1 In 4-quart saucepan or Dutch oven, place eggs in single layer. Add enough water to cover eggs by 1 inch. Heat to boiling. Immediately remove from heat; cover and let stand 15 minutes. Drain; rinse with cold water. Place eggs in bowl of ice water; let stand 10 minutes.

2 To remove shell, crack it by tapping egg gently all over; roll egg between hands to loosen shell. Peel, starting at large end.

3 Cut eggs lengthwise in half. Into medium bowl, slip out yolks; mash with fork. Stir dressing mix, mayonnaise and mustard into yolks.

4 Spoon or pipe the yolk mixture into the egg white halves. Sprinkle with chives. Refrigerate at least 30 minutes before serving.

**HIGH ALTITUDE (3500-6500 FT):** In Step 1, heat eggs to boiling and boil 5 minutes; remove from heat. Cover and let stand 15 minutes.

NUTRITION INFORMATION PER SERVING: Calories 60 • Total Fat 5g • Saturated Fat 1g • Cholesterol 105mg • Sodium 105mg • Total Carbohydrate 0g • Dietary Fiber 0g • Protein 3g. DIETARY EXCHANGES: 1/2 Medium-Fat Meat • 1/2 Fat.

*special touch*

*Shave a bit off the bottom of each egg white half so the filled eggs stay in place on the serving plate.*

# cheesy fish stick taco dogs

PREP TIME: 30 Minutes ✴ READY IN: 45 Minutes ✴ SERVINGS: 4

8 frozen battered or breaded fish sticks

1 can (8 oz.) Pillsbury® refrigerated crescent dinner rolls

1 tablespoon Old El Paso® taco seasoning mix (from 1-oz. pkg.)

4 slices (2/3 oz. each) American cheese, each cut into 4 strips

3 tablespoons Old El Paso® thick 'n chunky salsa

1 Heat oven to 375°F. Spray 15 x 10-inch pan with sides with cooking spray. Place fish sticks in single layer in pan. Bake 10 minutes, turning once.

2 Meanwhile, separate dough into 8 triangles. In shallow bowl, place taco seasoning mix. Lightly dip one side of each triangle into seasoning mix, coating evenly. Place triangles on work surface, seasoning side down.

3 Place 1 baked fish stick on shortest side of each triangle. Top each fish stick with 2 strips of cheese and about 1 teaspoon salsa. Starting with shortest side of each triangle, roll up dough around fish stick; place cheese-side up in same pan. Return to oven and bake 12 to 15 minutes longer or until golden brown.

NUTRITION INFORMATION PER SERVING: Calories 390 • Total Fat 23g • Saturated Fat 9g • Cholesterol 30mg • Sodium 1140mg • Total Carbohydrate 33g • Dietary Fiber 0g • Protein 13g. DIETARY EXCHANGES: 1-1/2 Starch • 1/2 Other Carbohydrate • 1 Very Lean Meat • 4-1/2 Fat • 2 Carb Choices.

# mango-mint fruit dip

PREP TIME: 10 Minutes ✳ READY IN: 10 Minutes ✳ SERVINGS: 16

1 cup chopped seeded peeled mango
  (about 1/2 medium)

1 teaspoon chopped fresh mint leaves

1 cup marshmallow creme

1 package (8 oz.) cream cheese, softened
  Assorted cut-up fresh fruit

1 In a food processor, place the chopped mango and mint. Cover and process about 10 seconds or until smooth.

2 Add marshmallow creme and cream cheese; process about 10 seconds or until well blended. Serve with fruit. Garnish with mint leaves, if desired.

NUTRITION INFORMATION PER SERVING: Calories 130 • Total Fat 5g • Saturated Fat 3g • Cholesterol 15mg • Sodium 55mg • Total Carbohydrate 19g • Dietary Fiber 2g • Protein 2g. DIETARY EXCHANGES: 1-1/2 Other Carbohydrate • 1/2 High-Fat Meat • 1 Carb Choice.

## kitchen tip

*Peeled mango strips are often available in the refrigerated section of the produce department. They can be used in place of fresh mango, but their flavor will differ slightly from that of fresh.*

chile-lime shrimp with creamy chipotle dip

# chile-lime shrimp with creamy chipotle dip

PREP TIME: 15 Minutes ✱ READY IN: 55 Minutes ✱ SERVINGS: 12

| | |
|---|---|
| 2 limes | 1/3 cup mayonnaise or salad dressing |
| 24 uncooked extra-large (16 to 20 per pound) deveined peeled shrimp with tail shells left on (about 1 1/2 lb.) | 2 tablespoons honey mustard |
| | 1 large chipotle chile in adobo sauce (from 7-oz. can), finely chopped (1 tablespoon) |
| 2 tablespoons olive or vegetable oil | 1 teaspoon adobo sauce |
| 1 clove garlic, finely chopped | 1 tablespoon chopped fresh cilantro |
| 1/2 teaspoon crushed red pepper flakes | |

1 Reserve 1 lime for garnish. Grate 1 teaspoon peel from other lime. Cut lime in half; squeeze enough juice to measure 2 tablespoons. Set peel and juice aside.

2 Butterfly each shrimp by cutting along the outside curve through the fleshiest part for about 1-1/2 inches, cutting almost to the inside curve. The shrimp should spread open.

3 In 1-gallon resealable food-storage plastic bag, mix oil, garlic, pepper flakes, lime juice and grated lime peel. Shake lightly to mix. Add shrimp. Seal bag; rotate to coat all of shrimp. Refrigerate 30 to 60 minutes to marinate.

4 Meanwhile, in small bowl, mix mayonnaise, honey mustard, chipotle chile and adobo sauce. Cover; refrigerate until serving.

5 Heat oven to 400°F. Remove shrimp from marinade; place in 15 x 10 x 1-inch baking pan. Open each shrimp, arranging in pan so that cut portion is on pan with tail tucked in. Discard marinade.

6 Bake 5 to 7 minutes, rearranging shrimp halfway through bake time, until shrimp are pink. Place on serving platter; sprinkle with cilantro. Spoon dip into bowl. Cut reserved lime into wedges. Garnish dip with wedges. Serve shrimp with dip. Store any remaining shrimp and dip in refrigerator.

NUTRITION INFORMATION PER SERVING: Calories 70 • Total Fat 6g • Saturated Fat 1g • Cholesterol 35mg • Sodium 95mg • Total Carbohydrate 0g • Dietary Fiber 0g • Protein 4g. DIETARY EXCHANGES: 1/2 Very Lean Meat • 1 Fat.

*cook's notes*

*If you don't want to butterfly the shrimp, you can just place them in the pan and bake, turning once, until they are pink in color.*

# apple snack stacks

PREP TIME: 15 Minutes ✱ READY IN: 45 Minutes ✱ SERVINGS 4

- 2 medium apples
- 4 tablespoons peanut butter, process cheese dip or sauce, or cream cheese

1 Wash apples; remove core, leaving apples whole. Fill center of each apple with about 2 tablespoons peanut butter, packing gently. Wrap each tightly in plastic wrap. Refrigerate until filling is set, about 30 minutes.

2 Cut each apple crosswise into 1/2-inch-thick slices. Divide the slices into 4 portions; wrap each portion tightly in plastic wrap. Refrigerate until serving time.

NUTRITION INFORMATION PER SERVING: Calories 150 • Total Fat 8g • Saturated Fat 1.5g • Cholesterol 0mg • Sodium 75mg • Total Carbohydrate 14g • Dietary Fiber 2g • Protein 4g. DIETARY EXCHANGES: 1 Fruit • 1/2 High-Fat Meat •1 Fat • 1 Carb Choice.

# layered italian dip with crisp wontons

PREP TIME: 30 Minutes ✳ READY IN: 40 Minutes ✳ SERVINGS: 14

| | |
|---|---|
| 14 | wonton skins (about 3-1/4-inch square) |
| | Cooking spray |
| 1 | can (15.5 oz.) great northern beans, drained, rinsed |
| 1/4 | cup shredded fresh Parmesan cheese |
| 1/4 | cup Caesar dressing |

| | |
|---|---|
| 1 | cup finely chopped pepperoni (about 4 oz.) |
| 1/2 | cup chopped drained pepperoncini peppers (bottled Italian peppers) |
| 3/4 | cup finely shredded Italian cheese blend (3 oz.) |
| 1 | tablespoon chopped fresh oregano leaves |

1 Heat oven to 400°F. Cut each wonton skin in half into 2 triangles. On 2 large ungreased cookie sheets, arrange wonton skins in single layer. Spray wontons with cooking spray. Bake about 6 minutes or until crisp; cool.

2 In food processor, place beans, Parmesan cheese and dressing. Cover; process until smooth. Spread mixture in ungreased 9-inch microwavable pie plate or quiche dish.

3 Top with pepperoni, pepperoncini peppers, cheese blend and oregano. Cover with microwavable plastic wrap.

4 Microwave on High 1-1/2 to 2 minutes, turning pan once halfway through cooking. Serve with crisp wontons.

**HIGH ALTITUDE (3500-6500 FT):** Heat oven to 375°F.

NUTRITION INFORMATION PER SERVING: Calories 150 • Total Fat 8g • Saturated Fat 3g • Cholesterol 20mg • Sodium 320mg • Total Carbohydrate 12g • Dietary Fiber 2g • Protein 7g. DIETARY EXCHANGES: 1 Starch • 1/2 Very Lean Meat • 1-1/2 Fat • 1 Carb Choice.

# peanutty rice cake rounds

PREP TIME: 20 Minutes  ❄  READY IN: 20 Minutes  ❄  SERVINGS: 6

| | |
|---|---|
| 1/4  cup creamy or crunchy peanut butter | 3  fresh whole strawberries |
| 1  teaspoon honey | 24  miniature rice cakes |

1  In medium bowl, mix the peanut butter and honey until well blended. Remove stems from the strawberries; cut each into 4 slices

2  Spread each rice cake with peanut butter mixture. Put 1 slice of strawberry on top of 12 of the rice cakes. Take the other 12 rice cakes and stack them, peanut butter-side down, on top of the strawberries.

NUTRITION INFORMATION PER SERVING: Calories 110 • Total Fat 6g • Saturated Fat 1g • Cholesterol 0mg • Sodium 80mg • Total Carbohydrate 10g • Dietary Fiber 1g • Protein 3g. DIETARY EXCHANGES:  1/2 Carb Choice.

# cucumber-hummus stacks

PREP TIME: 20 Minutes ✳ READY IN: 20 Minutes ✳ SERVINGS: 26

1 large cucumber (about 12 oz.), unpeeled

1 container (7 oz.) roasted red pepper hummus

2 tablespoons crumbled feta cheese

26 slices kalamata or ripe olives

1 Using tines of fork, score cucumber lengthwise on all sides. Cut cucumber into 26 (1/4-inch) slices. Blot dry with paper towel.

2 Spoon heaping teaspoon hummus on each cucumber slice. Sprinkle with feta cheese; top with olive slice.

NUTRITION INFORMATION PER SERVING: Calories 20 • Total Fat 1g • Saturated Fat 0g • Cholesterol 0mg • Sodium 50mg • Total Carbohydrate 2g • Dietary Fiber 0g • Protein 0g. DIETARY EXCHANGES: Free.

# rudolph nibblers with cinnamon-orange dip

PREP TIME: 15 Minutes ✳ READY IN: 15 Minutes ✳ SERVINGS: 8

- 1 package (8 oz.) cream cheese, softened
- 1/2 cup powdered sugar
- 1/4 cup frozen orange juice concentrate, thawed
- 1/4 teaspoon cinnamon
- 1/8 teaspoon nutmeg

- 1 pint (2 cups) fresh strawberries (small or cut in half)
- 1 red apple, cut into slices
- 1 green apple, cut into slices

1 In small bowl, beat the cream cheese and powdered sugar until smooth. Beat in the orange juice concentrate, cinnamon and nutmeg. Refrigerate until ready to serve. To serve, place bowl of dip on serving platter or tray. Arrange fruit around dip.

NUTRITION INFORMATION PER SERVING: Calories 180 • Total Fat 10g • Saturated Fat 6g • Cholesterol 30mg • Sodium 85mg • Total Carbohydrate 20g • Dietary Fiber 2g • Protein 3g. DIETARY EXCHANGES: 1/2 Starch • 1 Fruit • 1-1/2 Other Carbohydrate • 2 Fat.

# pretzel butterflies

PREP TIME: 35 Minutes ✳ READY IN: 1 Hour 5 Minutes ✳ SERVINGS: 20

- 2 cups (about 45) small pretzel twists
- 1/2 cup white vanilla chips or 2 oz. vanilla-flavored candy coating, cut into pieces

- 1/2 teaspoon vegetable oil
- 1/3 cup small round candy-coated fruit-flavored chewy candies (from 4 oz. bag)

1 Line large cookie sheet with waxed paper or parchment paper. To make 20 butterflies, arrange pretzel twists on cookie sheet in groups of 2 with single-hole sides of pretzels touching to form butterfly wings. Break remaining 5 pretzels into pieces for antennae; place 2 pieces at top of each butterfly between wings.

2 In 1-quart resealable freezer plastic bag, place vanilla chips and oil. Microwave on High 1 minute 20 seconds or until melted, squeezing bag to mix. Seal bag; cut small hole in bottom corner of bag.

3 Squeeze bag to pipe thin zigzag of melted chips between pretzels to resemble bodies of butterflies. Press pretzel pieces firmly into melted chips. Pipe melted chips into each hole in wings; top each with 1 candy. Let stand until set, about 30 minutes. Remove from waxed paper; store in tightly covered container.

NUTRITION INFORMATION PER SERVING: Calories 45 • Total Fat 0g • Saturated Fat 0g • Cholesterol 0mg • Sodium 50mg • Total Carbohydrate 11g • Dietary Fiber 0g • Protein 0g. DIETARY EXCHANGES: 1/2 Starch • 1 Carb Choice.

# berry sherbet punch

PREP TIME: 5 Minutes ✳ READY IN: 5 Minutes ✳ SERVINGS: 9

- 1 pint (2 cups) raspberry sherbet
- 1 quart (4 cups) cranberry juice cocktail, chilled

- 3-1/2 cups orange-flavored carbonated beverage, chilled

1 Scoop sherbet into small punch bowl or large pitcher. Add juice cocktail and carbonated beverage; mix lightly. Serve immediately.

NUTRITION INFORMATION PER SERVING: Calories 170 • Total Fat 1g • Saturated Fat 1g • Trans Fat • Cholesterol 3mg • Sodium 35mg • Total Carbohydrate 41g • Dietary Fiber 0g • Protein 0g. DIETARY EXCHANGES: 3 Fruit • 3 Other Carbohydrate.

# crescent sloppy joes

PREP TIME: 15 Minutes ✷ READY IN: 35 Minutes ✷ SERVINGS: 8

1/2 lb. lean (at least 80%) ground beef

1/4 cup barbecue sauce

1/4 cup shredded Cheddar cheese (1 oz.)

1 can (8 oz.) Pillsbury® refrigerated crescent dinner rolls

1 egg, beaten

1 teaspoon sesame seed

1 Heat oven to 375°F. In 10-inch skillet, brown ground beef over medium heat, stirring frequently, until thoroughly cooked; drain. Stir in barbecue sauce; cook 1 to 2 minutes, stirring occasionally, until thoroughly heated. Stir in cheese.

2 Unroll dough and separate into 4 rectangles; press each into 8 x 4-inch rectangle, firmly pressing perforations to seal. Cut each in half crosswise, making 8 squares.

3 Place about 2 rounded tablespoons ground beef mixture on center of each square. Fold dough over filling, forming triangles; press edges with fork to seal. With knife, cut small slits in tops for steam to escape. Place on ungreased cookie sheet. Brush with egg; sprinkle with sesame seeds.

4 Bake 11 to 18 minutes or until golden brown. Immediately remove crescents from the cookie sheet. Serve warm.

NUTRITION INFORMATION PER SERVING: Calories 190 • Total Fat 10g • Saturated Fat 4g • Cholesterol 45mg • Sodium 460mg • Total Carbohydrate 16g • Dietary Fiber 0g • Protein 9g. DIETARY EXCHANGES: 1 Starch • 1 Medium-Fat Meat • 1 Fat • 1 Carb Choice.

# citrus gazpacho with honey-lime cream

PREP TIME: 20 Minutes ✳ READY IN: 20 Minutes ✳ SERVINGS: 4

1 jar (26 oz.) refrigerated citrus salad
1 jar (16 oz.) chunky-style salsa
1-1/2 cups chopped green bell pepper
1-1/2 cups chopped seeded cucumber
2 cups tomato juice
1 cup chicken broth

1 tablespoon olive oil
1/2 cup chopped fresh cilantro
2 limes
1/2 to 1 cup reduced-fat dairy sour cream
1 tablespoon honey

1 Place citrus salad in large nonmetal bowl. With fork, break up fruit into small pieces. Add salsa, bell pepper, cucumber, tomato juice, broth and oil. Reserve 2 tablespoons cilantro. Add remaining cilantro to mixture in bowl; stir to combine.

2 Grate the peel from 1 lime; set aside. Squeeze juice from lime into small bowl. Add to fruit mixture in bowl; mix well. Refrigerate at least 2 hours to blend flavors.

3 In small bowl, combine the sour cream, honey and grated lime peel; mix well. Refrigerate until serving time.

4 To serve, cut remaining lime into thin slices; quarter each slice. Ladle gazpacho into individual shallow bowls. Top each serving with sour cream mixture. Sprinkle with reserved cilantro. Garnish with quartered lime slices. Store remaining gazpacho in refrigerator.

NUTRITION INFORMATION PER SERVING: Calories 380 • Total Fat 12g • Saturated Fat 5g • Cholesterol 30mg • Sodium 1570mg • Total Carbohydrate 61g • Dietary Fiber 4g • Protein 8g. DIETARY EXCHANGES: 3-1/2 Fruit • 3-1/2 Other Carbohydrate • 1 Vegetable • 1 Medium-Fat Meat • 1-1/2 Fat.

**Bake-Off**

ASHLEY SHEPARDSON
Chicago, Illinois
Bake-Off® Contest 40, 2002

*special touch*

*To make the soup a bit heartier, sprinkle servings with a few purchased croutons.*

# chicken and blue cheese bundles

PREP TIME: 35 Minutes ✳ READY IN: 50 Minutes ✳ SERVINGS: 4

| | |
|---|---|
| 1 tablespoon butter or margarine | 1/4 teaspoon dried thyme leaves |
| 1 medium onion, chopped (1/2 cup) | 1-3/4 cups chopped deli rotisserie chicken (without skin) |
| 1 cup chopped fresh mushrooms | |
| 1/4 cup dry white wine or chicken broth | 1/4 cup crumbled blue cheese (1 oz.) |
| 1/2 teaspoon dried rosemary leaves, crushed | 1 can (8 oz.) Pillsbury® refrigerated crescent dinner rolls |

1 Heat oven to 375°F. In 10-inch nonstick skillet, melt butter over medium heat. Add onion; cook 5 minutes, stirring occasionally. Add mushrooms; cook, stirring occasionally, until onions and mushrooms are tender.

2 Reduce heat to medium-low. Add the wine, rosemary and thyme; cook 4 to 5 minutes, stirring occasionally, until liquid has evaporated. Remove from heat. Stir in chicken and blue cheese.

3 Separate dough into 4 rectangles; press or roll each into 5-inch square, firmly pressing the perforations to seal. Spoon about 1/2 cup chicken mixture onto center of each dough square. Bring all 4 corners of dough up over chicken mixture; pinch seams to seal.

4 Place the bundles on an ungreased cookie sheet. Bake 11 to 14 minutes or until the crust is golden brown.

**HIGH ALTITUDE (3500-6500 FT):** In Step 4, bake 13 to 16 minutes.

NUTRITION INFORMATION PER SERVING: Calories 390 • Total Fat 21g • Saturated Fat 8g • Cholesterol 65mg • Sodium 610mg • Total Carbohydrate 25g • Dietary Fiber 1g • Protein 23g. DIETARY EXCHANGES: 1-1/2 Starch • 1/2 Other Carbohydrate • 2-1/2 Lean Meat • 2-1/2 Fat • 1-1/2 Carb Choices.

# asparagus melts with horseradish sauce

PREP TIME: 20 Minutes ✳ READY IN: 20 Minutes ✳ SERVINGS: 4

12 oz. fresh asparagus spears

2 mini baguettes (French rolls)

4 tablespoons horseradish sauce

2 slices red onion, halved, separated into strips

6 tomato slices, halved

3 slices (1-1/2 oz. each) mozzarella cheese, cut crosswise into strips

1 Break or cut off tough ends of asparagus. In 12 x 8-inch (2-quart) microwave-safe dish, arrange spears with tips in center. Add water; cover with microwave-safe plastic wrap. Microwave on High for 3 to 4 minutes or until asparagus is crisp-tender.

2 Meanwhile, cut baguettes in half lengthwise. Spread 1 tablespoon horseradish sauce evenly onto cut side of each baguette half. Top each baguette half with cooked asparagus, onion and tomato. Cut cheese into 1-inch-wide strips; arrange over tomato.

3 Place sandwiches on broiler pan or ungreased cookie sheet. Broil 4 to 6 inches from heat for 1 to 2 minutes or until cheese is melted.

NUTRITION INFORMATION PER SERVING: Calories 190 • Total Fat 9g • Saturated Fat 5g • Cholesterol 15mg • Sodium 350mg • Total Carbohydrate 15g • Dietary Fiber 2g • Protein 12g. DIETARY EXCHANGES: 1 Starch • 1 Other Carbohydrate • 1-1/2 Medium-Fat Meat.

*cook's notes*

*Homemade Dijon sauce can be used in place of the horseradish sauce: Stir together 1 tablespoon of Dijon mustard and 3 tablespoons of reduced-fat mayonnaise or salad dressing.*

# honey-mustard sweet onion blossoms

PREP TIME: 55 Minutes ✳ READY IN: 55 Minutes ✳ SERVINGS: 4

2 large sweet onions

1/2 cup honey-mustard dressing

1/2 teaspoon dried thyme leaves

1/2 cup garlic croutons, crushed

1 Heat gas or charcoal grill. Cut 4 (18 x 12-inch) sheets of heavy-duty foil. Cut off 1/4-inch-thick slice from both ends of each onion so they will sit flat; peel onions. Cut each onion in half cross-wise. With cut side up, make 4 cuts in each onion half, cutting to within 1/2 inch of bottom, to make 8 wedges.

2 Place onion half in center of each sheet of foil. Gently separate wedges slightly without break-ing apart at base. Spread 1 tablespoon of the dressing over each onion half, letting dressing drip between layers. Sprinkle each with thyme. Wrap each packet securely using double-fold seals, allowing room for heat expansion.

3 When grill is heated, place packets on gas grill over medium heat or on charcoal grill over medium coals; cover grill. Cook 15 to 20 minutes or just until onions are almost tender.

4 Remove packets from grill. Open packets carefully to allow steam to escape. Sprinkle each with crushed croutons. Return to grill, leaving packets open; cover grill. Cook 8 to 10 minutes longer or until onions are tender and lightly browned. Serve with remaining honey-mustard dressing.

**HIGH ALTITUDE (3500-6500 FT):** Place packets on gas grill over medium-low heat or on charcoal grill over medium-low coals; cover grill. Cook 20 to 25 minutes. Remove packets from grill, open packets and sprinkle with croutons; cook as directed above.

NUTRITION INFORMATION PER SERVING: Calories 150 • Total Fat 11g • Saturated Fat 1.5g • Cholesterol 0mg • Sodium 250mg • Total Carbohydrate 13g • Dietary Fiber 2g • Protein 1g. DIETARY EXCHANGES: 1/2 Other Carbohydrate • 1 Vegetable, 2 Fat • 1 Carb Choice.

# ham and cheese crescent sandwiches

PREP TIME: 10 Minutes ✳ READY IN: 25 Minutes ✳ SERVINGS: 4

1  can (8 oz.) Pillsbury® refrigerated crescent
   dinner rolls

4  thin slices cooked ham (3 oz.)
4  thin slices Cheddar cheese (3 oz.)

1  Heat oven to 375°F. Unroll dough and separate into 4 rectangles; place on ungreased cookie sheet. Press each into 6 x 5-inch rectangle, firmly pressing perforations to seal.

2  Place 1 ham slice and 1 cheese slice on one end of each rectangle. Fold dough in half over filling; press edges firmly to seal.

3  Bake sandwiches 10 to 13 minutes or until golden brown. Immediately remove from cookie sheet. Serve warm.

NUTRITION INFORMATION PER SERVING: Calories 320 • Total Fat 17g • Saturated Fat 7g • Cholesterol 35mg • Sodium 1130mg • Total Carbohydrate 27g • Dietary Fiber 0g • Protein 14g. DIETARY EXCHANGES: 2 Starch • 1 Medium-Fat Meat • 2 Fat • 2 Carb Choices.

# festive spinach dip

PREP TIME: 15 Minutes ✳ READY IN: 15 Minutes ✳ 20 SERVINGS: 2 tablespoons of dip each

1  box (9 oz.) Green Giant® frozen spinach
1  cup nonfat sour cream

1/2  cup reduced-calorie mayonnaise or salad
     dressing
1/3  cup Old El Paso® thick 'n chunky salsa

1  Cook spinach according to package directions; drain well and squeeze dry with paper towels. In medium bowl, separate spinach. With kitchen shears, cut any large pieces in half.

2  Stir in remaining ingredients until well mixed. Serve with assorted cut-up fresh vegetables or thinly sliced French bread.

NUTRITION INFORMATION PER SERVING: Calories 30 • Total Fat 2g • Saturated Fat 0g • Cholesterol 0mg • Sodium 120mg • Total Carbohydrate 2g • Dietary Fiber 0g • Protein 1g. DIETARY EXCHANGES: 1 Vegetable.

## cook's notes

You can also prepare this mulled cider in a large slow cooker and keep it warm for up to 2 hours. Your guests will love the spicy smell of cinnamon and cloves mingled with cranberry and apple.

# hot spiced cranberry cider

PREP TIME: 10 Minutes ✳ READY IN: 30 Minutes ✳ SERVINGS: 24

2  quarts (8 cups) apple cider
6  cups cranberry juice cocktail
1/4  cup packed brown sugar

4  cinnamon sticks
1-1/2  teaspoons whole cloves
1  orange, thinly sliced

1  In 5-quart saucepan, place all ingredients. Heat to boiling over high heat. Reduce heat to low; simmer 15 to 20 minutes to blend flavors.

2  With slotted spoon, remove cinnamon sticks, cloves and orange slices. To serve, ladle hot cider into mugs.

NUTRITION INFORMATION PER SERVING: Calories 90 • Total Fat 0g • Saturated Fat 0g • Cholesterol 0mg • Sodium 0mg • Total Carbohydrate 21g • Dietary Fiber 0g • Protein 0g. DIETARY EXCHANGES: 1 Fruit • 1/2 Other Carbohydrate • 1-1/2 Carb Choices.

ham and cheese crescent sandwiches

# spanish salsa with crispy french bread

PREP TIME: 20 Minutes ✳ READY IN: 40 Minutes ✳ SERVINGS: 32

**BREAD**

32 very thin diagonal slices French bread
Cooking spray

**SALSA**

1 cup finely chopped fresh mushrooms

1 tablespoon chopped fresh parsley

1 tablespoon balsamic or red wine vinegar

2 teaspoons dried basil leaves

1/4 teaspoon salt

6 plum (Roma) tomatoes, finely chopped

2 medium green onions, sliced (2 tablespoons)

1 jar (6 oz.) marinated artichoke hearts, drained, finely chopped

1 can (4-1/4 oz.) chopped ripe olives, drained

1 Heat oven to 325°F. Line cookie sheet with foil. Place bread slices on cookie sheet; spray lightly with cooking spray. Bake 7 to 10 minutes or until very crisp. Place bread slices on cooling rack; cool completely.

2 Meanwhile, in decorative bowl, mix salsa ingredients. Let stand at room temperature 20 minutes to blend flavors, or refrigerate until serving time. Serve salsa with crispy bread slices.

NUTRITION INFORMATION PER SERVING: Calories 30 • Total Fat 1g • Saturated Fat 0g • Cholesterol 0mg • Sodium 100mg • Total Carbohydrate 4g • Dietary Fiber 0g • Protein 0g. DIETARY EXCHANGES: 1/2 Other Carbohydrate.

# slow cooker spicy cheeseburger nachos

**PREP TIME:** 20 Minutes ✳ **READY IN:** 4 Hours 20 Minutes ✳ **SERVINGS:** 22

| | |
|---|---|
| 1 lb. lean (at least 80%) ground beef | 2 cans (10 oz. each) diced tomatoes with green chiles, drained |
| 1 clove garlic, minced | 1/2 cup chopped green onions (8 medium) |
| 2 boxes (16 oz. each) Mexican prepared cheese product with jalapeno peppers, cut into cubes | 22 oz. tortilla chips |

1 In 10-inch skillet, cook ground beef and garlic, stirring frequently, until beef is thoroughly cooked; drain. Spoon into 3-1/2- to 4-quart slow cooker. Add cheese and tomatoes; mix well.

2 Cover; cook on Low heat setting 3 to 4 hours, stirring after 2 hours. Before serving, stir in onions. Serve with tortilla chips.

NUTRITION INFORMATION PER SERVING: Calories 310 • Total Fat 18g • Saturated Fat 7g • Cholesterol 45mg • Sodium 870mg • Total Carbohydrate 24g • Dietary Fiber 1g • Protein 13g. DIETARY EXCHANGES: 1-1/2 Starch • 1 High-Fat Meat • 2 Fat • 1-1/2 Carb Choice.

# grapefruit citrus cooler

**PREP TIME:** 10 Minutes ✳ **READY IN:** 10 Minutes ✳ **SERVINGS:** 16

| | |
|---|---|
| 3-1/2 cups ruby red grapefruit juice, chilled | 1/2 cup sugar |
| 1/4 cup lemon juice | 4 cups club soda, chilled |
| 3 tablespoons lime juice | |

1 In large punch bowl or pitcher, combine juices and sugar; mix well. Just before serving, add club soda; stir gently. Serve over ice.

NUTRITION INFORMATION PER SERVING: Calories 50 • Total Fat 0g • Saturated Fat 0g • Cholesterol 0mg • Sodium 15mg • Total Carbohydrate 12g • Dietary Fiber 0g • Protein 0g. DIETARY EXCHANGES: 1 Other Carbohydrate • 1 Carb Choice.

*kitchen tip*

*One medium lemon and one medium lime yield the right amount of juice for this no-fuss beverage.*

# strawberry-orange fruit dip

**PREP TIME:** 15 Minutes ✳ **READY IN:** 15 Minutes ✳ 12 **SERVINGS:** 2 tablespoons of dip each

| | |
|---|---|
| 1 package (8 oz.) cream cheese, softened | 1/2 cup chopped strawberries (about 3 oz.) |
| 1/4 cup powdered sugar | Assorted fruit for dipping, as desired |
| 1/2 teaspoon grated orange peel | |

1 In small bowl, beat the cream cheese, powdered sugar and orange peel with electric mixer on low speed until smooth. Stir in the strawberries. Serve with assorted fruit. Cover and refrigerate any remaining dip.

NUTRITION INFORMATION PER SERVING: Calories 80 • Total Fat 7g • Saturated Fat 4g • Cholesterol 20mg • Sodium 55mg • Total Carbohydrate 4g • Dietary Fiber 0g • Protein 1g. DIETARY EXCHANGES: 1-1/2 Fat.

# picadillo empanadas

PREP TIME: 30 Minutes ✳ READY IN: 50 Minutes ✳ SERVINGS: 10

| | |
|---|---|
| 2 tablespoons vegetable oil | 1/2 teaspoon chicken bouillon granules |
| 1/2 cup finely chopped onion | 2 tablespoons slivered almonds |
| 2 cloves garlic, finely chopped | 2 tablespoons pitted chopped green olives, drained |
| 2/3 cup 1/8-inch cubes carrots | Raisins, if desired |
| 1 cup peeled 1/8-inch cubes red potatoes | 1 box Pillsbury® refrigerated pie crusts, softened as directed on box |
| 1/2 lb. lean (at least 80%) ground beef | |
| 1/2 cup tomato sauce | |

1   Heat oven to 350°F. In 10-inch skillet, heat oil over medium-high heat. Cook onion and garlic in oil 2 minutes. Stir in carrots and potatoes. Cook 4 minutes. Stir in beef. Cook until beef is brown; drain. Stir in sauce and bouillon granules. Cook until potatoes are tender and mixture thickens. Stir in almonds, green olives and raisins. Remove from heat; cool slightly.

2   On lightly floured surface, roll pie crusts into two 14-inch circles. Using 4-1/2-inch round cutter, cut 10 circles. Spoon 1 rounded tablespoonful filling onto half of each circle. Moisten edge of each with water. Fold in half; press edge with fork to seal. On ungreased cookie sheet, place 2 inches apart. Poke top of each once with fork to vent steam.

3   Bake about 20 minutes or until light golden brown. Store leftovers loosely covered in the refrigerator.

NUTRITION INFORMATION PER SERVING: Calories 290 • Total Fat 18g • Saturated Fat 5g • Cholesterol 20mg • Sodium 330mg • Total Carbohydrate 27g • Dietary Fiber 1g • Protein 6g. DIETARY EXCHANGES: 2 Starch • 3-1/2 Fat • 2 Carb Choices.

# bacon-crab dip

PREP TIME: 10 Minutes ✻ READY IN: 1 Hour 10 Minutes ✻ SERVINGS: 12

1 package (8 oz.) cream cheese, softened

1/2 cup sour cream

2 teaspoons prepared horseradish

1/8 teaspoon pepper

4 imitation crabmeat sticks, chopped (1 cup)

4 slices bacon, crisply cooked, crumbled

2 medium green onions, sliced (2 tablespoons)

Toasted bagels, cut into fourths or whole wheat crackers, if desired

Green onion, if desired

1 In medium bowl using electric mixer, beat cream cheese and sour cream on medium speed until smooth and fluffy. By hand, stir in remaining ingredients except bagels and green onion. Cover; refrigerate at least 1 hour to blend flavors. Place the dip in serving bowl. Serve with bagels. Cover and refrigerate any remaining dip.

NUTRITION INFORMATION PER SERVING: Calories 110 • Total Fat 10g • Saturated Fat 6g • Cholesterol 35mg • Sodium 220mg • Total Carbohydrate 2g • Dietary Fiber 0g • Protein 4g. DIETARY EXCHANGES: 1/2 Very Lean Meat • 2 Fat.

## kitchen tip

A 6-oz can crabmeat, drained, cartilage removed, can be substituted for imitation crabmeat sticks.

# pizza crisps

PREP TIME: 20 Minutes ✳ READY IN: 40 Minutes ✳ SERVINGS: 36

| | |
|---|---|
| 1-1/4 lb. lean (at least 80%) ground beef | 2 cups shredded Cheddar-American cheese blend (8 oz.) |
| 1/2 cup diced pepperoni (from 6-oz. pkg.) | 36 slices sourdough cocktail bread |
| 1 can (8 oz.) pizza sauce | |
| 1 cup shredded 6 cheese Italian cheese blend (4 oz.) | |

1 Heat oven to 350°F. In 10-inch skillet, cook ground beef over medium-high heat 5 to 7 minutes, stirring occasionally, until thoroughly cooked; drain. Stir in pepperoni and pizza sauce. Cook 2 to 3 minutes over medium heat until hot. Stir in Italian cheese blend and 1 cup of the Cheddar-American cheese blend until melted.

2 Arrange bread slices on 2 ungreased cookie sheets. Spread generous tablespoon of beef mixture on each slice. Top each with about 1 teaspoon of the remaining cheese. Bake 15 to 20 minutes or until thoroughly heated and crisp. Serve warm.

NUTRITION INFORMATION PER SERVING: Calories 80 • Total Fat 5g • Saturated Fat 2.5g • Cholesterol 20mg • Sodium 230mg • Total Carbohydrate 3g • Dietary Fiber 0g • Protein 6g. DIETARY EXCHANGES: 1 Medium-Fat Meat.

# bratwurst braids

PREP TIME: 15 Minutes ❋ READY IN: 35 Minutes ❋ SERVINGS: 4

1 can (8 oz.) Pillsbury® refrigerated crescent dinner rolls

4 teaspoons spicy brown mustard

1 can (8 oz.) sauerkraut, well drained on paper towels (1 cup)

4 fully cooked smoked bratwurst (thawed if frozen)

1 egg, beaten

1/2 teaspoon caraway seed

1 Heat oven to 375°F. Spray cookie sheet with cooking spray. Unroll dough and separate into 4 rectangles; place on cookie sheet. Press each into 6x4-inch rectangle, firmly pressing the perforations to seal.

2 Spread 1 teaspoon mustard over each rectangle to within 1/2 inch of all edges. Place 1/4 cup sauerkraut and 1 bratwurst lengthwise down center of each rectangle.

3 On long sides of each rectangle, make 5 cuts at an angle and 1 inch apart almost to edge of sauerkraut. For braided appearance, fold strips of dough at an angle across bratwurst with ends of strips slightly overlapping, alternating from side to side; press ends to seal. Brush tops with egg; sprinkle with caraway seed.

4 Bake 15 to 20 minutes or until deep golden brown. Immediately remove from cookie sheet. Serve warm with additional mustard, if desired.

NUTRITION INFORMATION PER SERVING: Calories 490 • Total Fat 34g • Saturated Fat 11g • Cholesterol 105mg • Sodium 1990mg • Total Carbohydrate 33g • Dietary Fiber 2g • Protein 16g. DIETARY EXCHANGES: 2 Starch • 1-1/2 High-Fat Meat • 4 Fat • 2 Carb Choices.

## kitchen tip

*Use cooked bratwurst because the uncooked variety will not cook completely in the short bake time. Be sure the bratwurst label indicates that it is "fully cooked."*

# roast beef rolls

PREP TIME: 10 Minutes ❋ READY IN: 10 Minutes ❋ SERVINGS: 24

6 slices cooked roast beef (from deli), 1/8 inch thick (about 3/4 lb.)

6 tablespoons chive-and-onion cream cheese spread (from 8-oz. container)

1-1/2 teaspoons prepared horseradish

12 snack-size dill pickles (about 2-1/4 inch)

1 On each slice of roast beef, spread 1 tablespoon cream cheese spread and 1/4 teaspoon horseradish.

2 Place 2 pickles, end to end, on one short side of each roast beef slice; roll up. Cut each roll crosswise into 4 pieces.

NUTRITION INFORMATION PER SERVING: Calories 50 • Total Fat 3g • Saturated Fat 1.5g • Cholesterol 15mg • Sodium 270mg • Total Carbohydrate 0g • Dietary Fiber 0g • Protein 4g. DIETARY EXCHANGES: 1/2 Medium-Fat Meat • 0 Carb Choice.

# Christmas Breads
# & Baked Goods

*Let the enticing aroma* of fresh-baked breads, golden biscuits and delectable coffee cakes bring warm smiles and comfort to your home during the frosty days of winter.

p. 43

p. 40

p. 60

p. 50

p. 41

cherry cream cheese
coffee cake p. 53

## cook's notes

*For a sweet treat, brush the shaped pretzels with melted butter and sprinkle with a mixture of cinnamon and sugar before baking. Skip the dip.*

# mini soft pretzels and dip

PREP TIME: 15 Minutes ✻ READY IN: 30 Minutes ✻ SERVINGS: 24

1 can (11 oz.) Pillsbury® refrigerated original breadsticks

1 egg, beaten

Kosher (coarse) salt, if desired

1 jar (5 oz.) pasteurized process cheese spread with bacon

2 tablespoons milk

1   Heat oven to 375°F. Unroll dough; separate into 12 breadsticks. Cut each in half lengthwise. Roll each breadstick lightly to form 10-inch-long rope.

2   To shape each pretzel, shape rope into a circle, overlapping dough about 2 inches from each end, leaving ends free. Take 1 end in each hand; twist once at point where dough overlaps. Lift ends over opposite side of circle into pretzel. On ungreased cookie sheet, place pretzels 1 inch apart. Brush each with beaten egg; sprinkle with salt.

3   Bake 13 to 15 minutes or until golden brown. Meanwhile, in small microwavable bowl, mix cheese spread and milk. Microwave on High 1 minute, stirring once halfway through cooking, until melted and hot. Remove pretzels from cookie sheet. Serve warm pretzels with warm cheese dip.

NUTRITION INFORMATION PER SERVING: Calories 60 • Total Fat 2.5g • Saturated Fat 1g • Cholesterol 15mg • Sodium 180mg • Total Carbohydrate 7g • Dietary Fiber 0g • Protein 2g. DIETARY EXCHANGES: 1/2 Starch • 1/2 Fat • 1/2 Carb Choice.

# maple pecan crescent twists

PREP TIME: 40 Minutes ✳ READY IN: 40 Minutes ✳ SERVINGS: 8

### ROLLS
- 1/2 cup finely chopped pecans
- 3 tablespoons granulated sugar
- 1 teaspoon ground cinnamon
- 1/8 teaspoon ground nutmeg
- 2 cans (8 oz. each) Pillsbury® refrigerated crescent dinner rolls
- 2 tablespoons butter or margarine, melted

### GLAZE
- 1/2 cup powdered sugar
- 1/4 teaspoon maple flavor
- 2 to 3 teaspoons milk

**JEAN OLSON**
Wallingford, Iowa
Bake-Off® Contest 35, 1992

1 Heat oven to 375°F. Spray 1 large or 2 small cookie sheets with cooking spray. In small bowl, mix pecans, granulated sugar, cinnamon and nutmeg.

2 Unroll both cans of dough; separate into 8 rectangles. Firmly press perforations to seal. Brush each rectangle with butter. Sprinkle 1 tablespoon pecan-sugar mixture evenly over each rectangle; press down lightly. Starting with long side, roll up each rectangle; pinch edges to seal.

3 With sharp knife, cut each roll in half lengthwise, forming 2 strips. With cut side up, carefully overlap strips 2 times to form each twist. Press ends together to seal. Place on cookie sheet. Sprinkle with any remaining pecan-sugar mixture.

4 Bake 10 to 15 minutes or until golden brown. In small bowl, mix all glaze ingredients, adding enough milk for desired drizzling consistency. Drizzle over warm rolls. Serve warm.

NUTRITION INFORMATION PER SERVING: Calories 340 • Total Fat 20g • Saturated Fat 6g • Cholesterol 10mg • Sodium 460mg • Total Carbohydrate 35g • Dietary Fiber 1g • Protein 5g. DIETARY EXCHANGES: 1 Starch • 1-1/2 Other Carbohydrate • 4 Fat • 2 Carb Choices.

# cheese crescent triangles

PREP TIME: 20 Minutes ✳ READY IN: 35 Minutes ✳ SERVINGS: 24

## cook's notes

*These triangles can be shaped up to 2 hours ahead; cover with plastic wrap and refrigerate. Just before serving, uncover and bake the triangles as directed.*

4 oz. tomato-basil feta cheese, finely crumbled (1 cup)

2 tablespoons finely chopped green onions (2 medium)

1 egg, well beaten

1 can (8 oz.) Pillsbury® refrigerated crescent dinner rolls or 1 can (8 oz.) Pillsbury® Crescent Recipe Creations® refrigerated seamless dough sheet

1 tablespoon grated Parmesan cheese

1 Heat the oven to 375°F. In small bowl, mix the feta cheese, green onions and 3 tablespoons of the beaten egg.

2 If using crescent rolls: Unroll dough and separate into 4 rectangles. Press perforations to seal. If using dough sheet: Unroll dough and cut into 4 rectangles.

3 Press each rectangle into 7-1/2 x 5-inch rectangle. Cut rectangle into 3 rows by 2 rows to make 6 (2-1/2-inch) squares. Top each dough square with a slightly rounded measuring teaspoon of feta cheese mixture. Fold dough over filling, forming triangle; press edges to seal. On ungreased cookie sheets, place triangles 2 inches apart. Repeat with remaining 3 dough rectangles and feta cheese mixture.

4 Brush tops with remaining beaten egg. Sprinkle lightly with Parmesan cheese. Bake 9 to 11 minutes or until golden brown. Serve warm.

NUTRITION INFORMATION PER SERVING: Calories 60 • Total Fat 3.5g • Saturated Fat 1.5g • Cholesterol 15mg • Sodium 150mg • Total Carbohydrate 4g • Dietary Fiber 0g • Protein 2g. DIETARY EXCHANGES: 1/2 Starch • 1/2 Fat.

# giant cinnamon-cheese danish

PREP TIME: 15 Minutes ✳ READY IN: 55 Minutes ✳ SERVINGS: 6

1 can (17.5 oz.) Pillsbury® Grands!® refrigerated cinnamon rolls with icing

1 package (8 oz.) cream cheese, softened

1/2 cup sugar

2 teaspoons sour cream

1 teaspoon lemon juice

1 teaspoon vanilla

**BETTY NICOSON**
Terre Haute, Indiana
Bake-Off® Contest 41, 2004

1 Heat oven to 350°F. Lightly grease 9-inch glass pie plate with shortening, or spray with Crisco® original no-stick cooking spray. Separate dough into 5 rolls; set icing aside. Unroll 1 roll into long strip of dough; reroll loosely and place in center of pie plate. Unroll second roll; loosely wrap around first roll, cinnamon side in. Replace any cinnamon that falls off. Repeat with remaining rolls, coiling dough in pie plate into spiral shape.

2 In small bowl, beat remaining ingredients except icing with electric mixer on medium speed until smooth. Spoon cream cheese mixture into decorating bag with tip or gallon-size resealable food-storage plastic bag with 1/2-inch hole cut in bottom corner. With tip or corner of bag about halfway down into rolls, pipe mixture between strips of dough, starting at center and working to edge of pan, using all of mixture.

3 Bake 25 to 35 minutes or until the center is thoroughly baked and edges are deep golden brown. Cool 5 minutes. Meanwhile, remove cover from icing; microwave on Medium (50%) 10 to 15 seconds or until thin enough to drizzle. Drizzle icing over warm coffee cake. Cut into wedges. Serve warm.

NUTRITION INFORMATION PER SERVING: Calories 480 • Total Fat 23g • Saturated Fat 11g • Cholesterol 45mg • Sodium 750mg • Total Carbohydrate 61g • Dietary Fiber 0g • Protein 6g. DIETARY EXCHANGES: 2-1/2 Starch • 1-1/2 Other Carbohydrate • 4 Fat • 4 Carb Choices.

# apricot-almond coffee cake

PREP TIME: 20 Minutes ✷ READY IN: 1 Hour 25 Minutes ✷ SERVINGS: 12

| | |
|---|---|
| 1 package (3 oz.) cream cheese, softened | 1/2 cup powdered sugar |
| 1/2 cup almond paste, crumbled | 2 teaspoons milk |
| 1 can (8 oz.) Pillsbury® refrigerated crescent dinner rolls | 1 tablespoon sliced almonds |
| 1/3 cup apricot preserves | |

1 Heat oven to 375°F. Grease cookie sheet with shortening or cooking spray. In small bowl, beat cream cheese with electric mixer on low speed until smooth and creamy. Beat in almond paste until well mixed.

2 Unroll dough onto cookie sheet; press into 13 x 7-inch rectangle, firmly pressing perforations to seal. Spoon cream cheese mixture lengthwise down center 1/3 of rectangle; spoon preserves on top of cheese mixture.

3 On each long side of dough rectangle, make cuts 1 inch apart to edge of filling. Fold opposite strips of dough over filling, and cross in center to make a braided appearance; seal ends.

4 Bake 18 to 22 minutes or until golden brown. Remove from cookie sheet to cooling rack. Cool completely, about 40 minutes.

5 In small bowl, mix powdered sugar and milk until smooth; drizzle over coffee cake. Garnish with sliced almonds.

NUTRITION INFORMATION PER SERVING: Calories 190 • Total Fat 9g • Saturated Fat 3g • Cholesterol 10mg • Sodium 170mg • Total Carbohydrate 24g • Dietary Fiber 1g • Protein 3g. DIETARY EXCHANGES: 1/2 Starch • 1 Other Carbohydrate • 2 Fat • 1-1/2 Carb Choices.

# artichoke-cheese braids

PREP TIME: 20 Minutes ✳ READY IN: 45 Minutes ✳ SERVINGS: 32

3/4 cup drained finely chopped artichoke hearts (from 14-oz. can), patted dry with paper towels

1/2 cup grated Parmesan cheese

2 tablespoons mayonnaise

1 can (8 oz.) Pillsbury® refrigerated crescent dinner rolls

1 jar (2 oz.) diced pimiento, drained, patted dry with paper towels

1 egg, beaten

1 teaspoon grated Parmesan cheese

1 Heat oven to 375°F. In small bowl, mix the artichokes, 1/2 cup Parmesan cheese and the mayonnaise.

2 Unroll dough and separate into 2 long rectangles; place crosswise on opposite ends of ungreased large cookie sheet. Press each into 11 x 4-1/2-inch rectangle; firmly press perforations to seal.

3 Spoon half of artichoke mixture lengthwise down center of each rectangle in 1-1/2-inch-wide strip. Top each evenly with pimiento.

4 On long sides of each rectangle, make 15 cuts about 3/4 inch apart almost to edge of artichoke mixture. For braided appearance, fold strips of dough at an angle halfway across artichoke mixture with ends of strips slightly overlapping, alternating from side to side; pinch to seal.

5 Bring ends of each braid together to form ring; press ends together to seal. Carefully brush tops of rings with egg; sprinkle with 1 teaspoon Parmesan cheese.

6 Bake 13 to 18 minutes or until deep golden brown. Cool 5 minutes. Carefully loosen the braids from cookie sheet with a wide spatula; slide onto a serving plate. Cut between strips into thin slices; serve warm.

NUTRITION INFORMATION PER SERVING: Calories 45 • Total Fat 2g • Saturated Fat 1g • Cholesterol 10mg • Sodium 135mg • Total Carbohydrate 4g • Dietary Fiber 0g • Protein 2g. DIETARY EXCHANGES: 1/2 Fat.

ELAINE A. JANAS
Columbia Heights, Minnesota
Bake-Off® Contest 39, 1996

### cook's notes

Lemon pie filling can be substituted for the lemon curd. Also, to quickly prepare the streusel, simply use a food processor to process until crumbly.

# lemon surprise coffee cake

PREP TIME: 30 Minutes ✳ READY IN: 2 Hours 40 Minutes ✳ SERVINGS: 12

**STREUSEL**
1/2 cup all-purpose flour
1/3 cup sugar
3 tablespoons butter or margarine
1/2 cup coconut

**COFFEE CAKE**
2-1/4 cups all-purpose flour
1 cup sugar
1/2 teaspoon baking powder
1/2 teaspoon baking soda
1/2 teaspoon salt
3/4 cup butter or margarine, softened
2/3 cup vanilla yogurt
2 teaspoons grated lemon peel
1 tablespoon lemon juice
1 egg
1 egg yolk
1/2 cup lemon curd

**GLAZE**
1/2 cup powdered sugar
1 teaspoon lemon juice
1 teaspoon water

1 Heat oven to 350°F. Grease and flour 10- or 9-inch springform pan. In medium bowl, mix 1/2 cup flour and 1/3 cup sugar. With fork or pastry blender, cut in 3 tablespoons butter until mixture looks like coarse crumbs. Stir in coconut; set aside.

2 In large bowl, mix 2-1/4 cups flour, 1 cup sugar, the baking powder, baking soda and salt. Add 3/4 cup butter, the yogurt, lemon peel, 1 tablespoon lemon juice, egg and yolk. Stir mixture with spoon until well blended.

3 Spread 2 cups of the batter in pan; sprinkle with 3/4 cup of the streusel. Drop lemon curd by 1/2 teaspoonfuls over streusel to within 1/2 inch of edge. Spoon remaining batter over lemon curd; sprinkle with remaining streusel.

4 Bake 50 to 60 minutes or until toothpick inserted in center comes out clean. Cool 10 minutes. Remove side of pan.

5 In small bowl, mix the glaze ingredients until smooth. Drizzle over the coffee cake. Cool 1 hour. Serve warm.

NUTRITION INFORMATION PER SERVING: Calories 420 • Total Fat 17g • Saturated Fat 10g • Cholesterol 75mg • Sodium 340mg • Total Carbohydrate 61g • Dietary Fiber 1g • Protein 5g. DIETARY EXCHANGES: 2 Starch • 2 Fruit • 4 Other Carbohydrate • 3 Fat.

# chive crescents

PREP TIME: 5 Minutes ✳ READY IN: 20 Minutes ✳ SERVINGS: 8

1 can (8 oz) Pillsbury® refrigerated crescent dinner rolls
1 tablespoon butter, melted
1/4 cup chopped fresh chives

1 Heat oven to 375°F. Unroll dough into 1 large rectangle; brush with butter. Separate dough into triangles; sprinkle buttered side of each with chives.

2 Starting with shortest side of each triangle, roll up dough to opposite point. Place point side down on ungreased cookie sheet, curving each into a crescent shape.

3 Bake 10 to 13 minutes or until golden brown. Immediately remove crescents from cookie sheet; serve warm.

NUTRITION INFORMATION PER SERVING: Calories 120 • Total Fat 7g • Saturated Fat 2.5g • Cholesterol 0mg • Sodium 230mg • Total Carbohydrate 11g • Dietary Fiber 0g • Protein 2g. DIETARY EXCHANGES: 1 Starch • 1 Fat • 1 Carb Choice.

lemon surprise coffee cake

# pizza biscuit wreath

**PREP TIME:** 20 Minutes ✳ **READY IN:** 40 Minutes ✳ **SERVINGS:** 10

2 cans (12 oz. each) Pillsbury® Grands!® Jr. Golden Layers® refrigerated buttermilk biscuits

60 small slices (1-1/2 inch) pepperoni (3-1/2 oz.)

5 sticks (3/4 oz. each) Colby-Monterey Jack cheese, each cut crosswise into 4 pieces

1 egg, beaten

2 tablespoons shredded Parmesan cheese

1/2 teaspoon Italian seasoning

1 can (8 oz.) pizza sauce

1 Heat oven to 375°F. Spray large cookie sheet with cooking spray. Separate 1 can of dough into 10 biscuits; keep second can refrigerated. Press each biscuit into 3-inch round.

2 Place 3 pepperoni slices and 1 piece of cheese on each dough round. Wrap the dough around the filling, pinching edges to seal and form a ball. Repeat with remaining can of dough, pepperoni and cheese.

3 Leaving a 4-inch hole in center, arrange 8 balls, seam side down and sides almost touching, into ring on cookie sheet. Arrange remaining 12 balls, sides almost touching, around outer edge of first ring. Brush rings with beaten egg. Sprinkle with Parmesan cheese and Italian seasoning.

4 Bake 18 to 20 minutes or until golden brown. Meanwhile, in small microwavable bowl, microwave pizza sauce, loosely covered, on High 45 to 60 seconds or until warm.

5 Carefully slide wreath from cookie sheet onto serving platter. Place bowl of pizza sauce in center of wreath. Garnish with fresh oregano, if desired. Serve warm.

**HIGH ALTITUDE (3500-6500 FT):** Heat oven to 350°F. Bake 25 to 27 minutes.

NUTRITION INFORMATION PER SERVING: Calories 350 • Total Fat 21g • Saturated Fat 7g • Cholesterol 40mg • Sodium 1090mg • Total Carbohydrate 30g • Dietary Fiber 1g • Protein 10g. DIETARY EXCHANGES: 1-1/2 Starch • 1/2 Other Carbohydrate • 1 High-Fat Meat • 2-1/2 Fat • 2 Carb Choices.

*cook's notes*

*You can also serve these tasty bite-size biscuits with your favorite salad dressing or dip.*

# simply super crescent cinnamon rolls

PREP TIME: 15 Minutes ✷ READY IN: 40 Minutes ✷ SERVINGS: 8

**FILLING**
- 2/3 cup finely chopped pecans
- 1/3 cup packed brown sugar
- 1/3 cup powdered sugar
- 1 teaspoon ground cinnamon
- 1/4 cup butter, softened

**ROLLS**
- 2 cans (8 oz. each) Pillsbury® refrigerated crescent dinner rolls

**GLAZE**
- 1 cup powdered sugar
- 1 tablespoon butter, softened
- 2 to 3 tablespoons milk

1 Heat oven to 375°F. Grease 13 x 9-inch pan. In small bowl, mix all filling ingredients. Unroll 1 can of the dough into 1 large rectangle; press into 13 x 7-inch rectangle, firmly pressing perforations to seal. Spread filling over rectangle.

2 Unroll second can of dough; press into 13 x 7-inch rectangle, firmly pressing perforations to seal. Place over filling; press dough onto filling. Cut stacked dough into 8 (13-inch) strips. Twist each strip 5 or 6 times, pressing extra filling into rolls. Shape each into a coil; place in pan.

3 Bake 20 to 25 minutes or until golden brown. Immediately remove from pan; place on wire rack. In small bowl, blend all glaze ingredients, adding enough milk for desired drizzling consistency; drizzle over warm rolls. Serve warm.

NUTRITION INFORMATION PER SERVING: Calories 450 • Total Fat 23g • Saturated Fat 7g • Cholesterol 20mg • Sodium 770mg • Total Carbohydrate 57g • Dietary Fiber 2g • Protein 5g. DIETARY EXCHANGES: 2 Starch • 2 Other Carbohydrate • 4 Fat • 4 Carb Choices.

**DOROTHY VEASEY**
Fort Wayne, Indiana
Bake-Off® Contest 24, 1973

# gingerbread bran muffins

PREP TIME: 20 Minutes ✷ READY IN: 45 Minutes ✷ SERVINGS: 12

**MUFFINS**
- 1 egg
- 1/4 cup sugar
- 1 cup buttermilk
- 1/3 cup vegetable oil
- 1/4 cup molasses
- 1-1/2 cups bran cereal shreds (do not use bran flakes)
- 1 cup all-purpose flour
- 1-1/2 teaspoons baking powder
- 1/2 teaspoon baking soda
- 1/2 teaspoon ground ginger
- 1/4 teaspoon salt
- 1/4 teaspoon ground cinnamon
- 1/4 teaspoon ground cloves

**TOPPING**
- 2 tablespoons sugar

1 In medium bowl, lightly beat egg. Add 1/4 cup sugar, the buttermilk, oil and molasses; beat well with wire whisk. Stir in cereal. Let stand 10 minutes.

2 In small bowl, mix all remaining muffin ingredients. Add to bran mixture; mix well. Bake immediately, or cover and refrigerate 8 hours or overnight.

3 Heat oven to 375°F. Place paper baking cup in each of 12 regular-size muffin cups. Divide batter evenly among muffin cups. Sprinkle each with 1/2 teaspoon sugar.

4 Bake 20 to 25 minutes or until tops spring back when touched lightly. Remove from pan. Serve warm or cool.

NUTRITION INFORMATION PER SERVING: Calories 180 • Total Fat 7g • Saturated Fat 1.5g • Cholesterol 20mg • Sodium 220mg • Total Carbohydrate 27g • Dietary Fiber 4g • Protein 3g. DIETARY EXCHANGES: 1/2 Starch • 1-1/2 Other Carbohydrate • 1 Fat • 2 Carb Choices.

*cook's notes*

*For more whole grain goodness, you can substitute 1/2 cup whole wheat flour for 1/2 cup of the all-purpose flour.*

*cook's notes*

*If making this bread ahead of time, store the foil-wrapped loaf in the refrigerator until it is ready to be placed on the grill.*

# pesto-cheese bread

PREP TIME: 20 Minutes ✱ READY IN: 20 Minutes ✱ SERVINGS: 12

- 1  loaf Italian bread (10 to 12 inch)
- 1/3  cup refrigerated basil pesto (from 7-oz. container)
- 3/4  cup shredded mozzarella cheese (3 oz.)

1  Heat gas or charcoal grill. Cut 18 x 18-inch sheet of heavy-duty foil. Cut loaf of bread in half lengthwise. Spread each half with pesto. Sprinkle with cheese.

2  Place bread, cheese sides together, on foil; wrap securely using double fold seals, allowing room for heat expansion.

3  Place wrapped bread on grill over medium heat. Cover grill; cook 10 to 12 minutes, rotating and turning over occasionally, until bread is warm and cheese is melted.

4  Carefully unwrap bread to allow steam to escape. Separate loaf into 2 halves; cut each into 6 pieces. Serve immediately.

**HIGH ALTITUDE (3500-6500 FT):** Cook over medium-low heat.

NUTRITION INFORMATION PER SERVING: Calories 140 • Total Fat 6g • Saturated Fat 2g • Cholesterol 5mg • Sodium 270mg • Total Carbohydrate 16g • Dietary Fiber 1g • Protein 5g. DIETARY EXCHANGES: 1 Starch • 1 Fat • 1 Carb Choice.

# meatball bubble biscuits

PREP TIME: 15 Minutes ✻ READY IN: 40 Minutes ✻ SERVINGS: 20

1 can (12 oz.) Pillsbury® Grands!® Jr. Golden Layers® refrigerated buttermilk biscuits

10 frozen cooked Italian-style meatballs (about 5 oz.), thawed, each cut in half

2 sticks (1 oz. each) string cheese, each cut into 10 pieces

1 tablespoon grated Parmesan cheese

1/2 teaspoon Italian seasoning

1/4 teaspoon garlic powder

1 cup marinara sauce, heated

*kitchen tip*

*The size of purchased meatballs varies. We used meatballs that weighed about 1/2 ounce each for this recipe.*

1 Heat oven to 375°F. Separate dough into 10 biscuits. Separate each biscuit into 2 layers. Press each biscuit layer into 3-inch round.

2 Place 1 meatball half, cut side up, and 1 string cheese piece in center of each dough round. Wrap dough around meatball and cheese, pressing edges to seal. In ungreased 8- or 9-inch round cake pan, place seam side down in single layer. Sprinkle evenly with Parmesan cheese, Italian seasoning and garlic powder.

3 Bake 20 to 25 minutes or until golden brown and biscuits are no longer doughy in center. Serve warm biscuits with warm marinara sauce for dipping.

NUTRITION INFORMATION PER SERVING: Calories 105 • Total Fat 5g • Saturated Fat 2g • Cholesterol 10mg • Sodium 330mg • Total Carbohydrate 11g • Dietary Fiber 0g • Protein 4g. DIETARY EXCHANGES: 1/2 Starch • 1/2 Other Carbohydrate • 1/2 Medium-Fat Meat • 1/2 Fat • 1 Carb Choice.

# cherry cream cheese coffee cake

PREP TIME: 20 Minutes ✳ READY IN: 1 Hour 15 Minutes ✳ SERVINGS: 12

| | |
|---|---|
| 1 package (3 oz.) cream cheese, softened | 1 can (8 oz.) Pillsbury® refrigerated crescent dinner rolls |
| 2 tablespoons granulated sugar | 1/2 cup powdered sugar |
| 1 teaspoon almond extract | 2 teaspoons milk |
| 1/4 cup sliced almonds | |
| 1/4 cup chopped maraschino cherries, well drained | |

1 Heat oven to 375°F. Grease cookie sheet with shortening. In small bowl, beat cream cheese and granulated sugar until light and fluffy. Stir in almond extract, almonds and cherries; set aside.

2 Unroll dough onto cookie sheet; press into 13 x 7-inch rectangle, firmly pressing perforations to seal. Spoon cream cheese mixture lengthwise down center 1/3 of rectangle.

3 On each long side of dough rectangle, make cuts 1 inch apart to edge of filling. Fold opposite strips of dough over filling and cross in center to form a braided appearance; seal ends.

4 Bake 18 to 22 minutes or until golden brown. Remove from cookie sheet to cooling rack. Cool completely, about 30 minutes.

5 In small bowl, mix powdered sugar and milk until smooth; drizzle over coffee cake. If desired, garnish with additional sliced almonds and cherries. Store in refrigerator.

NUTRITION INFORMATION PER SERVING: Calories 140 • Total Fat 7g • Saturated Fat 3g • Cholesterol 10mg • Sodium 170mg • Total Carbohydrate 16g • Dietary Fiber 0g • Protein 2g. DIETARY EXCHANGES: 1/2 Starch • 1/2 Other Carbohydrate • 1-1/2 Fat • 1 Carb Choice.

## cook's notes

*Frost a few cookies, then add the candy sprinkles as the white chocolate sets. For convenience, instead of frosting with melted white chocolate, you can roll the warm cookies in powdered sugar to coat them.*

# chocolate-orange shortbread bites

PREP TIME: 1 Hour ✳ READY IN: 1 Hour ✳ SERVINGS: 100

| | |
|---|---|
| 1 cup butter, softened | 1/4 cup miniature semisweet chocolate chips |
| 1/2 cup powdered sugar | 2 oz. white chocolate baking bar, chopped |
| 2 cups all-purpose flour | Candy sprinkles or small candy decors |
| 1 tablespoon grated orange peel | |

1 Heat oven to 325°F. In large bowl, beat butter and powdered sugar with electric mixer on medium speed about 1 minute or until fluffy. On low speed, beat in flour and orange peel until mixed. With spoon, stir in chocolate chips.

2 On work surface, pat dough into 6-1/2 x 6-1/2-inch square, 3/4-inch thick. With floured knife, cut 10 rows by 10 rows. Place squares 1/2-inch apart on ungreased cookie sheets.

3 Bake 18 to 22 minutes or until firm to touch and set. Remove from cookie sheets to cooling racks. Cool completely, about 10 minutes.

4 In small microwavable bowl, microwave baking bar on High 30 seconds; stir. If necessary, microwave in 10 second increments, stirring after each time until smooth. Spread melted baking bar over top of each cookie. Top with candy sprinkles.

NUTRITION INFORMATION PER SERVING: Calories 35 • Total Fat 2g • Saturated Fat 1.5g • Cholesterol 0mg • Sodium 15mg • Total Carbohydrate 3g • Dietary Fiber 0g • Protein 0g. DIETARY EXCHANGES: 1/2 Other Carbohydrate.

cherry cream cheese
coffee cake

**KAREN KWAN**
Belmont, California
Bake-Off® Contest 38, 1998

*cook's notes*

*To create your own substitute*

*for the garlic salt with parsley*

*blend, use a mixture of 1/2*

*teaspoon garlic salt plus*

*a dash of dried parsley*

*flakes.*

# cheddar twisters

PREP TIME: 10 Minutes ✳ READY IN: 35 Minutes ✳ SERVINGS: 8

| | |
|---|---|
| 2 cans (8 oz. each) Pillsbury® refrigerated crescent dinner rolls | 1 egg |
| 1-1/2 cups finely shredded sharp Cheddar cheese (6 oz.) | 1 teaspoon water |
| 1/4 cup chopped green onions (4 medium) | 2 teaspoons sesame seed |
| | 1/2 teaspoon garlic salt with parsley blend (from 4.8-oz. jar) |

1. Heat oven to 375°F. Lightly grease large cookie sheet. Unroll both cans of the dough and separate into 8 rectangles; firmly press perforations to seal.

2. In small bowl, mix cheese and onions. Spoon a scant 1/4 cup cheese mixture in 1-inch-wide strip lengthwise down center of each rectangle to within 1/4 inch of each end. Fold dough in half lengthwise to form long strip; firmly press edges to seal. Twist each strip 4 or 5 times; bring ends together to form ring and pinch to seal. Place on cookie sheet.

3. In another small bowl, beat egg and water until well blended; brush over dough. Sprinkle with sesame seed and garlic salt blend.

4. Bake 15 to 20 minutes or until golden brown. Immediately remove from the cookie sheet; cool 5 minutes. Serve warm.

NUTRITION INFORMATION PER SERVING: Calories 300 • Total Fat 16g • Saturated Fat 7g • Cholesterol 50mg • Sodium 850mg • Total Carbohydrate 28g • Dietary Fiber 1g • Protein 10g. DIETARY EXCHANGES: 2 Starch • 1/2 High-Fat Meat • 2 Fat • 2 Carb Choices.

# almond scones

PREP TIME: 20 Minutes ✳ READY IN: 50 Minutes ✳ SERVINGS: 12

| | |
|---|---|
| 2 cups all-purpose flour | 1/2 cup milk |
| 1/4 cup granulated sugar | 1/4 teaspoon almond extract |
| 2 teaspoons baking powder | 1 egg, beaten |
| 1/4 teaspoon salt | Sliced almonds, if desired |
| 6 tablespoons butter | Coarse sugar, if desired |
| 1/3 cup almond paste, cut into small pieces | |

1 Heat oven to 400°F. Lightly coat cookie sheet with cooking spray. In large bowl, mix flour, granulated sugar, baking powder and salt. With pastry blender or fork, cut in butter until mixture resembles coarse crumbs. Stir in almond paste, separating pieces to coat each with flour mixture.

2 In small bowl, mix milk, almond extract and egg until blended. Add to flour mixture. Stir just until dry ingredients are moistened.

3 On floured surface, gently knead dough about 6 times. Divide dough in half; shape each into ball. Pat each ball into 5-inch round with center higher than edges. Brush with milk; sprinkle with almonds and coarse sugar. Cut each round into 6 wedges; place 1 inch apart on cookie sheet. Bake 13 to 15 minutes or until light golden brown. Cool 10 minutes before serving.

NUTRITION INFORMATION PER SERVING: Calories 190 • Total Fat 8g • Saturated Fat 4g • Cholesterol 35mg • Sodium 180mg • Total Carbohydrate 24g • Dietary Fiber 1g • Protein 4g. DIETARY EXCHANGES: 1 Starch • 1/2 Other Carbohydrate • 1-1/2 Fat • 1-1/2 Carb Choices.

*cook's notes*

*Arrange the scone wedges on a cookie sheet, cover loosely with plastic wrap and refrigerate for up to an hour before baking.*

**MAUREEN MCBRIDE**
San Jose, California
Bake-Off® Contest 42, 2006

*kitchen tip*

Look for the parchment paper

with the other paper products

at your grocery store. It's

great for making cookies and

other items—and cleanup is

extra easy!

# crescent bear claws

PREP TIME: 20 Minutes ✳ READY IN: 45 Minutes ✳ SERVINGS: 6

### FILLING
- 1 egg
- 2 tablespoons milk
- 1 cup Progresso® plain bread crumbs
- 2 tablespoons granulated sugar
- 2 tablespoons butter or margarine, melted
- 1/4 cup water
- 2 teaspoons almond extract

### GLAZE
- 1/2 cup granulated sugar
- 1/4 cup water
- 1 tablespoon light corn syrup

### ROLLS
- 1 can (8 oz.) Pillsbury® refrigerated crescent dinner rolls or 1 can (8 oz.) Pillsbury® Crescent Recipe Creations® refrigerated seamless dough sheet
- 1/3 to 1/2 cup sliced almonds

### ICING
- 1 cup powdered sugar
- 2 tablespoons water

1 Heat oven to 375°F. Line cookie sheet with cooking parchment paper. In medium bowl, beat egg lightly with wire whisk. Place half of egg (about 1-1/2 tablespoons) in custard cup; beat in milk until blended, and set aside. To remaining egg in bowl, stir in remaining filling ingredients until well blended.

2 Meanwhile, in 1-quart heavy saucepan, mix glaze ingredients. Heat to boiling. Remove from heat; cool while making rolls.

3 On lightly floured work surface, unroll dough (if using crescent rolls, pinch seams to seal). Press into 12 x 8-inch rectangle. Spoon filling into 12 x 2-inch strip lengthwise down center 1/3 of dough. Fold 1/3 of dough over filling. Fold filling-topped section over last 1/3 of dough so seam is on bottom of folded dough. With hand, gently flatten 1-inch-wide strip of dough along one long side of folded dough. Cut folded dough crosswise into 6 (2-inch) pastries. Along flattened edge of each pastry, cut 1-inch-long cuts about 1/2 inch apart.

4 Lightly brush the egg-milk mixture over each pastry. Place almonds on plate; turn each pastry upside down onto almonds, and press gently so almonds stick to dough. Place almond side up on cookie sheet, spreading each cut slightly to form claw shape. Sprinkle remaining almonds over tops of pastries.

5 Bake 15 to 18 minutes or until golden brown. Remove to cooling rack; cool 5 minutes. Drizzle cooled glaze over each pastry. In another small bowl, mix the icing ingredients until smooth (if icing is too thick, add 1/2 teaspoon water at a time until drizzling consistency). Drizzle icing over cooled pastries.

**HIGH ALTITUDE (3500-6500 FT):** Bake 14 to 17 minutes.

NUTRITION INFORMATION PER SERVING: Calories 440 • Total Fat 15g • Saturated Fat 5g • Cholesterol 45mg • Sodium 370mg • Total Carbohydrate 71g • Dietary Fiber 0g • Protein 5g. DIETARY EXCHANGES: 1-1/2 Starch • 3 Other Carbohydrate • 3 Fat • 5 Carb Choices.

# strawberry-orange butterfly biscuits

PREP TIME: 20 Minutes ✻ READY IN: 40 Minutes ✻ SERVINGS: 8

1 can (16.3 oz.) Pillsbury® Grands!® flaky
  layers refrigerated original biscuits

3 tablespoons strawberry preserves

  Grated peel of 1 medium orange
  (1 to 2 tablespoons)

1 heaping tablespoon coarse white
  sparkling sugar

1/2 cup whipping cream

  2 teaspoons granulated sugar

1/4 teaspoon vanilla, if desired

1-1/2 pints (3 cups) fresh strawberries, sliced

*kitchen tip*

*Regular granulated sugar*

*can be substituted for the*

*sparkling sugar.*

1  Heat oven to 350°F. Spray large cookie sheet with cooking spray. Separate dough into 8 biscuits.
   Separate each biscuit into 2 layers; spread about 1/2 teaspoon preserves between layers, then put
   biscuits back together. Pinch edges together to seal. Cut biscuits in half. Place 2 halves on cookie
   sheet with round edges overlapping slightly to look like butterfly; press together where round
   edges touch. Make 7 more butterfly biscuits.

2  Spread remaining preserves on tops of biscuits; sprinkle each with orange peel and about 1/2
   teaspoon sparkling sugar.

3  Bake 12 to 15 minutes or until golden brown. Cool 5 minutes. Meanwhile, beat whipping cream
   with electric mixer on high speed until soft peaks form. Beat in granulated sugar and vanilla.

4  To serve, arrange strawberry slices on tops of butterfly biscuits for wings; pipe whipped cream to
   form body and antenna of each butterfly.

NUTRITION INFORMATION PER SERVING: Calories 290 • Total Fat 14g • Saturated Fat 5g • Cholesterol 15mg • Sodium 560mg •
Total Carbohydrate 38g • Dietary Fiber 1g • Protein 5g. DIETARY EXCHANGES: 1-1/2 Starch • 1 Other Carbohydrate • 2-1/2 Fat •
2-1/2 Carb Choices.

cheese steak crescent braids

# cheese steak crescent braids

PREP TIME: 35 Minutes ✳ READY IN: 1 Hour 5 Minutes ✳ SERVINGS: 6

1 tablespoon butter or margarine

4 portions thinly sliced frozen sandwich steaks (from 12.25-oz. box), cut crosswise into 1/2-inch strips

1 large green bell pepper, cut into thin bite-size strips (1-1/2 cups)

1 medium onion, chopped (1/2 cup)

2 cans (8 oz. each) Pillsbury® refrigerated crescent dinner rolls

1 cup shredded mozzarella cheese (4 oz.)

1 egg, beaten, if desired

1 Heat oven to 350°F. In 10-inch skillet, melt butter over medium-high heat. Add steak strips; cook 8 to 10 minutes, stirring frequently, until no longer pink. Remove steak from skillet; place on plate. Add bell pepper and onion to skillet; cook about 5 minutes, stirring occasionally, until crisp-tender. Return cooked steak to skillet; mix well. If desired, add salt and pepper to taste.

2 Unroll 1 can of dough onto ungreased cookie sheet, firmly press perforations and edges to seal. Press or roll into 13 x 7-inch rectangle.

3 Spoon heaping cup of steak mixture in 2-inch-wide strip lengthwise down center of dough to within 1/4 inch of each end. Sprinkle 1/2 cup of the cheese over steak mixture.

4 Make cuts 1 inch apart on long sides of rectangle just to edge of filling. For braided appearance, fold strips of dough at an angle halfway across filling with ends slightly overlapping, alternating from side to side. Fold ends of braid under to seal. On second ungreased cookie sheet, repeat with remaining can of dough, steak mixture and cheese. Brush braids with beaten egg.

5 Bake 16 to 22 minutes or until golden brown, switching position of cookie sheets in oven halfway through baking. Cool 1 minute; remove braids from cookie sheets. Let stand 5 minutes before serving. Cut into slices.

NUTRITION INFORMATION PER SERVING: Calories 410 • Total Fat 23g • Saturated Fat 9g • Cholesterol 35mg • Sodium 710mg • Total Carbohydrate 32g • Dietary Fiber 1g • Protein 19g. DIETARY EXCHANGES: 1-1/2 Starch • 1/2 Other Carbohydrate • 2 Medium-Fat Meat • 2-1/2 Fat • 2 Carb Choices.

**CINDY JOY**
Alameda, California
Bake-Off® Contest 33, 1988

*kitchen tip*

*Bell peppers—whether green, red or yellow—are rich in vitamin C, so try to work them into your dishes whenever possible.*

# peach crescent palmiers

PREP TIME: 20 Minutes ✳ READY IN: 35 Minutes ✳ SERVINGS: 16

3 tablespoons sugar

1 can (8 oz.) Pillsbury® refrigerated crescent dinner rolls

2 tablespoons butter or margarine, melted

3/4 cup pineapple cream cheese spread

1-2/3 cups thinly sliced peaches, halved

1 Heat oven to 375°F. On cutting board sprinkled with 1-1/2 tablespoons of the sugar, separate dough into 4 rectangles; firmly press perforations to seal. Lightly press dough into sugar. Brush rectangles with about 1 tablespoon of the melted butter; sprinkle with remaining sugar.

2 Using 2 rectangles, place one rectangle on top of the other. Starting with the shortest sides, roll up both ends jelly-roll fashion to meet in center. Cut into 8 slices. Repeat with the remaining 2 rectangles, forming 16 slices in all. Place, cut side down, 2 inches apart on ungreased cookie sheets. Brush with remaining melted butter.

3 Bake 10 to 13 minutes or until golden brown. Gently recoil cookie if necessary. Immediately remove from cookie sheets. Cool completely. Place cookies on serving plate. Place dollop of cream cheese spread on each cookie. Top each with sliced peaches.

NUTRITION INFORMATION PER SERVING: Calories 120 • Total Fat 8g • Saturated Fat 4g • Cholesterol 15mg • Sodium 200mg • Total Carbohydrate 10g • Dietary Fiber 0g • Protein 2g. DIETARY EXCHANGES: 1/2 Starch • 1-1/2 Fat • 1/2 Carb Choice.

# banana-strawberry muffins

PREP TIME: 15 Minutes ✳ READY IN: 40 Minutes ✳ SERVINGS: 12

| | |
|---|---|
| 2/3 cup sugar | 1 2/3 cups all-purpose flour |
| 1/2 cup oil | 1 teaspoon baking soda |
| 2 eggs | 1/2 teaspoon salt |
| 2/3 cup mashed ripe bananas | 3/4 cup finely chopped fresh strawberries |
| 1 teaspoon vanilla | |

1 Heat oven to 375°F. Line 12 muffin cups with paper baking cups. In medium bowl, combine sugar, oil and eggs; blend well. Stir in bananas and vanilla.

2 Add flour, baking soda and salt to sugar mixture; stir just until combined. Stir in strawberries. Spoon batter evenly into paper-lined muffin cups.

3 Bake 17 to 21 minutes or until toothpick inserted in center comes out clean. Immediately remove from muffin cups. Serve warm or cool.

**HIGH ALTITUDE (3500-6500 FT):** Increase flour to 1 2/3 cups plus 1 tablespoon. Spoon batter evenly into 14 muffin cups. Bake as directed above.

NUTRITION INFORMATION PER SERVING: Calories 210 • Total Fat 10g • Saturated Fat 1g • Cholesterol 35mg • Sodium 200mg • Total Carbohydrate 28g • Dietary Fiber 1g • Protein 3g. DIETARY EXCHANGES: 1 Starch • 1 Fruit • 2 Other Carbohydrate • 2 Fat.

## kitchen tip

*For the best banana-flavored baked goods, use ripe bananas with just a few dark spots on the peel. One large or 2 small bananas yield about 2/3 cup mashed.*

## cook's notes

*The gumdrops cut easily with floured kitchen scissors. If you have large gumdrops, just cut them into small pieces instead of in half.*

# gumdrop spice muffins

PREP TIME: 20 Minutes ✳ READY IN: 55 Minutes ✳ SERVINGS: 12

| | |
|---|---|
| 2 cups all-purpose flour | 1 cup small gumdrops, each cut in half |
| 2/3 cup sugar | 3/4 cup milk |
| 3 teaspoons baking powder | 1/3 cup oil |
| 1/2 teaspoon ground cinnamon | 1 egg, beaten |
| 1/2 teaspoon salt | 4 teaspoons sugar |

1 Heat oven to 400°F. Line 12 regular-size muffin cups with paper baking cups. In large bowl with wooden spoon, mix flour, 2/3 cup sugar, baking powder, cinnamon and salt. Reserve 36 gumdrop halves for topping. Stir remaining gumdrops into flour mixture until coated.

2 Stir in milk, oil and egg just until dry ingredients are moistened. Spoon into muffin cups, filling 3/4 full. Sprinkle batter with 4 teaspoons sugar. Place 3 gumdrop halves on top of each muffin.

3 Bake 20 to 25 minutes or until toothpick inserted in center comes out clean. Cool in pan 10 minutes. Serve warm or cool.

**HIGH ALTITUDE (3500-6500 FT):** Decrease baking powder to 1-3/4 teaspoons.

NUTRITION INFORMATION PER SERVING: Calories 250 • Total Fat 7g • Saturated Fat 1g • Cholesterol 20mg • Sodium 240mg • Total Carbohydrate 45g • Dietary Fiber 0g • Protein 3g. DIETARY EXCHANGES: 1 Starch • 2 Other Carbohydrate • 1 Fat • 3 Carb Choices.

# lemon-almond breakfast pastry

PREP TIME: 20 Minutes ✸ READY IN: 1 Hour 10 Minutes ✸ SERVINGS: 16

### FILLING

- 1/2 cup butter or margarine, softened
- 1 roll (7 oz.) almond paste, broken into small pieces
- 2 eggs
- 5 teaspoons all-purpose flour
- 1 to 2 teaspoons grated lemon peel

### CRUST

- 1 box Pillsbury® refrigerated pie crusts, softened as directed on box
- 1 egg, beaten
- 1 tablespoon milk
- 2 tablespoons sugar

**SHARON RICHARDSON**
Dallas, Texas
Bake-Off® Contest 33, 1988

1 In small bowl with spoon or food processor, beat or process butter and almond paste until smooth. Add 2 eggs; beat or process until well blended. By hand, stir in flour and lemon peel just until blended. Cover; place in freezer until mixture is thick, 20 to 30 minutes.

2 Remove 1 pie crust from pouch; place crust flat on work surface. If necessary, press out folds or creases. Cut 1-inch circle from center of crust. With very sharp knife, and curving motions, decoratively score crust in pinwheel design (do not cut through crust or filling will leak out).

3 Heat oven to 400°F. Place remaining pie crust flat on work surface. If necessary, press out folds or creases. Place crust on ungreased 12-inch pizza pan or cookie sheet.

4 Spread cold filling over crust to within 2 inches of edge. Brush edge with beaten egg. Carefully place scored crust over filled bottom crust. Press edges to seal; flute. In small bowl, mix remaining beaten egg and milk; brush over pastry. Sprinkle with sugar.

5 Bake 22 to 27 minutes or until golden brown. Cut into wedges; serve warm. Store in the refrigerator.

**HIGH ALTITUDE (3500-6500 FT):** Bake at 400°F 24 to 29 minutes.

NUTRITION INFORMATION PER SERVING: Calories 240 • Total Fat 16g • Saturated Fat 7g • Cholesterol 60mg • Sodium 180mg • Total Carbohydrate 21g • Dietary Fiber 0g • Protein 3g. DIETARY EXCHANGES: 1 Starch • 1/2 Other Carbohydrate • 3 Fat • 1-1/2 Carb Choices.

# Seasonal Soups, Sides & Salads

*Round out your* holiday meals perfectly and make menu planning a snap with this delightful assortment of simmering soups, hearty side dishes and colorful salads.

p. 73

p. 66

p. 75

p. 90

p. 80

chicken soup italiano p. 83

*special touch*

To add zesty seasonal flavor
to this salad, add sections
of fresh citrus, such as fresh
oranges, clementines or
grapefruit.

# gingered fresh fruit salad

**PREP TIME:** 25 Minutes  ✳  **READY IN:** 25 Minutes  ✳  **SERVINGS:** 8

**DRESSING**

2 tablespoons honey

1 teaspoon chopped crystallized ginger

1/4 teaspoon grated lime peel

2 tablespoons fresh lime juice

**SALAD**

2 cups fresh pineapple cubes

1 cup watermelon cubes

1 cup cantaloupe cubes

1 cup seedless green grapes

1 pint (2 cups) fresh raspberries

1 In 1-cup microwavable measuring cup, mix dressing ingredients. Microwave uncovered on High 20 to 30 seconds or until hot. Cool completely, about 15 minutes.

2 In very large bowl, mix all of the salad ingredients. Pour the dressing over the fruit and toss gently to coat.

NUTRITION INFORMATION PER SERVING: Calories 90 • Total Fat 0g • Saturated Fat 0g • Cholesterol 0mg • Sodium 5mg • Total Carbohydrate 20g • Dietary Fiber 3g • Protein 1g. DIETARY EXCHANGES: 1 Fruit • 1/2 Other Carbohydrate • 1 Carb Choice.

# squash and mushroom soup

PREP TIME: 45 Minutes ✳ READY IN: 50 Minutes ✳ SERVINGS: 6

1 butternut squash (3 lb.)
1 tablespoon butter or margarine
1 medium onion, chopped (1/2 cup)
1 package (8 oz.) sliced fresh mushrooms (3 cups)
3 cloves garlic, minced
1 teaspoon salt

1/2 teaspoon ground ginger
1/4 teaspoon ground cumin
1/4 teaspoon black pepper
   Dash ground red pepper (cayenne)
2 cans (14 oz. each) chicken broth
1 cup half-and-half

1 Cut squash in half lengthwise; remove seeds. Cover each squash half with microwavable plastic wrap; place on microwavable plate. Microwave on High 8 to 16 minutes or until fork-tender. Cool 10 to 15 minutes before handling.

2 Meanwhile, in 4-quart Dutch oven, melt butter over medium heat. Add onion and mushrooms; cook about 10 minutes, stirring occasionally, until tender. Stir in garlic, salt, ginger, cumin, black pepper and ground red pepper. Add broth; heat to boiling over high heat. Reduce heat to low; simmer uncovered 5 minutes to blend flavors.

3 Scoop flesh from cooled squash into blender or food processor. Add half-and-half; blend until smooth. Stir squash mixture into mushroom mixture in Dutch oven. Simmer uncovered 10 minutes longer, stirring occasionally, until thoroughly heated.

NUTRITION INFORMATION PER SERVING: Calories 190 • Total Fat 8g • Saturated Fat 4g • Cholesterol 20mg • Sodium 1030mg • Total Carbohydrate 23g • Dietary Fiber 3g • Protein 7g. DIETARY EXCHANGES: 1-1/2 Starch • 1-1/2 Fat • 1-1/2 Carb Choices.

## cook's notes

If you'd prefer to bake the squash in the oven, place it cut side down in a shallow pan and bake at 400°F for 35 to 45 minutes.

# mojito shrimp salad in biscuit bowls

PREP TIME: 15 Minutes ✳ READY IN: 35 Minutes ✳ SERVINGS: 5

### BISCUIT BOWLS
- 1 can (10.2 oz.) Pillsbury® Grands!® flaky layers refrigerated original biscuits

### DRESSING
- 1/4 cup olive or canola oil
- 2 tablespoons chopped fresh mint leaves
- 1 tablespoon honey
- 1 teaspoon grated lime peel
- 2 tablespoons fresh lime juice
- 1/4 teaspoon rum extract
- 1 small clove garlic, finely chopped

### SALAD
- 12 oz. cooked deveined peeled medium (32 count) shrimp, tail shells removed
- 1/2 cup fresh sweet peas (from pods)
- 1 can (11 oz.) mandarin orange segments, drained
- 5 cups torn leaf lettuce
- 2 medium green onions, sliced (2 tablespoons)

1 Heat oven to 350°F. On ungreased large cookie sheet, turn 5 (6-oz) custard cups upside down; spray outsides of cups with cooking spray. Separate dough into 5 biscuits; press each to form 6-inch circle. Press each biscuit over bottom and around side of each cup. Using fingers, press dough around each cup, forming bowl.

2 Bake 15 to 18 minutes or until golden brown. Carefully remove custard cups. Cool biscuit bowls completely, about 5 minutes.

3 Meanwhile, in large bowl, mix dressing ingredients with wire whisk. Fold shrimp into dressing; set aside. In small microwavable bowl, microwave peas about 30 seconds or just until heated through. Refrigerate while biscuit bowls cool.

4 Place biscuit bowls on serving plates. Fold peas, orange segments, lettuce and onions into shrimp and dressing. Spoon into biscuit bowls. Serve immediately.

NUTRITION INFORMATION PER SERVING: Calories 390 • Total Fat 21g • Saturated Fat 3.5g • Cholesterol 135mg • Sodium 720mg • Total Carbohydrate 31g • Dietary Fiber 1g • Protein 20g. DIETARY EXCHANGES: 2 Starch • 2 Very Lean Meat • 3-1/2 Fat • 2 Carb Choices.

# bean and barley vegetable soup

PREP TIME: 30 Minutes ✳ READY IN: 30 Minutes ✳ SERVINGS: 4

- 2 teaspoons olive oil
- 2 cups ready-to-eat baby-cut carrots, thinly sliced
- 2 medium celery stalks, thinly sliced (about 1 cup)
- 1 medium onion, chopped (1/2 cup)
- 1/2 cup uncooked quick-cooking barley
- 1 can (15.5 oz.) great northern beans, drained, rinsed
- 1 can (14.5 oz.) diced tomatoes with basil, garlic and oregano, undrained
- 1 can (8 oz.) no-salt-added tomato sauce
- 2-1/2 cups water

1 In 3-quart saucepan, heat oil over medium-high heat. Add the carrots, celery and onion; cook 3 minutes, stirring frequently, until vegetables are crisp-tender.

2 Stir in remaining ingredients. Heat to boiling. Reduce heat to medium; cover and cook 15 to 20 minutes, stirring occasionally, until vegetables and barley are tender.

NUTRITION INFORMATION PER SERVING: Calories 300 • Total Fat 3.5g • Saturated Fat 0.5g • Cholesterol 0mg • Sodium 220mg • Total Carbohydrate 55g • Dietary Fiber 13g • Protein 11g. DIETARY EXCHANGES: 3 Starch • 2 Vegetable • 1/2 Fat • 3-1/2 Carb Choices.

mojito shrimp salad in biscuit bowls

## slow cooker two-potato vegetable soup

PREP TIME: 20 Minutes ✳ READY IN: 12 Hours 35 Minutes ✳ SERVINGS: 4

1 large dark-orange sweet potato, peeled, cut into 1/2-inch cubes (1-1/4 cups)

1 medium russet or baking potato, cut into 1/2-inch cubes (1 cup)

1/4 cup chopped onion (1/2 medium)

1 can (14.5 oz.) diced tomatoes with basil, garlic and oregano, undrained

2-1/2 cups water

3/4 teaspoon salt

2 vegetarian vegetable bouillon cubes

2 cups frozen peas and carrots (from 1-lb. bag), thawed

1 In 3- to 4-quart slow cooker, mix all ingredients except peas and carrots. Cover and cook on Low setting 8 to 12 hours.

2 About 15 minutes before serving, stir thawed peas and carrots into soup. Cover; cook on Low setting 15 minutes longer or until peas and carrots are thoroughly heated.

NUTRITION INFORMATION PER SERVING: Calories 130 • Total Fat 0.5g • Saturated Fat 0g • Cholesterol 0mg • Sodium 1220mg • Total Carbohydrate 27g • Dietary Fiber 5g • Protein 5g. DIETARY EXCHANGES: 1 Starch • 1 Vegetable • 2 Carb Choices.

# chive and onion mashed potato triangles

PREP TIME: 30 Minutes ✳ READY IN: 1 Hour ✳ SERVINGS: 24

**DIP**

- 1/4 cup chive and onion cream cheese spread, softened
- 2 tablespoons milk
- 2 teaspoons Dijon mustard

  Chopped chives or green onions, if desired

**TRIANGLES**

- 1/2 cup Green Giant® frozen roasted potatoes with garlic & herb sauce (use 2 sauce chips)
- 1/4 cup chive and onion cream cheese spread, softened
- 1 can (8 oz.) Pillsbury® refrigerated crescent dinner rolls

1 Heat oven to 375°F. In small bowl, mix 1/4 cup cream cheese spread, the milk and mustard with wire whisk until smooth. Refrigerate until serving time.

2 In small microwavable bowl, place potatoes. Microwave 4 to 7 minutes or until potatoes are tender and sauce chips are melted, stirring once during cooking. Cool slightly, 10 to 15 minutes. With potato masher or electric mixer on medium speed, mash potatoes. Beat in 1/4 cup cream cheese spread until well blended.

3 Remove half of dough in rolled section from can; refrigerate remaining half of dough in can. Unroll dough and separate into 2 rectangles; press each into 7-1/2 x 5-inch rectangle; firmly press perforations to seal. Cut each rectangle into 6 (2-1/2-inch) squares. Repeat with remaining half of dough.

4 Place 1 rounded teaspoon potato mixture on each square. Fold 1 corner to the opposite corner, forming triangle; press edges to seal. Place on ungreased cookie sheet.

5 Bake 9 to 12 minutes or until golden brown. Sprinkle dip with chopped chives. Serve the warm triangles with dip.

NUTRITION INFORMATION PER SERVING: Calories 50 • Total Fat 3.5g • Saturated Fat 1.5g • Cholesterol 0mg • Sodium 130mg • Total Carbohydrate 4g • Dietary Fiber 0g • Protein 1g. DIETARY EXCHANGES: 1/2 Other Carbohydrate • 1/2 Fat.

*kitchen tip*

*Make the triangles up to 2 hours ahead of time; cover with plastic wrap and refrigerate. Uncover and bake just before serving.*

# carved watermelon bowl

PREP TIME: 45 Minutes ✳ READY IN: 45 Minutes ✳ SERVINGS: 30

- 1 large watermelon
- 20 cups cut-up fresh or canned fruit

1 To carve a melon bowl, cut off top 1/4 of melon. Being careful not to cut through to the melon, cut a thin slice from bottom of melon so it will sit flat. Scoop out the watermelon, leaving 1/2- to 1-inch-thick shell. Carve decorations into side of melon if desired.

2 Wrap melon bowl in plastic wrap to keep moist; refrigerate until ready to fill. At serving time, fill with cut-up fruit.

NUTRITION INFORMATION PER SERVING: Calories 50 • Total Fat 0g • Saturated Fat 0g • Cholesterol 0mg • Sodium 0mg • Total Carbohydrate 10g • Dietary Fiber 1g • Protein 0g. DIETARY EXCHANGES: 1 Fruit • 1/2 Carb Choice.

*cook's notes*

*Pumpkin-carving tools work really well for carving watermelon. If you don't have any, use a small, sharp paring knife.*

# tropical fruit salad with poppy seed dressing

**PREP TIME:** 20 Minutes ✳ **READY IN:** 20 Minutes ✳ **SERVINGS:** 6

## cook's notes

*You could easily substitute 3/4 cup refrigerated poppy seed dressing for the dressing mixture in this recipe.*

### DRESSING

- 1/2 cup plain yogurt
- 2 tablespoons apricot preserves or orange marmalade
- 1/4 teaspoon poppy seed

### SALAD

- 1 small pineapple, peeled, cored and cut into wedges
- 1 mango or papaya, peeled, seeded and sliced (about 1-1/2 cups)
- 1 medium banana, sliced (about 3/4 cup)
- 2 kiwifruit, peeled, sliced (about 2/3 cup)
- 1/2 cup seedless red grapes
- 2 tablespoons coconut, toasted if desired

1 In small bowl, mix dressing ingredients. On serving platter, arrange fruit in decorative pattern; sprinkle with coconut. Drizzle dressing over salad.

NUTRITION INFORMATION PER SERVING: Calories 160 • Total Fat 1.5g • Saturated Fat 1g • Cholesterol 0mg • Sodium 25mg • Total Carbohydrate 33g • Dietary Fiber 3g • Protein 2g. DIETARY EXCHANGES: 1 Fruit • 1 Other Carbohydrate • 1/2 Fat • 2 Carb Choices.

# mexicorn®-topped tomatoes

PREP TIME: 20 Minutes ✳ READY IN: 20 Minutes ✳ SERVINGS: 6

1 can (11 oz.) vacuum-packed whole kernel corn with red and green peppers, drained

1 can (4.5 oz.) chopped green chiles, drained

1/2 cup finely chopped fresh or refrigerated mango

2 tablespoons finely chopped green onions (2 medium)

2 tablespoons sliced ripe olives

1 tablespoon finely chopped fresh cilantro

1 tablespoon chopped chipotle chile in adobo sauce (from 7-oz. can)

1 tablespoon lime juice (1/2 medium)

1 teaspoon olive oil

4 large firm ripe tomatoes, cut crosswise into 1/4-inch-thick slices

Pumpkin seeds

**ROXANNE CHAN**
Albany, California
Bake-Off® Contest 42, 2006

1 In a medium bowl, mix the first nine ingredients together. On a serving platter, arrange the tomato slices so they are overlapping.

2 Spoon the corn mixture down the center of tomatoes. Sprinkle with pumpkin seeds.

NUTRITION INFORMATION PER SERVING: Calories 110 • Total Fat 2.5g • Saturated Fat 0g • Cholesterol 0mg • Sodium 300mg • Total Carbohydrate 18g • Dietary Fiber 3g • Protein 3g. DIETARY EXCHANGES: 1/2 Starch • 1/2 Other Carbohydrate • 1 Vegetable • 1/2 Fat • 1 Carb Choice.

## cook's notes

*Winter squash has very hard outer skin, and is difficult to cut when uncooked.*

*Microwaving the squash for a short period of time softens the skin and makes it easier to cut.*

# orange caramelized squash rings

**PREP TIME:** 15 Minutes ❋ **READY IN:** 1 Hour 15 Minutes ❋ **SERVINGS:** 4

| | |
|---|---|
| 2 medium acorn squash | 2 tablespoons orange marmalade |
| 2 tablespoons butter, melted | 2 tablespoons packed brown sugar |

1. Heat oven to 350°F. Wash squash; pierce several times with fork. Place squash on microwavable paper towel in microwave oven. Microwave on High 5 to 6 minutes, turning and rotating twice, until skin starts to soften. Let stand in microwave about 5 minutes to cool slightly.

2. Cut off small portion of each end of each squash. Cut each squash into 4 rings (about 1-inch thick); remove seeds. Place rings in ungreased 15 x 10 x 1-inch pan, overlapping slightly if necessary. Brush tops with 1/2 of the butter. Turn; brush with remaining butter.

3. Bake 30 minutes. In small bowl, mix marmalade and brown sugar. Brush over top of squash. Bake 10 minutes. Turn slices over; brush with remaining mixture. Bake 5 to 10 minutes longer or until squash is tender.

NUTRITION INFORMATION PER SERVING: Calories 210 • Total Fat 6g • Saturated Fat 3.5g • Cholesterol 15mg • Sodium 55mg • Total Carbohydrate 36g • Dietary Fiber 7g • Protein 2g. DIETARY EXCHANGES: 1 Starch • 1-1/2 Other Carbohydrate • 1 Fat • 2-1/2 Carb Choices.

# warm grilled veggie sandwiches

**PREP TIME:** 1 Hour ❋ **READY IN:** 1 Hour ❋ **SERVINGS:** 4

| | |
|---|---|
| 1 medium zucchini, cut in half crosswise, cut lengthwise into 1/4-inch-thick strips | 1 tablespoon chopped fresh oregano |
| | 1 clove garlic, minced |
| 1/4 medium red bell pepper, seeded, cut into 1/2-inch-wide strips | 1/2 loaf French bread (about 11 inch) |
| 1/2 red onion, cut into 3/4-inch-thick slices | 1/4 cup ranch dressing |
| 1 tablespoon olive oil | 3 thin slices (1/2 oz. each) Swiss cheese (from deli) |

1. Heat gas or charcoal grill. In 8-inch (2-quart) glass baking dish, mix zucchini, bell pepper and onion. Drizzle with oil; toss to coat. With tongs, place vegetables in grill basket.

2. When grill is heated, place grill basket on gas grill over medium heat or on charcoal grill over medium coals; cover grill. Cook 15 to 20 minutes, stirring occasionally, until vegetables are crisp-tender. Remove grill basket from grill; place vegetables in 8-inch dish. Stir in oregano and garlic.

3. Cut 18 x 18-inch sheet of heavy-duty foil; lightly spray foil with cooking spray. Cut loaf of bread in half lengthwise. Spread cut sides of bread with dressing.

4. Top bottom half with grilled vegetable mixture. Place cheese slices diagonally over vegetables, overlapping slightly. Cover with top half of bread. Place on foil; wrap securely using double-fold seals, allowing room for heat expansion.

5. Reduce gas grill to low heat or adjust coals for low heat. Place wrapped loaf on grill; cover grill. Cook 7 to 10 minutes or until warm. Carefully unwrap loaf to allow steam to escape. Cut loaf into 4 sandwiches.

NUTRITION INFORMATION PER SERVING: Calories 230 • Total Fat 9g • Saturated Fat 2.5g • Cholesterol 5mg • Sodium 400mg • Total Carbohydrate 30g • Dietary Fiber 2g • Protein 7g. DIETARY EXCHANGES: 2 Starch • 1-1/2 Fat • 2 Carb Choices.

# spinach tortellini soup

PREP TIME: 30 Minutes ✳ READY IN: 30 Minutes ✳ SERVINGS: 6

2 tablespoons olive or vegetable oil

1-1/2 cups chopped onions

4 garlic cloves, minced

1 (8-oz.) package sliced fresh mushrooms (3 cups)

4 (14-1/2-oz.) cans ready-to-serve chicken broth with 1/3 less sodium

1 (9-oz.) package refrigerated cheese-filled tortellini

3 cups chopped fresh spinach

1-1/3 oz. (1/3 cup) shredded fresh Parmesan cheese

1 Heat oil in large saucepan over medium-high heat until hot. Add onions; cook and stir 2 to 3 minutes or until tender. Add garlic and mushrooms; cook and stir 2 minutes.

2 Add broth; bring to a boil. Add tortellini; return to a boil. Boil 5 to 7 minutes or until tortellini are of desired doneness.

3 Stir in spinach; cook 1 to 2 minutes or just until wilted. To serve, spoon soup into individual soup bowls. Top each serving with cheese.

NUTRITION INFORMATION PER SERVING: Calories 260 • Total Fat 10g • Saturated Fat 3g • Cholesterol 25mg • Sodium 900mg • Total Carbohydrate 29g • Dietary Fiber 3g • Protein 13g. DIETARY EXCHANGES: 1-1/2 Starch • 1-1/2 Other Carbohydrate • 1 Vegetable • 1 Medium-Fat Meat • 1 Fat.

zesty tomato-crab bisque

# zesty tomato-crab bisque

PREP TIME: 20 Minutes ✳ READY IN: 20 Minutes ✳ SERVINGS: 12

2 cans (19 oz. each) Progresso® vegetable classics hearty tomato soup

1 can (7 oz.) Old El Paso® chopped green chiles

1 cup whipping cream

1 teaspoon seafood seasoning (from 6-oz. container)

3/4 cup chopped cooked crabmeat
Fresh thyme sprigs, if desired

1 In 3-quart saucepan, heat soup and chilies to boiling over medium heat. Reduce heat to low; beat in whipping cream and seasoning with wire whisk until blended. Cook just until hot (do not boil). Stir in crabmeat.

2 Ladle the soup into small mugs or demitasse cups. Top each serving with thyme.

NUTRITION INFORMATION PER SERVING: Calories 110 • Total Fat 7g • Saturated Fat 4g • Cholesterol 30mg • Sodium 720mg • Total Carbohydrate 10g • Dietary Fiber 1g • Protein 3g. DIETARY EXCHANGES: 1/2 Other Carbohydrate • 1/2 Very Lean Meat • 1-1/2 Fat • 1/2 Carb Choice.

*special touch*

*To make the bisque extra special, serve with celery ribs with leaves for stirring.*

# cheesy potatoes

PREP TIME: 20 Minutes ✳ READY IN: 1 Hour 5 Minutes ✳ SERVINGS: 18

**POTATOES**

1 bag (32 oz.) frozen southern-style diced hash-brown potatoes

2 cups shredded Colby, Cheddar or Monterey Jack cheese (8 oz.)

1 container (16 oz.) sour cream

1 can (10-3/4 oz.) condensed cream of mushroom soup

1/4 cup chopped onion (1/2 medium)

1/4 cup butter or margarine, melted

1 teaspoon salt

1/4 teaspoon pepper

**TOPPING**

1/4 cup butter or margarine

2 cups crushed corn flakes cereal

1 Heat oven to 350°F. Spray 13 x 9-inch (3-quart) glass baking dish with cooking spray. In large microwavable bowl, microwave potatoes on Defrost 12 to 15 minutes or until thawed, stirring once or twice. Stir in all remaining potato ingredients; spread in baking dish.

2 In small microwavable bowl, microwave 1/4 cup butter on High 30 to 60 seconds or until melted. Stir in crushed cereal; sprinkle evenly over potato mixture. Bake 30 to 45 minutes or until browned and bubbly around edges.

**HIGH ALTITUDE (3500-6500 FT):** Heat oven to 375°F. Continue as directed above.

NUTRITION INFORMATION PER SERVING: Calories 235 • Total Fat 15g • Saturated Fat 9g • Cholesterol 45mg • Sodium 410mg • Total Carbohydrate 19g • Dietary Fiber 1g • Protein 6g. DIETARY EXCHANGES: 1 Starch • 1/2 High-Fat Meat • 2 Fat • 1 Carb Choice.

*cook's notes*

*For an even creamier texture, substitute processed cheese product (the foil-wrapped cheese in a box), cubed, for some of the shredded cheese in this recipe.*

# baked tomatoes with zucchini

PREP TIME: 20 Minutes ✳ READY IN: 1 Hour ✳ SERVINGS: 6

6 medium tomatoes

2 medium zucchini, unpeeled, cut into
1/4-inch slices

4 cloves garlic, minced

1 teaspoon parsley flakes

1/4 teaspoon salt

1/4 teaspoon pepper

3 tablespoons olive oil

1 Heat oven to 400°F. Place tomatoes stem side down on cutting board. Cut each tomato into 8 wedges, cutting to about 1/2 inch from bottom (not all the way through). Place tomatoes, cut side up, in ungreased 12 x 8-inch (2-quart) glass baking dish. Insert 2 zucchini slices between each slice in each tomato.

2 In a small bowl, mix remaining ingredients; drizzle over tomatoes. Bake uncovered 30 to 40 minutes or until tomatoes are slightly soft. Serve tomatoes with slotted spoon.

NUTRITION INFORMATION PER SERVING: Calories 110 • Total Fat 7g • Saturated Fat 1g • Cholesterol 0mg • Sodium 110mg • Total Carbohydrate 8g • Dietary Fiber 3g • Protein 2g. DIETARY EXCHANGES: 1 Vegetable • 1-1/2 Fat • 1/2 Carb Choice.

# layered picnic potato salad

PREP TIME: 20 Minutes ✳ READY IN: 20 Minutes ✳ SERVINGS: 15

1-1/2  cups Green Giant® frozen sweet peas
(from 1-lb. bag)

1  jar (2 oz.) diced pimientos, drained

3  pints deli potato salad (6 cups)

1 Cook the peas as directed on package. Drain; rinse with cold water until cool. Line 9 x 5-inch loaf pan with plastic wrap.

2 Stir the pimientos into potato salad. Spoon and spread half of potato salad into pan; top with peas. Spoon and carefully spread remaining potato salad evenly over peas; press gently.

3 Serve immediately or refrigerate until serving time. To serve, invert onto serving platter. Peel off plastic wrap.

NUTRITION INFORMATION PER SERVING: Calories 150 • Total Fat 9g • Saturated Fat 1.5g • Cholesterol 10mg • Sodium 260mg • Total Carbohydrate 15g • Dietary Fiber 2g • Protein 2g. DIETARY EXCHANGES: 1 Starch • 1-1/2 Fat • 1 Carb Choice.

## kitchen tip

When purchasing deli potato salad for this recipe, choose the most basic, creamy salad with small pieces that will hold together when molded in the pan.

# chicken salad cups

PREP TIME: 10 Minutes ✳ READY IN: 30 Minutes ✳ SERVINGS: 2

- 2 Pillsbury® Grands!® frozen buttermilk biscuits (from 25-oz. bag)
- 3/4 cup chopped cooked chicken
- 2 tablespoons shredded Cheddar cheese
- 2 teaspoons chopped toasted sliced almonds
- 2 teaspoons chopped green onions
- 1 tablespoon mayonnaise or salad dressing
  Dash ground ginger
  Sesame seeds, if desired

1 Heat oven to 375°F. Lightly grease 2 jumbo muffin cups. Place biscuits on microwavable plate. Microwave uncovered on High 30 to 40 seconds, turning biscuits over halfway through microwave time, until soft enough to press into rounds.

2 In small bowl, mix chicken, cheese, almonds, green onions, mayonnaise and ginger until well blended. Press each biscuit to cover the bottom and side of muffin cup. Spoon chicken mixture into biscuit cups. Sprinkle with sesame seeds. Bake 16 to 21 minutes or until the edges are deep golden brown.

NUTRITION INFORMATION PER SERVING: Calories 360 • Total Fat 21g • Saturated Fat 5g • Cholesterol 55mg • Sodium 690mg • Total Carbohydrate 23g • Dietary Fiber 0g • Protein 21g. DIETARY EXCHANGES: 1-1/2 Starch • 2-1/2 Lean Meat • 2-1/2 Fat • 1-1/2 Carb Choices.

# ham and asparagus chowder

PREP TIME: 20 Minutes ✳ READY IN: 20 Minutes ✳ SERVINGS: 4

1-1/2 cups cubed unpeeled red potatoes
  1/2 cup water
1-1/2 cups 1-1/2-inch pieces fresh asparagus
    spears
1-1/2 cups cubed cooked ham

1 can (10-3/4 oz.) condensed cream
  of mushroom soup
1 cup milk
  Freshly ground pepper, if desired

1  In 2-quart saucepan, heat potatoes and water to boiling. Reduce heat to medium. Cover; cook about 5 minutes or until potatoes are crisp-tender.

2  Add the asparagus and ham. Cover; cook 3 to 5 minutes or until thoroughly heated. Stir in the soup and the milk.

3  Heat to boiling over high heat, stirring occasionally. Sprinkle with pepper before serving.

NUTRITION INFORMATION PER SERVING: Calories 230 • Total Fat 9g • Saturated Fat 3g • Cholesterol 30mg • Sodium 1120mg • Total Carbohydrate 23g • Dietary Fiber 2g • Protein 15g. DIETARY EXCHANGES: 1 Starch • 1/2 Other Carbohydrate • 1-1/2 Very Lean Meat • 1-1/2 Fat • 1-1/2 Carb Choices.

## cook's notes

One box (9 oz.) Green Giant® frozen asparagus cuts can be substituted for the fresh. There's no need to thaw it before adding it with the ham.

# white chicken chili

PREP TIME: 30 Minutes ✳ READY IN: 30 Minutes ✳ SERVINGS: 9

1 tablespoon vegetable oil
1 large onion, chopped (1 cup)
2 cloves garlic, finely chopped
1 lb. boneless skinless chicken breasts,
  cut into bite-size pieces
5-1/4 cups chicken broth (from two
    32-oz. cartons)
2 cans (15 oz. each) cannellini beans, drained

2 cans (4.5 oz. each) chopped green chiles,
  drained
1 teaspoon dried oregano leaves
1/2 teaspoon ground cumin
  Dash ground red pepper (cayenne),
  if desired
1-1/2 cups shredded Monterey Jack cheese
  (6 oz.), if desired
  Chopped fresh cilantro, if desired

1  In 4-quart Dutch oven, heat oil over medium-high heat until hot. Add onion, garlic and chicken; cook and stir until chicken is no longer pink.

2  Stir in remaining ingredients except cheese and cilantro. Heat to boiling. Reduce heat to low; simmer 10 to 15 minutes to blend flavors, stirring occasionally. Serve with cheese and cilantro.

NUTRITION INFORMATION PER SERVING: Calories 200 • Total Fat 4.5g • Saturated Fat 1g • Cholesterol 30mg • Sodium 710mg • Total Carbohydrate 20g • Dietary Fiber 5g • Protein 20g. DIETARY EXCHANGES: 1 Starch • 1/2 Vegetable • 2-1/2 Very Lean Meat • 1/2 Fat • 1 Carb Choice.

## kitchen tip

Stock up on chicken breasts when they are on sale, because you will be making this chili often for family and friends. If ground turkey is on sale, you may want to use a pound of it instead of the chicken breast.

# grilled caesar steak and potato salad

PREP TIME: 45 Minutes ✳ READY IN: 45 Minutes ✳ SERVINGS: 8

| | |
|---|---|
| 2 lb. boneless beef sirloin steak (1 inch thick) | Cooking spray |
| 2 tablespoons refrigerated Caesar dressing | 2/3 cup shredded Parmesan cheese (2-2/3 oz.) |
| 3/4 teaspoon salt | 2/3 cup refrigerated Caesar dressing |
| 1/4 teaspoon pepper | Chopped romaine lettuce, if desired |
| 2 packages (1 lb. 4 oz. each) refrigerated new potato wedges | 1/2 cup sliced green onions (8 medium) |

1 Heat gas or charcoal grill. Brush steak with 2 tablespoons dressing; sprinkle with 1/4 teaspoon of the salt and the pepper.

2 Cut 4 (18 x 12-inch) sheets of heavy-duty foil. Generously spray half of one side of each foil sheet with cooking spray. Place 1/4 of potatoes evenly in center of each sprayed portion of foil. Generously spray potatoes with cooking spray; sprinkle with remaining 1/2 teaspoon salt. Fold unsprayed half of foil loosely over potatoes so edges meet; seal edges with tight 1/2-inch folds and fold again.

3 When grill is heated, place packets on gas grill over medium-high heat or on charcoal grill over medium-high coals; cover grill. Cook packets 10 minutes, turning over several times. Place steak on grill with packets; cook 10 to 15 minutes longer, turning steak over once or twice and turning packets several times, until steak is desired doneness and potatoes are tender.

4 In large bowl, toss cooked potatoes, cheese and 2/3 cup dressing. Cut steak across grain into thin slices. Divide potato mixture evenly onto serving plates; top each with steak slices and sprinkle with onions.

**HIGH ALTITUDE (3500-6500 FT):** Cook packets and steak on gas grill over medium-low heat or on charcoal grill over medium-low coals. Continue as directed above.

NUTRITION INFORMATION PER SERVING: Calories 400 • Total Fat 21g • Saturated Fat 5g • Cholesterol 65mg • Sodium 1020mg • Total Carbohydrate 27g • Dietary Fiber 4g • Protein 29g. DIETARY EXCHANGES: 2 Starch • 3 Lean Meat • 2 Fat • 2 Carb Choices.

# smoked turkey and rice soup

PREP TIME: 35 Minutes ✳ READY IN: 35 Minutes ✳ SERVINGS: 6

| | |
|---|---|
| 2 stalks celery, sliced | 2 cups water |
| 2 medium carrots, thinly sliced | 2 cans (14-1/2 oz. each) fat-free chicken broth with 1/3 less sodium |
| 1 cup sliced fresh mushrooms | 1 package (6.2 oz.) fast-cooking long-grain and wild rice mix |
| 8 oz smoked turkey breast, cut into 1/2-inch cubes | |

1 In large saucepan, combine all ingredients; mix well. Bring to a boil. Reduce heat; cover and simmer 8 to 10 minutes or until rice and vegetables are tender.

NUTRITION INFORMATION PER SERVING: Calories 160 • Total Fat 1g • Saturated Fat 0g • Cholesterol 15mg • Sodium 0mg • Total Carbohydrate 25g • Dietary Fiber 2g • Protein 12g. DIETARY EXCHANGES: 1-1/2 Starch • 1-1/2 Other Carbohydrate • 1 Very Lean Meat.

*cook's notes*

One 4.5-ounce jar of Green Giant® sliced mushrooms, drained, can be used in place of the sliced fresh mushrooms.

grilled caesar steak and potato salad

# speedy honey-lime fruit salad

PREP TIME: 5 Minutes ✳ READY IN: 5 Minutes ✳ SERVINGS: 8

1/2 cup refrigerated coleslaw dressing
3 tablespoons honey
1 teaspoon grated lime peel

1-1/2 teaspoons fresh lime juice
2 quarts (8 cups) fresh fruit salad (from deli)

1 In small bowl, mix coleslaw dressing, honey, lime peel and lime juice until well blended.

2 Just before serving, in large serving bowl, gently mix fruit salad and dressing mixture to coat.

NUTRITION INFORMATION PER SERVING: Calories 205 • Total Fat 8g • Saturated Fat 1g • Cholesterol 5mg • Sodium 85mg • Total Carbohydrate 32g • Dietary Fiber 3g • Protein 1g. DIETARY EXCHANGES: 1-1/2 Fruit • 1/2 Other Carbohydrate • 1-1/2 Fat • 2 Carb Choices.

# chicken soup italiano

**PREP TIME:** 40 Minutes ✳ **READY IN:** 40 Minutes ✳ **SERVINGS:** 4

1 tablespoon olive or vegetable oil

1/2 medium red or green bell pepper, chopped

1 small onion, chopped

1 small zucchini, coarsely chopped

1 garlic clove, minced

2 cups cubed cooked chicken

1 cup water

1 teaspoon dried Italian seasoning

1/8 teaspoon pepper

3-1/2 cups Progresso® chicken broth
(from 32-oz. carton)

2-1/4 oz. (1/2 cup) uncooked ditalini
(short macaroni tubes)

1 oz. (1/4 cup) shredded fresh Parmesan
cheese

1 Heat oil in large saucepan over medium-high heat until hot. Add bell pepper, onion, zucchini and
garlic; cook and stir 3 minutes or until vegetables are crisp-tender.

2 Add all remaining ingredients except ditalini and cheese. Bring to a boil. Add ditalini; cook 12 to 15
minutes or until ditalini is tender, stirring occasionally. Sprinkle individual servings with cheese.

NUTRITION INFORMATION PER SERVING: Calories 290 • Total Fat 12g • Saturated Fat 3g • Cholesterol 65mg • Sodium 830mg • Total
Carbohydrate 16g • Dietary Fiber 1g • Protein 30g. DIETARY EXCHANGES: 1 Starch • 4 Lean Meat.

fresh sugar snaps with sesame

# fresh sugar snaps with sesame

PREP TIME: 10 Minutes ✳ READY IN: 10 Minutes ✳ SERVINGS: 24

| | |
|---|---|
| 1 teaspoon soy sauce | 1 bag (8 oz.) fresh sugar snap peas, ends trimmed (2 cups) |
| 1/4 teaspoon roasted sesame oil | 1/2 teaspoon black sesame seed |

1 In a medium bowl, stir together the soy sauce and the sesame oil. Add the sugar snap peas and stir to coat.

2 Arrange the snap peas on a serving platter and sprinkle with the black sesame seeds.

3 Serve the sugar snap peas with toothpicks or cocktail forks.

NUTRITION INFORMATION PER SERVING: Calories 0 • Total Fat 0g • Saturated Fat 0g • Cholesterol 0mg • Sodium 15mg • Total Carbohydrate 0g • Dietary Fiber 0g • Protein 0g. DIETARY EXCHANGES: Free.

*cook's notes*

*Don't forget to check the sugar snap peas—the string that runs along the spine of each may need to be removed.*

# honey-mustard chicken salad

PREP TIME: 20 Minutes ✳ READY IN: 20 Minutes ✳ SERVINGS: 10

| | |
|---|---|
| 4 cups shredded romaine lettuce | 1 can (11 oz.) Green Giant® Mexicorn® whole kernel corn with red and green peppers, drained |
| 1 bag (16 oz.) coleslaw blend | |
| 4 cups diced cooked chicken | 1 cup honey-mustard dressing |
| 1/2 cup sliced green onions (about 8 medium) | 1 can (11 oz.) mandarin orange segments, drained |
| 2 packages (3 oz. each) oriental-flavor ramen noodle soup mix | 1/2 cup slivered almonds, toasted if desired |

1 In very large (6-quart) bowl, mix the lettuce, coleslaw blend, chicken, onions, noodles from soup mix and corn.

2 In small bowl, mix dressing and contents of 1 seasoning packet from soup mix (discard remaining seasoning packet or save for another use). Pour dressing over salad; toss to mix.

3 Gently stir in the mandarin orange segments. Spoon the salad into large serving bowl; sprinkle with almonds.

NUTRITION INFORMATION PER SERVING: Calories 310 • Total Fat 16g • Saturated Fat 3.5g • Cholesterol 50mg • Sodium 490mg • Total Carbohydrate 24g • Dietary Fiber 3g • Protein 19g. DIETARY EXCHANGES: 1 Starch • 1/2 Other Carbohydrate • 2-1/2 Lean Meat • 1-1/2 Fat • 1-1/2 Carb Choices.

*special touch*

*To add some flair to individual servings of the salad, scoop it into washed and dried lettuce leaves. Iceberg and butter lettuce leaves both work well.*

# crispy-topped meatballs and baked beans

PREP TIME: 10 Minutes ✸ READY IN: 1 Hour 5 Minutes ✸ SERVINGS: 6

| | |
|---|---|
| 1 (16 oz.) can baked beans, undrained | 1/4 cup barbecue sauce |
| 1 (15 oz.) can kidney beans, drained | 12 frozen cooked Italian meatballs (about 5 oz.) |
| 1-1/2 cups Green Giant® frozen cut green beans | |
| 1/2 cup frozen chopped onion | 1 (1-3/4-oz.) can shoestring potatoes (about 1 cup) |

1 Heat oven to 375°F. Spray a shallow 2-quart casserole with nonstick cooking spray. In the sprayed casserole, combine all ingredients except the shoestring potatoes; mix well. Cover. Bake covered at 375°F. for 30 minutes.

2 Uncover casserole; sprinkle evenly with shoestring potatoes, pressing lightly. Bake uncovered an additional 20 to 25 minutes or until bubbly and thoroughly heated.

NUTRITION INFORMATION PER SERVING: Calories 355 • Total Fat 13g • Saturated Fat 5g • Cholesterol 65mg • Sodium 950mg • Total Carbohydrate 47g • Dietary Fiber 9g • Protein 22g. DIETARY EXCHANGES: 2-1/2 Starch • 2 Medium-Fat Meat • 1/2 Fat • 2-1/2 Carb Choices.

# broccoli alfredo soup

PREP TIME: 20 Minutes ✳ READY IN: 20 Minutes ✳ SERVINGS: 2

1/2  cup water
  1  bag (1 lb.) Green Giant® frozen broccoli cuts
  1  cup Alfredo pasta sauce (from 16-oz. jar)

1/2  cup milk
1/8  teaspoon pepper
     Shredded carrot, if desired

1 In 2-quart saucepan, heat water to boiling over high heat. Add broccoli; return to boiling. Reduce heat to medium-low; cover and simmer 3 to 5 minutes or until broccoli is tender. Do not drain.

2 In blender, place about 1 cup of the broccoli and water mixture. Cover; blend until smooth.

3 To broccoli mixture in saucepan, stir in pureed broccoli, Alfredo sauce, milk and pepper. Cook uncovered 3 to 4 minutes, stirring frequently, until thoroughly heated. Sprinkle shredded carrot over individual servings.

NUTRITION INFORMATION PER SERVING: Calories 510 • Total Fat 39g • Saturated Fat 22g • Cholesterol 120mg • Sodium 560mg • Total Carbohydrate 22g • Dietary Fiber 6g • Protein 18g. DIETARY EXCHANGES: 1/2 Starch • 1/2 Other Carbohydrate • 2 Vegetable • 2 High-Fat Meat • 4-1/2 Fat • 1-1/2 Carb Choices.

*special touch*

*Pop a couple of Pillsbury® frozen crusty French dinner rolls in the oven to heat and serve with this creamy soup.*

# mac 'n cheese soup

PREP TIME: 20 Minutes ✳ READY IN: 30 Minutes ✳ SERVINGS: 4

1-1/2  cups water

1  box (12 oz.) shells and cheese dinner mix

2  cups milk

1  cup Green Giant® frozen sweet peas (from 1-lb. bag)

4  hot dogs, thinly sliced

1  In 2-quart saucepan, heat water to boiling. Add shells from mix; cook uncovered over medium heat 7 to 10 minutes, stirring frequently, until shells are tender. Do not drain.

2  Carefully stir in the cheese packet from the boxed mix. Add the milk, sweet peas and thinly sliced hot dogs.

3  Cook uncovered 5 to 10 minutes longer, stirring occasionally, until soup is thoroughly heated.

**HIGH ALTITUDE (3500-6500 FT):** Add up to 1/2 cup additional water if soup gets too thick.

NUTRITION INFORMATION PER SERVING: Calories 540 • Total Fat 18g • Saturated Fat 7g • Cholesterol 45mg • Sodium 1290mg • Total Carbohydrate 70g • Dietary Fiber 3g • Protein 24g. DIETARY EXCHANGES: 3-1/2 Starch • 1 Other Carbohydrate • 1/2 Low-Fat Milk • 1-1/2 High-Fat Meat • 4-1/2 Carb Choices.

# mixed vegetable clam chowder

PREP TIME: 10 Minutes ✳ READY IN: 10 Minutes ✳ SERVINGS: 2

1  can (18.5 oz.) Progresso® New England clam chowder

1  cup frozen mixed vegetables, thawed

1/8  teaspoon dried thyme leaves

2  tablespoons shredded Cheddar cheese

1  In 2-quart saucepan, stir together all ingredients except cheese. Cook over medium heat until hot, stirring frequently.

2  To serve, ladle chowder into bowls; sprinkle with cheese.

NUTRITION INFORMATION PER SERVING: Calories 300 • Total Fat 13g • Saturated Fat 4.5g • Cholesterol 20mg • Sodium 1050mg • Total Carbohydrate 34g • Dietary Fiber 6g • Protein 11g. DIETARY EXCHANGES: 1 Starch • 1 Other Carbohydrate • 1 Vegetable • 1 High-Fat Meat • 1 Fat • 2 Carb Choices.

# cucumber and tomato salad caprese

**PREP TIME:** 20 Minutes ✳ **READY IN:** 20 Minutes ✳ **SERVINGS:** 12

| | |
|---|---|
| 1 large red tomato, sliced | 1 tablespoon lemon juice |
| 1 large yellow tomato, sliced | 1/8 teaspoon salt |
| 1 medium cucumber, sliced | 1/8 teaspoon freshly ground black pepper |
| 8 oz fresh mozzarella cheese, sliced | 1/3 cup coarsely chopped fresh basil or lemon basil leaves |
| 2 tablespoons extra-virgin olive oil | |

1 On a large serving platter, arrange rows of tomato, cucumber and mozzarella cheese slices so that they overlap, as shown above.

2 In small bowl, mix olive oil, lemon juice, salt and pepper. Drizzle dressing over the cheese sand vegetables. Sprinkle with basil.

*cook's notes*

To chop the fresh basil, place it in a glass measuring cup and snip it a few times with kitchen scissors.

NUTRITION INFORMATION PER SERVING: Calories 170 • Total Fat 12g • Saturated Fat 5g • Cholesterol 20mg • Sodium 250mg • Total Carbohydrate 5g • Dietary Fiber 1g • Protein 11g. DIETARY EXCHANGES: 1 Vegetable • 1-1/2 Medium-Fat Meat • 1 Fat • 1/2 Carb Choice.

# southwestern shrimp taco salad

PREP TIME: 15 Minutes ✳ READY IN: 15 Minutes ✳ SERVINGS: 4

1/2 cup Southwestern sour cream dip (from 15.5-oz. container)

1/2 cup Old El Paso® thick 'n chunky salsa

1 bag (10 oz.) romaine and leaf lettuce

12 oz cooked deveined shelled medium shrimp, tail shells removed

1 cup shredded Mexican cheese blend (4 oz.)

1 In large bowl, mix sour cream dip and salsa. Add lettuce, shrimp and 1/2 cup of the cheese; toss to coat well. Divide salad evenly onto serving plates. Sprinkle with remaining 1/2 cup cheese.

NUTRITION INFORMATION PER SERVING: Calories 270 • Total Fat 15g • Saturated Fat 9g • Cholesterol 200mg • Sodium 850mg • Total Carbohydrate 8g • Dietary Fiber 1g • Protein 26g. DIETARY EXCHANGES: 1 Vegetable • 3-1/2 Lean Meat • 1 Fat • 1/2 Carb Choices.

# easy chunky tomato soup

PREP TIME: 25 Minutes  *  READY IN: 25 Minutes  *  SERVINGS: 4

2 tablespoons vegetable oil

1 medium onion, chopped (1/2 cup)

2 tablespoons all-purpose flour

1/2 cup milk

1 jar (26 to 28 oz.) tomato pasta sauce

1 can (14.5 oz.) diced tomatoes with basil, garlic and oregano, undrained

1 can (14 oz.) chicken broth

3/4 cup finely shredded Cheddar-American cheese blend (3 oz.)

1 In 4-quart saucepan, heat oil over medium heat. Add onion; cook and stir until softened. Add flour; cook and stir until moistened. Gradually add milk, cooking and stirring about 2 minutes or until smooth and bubbly.

2 Stir in pasta sauce, tomatoes and broth. Cover; cook over medium heat about 15 minutes, stirring frequently, just until mixture boils. Top each serving with 3 tablespoons cheese.

NUTRITION INFORMATION PER SERVING: Calories 430 • Total Fat 22g • Saturated Fat 7g • Cholesterol 25mg • Sodium 1630mg • Total Carbohydrate 46g • Dietary Fiber 4g • Protein 12g. DIETARY EXCHANGES: 2 Starch • 1 Other Carbohydrate • 1 Medium-Fat Meat • 3 Fat • 3 Carb Choices.

*special touch*

*Serve the soup with grilled cheese sandwiches or Pillsbury® refrigerated breadsticks sprinkled with Parmesan cheese before baking.*

# Yuletide Entrees

*Creating scrumptious meals* is easy when you start with these mouthwatering main courses that feature tender cuts of beef, juicy poultry, robust casseroles and more.

p. 111

p. 120

p. 99

p. 100

p. 103

tomato-basil linguine
with chicken p. 133

# herbed alfredo sauce over linguine

PREP TIME: 30 Minutes ✳ READY IN: 30 Minutes ✳ SERVINGS: 5

12 oz. uncooked linguine or 2 packages (9 oz. each) refrigerated linguine

2 teaspoons butter or margarine

1 teaspoon olive oil

3 large cloves garlic, minced

1/2 cup finely chopped red bell pepper (1 small)

1/3 cup sliced green onions (about 5 medium)

1/3 cup chopped fresh parsley or 3 teaspoons dried parsley flakes

1/4 cup all-purpose flour

2 cans (12 oz. each) evaporated low-fat milk

1 teaspoon dried basil leaves

1/2 teaspoon dried oregano leaves

1/2 teaspoon salt

1/3 cup grated Parmesan cheese

1 In 4-quart Dutch oven, cook linguine as directed on package. Drain; return to Dutch oven and cover to keep warm.

2 Meanwhile, in 10-inch nonstick skillet, melt butter with oil over medium heat. Add garlic; cook and stir 1 minute. Add bell pepper, onions, parsley and flour; cook and stir 1 minute. Gradually stir in milk until well blended. Heat to boiling, stirring constantly. Cook 6 to 10 minutes, stirring frequently, until sauce is bubbly and thickened.

3 Remove skillet from heat. Stir in basil, oregano and salt. Pour sauce over linguine; toss gently to coat. Sprinkle with cheese.

NUTRITION INFORMATION PER SERVING: Calories 510 • Total Fat 12g • Saturated Fat 6g • Cholesterol 35mg • Sodium 820mg • Total Carbohydrate 78g • Dietary Fiber 5g • Protein 24g. DIETARY EXCHANGES: 3-1/2 Starch • 1 Other Carbohydrate • 1 Low-Fat Milk • 1/2 Lean Meat • 1/2 Fat • 5 Carb Choices.

# pot roast with sweet potatoes and parsnips

PREP TIME: 35 Minutes ✳ READY IN: 2 Hours 50 minutes ✳ SERVINGS: 8

1 tablespoon vegetable oil

1 boneless beef chuck roast (3 to 3-1/2 lb.)

1/2 teaspoon salt

1/4 teaspoon pepper

1 medium onion, chopped (1/2 cup)

1 can (14 oz.) beef broth

2 tablespoons molasses

1 teaspoon dried thyme leaves

2 medium dark-orange sweet potatoes (about 1 lb.), peeled, cut into 2-inch pieces (3 cups)

3 medium parsnips, peeled, cut into 1-inch-thick slices (2 cups)

1/4 cup all-purpose flour

1/4 cup water

1 Heat oven to 350°F. In 12-inch nonstick skillet, heat oil over medium-high heat. Add beef roast; cook until browned on both sides. Place the roast in center of ungreased shallow roasting pan or 13 x 9-inch (3-quart) glass baking dish. Sprinkle with salt and pepper.

2 In same skillet, cook onion over medium-high heat 4 to 6 minutes, stirring occasionally, until tender. Stir in broth, molasses and thyme. Heat to boiling. Boil 5 minutes, stirring occasionally. Pour broth mixture over roast. Cover tightly with foil.

3 Bake 1 hour. Place sweet potatoes and parsnips around roast; bake 1 to 1-1/4 hours longer or until roast and vegetables are fork-tender.

4 Remove roast and vegetables from pan, reserving juices. Pour juices into 2-quart saucepan. In small bowl, mix flour and water until smooth. Place saucepan with drippings over medium heat; gradually stir in flour mixture, cooking and stirring, until mixture comes to a full boil. Boil 1 minute, stirring constantly, until thickened. Cut roast into slices; serve with vegetables and gravy.

NUTRITION INFORMATION PER SERVING: Calories 450 • Total Fat 22g • Saturated Fat 8g • Cholesterol 105mg • Sodium 450mg • Total Carbohydrate 27g • Dietary Fiber 3g • Protein 37g. DIETARY EXCHANGES: 1 Starch • 1 Other Carbohydrate • 5 Lean Meat • 1 Fat • 2 Carb Choices.

## kitchen tip

*Parsnips are a white root vegetable that look like a thick carrot. They are commonly coated with wax, which should be removed with a vegetable peeler.*

# orange chicken stir-fry

**PREP TIME:** 10 Minutes ✳ **READY IN:** 20 Minutes ✳ **SERVINGS:** 4

| | |
|---|---|
| 2 cups uncooked instant rice | 1/4 teaspoon garlic powder |
| 2 cups water | 1 lb. chicken breast strips for stir-fry |
| 3 tablespoons frozen (thawed) orange juice concentrate | 1 bag (1 lb.) frozen broccoli, carrots and water chestnuts, thawed, drained |
| 2 tablespoons low-sodium soy sauce | Green onions, if desired |
| 1/2 teaspoon cornstarch | |

1 Cook rice in water as directed on package, omitting the salt.

2 Meanwhile, in small bowl, mix orange juice concentrate, soy sauce, cornstarch and garlic powder until smooth.

3 Heat 10-inch nonstick skillet over medium-high heat. Add chicken; cook 5 to 8 minutes, stirring frequently, until chicken is no longer pink in center.

4 Stir in the orange juice concentrate mixture and vegetables. Reduce heat to medium; cover and cook 6 to 8 minutes, stirring occasionally, until vegetables are crisp-tender. Serve over the cooked rice. Garnish with onions if desired.

NUTRITION INFORMATION PER SERVING: Calories 390 • Total Fat 5g • Saturated Fat 1g • Cholesterol 70mg • Sodium 340mg • Total Carbohydrate 55g • Dietary Fiber 4g • Protein 32g. DIETARY EXCHANGES: 1 Other Carbohydrate • 1 Vegetable • 3 Very Lean Meat • 3-1/2 Carb Choices.

# spinach and basil-stuffed pork tenderloin

PREP TIME: 20 Minutes ✷ READY IN: 1 Hour ✷ SERVINGS: 6

**STUFFING**

- 1 tablespoon olive or vegetable oil
- 1 large clove garlic, minced
- 1 box (9 oz.) Green Giant® frozen spinach, thawed, well drained
- 1/3 cup chopped fresh or 4-1/2 teaspoons dried basil leaves
- 1/4 teaspoon salt
- 1/8 teaspoon pepper
- 1 egg

**PORK TENDERLOIN**

- 2 pork tenderloins (1-1/2 lb.)
- 1 tablespoon olive or vegetable oil
- 1 large clove garlic, minced
- 1 teaspoon fennel seed, crushed

*cook's notes*

Crush the fennel seed with a mortar and pestle or place it in a plastic bag and crush with a rolling pin.

1 Heat oven to 375°F. In 8-inch skillet, heat 1 tablespoon oil over medium-high heat. Add 1 minced clove of garlic; cook and stir 30 to 60 seconds or until garlic is tender. Remove from heat. Stir in remaining stuffing ingredients.

2 Butterfly each pork tenderloin by making lengthwise cut 3/4 of the way through, being careful not to cut tenderloin into 2 pieces. Open each tenderloin and lay flat. If desired, sprinkle cut sides of each with salt and pepper.

3 Spread stuffing evenly over cut side of 1 tenderloin. Place second tenderloin, cut side down, over stuffing (to ensure even cooking, place wide end of 1 tenderloin at narrow end of the other). Tie at intervals with cotton string.

4 In small bowl, mix 1 tablespoon oil, 1 minced clove of garlic and the fennel seed. Brush tenderloin with oil mixture; place on rack in shallow roasting pan.

5 Bake uncovered 35 to 45 minutes or until pork has slight blush of pink in center and meat thermometer inserted in center of pork reads 160°F. Remove string before cutting into slices.

NUTRITION INFORMATION PER SERVING: Calories 210 • Total Fat 10g • Saturated Fat 2.5g • Cholesterol 105mg • Sodium 180mg • Total Carbohydrate 2g • Dietary Fiber 1g • Protein 28g. DIETARY EXCHANGES: 4 Very Lean Meat • 1-1/2 Fat.

# tiny ham and pineapple pot pies

PREP TIME: 40 Minutes ✳ READY IN: 1 Hour ✳ SERVINGS: 16

| | |
|---|---|
| 1/2 cup finely chopped cooked ham | 1/2 teaspoon ground mustard |
| 1/2 cup finely shredded Swiss cheese (2 oz.) | 1 box Pillsbury® refrigerated pie crusts, softened as directed on box |
| 1/2 cup canned crushed pineapple, well drained | |
| 1 tablespoon finely chopped green onions | 1 egg, beaten |
| | 1 teaspoon sesame seeds, if desired |

1 Heat oven to 450°F. (425°F. for dark or nonstick pans). In small bowl, mix ham, cheese, pineapple, onions and mustard; set aside.

2 Remove pie crusts from pouches; unroll crusts on work surface. From each crust, cut 8 (3-inch) rounds and 8 (2-inch) rounds, rerolling crusts if necessary. In 16 ungreased mini muffin cups, press 3-inch rounds in bottoms and up sides so edges of crusts extend slightly over sides of cups.

3 Spoon about 1 rounded tablespoon ham mixture into each crust-lined cup. Brush crust edges lightly with beaten egg.

4 Cut a small vent in each 2-inch crust round. Place 1 round over filling in each cup; press crust edges together, pushing toward cup so crust does not extend over sides. Brush top crusts with beaten egg. Sprinkle with sesame seeds.

5 Bake 10 to 14 minutes or until crust is deep golden brown. Remove from muffin cups. Let stand 5 minutes before serving.

NUTRITION INFORMATION PER SERVING: Calories 120 • Total Fat 7g • Saturated Fat 3g • Cholesterol 25mg • Sodium 160mg • Total Carbohydrate 11g • Dietary Fiber 0g • Protein 3g. DIETARY EXCHANGES: 1 Starch • 1 Fat • 1 Carb Choice.

# chicken cordon bleu lasagna

PREP TIME: 25 Minutes ✽ READY IN: 1 Hour 40 Minutes ✽ SERVINGS: 9

2 eggs
1 container (15 oz.) ricotta cheese
2 cottage cheese
1/2 cup grated Parmesan cheese
1/4 cup chopped fresh parsley
2 cups diced (1/4- to 1/2- inch) cooked chicken

2 cups diced (1/4- to 1/2- inch) cooked ham
1/4 teaspoon garlic powder
1 jar (16 oz.) creamy garlic Alfredo sauce
6 uncooked lasagna noodles
2 cups shredded mozzarella cheese (8 oz.)
1 cup shredded Swiss cheese (4 oz.)
2 tablespoons chopped fresh parsley

1 Heat oven to 350°F. In medium bowl, beat eggs. Stir in ricotta, cottage and Parmesan cheeses and 1/4 cup parsley; set aside.

2 In another medium bowl, mix the chicken, ham, garlic powder and Alfredo sauce. In an ungreased 13 x 9-inch (3-quart) glass baking dish, spread about 1/2 cup chicken mixture.

3 Top chicken mixture with 3 uncooked noodles, half of the cheese mixture, half of the remaining chicken mixture and half each of the mozzarella and Swiss cheeses. Repeat layers starting with noodles, ending with Swiss cheese. Cover tightly with foil.

4 Bake 1 hour or until very hot and bubbly. Let stand covered 15 minutes before serving. Sprinkle with 2 tablespoons parsley.

**HIGH ALTITUDE** (3500-6500 ft): Add 1/3 cup water to chicken mixture. Continue as directed above.

NUTRITION INFORMATION PER SERVING: Calories 585 • Total Fat 37g • Saturated Fat 21g • Cholesterol 190mg • Sodium 1130mg • Total Carbohydrate 19g • Dietary Fiber 0g • Protein 44g. DIETARY EXCHANGES: 1 Starch • 6 Medium-Fat Meat • 1 Fat • 1 Carb Choice.

*cook's notes*

*Cordon Bleu is a French dish*
*combining chicken or veal*
*with ham or prosciutto and*
*Swiss or Gruyère cheese.*
*In this recipe, those flavors*
*are simplified to produce a*
*luscious lasagna.*

# salmon with lemon butter and pineapple salsa

PREP TIME: 10 Minutes ✽ READY IN: 20 Minutes ✽ SERVINGS: 4

1/4 cup butter or margarine, softened
4 teaspoons grated lemon peel
2 teaspoons lemon juice
1 cup chopped fresh pineapple
3 tablespoons chopped fresh cilantro

2 tablespoons finely chopped red onion
1 teaspoon finely chopped jalapeño pepper, if desired
4 salmon fillets, about 1 inch thick (1-1/2 lb.)
1/4 teaspoon salt

1 Heat oven to 375°F. In small bowl, mix butter, lemon peel and lemon juice; set aside. In medium bowl, mix pineapple, cilantro, onion and jalapeño; refrigerate until serving time.

2 Line 13 x 9-inch pan with foil. Place salmon, skin side down, in pan; sprinkle with salt. Bake 8 to 10 minutes or until fish flakes easily with a fork. Immediately top salmon with butter mixture. Serve with pineapple salsa.

NUTRITION INFORMATION PER SERVING: Calories 360 • Total Fat 21g • Saturated Fat 9g • Cholesterol 140mg • Sodium 330mg • Total Carbohydrate 6g • Dietary Fiber 0g • Protein 37g. DIETARY EXCHANGES: 1/2 Fruit • 5 Lean Meat • 1-1/2 Fat • 1/2 Carb Choice.

*cook's notes*

*If you prefer halibut, go*
*ahead and substitute it for*
*the salmon. Just follow the*
*guidelines for the thickness*
*and weight called for in*
*the recipe.*

# chicken phyllo bundles

PREP TIME: 30 Minutes ✳ READY IN: 55 Minutes ✳ SERVINGS: 8

| | |
|---|---|
| 1/2 cup julienne (matchstick-cut) carrots | 1 package (6.5 oz.) garlic-and-herbs spreadable cheese, softened |
| 2 cups cut-up cooked chicken | 1 box (16 oz. 40 sheets) frozen phyllo (filo) pastry sheets (14 x 9 inch), thawed |
| 1/2 cup shredded Swiss cheese (2 oz.) | Buttered flavored cooking spray |
| 4 medium green onions, thinly sliced (1/4 cup) | |
| 1 box (9 oz.) Green Giant® frozen asparagus cuts, thawed, drained | |

1 Heat oven to 375°F. In small microwavable bowl, place carrots. Cover; microwave on High about 1 minute or until tender. Meanwhile, in medium bowl, gently mix chicken, Swiss cheese, onions, asparagus and spreadable cheese. Stir in carrots.

2 To make 1 bundle, layer 5 phyllo pastry sheets, generously spraying each layer with cooking spray (sheets can be stacked randomly). Keep remaining pastry sheets covered with damp cloth until needed to prevent dough from drying out. Place about 1/2 cup chicken mixture in center of stack of pastry. With both hands, lift pastry stack towards center and twist in center to make bundle (pastry may tear a little). Spray outside of each bundle generously with cooking spray; place on ungreased large cookie sheet. Repeat to make 7 more bundles.

3 Bake 20 to 25 minutes or until pastry is browned and crisp.

**HIGH ALTITUDE** (3500-6500 ft): Bake 22 to 27 minutes.

NUTRITION INFORMATION PER SERVING: Calories 350 • Total Fat 14g • Saturated Fat 7g • Cholesterol 60mg • Sodium 310mg • Total Carbohydrate 38g • Dietary Fiber 2g • Protein 19g. DIETARY EXCHANGES: 2-1/2 Starch • 1-1/2 Lean Meat • 1-1/2 Fat • 2-1/2 Carb Choices.

# sweet-and-sour meat loaf

PREP TIME: 20 Minutes ✳ READY IN: 1 Hour 30 Minutes ✳ SERVINGS: 6

**MEAT LOAF**

| | |
|---|---|
| 1 egg | 1/2 teaspoon garlic-pepper blend |
| 1 lb. lean (at least 80%) ground beef | 1/4 teaspoon salt |
| 1/2 lb. lean ground pork | **TOPPING** |
| 1/2 cup Progresso® plain bread crumbs | 4 tablespoons purchased sweet-and-sour sauce |
| 1/4 cup purchased sweet-and-sour sauce | 3 or 4 green or red bell pepper rings |
| 1 tablespoon instant minced onion | 3 or 4 drained canned pineapple slices |

1 Heat oven to 350°F. Beat egg in large bowl. Add all remaining meat loaf ingredients; mix well. Press mixture firmly in ungreased 8 x 4-inch loaf pan. Bake at 350°F. for 40 minutes.

2 Remove meat loaf from oven. Spread about 3 tablespoons sweet-and-sour sauce over loaf. Arrange bell pepper rings and pineapple slices over sauce. Brush with remaining tablespoon sauce.

3 Return to oven; bake an additional 25 to 30 minutes or until meat loaf is thoroughly cooked in center and meat thermometer registers 160°F. Cover with foil; let stand 5 minutes before cutting meat loaf into slices.

NUTRITION INFORMATION PER SERVING: Calories 315 • Total Fat 19g • Saturated Fat 7g • Cholesterol 140mg • Sodium 300mg • Total Carbohydrate 13g • Dietary Fiber 1g • Protein 24g. DIETARY EXCHANGES: 1 Fruit • 1 Other Carbohydrate • 3-1/2 Medium-Fat Meat.

chicken phyllo bundles

# southwestern pork and vegetable stew

PREP TIME: 50 Minutes ❋ READY IN: 50 Minutes ❋ SERVINGS: 5

| | |
|---|---|
| 1 tablespoon oil | 1/2 medium red bell pepper, coarsely chopped |
| 1 lb. boneless pork shoulder roast, cut into 3/4-inch pieces | 1 can (14.5 oz.) white hominy, drained, rinsed |
| 1 medium onion, coarsely chopped (1/2 cup) | 1 can (14 oz.) chicken broth |
| 1 garlic clove, minced | 1 can (4.5 oz.) Old El Paso® chopped green chiles |
| 1/2 lb. small red potatoes, cut into 1/2-inch pieces (1-1/2 cups) | 1 tablespoon chili powder |
| 1 cup Green Giant® Niblets® frozen corn | 1 teaspoon dried oregano leaves |
| 1/2 medium green bell pepper, coarsely chopped | 1 teaspoon cumin |

1 Heat oil in large saucepan or Dutch oven over medium-high heat until hot. Add pork; cook 3 to 4 minutes or until browned, stirring frequently. Add the onion and garlic; cook and stir 1 to 2 minutes or until onion is crisp-tender.

2 Add all remaining ingredients; mix well. Bring to a boil. Reduce heat; cover and simmer 18 to 20 minutes or until potatoes are tender and pork is no longer pink in center, stirring occasionally.

NUTRITION INFORMATION PER SERVING: Calories 365 • Total Fat 15g • Saturated Fat 5g • Cholesterol 60mg • Sodium 690mg • Total Carbohydrate 33g • Dietary Fiber 5g • Protein 29g. DIETARY EXCHANGES: 2 Starch • 3 Lean Meat • 1 Fat • 2 Carb Choices.

# roast cornish hen with vegetables

PREP TIME: 15 Minutes ✳ READY IN: 1 Hour 5 Minutes ✳ SERVINGS: 2

- 1 Cornish game hen (24 oz.), thawed if frozen
- 1 teaspoon garlic salt
- 1 teaspoon chili powder
- 1/2 teaspoon ground ginger
- 1/2 teaspoon ground cumin

- 2 tablespoons olive or vegetable oil
- 1 medium dark-orange sweet potato, peeled, cut into 1-inch pieces (2 cups)
- 2 small red potatoes, quartered
- 1 small green bell pepper, cut into 1-inch pieces (1 cup)

1 Heat oven to 400°F. Spray 11 x 7-inch (2-quart) glass baking dish with cooking spray. Remove and discard neck and giblets from game hen. With kitchen scissors, cut hen in half; place halves, skin side up, in baking dish.

2 In medium bowl, mix garlic salt, chili powder, ginger, cumin and oil. Brush hen halves with 1 tablespoon of the oil mixture. To remaining mixture in bowl, add sweet potatoes, red potatoes and bell pepper; toss to coat. Arrange vegetables around hen halves in dish.

3 Bake 40 to 50 minutes or until hen halves are fork-tender and juices run clear, and vegetables are tender.

NUTRITION INFORMATION PER SERVING: Calories 820 • Total Fat 48g • Saturated Fat 11g • Cholesterol 240mg • Sodium 640mg • Total Carbohydrate 51g • Dietary Fiber 7g • Protein 46g. DIETARY EXCHANGES: 3 Starch • 1/2 Vegetable • 5 Medium-Fat Meat • 4 Fat • 3-1/2 Carb Choices.

## cook's notes

*It's easier to thinly slice pork if it's partially frozen. Freeze the pork for about 30 minutes before cutting it.*

# sweet and sour pork

PREP TIME: 25 Minutes ✳ READY IN: 25 Minutes ✳ SERVINGS: 4

2 cups hot cooked rice

1 lb. pork tenderloin, cut crosswise into thin slices

1 green bell pepper, cut into 1 x 1-inch pieces

1 can (20 oz.) pineapple chunks in unsweetened juice, drained

1/2 cup sweet and sour sauce

1/4 teaspoon ground ginger

1 While rice is cooking, spray large skillet with nonstick cooking spray. Heat over medium-high heat until hot. Add pork; cook and stir 3 to 5 minutes or until no longer pink.

2 Add bell pepper; cook and stir 4 to 6 minutes or until crisp-tender. Stir in pineapple, sweet and sour sauce and ginger; cook and stir until thoroughly heated. Serve over rice.

NUTRITION INFORMATION PER SERVING: Calories 320 • Total Fat 4g • Saturated Fat 1g • Cholesterol 65mg • Sodium 150mg • Total Carbohydrate 44g • Dietary Fiber 2g • Protein 26g. DIETARY EXCHANGES: 2 Starch • 1 Fruit • 3 Other Carbohydrate • 2 Lean Meat.

# sesame asian grilled cornish hen halves

PREP TIME: 1 Hour ✳ READY IN: 5 Hours ✳ SERVINGS: 4

2 Cornish game hens (24 oz. each), thawed if frozen

1/3 cup soy sauce

2 tablespoons packed brown sugar

2 cloves garlic, minced

1 tablespoon sesame seeds

1 With kitchen scissors, cut game hens in half lengthwise; rinse well. In large nonmetal dish or resealable food-storage bag, place hen halves. In 1-cup glass measuring cup, mix soy sauce, brown sugar and garlic; pour over hen halves. Stir or turn bag to coat. Cover dish or seal bag; refrigerate at least 4 hours, stirring or turning occasionally, to marinate.

2 Heat gas or charcoal grill. Remove hen halves from marinade; discard marinade. Sprinkle skin side of hen halves with sesame seeds.

3 When grill is heated, place hen halves, skin side up, on gas grill over medium heat or on charcoal grill over medium coals; cover grill. Cook 30 to 40 minutes, turning hen halves twice, until fork-tender and juices run clear.

**HIGH ALTITUDE (3500-6500 FT):** Place hen halves, skin side up, on gas grill over low heat or on charcoal grill over low coals; cover grill. Cook using times above as a guide, turning hen halves twice.

NUTRITION INFORMATION PER SERVING: Calories 260 • Total Fat 18g • Saturated Fat 5g • Cholesterol 120mg • Sodium 350mg • Total Carbohydrate 3g • Dietary Fiber 0g • Protein 21g. DIETARY EXCHANGES: 3 Lean Meat • 2 Fat.

# southwestern chili shrimp

PREP TIME: 20 Minutes ✳ READY IN: 20 Minutes ✳ SERVINGS: 4

**SHRIMP**

2 tablespoons butter or margarine, melted

1-1/2 teaspoons chili powder

1/2 teaspoon garlic salt

1/2 teaspoon ground cumin

2 teaspoons lime juice

1-1/2 lb. uncooked deveined peeled large shrimp, tail shells removed, if desired

**SAUCE**

1/4 cup mayonnaise or salad dressing

1/4 cup guacamole

2 tablespoons chopped fresh cilantro

1 Heat gas or charcoal grill. In large bowl, mix melted butter, chili powder, garlic salt, cumin and lime juice. Add shrimp; toss to coat. Thread shrimp on six 15-inch metal skewers, leaving space between each.

2 Place on grill over medium heat. Cover grill; cook 5 to 10 minutes, turning 2 to 3 times, until shrimp are pink. In small bowl, mix sauce ingredients. Serve sauce with shrimp.

3 Closed Contact Grill Directions: Heat closed contact grill for 5 minutes. Meanwhile, in large bowl, mix melted butter, chili powder, garlic salt, cumin and lime juice. Add shrimp; toss to coat. With slotted spoon, place shrimp on bottom grill surface. Close grill; cook 4 to 6 minutes or until shrimp are pink. In small bowl, mix sauce ingredients. Serve sauce with shrimp.

NUTRITION INFORMATION PER SERVING: Calories 300 • Total Fat 20g • Saturated Fat 6g • Cholesterol 265mg • Sodium 600mg • Total Carbohydrate 3g • Dietary Fiber 1g • Protein 27g. DIETARY EXCHANGES: 4 Very Lean Meat • 3-1/2 Fat.

*cook's notes*

*To devein shrimp, use a sharp pointed knife to cut a slit along the back curve of the shrimp. Pull out the dark vein, and rinse the shrimp under cold water.*

# short ribs in red wine

PREP TIME: 20 Minutes ✳ READY IN: 7 Hours 35 Minutes ✳ SERVINGS: 6

2   tablespoons olive or vegetable oil
3   lb. bone-in beef short ribs
1/4   teaspoon salt
1/4   teaspoon pepper
1   can (14.5 oz.) stewed tomatoes, undrained
1   medium onion, chopped (1/2 cup)
2   tablespoons tomato paste

1/2   cup red wine or Progresso® beef flavored broth
1/2   cup Progresso® beef flavored broth (from 32-oz. carton)
1   tablespoon Worcestershire sauce
1/4   cup water
2   tablespoons cornstarch

1   In 12-inch skillet, heat oil over medium-high heat. Add short ribs; sprinkle with salt and pepper. Cook 4 to 6 minutes, turning occasionally, until browned.

2   In 3- to 4-quart slow cooker, place tomatoes, onion and tomato paste; stir. Add ribs, wine, broth and Worcestershire sauce. Cover; cook on Low heat setting 7 to 9 hours.

3   Remove ribs and bones from cooker; cover ribs to keep warm. Discard bones. Spoon off any fat from mixture in cooker. In small bowl, mix water and cornstarch; stir into mixture in cooker. Increase heat setting to High. Cover; cook 10 to 15 minutes longer or until sauce is thickened. Serve over ribs.

NUTRITION INFORMATION PER SERVING: Calories 270 • Total Fat 18g • Saturated Fat 6g • Cholesterol 70mg • Sodium 490mg • Total Carbohydrate 10g • Dietary Fiber 1g • Protein 18g. DIETARY EXCHANGES: 1/2 Other Carbohydrate • 2-1/2 Medium-Fat Meat • 1 Fat • 1/2 Carb Choice.

# creamy potatoes and pork chops

PREP TIME: 20 Minutes ✳ READY IN: 1 Hour 15 Minutes ✳ SERVINGS: 4

- 4 bone-in pork loin chops, trimmed of fat
- 1/2 teaspoon seasoned salt
- 1 can (10 3/4 oz.) condensed cream of mushroom soup
- 1-1/4 cups milk
- 1 tablespoon Worcestershire sauce
- 1 package (1 lb. 4 oz.) refrigerated new potato wedges with skins
- 1 cup Green Giant® frozen sweet peas

1 Heat oven to 350°F. Sprinkle pork chops with seasoned salt. Spray large nonstick skillet with nonstick cooking spray. Heat over medium-high heat until hot. Add pork chops; brown well on both sides.

2 In 13 x 9-inch (3-quart) glass baking dish, combine soup, milk and Worcestershire sauce; mix until smooth. Add potatoes and peas; stir until coated. Place browned pork chops over potato mixture. Cover with foil.

3 Bake at 350°F. for 30 minutes. Uncover; bake an additional 20 to 25 minutes or until potatoes and pork chops are tender.

NUTRITION INFORMATION PER SERVING: Calories 410 • Total Fat 16g • Saturated Fat 6g • Cholesterol 80mg • Sodium 900mg • Total Carbohydrate 32g • Dietary Fiber 5g • Protein 35g. DIETARY EXCHANGES: 1-1/2 Starch • 1/2 Fruit • 2 Other Carbohydrate • 4-1/2 Lean Meat • 1/2 Fat.

# baja pie

PREP TIME: 20 Minutes ✷ READY IN: 1 Hour 5 Minutes ✷ SERVINGS: 6

- 5 corn tortillas (6 inch)
- 1 tablespoon butter or margarine, melted
- 2 cups shredded deli rotisserie chicken (from 2- to 2-1/2-lb. chicken)
- 1 can (15 oz.) Progresso® black beans, drained, rinsed
- 1 cup Old El Paso® thick 'n chunky salsa

- 2 tablespoons Old El Paso® taco seasoning mix (from 1-oz. pkg.)
- 1-1/2 cups shredded Cheddar cheese (6 oz.)
- 1 medium tomato, cut into 6 slices
- 1 medium avocado, pitted, peeled and chopped

1. Heat oven to 325°F. In 9-inch glass pie plate, arrange tortillas, overlapping and extending to edge or slightly over edge of plate. Brush edges of tortillas with melted butter.

2. In large bowl, mix chicken, beans, salsa, taco seasoning mix and 1/2 cup of the cheese. Spoon chicken mixture onto tortillas.

3. Bake 25 to 30 minutes or until hot. Sprinkle with remaining 1 cup cheese. Bake 2 to 4 minutes longer or until cheese begins to melt. Top with tomato and avocado.

**HIGH ALTITUDE (3500-6500 FT):** Increase first bake time from 28 to 33 minutes.

NUTRITION INFORMATION PER SERVING: Calories 430 • Total Fat 20g • Saturated Fat 9g • Cholesterol 75mg • Sodium 1010mg • Total Carbohydrate 35g • Dietary Fiber 10g • Protein 27g. DIETARY EXCHANGES: 2 Starch • 3 Very Lean Meat • 3-1/2 Fat • 2 Carb Choices.

# manicotti al forno

PREP TIME: 35 Minutes ✳ READY IN: 1 Hour 25 Minutes ✳ SERVINGS: 6

12 uncooked manicotti pasta shells

1 lb. bulk Italian pork sausage

2 large cloves garlic, finely chopped

1 teaspoon dried oregano leaves

1 jar (26 oz.) tomato pasta sauce

1 can (14.5 oz.) diced tomatoes with Italian-style herbs, drained

1 egg

1 container (15 oz.) part-skim ricotta cheese

3 cups shredded Italian cheese blend or mozzarella cheese (12 oz.)

1/4 cup fresh basil leaves, cut into strips

1 Heat oven to 350°F. Cook the pasta shells as directed on package. Drain and rinse with cold water to cool.

2 Meanwhile, in 12-inch skillet, cook sausage, garlic and oregano over medium heat 8 to 10 minutes, stirring occasionally, until sausage is no longer pink; drain. Stir in pasta sauce and tomatoes. Spread 1 cup of the meat sauce in ungreased 13 x 9-inch (3-quart) glass baking dish.

3 In medium bowl, beat egg. Stir in ricotta cheese and 2 cups of the Italian cheese blend. Spoon cheese mixture into gallon-size food-storage plastic bag; seal bag. Cut 1-inch hole in one bottom corner of bag. Squeeze bag to pipe about 1/4 cup cheese mixture into each pasta shell. Arrange stuffed shells over meat sauce in dish. Pour remaining meat sauce evenly over shells.

4 Cover dish with foil. Bake 35 to 40 minutes or until hot and bubbly. Top with remaining 1 cup Italian cheese blend. Bake uncovered 5 to 10 minutes longer or until cheese is melted. Sprinkle basil over top before serving.

**HIGH ALTITUDE (3500-6500 FT):** In Step 4, bake covered 40 to 45 minutes. Top with remaining 1 cup Italian cheese blend. Bake uncovered 20 minutes longer.

NUTRITION INFORMATION PER SERVING: Calories 700 • Total Fat 36g • Saturated Fat 17g • Cholesterol 135mg • Sodium 1970mg • Total Carbohydrate 57g • Dietary Fiber 4g • Protein 37g. DIETARY EXCHANGES: 3 Starch • 1 Other Carbohydrate • 4 High-Fat Meat • 4 Carb Choices.

*special touch*

*Serve with a marinated vegetable salad, warm garlic breadsticks and ice cream with a berry sauce.*

herb-stuffed flank steak

# herb-stuffed flank steak

PREP TIME: 50 Minutes ✳ READY IN: 4 Hours 50 Minutes ✳ SERVINGS: 6

**MARINADE**

- 3 tablespoons dry red wine
- 3 tablespoons olive oil
- 1 tablespoon fresh lemon juice
- 1 teaspoon beef-flavor instant bouillon
- 1 large clove garlic, minced

**STEAK**

- 1 beef flank steak (2 lb.)

**STUFFING**

- 3 tablespoons olive oil
- 1/4 cup finely chopped onion (1/2 medium)
- 3 cloves garlic, thinly sliced
- 2 tablespoons chopped fresh parsley
- 2 tablespoons Progresso® plain bread crumbs
- 1 teaspoon grated lemon peel

1 In large, shallow nonmetal dish or resealable plastic bag, mix all marinade ingredients. Make pocket in side of flank steak by cutting lengthwise almost but not completely through opposite side. Add steak to marinade; turn to coat. Cover dish or seal bag; refrigerate at least 4 hours or overnight to marinate.

2 In 8-inch skillet, heat oil over medium heat. Add onion; cook 2 minutes, stirring occasionally, until tender. Stir in garlic and parsley; cook and stir 1 minute. Add bread crumbs and lemon peel; cook and stir 1 minute. Remove from heat.

3 Heat grill. Remove steak from marinade; discard marinade. Fill pocket in steak with stuffing. Secure opening with toothpicks.

4 Place steak on gas grill over medium heat; cover grill. Cook 12 to 20 minutes, turning once, until steak is desired doneness. Cut steak across grain into 1/2-inch-thick slices.

**HIGH ALTITUDE (3500-6500 FT):** Place steak on gas grill over medium-low heat or on charcoal grill over medium-low coals; cover grill. Cook using times above as a guide, turning once.

NUTRITION INFORMATION PER SERVING: Calories 320 • Total Fat 19g • Saturated Fat 5g • Cholesterol 85mg • Sodium 135mg • Total Carbohydrate 3g • Dietary Fiber 0g • Protein 33g. DIETARY EXCHANGES: 5 Lean Meat • 1 Fat.

# tomato-basil meat loaves

PREP TIME: 20 Minutes ✳ READY IN: 1 Hour 10 Minutes ✳ SERVINGS: 8

- 3 eggs
- 2 lb. lean (at least 80%) ground beef
- 1/2 cup Progresso® Italian style bread crumbs
- 1 cup chopped Italian plum tomatoes (3 medium)
- 1/2 cup finely chopped onion (1 medium)
- 1/2 cup ketchup
- 2 teaspoons dried basil leaves
- 1/2 teaspoon salt

1 Heat oven to 350°F. In large bowl, beat eggs. Stir in all remaining ingredients until well blended. On large sheet of waxed paper, shape mixture into 4 (6-1/2 x 3-inch) loaves. Wrap 3 meat loaves tightly in heavy-duty foil; freeze up to 2 months.

2 Place 1 loaf in ungreased shallow baking pan; bake 40 to 50 minutes or until thoroughly cooked in center and meat thermometer reads 160°F. Let meat loaf stand 5 minutes before serving.

3 To thaw frozen meat loaf, place in refrigerator for 24 hours, or unwrap, place on microwavable plate and microwave on Defrost about 10 minutes or until thawed. Bake meat loaf as directed above.

NUTRITION INFORMATION PER SERVING: Calories 280 • Total Fat 15g • Saturated Fat 6g • Cholesterol 150mg • Sodium 460mg • Total Carbohydrate 11g • Dietary Fiber 0g • Protein 24g. DIETARY EXCHANGES: 1 Starch • 3 Medium-Fat Meat • 1/2 Fat • 1 Carb Choice.

*cook's notes*

*Italian plum tomatoes have less juice and are firmer than regular tomatoes, making them perfect for meat loaf.*

## cook's notes

*Don't have chicken tenders?*

*Just cut 4 boneless skinless*

*chicken breasts into long*

*strips to make about*

*14 pieces.*

# pesto-chicken manicotti

PREP TIME: 20 Minutes ❋ READY IN: 1 Hour 15 Minutes ❋ SERVINGS: 7

| | |
|---|---|
| 1 jar (16 oz.) Alfredo pasta sauce | 1 teaspoon Italian seasoning |
| 1-1/2 cups water | 14 uncooked manicotti pasta shells (8 oz.) |
| 1 teaspoon garlic powder | 2 cups shredded mozzarella cheese (8 oz.) |
| 1 package (1-1/4 lb.) uncooked chicken breast tenders (not breaded, 14 tenders) | 1 large tomato, chopped (1 cup) |
| | 1/3 cup basil pesto |

1 Heat oven to 375°F. Meanwhile, in medium bowl, mix the pasta sauce, water and garlic powder. In an ungreased 13 x 9-inch (3-quart) glass baking dish, spread about one-third (1 cup) of the pasta sauce mixture.

2 In medium bowl, sprinkle chicken tenders with Italian seasoning. Stuff chicken into uncooked manicotti shells. Place shells on pasta sauce in baking dish. Pour remaining pasta sauce mixture evenly over shells, covering completely.

3 Cover with foil. Bake 45 to 50 minutes or until pasta shells are tender. Sprinkle with the cheese. Bake uncovered 2 to 4 minutes longer or until the cheese is melted. Sprinkle with tomato. Serve with pesto.

**HIGH ALTITUDE (3500-6500 FT):** Increase first bake time to 60 to 65 minutes.

NUTRITION INFORMATION PER SERVING: Calories 600 • Total Fat 34g • Saturated Fat 18g • Cholesterol 120mg • Sodium 610mg • Total Carbohydrate 35g • Dietary Fiber 2g • Protein 37g. DIETARY EXCHANGES: 2-1/2 Starch • 4 Lean Meat • 4 Fat • 2 Carb Choices.

# stuffed chicken breasts cordon bleu

PREP TIME: 15 Minutes ❋ READY IN: 45 Minutes ❋ SERVINGS: 4

| | |
|---|---|
| 4 large boneless skinless chicken breasts (1-1/4 to 1-1/2 lb.) | 2 tablespoons real bacon pieces (from 2.8-oz. pkg.) |
| 1/4 cup finely shredded Swiss cheese (1 oz.) | 2 tablespoons butter, melted |
| 1/4 cup finely chopped ham (1 oz.) | 1/3 cup Progresso® plain dry bread crumbs |

1 Heat oven to 350°F. To form pocket in each chicken breast, cut 3-inch-long slit in thick side of each breast, cutting into breast about 2 inches and to within 1/2 inch of opposite side.

2 In small bowl, mix cheese, ham and bacon. Spoon evenly into pockets in chicken; secure openings with toothpicks.

3 Place melted butter in shallow dish. Place bread crumbs on sheet of waxed paper. Dip each stuffed chicken breast in butter; roll in bread crumbs to coat. Place in ungreased 8-inch square (2-quart) glass baking dish. Sprinkle any remaining bread crumbs over chicken.

4 Bake 30 minutes or until juice of chicken is clear when center of thickest part is cut (170°F.). Remove toothpicks before serving.

**HIGH ALTITUDE (3500-6500 FT):** Heat oven to 375°F. Bake 40 minutes.

NUTRITION INFORMATION PER SERVING: Calories 300 • Total Fat 15g • Saturated Fat 6g • Cholesterol 115mg • Sodium 360mg • Total Carbohydrate 7g • Dietary Fiber 0g • Protein 37g. DIETARY EXCHANGES: 1/2 Starch • 5 Very Lean Meat • 2-1/2 Fat • 1/2 Carb Choice.

## cook's notes

*To quickly melt butter, place*

*butter in a microwave-safe*

*pie plate. Microwave 30*

*seconds. Use for dipping*

*the chicken.*

# lasagna roll-ups

**PREP TIME:** 30 Minutes ✳ **READY IN:** 1 Hour 20 Minutes ✳ **SERVINGS:** 8

8 uncooked lasagna noodles

1/2 lb. lean ground turkey

2 cloves garlic, minced

1 jar (26 oz.) tomato pasta sauce

2 teaspoons Italian seasoning

1/2 teaspoon fennel seed, if desired

1 cup part-skim ricotta or cottage cheese

1/2 cup shredded carrot (1 small)

1 box (9 oz.) Green Giant® frozen spinach, thawed, drained and squeezed dry

2 egg whites or 1 egg

1 cup shredded mozzarella cheese (4 oz.)

1 Heat oven to 350°F. Cook lasagna noodles as directed on package. Drain; rinse with hot water. Meanwhile, in 10-inch skillet, cook ground turkey and garlic over medium-high heat, stirring frequently, until turkey is no longer pink; drain, if necessary. Stir in pasta sauce, Italian seasoning and fennel. Reduce heat to low; simmer uncovered about 15 minutes, stirring occasionally.

2 In small bowl, mix ricotta cheese, carrot, spinach and egg whites. Spread each cooked lasagna noodle with generous 1/4 cup spinach filling to within 1 inch of one short end. Roll up firmly toward unfilled end.

3 Reserve 1-1/2 cups sauce. In ungreased 12 x 8-inch (2-quart) glass baking dish, pour remaining sauce. Arrange roll-ups, seam side down, in sauce. Pour reserved sauce over roll-ups.

4 Cover tightly with foil; bake 30 to 40 minutes or until hot and bubbly. Sprinkle with mozzarella cheese; bake uncovered 3 to 5 minutes longer or until cheese is melted. Let stand 5 minutes before serving.

**HIGH ALTITUDE (3500-6500 FT):** Heat oven to 375°F.

NUTRITION INFORMATION PER SERVING: Calories 320 • Total Fat 11g • Saturated Fat 4.5g • Cholesterol 35mg • Sodium 700mg • Total Carbohydrate 37g • Dietary Fiber 3g • Protein 19g. DIETARY EXCHANGES: 2 Starch • 1/2 Other Carbohydrate • 2 Medium-Fat Meat • 2-1/2 Carb Choices.

## fish fillets primavera

PREP TIME: 15 Minutes  ✳  READY IN: 30 Minutes  ✳  SERVINGS: 4

*cook's notes*

*Any white-fleshed, mild-flavored fish, such as flounder, haddock or whitefish, can be used in place of the orange roughy.*

| | |
|---|---|
| 3 tablespoons margarine or butter | 1 cup julienne (2 x1/8 x 1/8-inch) carrots |
| 4 fresh or frozen orange roughy fish fillets (4 to 5 oz. each), thawed | 1 cup sliced fresh mushrooms or 1 jar (2.5 oz.) Green Giant® sliced mushrooms, drained |
| 1 tablespoon lemon juice | |
| Dash salt and pepper | 1/2 cup diagonally sliced celery |
| 1 garlic clove, minced | 1/4 teaspoon salt |
| 1-1/2 cups fresh broccoli florets | 1/4 teaspoon dried basil leaves |
| 1 cup fresh cauliflower florets | 1/4 cup grated Parmesan cheese |

1 Heat oven to 450°F. In oven, melt 2 tablespoons of the margarine in 13 x 9-inch (3 quart) baking dish. Place fish in melted margarine; turn to coat. Sprinkle with lemon juice, salt and pepper. Bake at 450°F. for 5 minutes. Remove from oven.

2 While fish is baking, in large skillet, melt remaining 1 tablespoon margarine over medium-high heat. Add garlic; cook until lightly browned. Add all remaining ingredients except Parmesan cheese. Cook and stir 5 to 6 minutes or until vegetables are crisp-tender.

3 Spoon hot vegetables in center of baking dish, moving fish to ends of dish. Sprinkle with Parmesan cheese. Return to oven; bake an additional 3 to 5 minutes or until fish flakes easily with fork.

NUTRITION INFORMATION PER SERVING: Calories 240 • Total Fat 12g • Saturated Fat 3g • Cholesterol 35mg; Sodium 510mg • Total Carbohydrate 8g • Dietary Fiber 3g • Protein 26g. DIETARY EXCHANGES: 1 Vegetable • 3-1/2 Very Lean Meat • 2 Fat.

# pepper-rubbed steaks with caramelized onions

PREP TIME: 20 Minutes ✳ READY IN: 20 Minutes ✳ SERVINGS: 4

1 large sweet onion (Maui, Texas Sweet or Walla Walla), thinly sliced, separated into rings

1 tablespoon sugar

2 tablespoons water

1 tablespoon balsamic vinegar

1/2 to 1 teaspoon seasoned pepper blend

4 boneless beef strip steaks, 1/2 to 3/4-inch thick (4 oz. each), trimmed of fat

1 Heat 12-inch nonstick skillet over medium heat. Add onion; cook 3 to 4 minutes, stirring frequently, just until it begins to brown. Stir in sugar and water. Reduce heat to medium-low; cover and cook 6 to 8 minutes, stirring frequently, until onion is tender and golden. Remove from heat; stir in vinegar.

2 Meanwhile, heat a closed contact grill for 5 minutes. Rub the seasoned pepper blend on both sides of each steak.

3 When grill is heated, place steaks on bottom grill surface. Close grill; cook 3 to 5 minutes or until desired doneness. Serve steaks with onions.

NUTRITION INFORMATION PER SERVING: Calories 190 • Total Fat 4g • Saturated Fat 1.5g • Cholesterol 75mg • Sodium 40mg • Total Carbohydrate 7g • Dietary Fiber 0g • Protein 30g. DIETARY EXCHANGES: 1/2 Other Carbohydrate • 4 Very Lean Meat • 1/2 Fat • 1/2 Carb Choice.

*cook's notes*

*Lean beef can be part of a healthful diet. It contains iron, folic acid and vitamin B-12, all of which are important nutrients!*

# layered italian meat loaf

PREP TIME: 15 Minutes ✳ READY IN: 1 Hour 30 Minutes ✳ SERVINGS: 6

1-1/2  lb. lean (at least 80%) ground beef

1  can (8 oz.) tomato sauce with basil, garlic and oregano

1  egg

3/4  cup Progresso® Italian style bread crumbs

1  teaspoon garlic powder

1/4  teaspoon pepper

1  cup shredded Italian cheese blend (4 oz.)

1  box (9 oz.) Green Giant® frozen spinach, thawed, well drained

1 Heat oven to 350°F. Spray 9 x 5-inch loaf pan with cooking spray or grease with shortening. In large bowl, mix ground beef, 1/2 cup of the tomato sauce, the egg, bread crumbs, garlic powder and pepper. Pat half of meat mixture in pan.

2 Sprinkle 1/2 cup of the cheese over meat mixture. Spread spinach over cheese; sprinkle with remaining 1/2 cup cheese. Pat remaining meat mixture on top of cheese. Insert ovenproof meat thermometer so tip is in center of loaf.

3 Bake uncovered 1 hour to 1 hour 15 minutes or until thoroughly cooked in center and the thermometer reads 160°F. Run knife around edges of pan. Place serving platter upside down over pan; turn platter and pan over. Remove pan.

4 In small microwavable bowl, microwave remaining tomato sauce, loosely covered, on High 30 to 60 seconds or until hot; pour over top of meat loaf.

NUTRITION INFORMATION PER SERVING: Calories 350 • Total Fat 19g • Saturated Fat 8g • Cholesterol 120mg • Sodium 700mg • Total Carbohydrate 15g • Dietary Fiber 2g • Protein 29g. DIETARY EXCHANGES: 1 Starch • 3-1/2 Medium-Fat Meat • 1 Carb Choice.

# grilled chicken-asparagus bundles

**PREP TIME:** 45 Minutes ✳ **READY IN:** 45 Minutes ✳ **SERVINGS:** 4

8 fresh asparagus spears (about 6 oz.), trimmed

4 boneless skinless chicken breast halves (about 1-1/4 lb.)

1/4 cup mayonnaise

1 teaspoon dried tarragon leaves

1 teaspoon Dijon mustard

1/4 teaspoon garlic salt

1 Heat gas or charcoal grill. Place asparagus on shallow microwavable plate; cover with vented microwavable plastic wrap. Microwave on High 1 to 2 minutes or until crisp-tender. Uncover and cool.

2 Between 2 pieces of plastic wrap or waxed paper, place 1 chicken breast half. With flat side of meat mallet or rolling pin and working from center, gently pound chicken until about 1/4 inch thick; remove wrap. Repeat with remaining chicken breast halves.

3 In small bowl, mix mayonnaise, tarragon, mustard and garlic salt; reserve 1 tablespoon. Divide remaining mixture evenly onto chicken breast halves; spread evenly to within 1/2 inch of edges.

4 Place asparagus spears crosswise on each chicken breast half. Wrap chicken around asparagus; secure each with toothpick.

5 When grill is heated, place chicken bundles, toothpick side up, on gas grill over medium heat or on charcoal grill over medium coals; cover grill. Cook 10 to 12 minutes, rotating bundles twice to cook both ends (do not turn upside down), until chicken is fork-tender and juices run clear. Before serving, remove toothpicks; top each with reserved mayonnaise mixture.

**HIGH ALTITUDE (3500-6500 FT):** Place chicken bundles, toothpick side up, on gas grill over medium-low heat or on charcoal grill over medium-low coals; cover grill. Cook 12 to 14 minutes, rotating bundles twice to cook both ends (do not turn upside down).

NUTRITION INFORMATION PER SERVING: Calories 270 • Total Fat 16g • Saturated Fat 3g • Cholesterol 95mg • Sodium 250mg • Total Carbohydrate 2g • Dietary Fiber 0g • Protein 32g. DIETARY EXCHANGES: 4-1/2 Very Lean Meat • 2-1/2 Fat.

# italian vegetarian lasagna

PREP TIME: 40 Minutes ✳ READY IN: 1 Hour 20 Minutes ✳ SERVINGS: 8

| | |
|---|---|
| 12 uncooked lasagna noodles | 2 cups chopped fresh spinach |
| 1/2 cup dry sherry or unsweetened apple juice | 1 teaspoon dried basil leaves |
| 1 medium onion, finely chopped (1/2 cup) | 1/2 teaspoon dried oregano leaves |
| 1 package (8 oz.) sliced fresh mushrooms (about 3 cups) | 1 container (15 oz.) reduced-fat ricotta cheese |
| 2 large zucchini, shredded (about 4 cups) | 1 cup fat-free or reduced-fat cottage cheese |
| 2 medium red or green bell peppers, chopped (1 cup) | 1/4 cup grated Parmesan cheese |
| 1/2 teaspoon salt | 1 can (8 oz.) tomato sauce |
| | 1 cup shredded mozzarella cheese (4 oz.) |

1 Heat oven to 425°F. Spray 13 x 9-inch (3-quart) glass baking dish with cooking spray. Cook and drain lasagna noodles as directed on package. Rinse with cold water to cool; drain well.

2 Meanwhile, in 12-inch nonstick skillet or 4-quart Dutch oven, heat sherry to boiling over medium-high heat. Add onion; cook 3 minutes, stirring frequently. Stir in mushrooms, zucchini, bell peppers and salt. Cook 5 minutes, stirring occasionally. Stir in spinach, basil and oregano. Cook 2 minutes. Remove from heat; drain well. In medium bowl, mix ricotta, cottage and Parmesan cheeses.

3 Place 3 noodles in bottom of baking dish. Top with 1/3 of ricotta mixture and 1/3 of vegetable mixture. Repeat layers 2 more times. Top with remaining 3 lasagna noodles, the tomato sauce and mozzarella cheese.

4 Spray sheet of foil with cooking spray; place sprayed side down over baking dish. Bake 25 to 30 minutes or until bubbly around edges. Uncover; bake 5 minutes longer or until top is light golden brown. Let stand 5 minutes before serving.

NUTRITION INFORMATION PER SERVING: Calories 320 • Total Fat 9g • Saturated Fat 5g • Cholesterol 30mg • Sodium 700mg • Total Carbohydrate 38g • Dietary Fiber 3g • Protein 21g. DIETARY EXCHANGES: 1-1/2 Starch • 3 Vegetable • 1-1/2 Medium-Fat Meat • 2-1/2 Carb Choices.

# crescent-topped burger bake

PREP TIME: 20 Minutes ✳ READY IN: 40 Minutes ✳ SERVINGS: 8

1-1/2  lb. lean (at least 80%) ground beef

1/4  cup chopped onion (1/2 medium)

3  cups frozen southern-style hash-brown potatoes (from 32-oz. bag)

1  bag (1 lb.) Green Giant® frozen mixed vegetables

2  jars (12 oz. each) beef gravy

1/2  teaspoon salt

1/4  teaspoon pepper

1  can (8 oz.) Pillsbury® refrigerated crescent dinner rolls

1  Heat oven to 375°F. In 12-inch skillet or Dutch oven, cook ground beef and onion over medium-high heat, stirring frequently, until beef is thoroughly cooked; drain.

2  Stir in potatoes, frozen vegetables and gravy. Heat to boiling. Reduce heat to medium; cover and cook 8 to 10 minutes, stirring occasionally, until vegetables are crisp-tender. Stir in salt and pepper.

3  Into ungreased 2-1/2- to 3-quart casserole or 13 x 9-inch (3-quart) glass baking dish, spoon hot beef and vegetable mixture.

4  Unroll dough; separate into 8 triangles. Place triangles over hot mixture with points toward center of casserole. Bake 14 to 17 minutes or until crescents are golden brown and mixture is bubbly around edges.

NUTRITION INFORMATION PER SERVING: Calories 420 • Total Fat 18g • Saturated Fat 7g • Cholesterol 50mg • Sodium 1040mg • Total Carbohydrate 41g • Dietary Fiber 5g • Protein 24g. DIETARY EXCHANGES: 3 Starch • 2 Medium-Fat Meat • 1 Fat • 2-1/2 Carb Choices.

# italian cheese-stuffed meat loaf

PREP TIME: 30 Minutes ✳ READY IN: 1 Hour 40 Minutes ✳ SERVINGS: 6

2  eggs

1-1/2  lb. lean (at least 80%) ground beef

2  cups soft French bread crumbs

1/2  cup shredded Parmesan cheese (2 oz.)

1/4  cup chopped fresh basil or 1-1/2 teaspoons dried basil leaves

1/2  teaspoon salt

1/4  teaspoon pepper

4  cloves garlic, minced

1  can (8 oz.) pizza sauce

1-1/2  cups shredded provolone cheese (6 oz.)

1  jar (7.25 oz.) roasted red bell peppers, drained, chopped

1/4  cup chopped ripe olives

1  Heat oven to 375°F. Line 15 x 10 x 1-inch pan with foil; spray foil with cooking spray. In large bowl, beat eggs. Stir in ground beef, bread crumbs, Parmesan cheese, basil, salt, pepper, garlic and 1/2 cup of the pizza sauce until well combined.

2  On large sheet of foil, shape beef mixture into 12 x 10-inch rectangle. Top evenly with provolone cheese, roasted peppers and olives to within 1/2 inch of edges. Starting with one 10-inch side, roll up; press seam to seal. Place seam side down in pan.

3  Bake 40 minutes. Spoon remaining pizza sauce over loaf. Insert meat thermometer so bulb reaches center of loaf. Bake 15 to 20 minutes longer or until loaf is thoroughly cooked in center and thermometer reads 160°F. Let stand 10 minutes before slicing.

NUTRITION INFORMATION PER SERVING: Calories 320 • Total Fat 19g • Saturated Fat 9g • Cholesterol 125mg • Sodium 720mg • Total Carbohydrate 10g • Dietary Fiber 1g • Protein 26g. DIETARY EXCHANGES: 1/2 Other Carbohydrate • 3-1/2 Medium-Fat Meat • 1/2 Fat • 1/2 Carb Choice.

### cook's notes

*To cut basil into strips, stack several basil leaves, roll them up tight, and slice crosswise with a sharp knife. Fluff with fingertips to separate.*

# seafood and asparagus manicotti

PREP TIME: 30 Minutes ✽ READY IN: 1 Hour 10 Minutes ✽ SERVINGS: 6

12 uncooked manicotti pasta shells (from 8-oz. pkg.)

1 jar (26 oz.) tomato pasta sauce

1/4 cup dry white wine or non-alcoholic white wine

3/4 cup half-and-half

1 package (6 oz.) frozen cooked salad shrimp, thawed

6 oz. refrigerated imitation crabmeat sticks (from 12-oz. pkg.), cut into 1/4-inch pieces

1 box (9 oz.) Green Giant® frozen asparagus cuts, thawed, coarsely chopped

1/2 cup chopped sun-dried tomatoes in oil, drained

1/3 cup cream cheese, softened

2 cups shredded mozzarella cheese (8 oz.)

1/4 cup lightly packed cut-up strips fresh basil leaves

1 Heat oven to 350°F. Cook and drain pasta as directed on package. Meanwhile, in 2-quart saucepan, heat tomato sauce and wine to boiling over medium heat. Reduce heat to low; simmer 4 minutes. Remove from heat; stir in half-and-half. In ungreased 13 x 9-inch (3-quart) glass baking dish, spread 1 cup of the tomato sauce.

2 In medium bowl, mix shrimp, imitation crabmeat, asparagus, sun-dried tomatoes, cream cheese and 1/2 cup of the mozzarella cheese. Spoon about 1/4 cup seafood mixture into each pasta shell. Arrange in baking dish. Pour remaining tomato sauce evenly over shells. Cover dish with foil.

3 Bake 25 to 30 minutes or until hot. Top with the remaining 1-1/2 cups mozzarella cheese. Bake uncovered 5 to 10 minutes longer or until cheese is melted. Sprinkle with basil before serving.

**HIGH ALTITUDE (3500-6500 FT):** Heat oven to 375°F. Bake 10 to 15 minutes after adding cheese.

NUTRITION INFORMATION PER SERVING: Calories 550 • Total Fat 23g • Saturated Fat 11g • Cholesterol 95mg • Sodium 1290mg • Total Carbohydrate 58g • Dietary Fiber 4g • Protein 29g. DIETARY EXCHANGES: 2-1/2 Starch • 1 Other Carbohydrate • 1 Vegetable • 2-1/2 Very Lean Meat • 4 Fat • 4 Carb Choices.

# easy chicken chilaquiles skillet

PREP TIME: 25 Minutes ✽ READY IN: 40 Minutes ✽ SERVINGS: 4

1 lb. boneless skinless chicken breasts, cut into 3/4-inch pieces

1/2 teaspoon garlic salt

2 teaspoons vegetable oil

1 can (14.5 oz.) diced tomatoes with green chiles, undrained

1 can (15 oz.) spicy chili beans

1-1/2 cups Green Giant® frozen corn (from 1-lb. bag)

1/2 cup water

2 cups tortilla chips, broken slightly

1 cup shredded Mexican cheese blend (4 oz.)

1 In medium bowl, mix chicken and garlic salt to coat. In 10-inch nonstick skillet, heat oil over medium-high heat. Add chicken; cook 3 to 5 minutes, stirring frequently, until browned. Stir in tomatoes, beans, corn and water. Reduce heat to medium-low; cover and cook 10 minutes.

2 Gently stir in chips. Cook uncovered 5 to 10 minutes, stirring occasionally, until chicken is no longer pink in center and corn is tender. Sprinkle cheese over top; cover and cook 2 to 3 minutes longer or until cheese is melted.

NUTRITION INFORMATION PER SERVING: Calories 510 • Total Fat 19g • Saturated Fat 8g • Cholesterol 100mg • Sodium 1510mg • Total Carbohydrate 42g • Dietary Fiber 8g • Protein 42g. DIETARY EXCHANGES: 2 Starch • 1/2 Other Carbohydrate • 1 Vegetable • 5 Very Lean Meat • 3 Fat • 3 Carb Choices.

seafood and asparagus manicotti

## cook's notes

To split game hens, use a heavy-duty kitchen scissors or place the hens on a cutting board and use a large knife to cut through the birds.

# cornish hens with apple-raisin stuffing

PREP TIME: 30 Minutes ✹ READY IN: 1 Hour 45 Minutes ✹ SERVINGS: 8

### STUFFING

- 3 tablespoons butter or margarine
- 1/2 cup chopped green onions (8 medium)
- 1 red baking apple, unpeeled, chopped
- 4 cups unseasoned dry bread cubes
- 1/2 cup raisins
- 1/4 teaspoon salt
- 1/4 teaspoon ground allspice
- 1/4 cup apple juice

### CORNISH HENS

- 4 Cornish game hens (24 oz. each), thawed if frozen
- 1/4 teaspoon salt
- 1/8 teaspoon pepper
- 1/4 cup apple jelly
- 2 tablespoons butter or margarine

1 Heat oven to 350°F. In 10-inch skillet, melt 3 tablespoons butter over medium-high heat. Add onions and apple; cook and stir until tender. Stir in remaining stuffing ingredients. In ungreased 15 x 10 x 1-inch pan, spread stuffing.

2 Split each game hen in half. Sprinkle lightly with salt and pepper. Place the hen halves, skin side up, over stuffing. In 1-quart saucepan, melt the jelly with 2 tablespoons butter over low heat; brush over hens.

3 Bake uncovered 1 hour to 1 hour 15 minutes or until hens are fork-tender and juice is clear when thickest part is cut to bone (180°F.).

NUTRITION INFORMATION PER SERVING: Calories 810 • Total Fat 44g • Saturated Fat 14g • Cholesterol 260mg • Sodium 780mg • Total Carbohydrate 57g • Dietary Fiber 2g • Protein 48g. DIETARY EXCHANGES: 3 Starch • 1/2 Fruit • 1/2 Other Carbohydrate • 5-1/2 Lean Meat • 5 Fat • 4 Carb Choices.

# sweet plum-pork stir-fry

PREP TIME: 35 Minutes  ✳  READY IN: 35 Minutes  ✳  SERVINGS: 4

1 cup uncooked instant white rice

1-1/4 cups water

3/4 lb. pork tenderloin

2 tablespoons oil

1 medium sweet onion (such as Walla Walla or Maui), cut into thin wedges (3/4 cup)

1 medium carrot, diagonally sliced (1/2 cup)

1 medium red bell pepper, cut into thin bite-sized strips

1 cup fresh snow pea pods, trimmed

1/3 cup plum jelly or jam

1 tablespoon soy sauce

1 tablespoon cornstarch

1/2 teaspoon ginger

1/4 teaspoon salt

1 Cook rice in 1 cup of the water as directed on package. Meanwhile, cut tenderloin into 1/4-inch thick slices; cut slices into thin bite-sized strips. Heat 1 tablespoon of the oil in wok or 12-inch skillet over medium-high heat until hot. Add pork; cook and stir 4 to 5 minutes or until pork is no longer pink in center. Remove pork from wok; place on plate and cover to keep warm.

2 Add remaining tablespoon oil to wok. Add onion and carrot; cook and stir 3 minutes. Add bell pepper and pea pods; cook and stir an additional 2 to 3 minutes or until vegetables are crisp-tender.

3 In small bowl, mix jelly, soy sauce, cornstarch, ginger, salt and remaining 1/4 cup water until smooth. Add jelly mixture and return pork to wok; cook and stir an additional 2 minutes or until sauce has thickened. Serve over rice.

**HIGH ALTITUDE (3500-6500 FT):** Cook rice using high altitude directions on package. Increase water in jelly mixture to 1/2 cup.

NUTRITION INFORMATION PER SERVING: Calories 390 • Total Fat 11g • Saturated Fat 2g • Cholesterol 55mg • Sodium 750mg • Total Carbohydrate 50g • Dietary Fiber 2g • Protein 23g. DIETARY EXCHANGES: 2 Starch • 1 Other Carbohydrate • 2-1/2 Lean Meat • 1/2 Fat • 3 Carb Choices.

## kitchen tip

*Maui onions, from the Hawaiian Islands, are sweet, mild and white to pale yellow, and are in season from April to July. Walla Walla onions, from Walla Walla, Washington, are also yellow and sweet, and are available from June through September.*

# apricot-glazed chicken breasts with almond couscous

PREP TIME: 25 Minutes ✳ READY IN: 25 Minutes ✳ SERVINGS: 4

4 boneless skinless chicken breasts (about 1 lb.)
1/2 teaspoon of garlic powder
1/4 teaspoons pepper
1/8 teaspoon ground red pepper (cayenne)
2 tablespoons apricot preserves

1 cup chicken broth
1 tablespoon butter or margarine
1 cup uncooked couscous
2 tablespoons slivered almonds, toasted, if desired

1 Set oven control to broil. Spray rack in broiler pan with cooking spray. To flatten each chicken breast, place between 2 pieces of plastic wrap or waxed paper. Working from center, gently pound chicken with rolling pin or flat side of meat mallet until 1/4 inch thick.

2 In small bowl, mix garlic powder, pepper and ground red pepper. Sprinkle on both sides of chicken; place on rack in pan.

3 Broil 4 to 6 inches from heat 5 to 7 minutes or until chicken is no longer pink in center. Brush with half of apricot preserves; broil 1 minute longer or until preserves are bubbly. Brush with remaining preserves before serving.

4 Meanwhile, in 2-quart saucepan, heat broth and butter to boiling. Stir in couscous and almonds. Remove from heat; cover and let stand 5 minutes. Fluff couscous with fork before serving with glazed chicken.

NUTRITION INFORMATION PER SERVING: Calories 380 • Total Fat 9g • Saturated Fat 3g • Cholesterol 75mg • Sodium 340mg • Total Carbohydrate 42g • Dietary Fiber 3g • Protein 32g. DIETARY EXCHANGES: 2-1/2 Starch • 1/2 Other Carbohydrate • 3-1/2 Very Lean Meat • 1 Fat • 3 Carb Choices.

# chicken-chile casserole

PREP TIME: 25 Minutes ✳ READY IN: 55 Minutes ✳ SERVINGS: 6

2 cups frozen bell pepper and onion stir-fry (from 1-lb. bag)
1 1/2 cups Green Giant® Niblets® frozen corn (from 1-lb. bag)
1 container (18 oz.) Old El Paso® refrigerated taco sauce with seasoned chicken

1 can (15.5 oz.) kidney beans, drained, rinsed
1/2 cup Old El Paso® thick 'n chunky salsa
1 can (8 oz.) Pillsbury® refrigerated crescent dinner rolls
1 tablespoon butter or margarine, melted
1 tablespoon yellow cornmeal

1 Heat oven to 375°F. In 12-inch nonstick skillet, cook bell pepper and onion stir-fry over medium-high heat 2 minutes, stirring frequently and breaking up larger pieces.

2 Stir in corn, taco sauce with seasoned chicken, beans and salsa. Heat to boiling. Reduce heat to medium-low; cook 5 to 8 minutes, stirring occasionally, until corn is tender. Spoon mixture into ungreased 8-inch square (2-quart) glass baking dish.

3 Remove dough from can in rolled section; cut roll into 12 slices, then cut each slice in half crosswise. Arrange half roll slices, curved side up, around outside edge of dish, overlapping slightly. Brush half roll slices with butter; sprinkle with cornmeal. Bake 23 to 28 minutes or until roll slices are deep golden brown and mixture is bubbly.

NUTRITION INFORMATION PER SERVING: Calories 380 • Total Fat 11g • Saturated Fat 3g • Cholesterol 45mg • Sodium 1380mg • Total Carbohydrate 55g • Dietary Fiber 9g • Protein 18g. DIETARY EXCHANGES: 3-1/2 Starch • 1 Very Lean Meat • 1-1/2 Fat • 3 Carb Choices.

# chicken waikiki

PREP TIME: 35 Minutes ✳ READY IN: 1 Hour 20 Minutes ✳ SERVINGS: 6

| | |
|---|---|
| 3-1/2 cups chicken broth | 1/3 cup cider vinegar |
| 1-1/2 cups uncooked regular long-grain white rice | 2 tablespoons soy sauce |
| 1 can (20 oz.) pineapple chunks in juice | 1 medium red bell pepper, cut into 1-inch pieces (1 cup) |
| 1 cup sugar | 1 medium green bell pepper, cut into 1-inch pieces (1 cup) |
| 3 tablespoons cornstarch | |
| 1 tablespoon grated gingerroot or 1/2 teaspoon ground ginger | 6 boneless skinless chicken breasts (about 1-1/2 lb.) |

1  Heat oven to 350°F. Spray 13 x 9-inch (3-quart) glass baking dish with cooking spray. In 2-quart saucepan, heat 3 cups of the broth to boiling over high heat. Add rice; reduce heat to medium-low. Cover; simmer about 20 minutes or until liquid is absorbed.

2  Meanwhile, drain pineapple juice into 2-cup measuring cup; add remaining 1/2 cup broth to make 1-1/4 cups. In another 2-quart saucepan, mix pineapple liquid, sugar, cornstarch, gingerroot, vinegar and soy sauce. Heat to boiling over high heat. Cook about 2 minutes, stirring constantly. Remove from heat. Stir in bell peppers and pineapple.

3  Cut chicken into 2-1/2 x 1-inch strips. Spread rice in baking dish; arrange chicken strips over rice. Pour pineapple mixture over chicken and rice. Cover dish with foil. Bake about 45 minutes or until the chicken is no longer pink in center and mixture is bubbly.

NUTRITION INFORMATION PER SERVING: Calories 560 • Total Fat 5g • Saturated Fat 1.5g • Cholesterol 70mg • Sodium 960mg • Total Carbohydrate 96g • Dietary Fiber 2g • Protein 33g. DIETARY EXCHANGES: 2 Starch • 1/2 Fruit, 4 Other Carbohydrate • 4 Very Lean Meat • 6-1/2 Carb Choices.

## kitchen tip

*Purchase fresh gingerroot in the produce section of the grocery store. Buy a piece that's large enough to hold in your hand for easy grating. Freeze any leftover root for use in future recipes.*

# patchwork pot pie

PREP TIME: 15 Minutes  ✳  READY IN: 1 Hour 35 Minutes  ✳  SERVINGS: 6

2　cups diced (1/4 to 1/2 inch) cooked turkey breast

2　cups refrigerated cooked diced potatoes with onions (from 20-oz. bag)

2　cups Green Giant® Valley Fresh Steamers™ frozen mixed vegetables

1　jar (4.5 oz.) Green Giant® sliced mushrooms, drained

1/2　cup sour cream

1　jar (12 oz.) turkey gravy

1/4　teaspoon dried sage laves

1　Pillsbury® refrigerated pie crust, softened as directed on box

1　Heat oven to 375°F. Spray 3-quart casserole with cooking spray. In large bowl, mix turkey, potatoes, frozen vegetables, mushrooms, sour cream, gravy and sage; spoon mixture into casserole.

2　Unroll pie crust. Cut into 1-1/2-inch wide strips, then cut in opposite direction, making 1-1/2-inch square pieces (not all will be perfectly square). Starting with rounded-edge pieces around edge of casserole, cover top of mixture with pie crust pieces, overlapping each piece (see photo). Bake 1 hour 15 minutes to 1 hour 20 minutes or until crust is golden brown and edges are bubbly.

**HIGH ALTITUDE (3500-6500 FT):** Thaw frozen vegetables before adding to casserole.

NUTRITION INFORMATION PER SERVING: Calories 390 • Total Fat 18g • Saturated Fat 7g • Cholesterol 60mg • Sodium 760mg • Total Carbohydrate 40g • Dietary Fiber 4g • Protein 19g. DIETARY EXCHANGES: 2 Starch • 1/2 Other Carbohydrate • 1 Vegetable • 1-1/2 Very Lean Meat • 3 Fat • 2-1/2 Carb Choices.

# fish fillets with herbed tartar sauce

PREP TIME: 20 Minutes ✳ READY IN: 20 Minutes ✳ SERVINGS: 4

| | |
|---|---|
| 1 egg | 1/3 cup tartar sauce |
| 1/2 cup Progresso® Italian style bread crumbs | 1/4 cup chopped tomato |
| 3 tablespoons olive oil | 1/2 teaspoon dried basil leaves |
| 1 lb. mild-flavored fish fillets (about 1/2 inch thick), cut into 4 serving pieces | |

1 In shallow dish or pie plate, beat egg with wire whisk. In another shallow dish or pie plate, place bread crumbs.

2 In 12-inch skillet, heat oil over medium heat. Dip fish into egg, then coat with bread crumbs; place in skillet. Cook 8 to 10 minutes, turning once, until browned on both sides and fish flakes easily with fork. In small bowl, mix tartar sauce, tomato and basil; serve with fish.

NUTRITION INFORMATION PER SERVING: Calories 370 • Total Fat 24g • Saturated Fat 3.5g • Cholesterol 120mg • Sodium 440mg • Total Carbohydrate 12g • Dietary Fiber 0g • Protein 25g. DIETARY EXCHANGES: 1 Starch • 3 Lean Meat • 3 Fat • 1 Carb Choice.

**kitchen tip**

*Fish that would work well in this recipe include cod, walleye, perch, sole or any other mild flavored fillets.*

# hearty multi-bean chili

PREP TIME: 1 Hour 10 Minutes ✳ READY IN: 1 Hour 10 Minutes ✳ SERVINGS: 12

| | |
|---|---|
| 2 tablespoons oil | 2 cans (15 oz. each) black beans, drained, rinsed |
| 2 medium onions, chopped | 2 cans (15 oz. each) black-eyed peas, drained, rinsed |
| 2 carrots, chopped | |
| 1 medium green bell pepper, chopped | 1 can (15 oz.) tomato sauce |
| 3 garlic cloves, minced | 1 tablespoon sugar |
| 2 cans (28 oz. each) diced tomatoes, undrained | 2 to 3 tablespoons chili powder |
| 2 cans (15.5 oz. each) kidney beans, drained, rinsed | 1 tablespoon cumin |
| | 1 teaspoon fennel seed, crushed |
| 2 cans (15.5 oz. each) pinto beans, drained, rinsed | |

1 Heat oil in 6-quart stockpot or Dutch oven over medium-high heat until hot. Add onions, carrots, bell pepper and garlic; cook and stir 4 minutes.

2 Add all remaining ingredients; mix well. Bring to a boil. Reduce heat; cover and simmer 40 to 50 minutes or until vegetables are tender and flavors are blended, stirring frequently.

NUTRITION INFORMATION PER SERVING: Calories 320 • Total Fat 4g • Saturated Fat 0g • Cholesterol 0mg • Sodium 950mg • Total Carbohydrate 56g • Dietary Fiber 13g • Protein 16g. DIETARY EXCHANGES: 3-1/2 Starch • 3-1/2 Other Carbohydrate • 1 Vegetable • 1 Very Lean Meat • 1/2 Fat.

**cook's notes**

*Offer bowls of garnishes with this chili. Sour cream, finely shredded Cheddar cheese, diced avocado, chopped onion, fresh chunky salsa and chopped fresh cilantro all make good toppings.*

# stuffed cabbage rolls

PREP TIME: 1 Hour 15 Minutes ✳ READY IN: 2 Hours 15 Minutes ✳ SERVINGS: 8

| | |
|---|---|
| 1 cup water | 1/2 teaspoon salt |
| 1/2 cup uncooked regular long-grain white rice | 1/4 teaspoon dried oregano leaves |
| 1 medium head cabbage, core removed | 1/4 teaspoon pepper |
| 2 eggs | 1 can (15 oz.) tomato sauce |
| 1 lb. lean (at least 80%) ground beef | 3/4 cup grated Parmesan cheese |
| 1/3 cup chopped onion | |

1 Heat oven to 375°F. Spray 13 x 9-inch (3-quart) glass baking dish with cooking spray. In 2-quart saucepan, heat water and rice to boiling. Reduce heat to low; cover and cook 12 to 14 minutes or until rice is tender. Remove from heat.

2 Meanwhile, in 6-quart Dutch oven, cook whole head of cabbage in enough boiling water to cover, about 3 minutes or just until outer leaves are softened. Remove cabbage from water; remove as many leaves as can easily be removed. Return cabbage to water; repeat process until 16 leaves are removed.

3 In large bowl, beat eggs. Stir in beef, onion, salt, oregano, pepper and cooked rice. For each roll, place about 3 tablespoons beef mixture in cooked cabbage leaf; roll up, tucking in ends to completely cover mixture. Place seam side down in baking dish. Pour tomato sauce over rolls. Sprinkle with Parmesan cheese.

4 Cover tightly with foil; bake 50 to 60 minutes or until bubbly around edges, cheese is melted and beef is thoroughly cooked.

**HIGH ALTITUDE (3500-6500 FT):** Heat oven to 400°F.

NUTRITION INFORMATION PER SERVING: Calories 250 • Total Fat 11g • Saturated Fat 4.5g • Cholesterol 95mg • Sodium 630mg • Total Carbohydrate 21g • Dietary Fiber 3g • Protein 18g. DIETARY EXCHANGES: 1/2 Starch • 1/2 Other Carbohydrate • 1 Vegetable • 2 Medium-Fat Meat • 1-1/2 Carb Choices.

# rolled italian meat loaf

**PREP TIME:** 15 Minutes ✳ **READY IN:** 1 Hour 40 Minutes ✳ **SERVINGS:** 8

1-1/4 lb. extra-lean (at least 90%) ground beef

3/4 lb. bulk Italian sausage

1 egg

1 can (8 oz.) pizza sauce

1/4 cup Progresso® Italian style bread crumbs

1/4 teaspoon pepper

2 cups shredded 6 cheese Italian cheese blend (8 oz.)

2 cups loosely packed fresh spinach leaves

1 Heat oven to 350°F. In large bowl, mix ground beef, sausage, egg, 1/2 cup of the pizza sauce, the bread crumbs and pepper.

2 On foil, pat mixture to 12 x 8-inch rectangle. Sprinkle evenly with cheese; gently press into meat. Top with spinach. Starting at short end, roll up tightly, using foil to start roll and tucking in spinach leaves; seal ends. Place seam side down in ungreased 12 x 8-inch (2 quart) glass baking dish.

3 Bake 1 hour. Spread remaining pizza sauce over top. Bake 15 minutes longer or until thermometer inserted in meat loaf reads 160°F. Let stand 5 to 10 minutes before serving.

NUTRITION INFORMATION PER SERVING: Calories 330 • Total Fat 22g • Saturated Fat 10g • Cholesterol 120mg • Sodium 900mg • Total Carbohydrate 6g • Dietary Fiber 0g • Protein 29g. DIETARY EXCHANGES: 1/2 Other Carbohydrate • 4 Medium-Fat Meat • 1/2 Carb Choice.

*cook's notes*

*Use foil to make rolling the meat loaf easier. Then, using the foil, transfer the meat loaf to the pan and bake on the foil to make cleanup quicker.*

orange soda grilled chicken

# orange soda grilled chicken

PREP TIME: 15 Minutes ✽ READY IN: 1 Hour 45 Minutes ✽ SERVINGS: 4

**CHICKEN**
- 1 (3-1/2 to 4-lb.) whole roasting chicken
- 1 teaspoon coarse salt
- 1 teaspoon brown sugar
- 1 teaspoon chili powder
- 1/4 cup orange marmalade

- 1 (12-oz.) clean can orange-flavored carbonated beverage

**SAUCE**
- 1/3 cup orange marmalade
- Reserved carbonated beverage
- 2 teaspoons oil

**cook's notes**

*The chicken, can, and the liquid inside the can all will become very hot; use oven mitts to remove the can from the chicken.*

1 Heat grill for indirect cooking as directed by manufacturer. Remove and discard neck and giblets from chicken cavity. Rinse chicken and pat dry with paper towels.

2 In small bowl, combine salt, brown sugar and chili powder; mix well. Rub 1-1/2 teaspoons salt mixture inside chicken. Add 1/4 cup marmalade to remaining salt mixture; mix well. Set aside.

3 Open beverage can; measure out 2/3 cup beverage. Set aside 3 tablespoons of the beverage and reserve remainder for another use. Add 2 teaspoons of the reserved orange-flavored beverage to marmalade mixture, stirring until brushing consistency. Spray outside of half-full can of beverage with nonstick cooking spray; set in shallow baking pan. Carefully set chicken cavity over can, pushing until chicken balances in pan. Rub skin of chicken with oil.

4 When ready to grill, use tongs and spatula to remove chicken and can from pan and set on grill for indirect cooking, making sure chicken is balanced. Cover grill. Cook 1-1/4 to 1-1/2 hours or until chicken juices run clear and instant-read thermometer inserted in thickest part of thigh registers 180°F. During last 30 minutes of cooking time, brush chicken with marmalade mixture.

5 With thick hot pads and tongs, carefully remove chicken and can from grill to clean baking pan or platter. Twist can to remove from chicken. Discard any beverage left in can. Let stand 5 minutes before carving. In small microwave-safe bowl, combine 1/3 cup marmalade and remaining 2 tablespoons plus 1 teaspoon carbonated beverage; mix well. Microwave on High for 30 seconds or until warm. Serve marmalade mixture with chicken.

NUTRITION INFORMATION PER SERVING: Calories 520 • Total Fat 26g • Saturated Fat 7g • Cholesterol 150mg • Sodium 530mg • Total Carbohydrate 24g • Dietary Fiber 0g • Protein 47g. DIETARY EXCHANGES: 1-1/2 Starch • 1-1/2 Other Carbohydrate • 1-1/2 Fat • 1-1/2 Carb Choices.

# jerk-seasoned chicken and pepper saute

PREP TIME: 20 Minutes ✽ READY IN: 20 Minutes ✽ SERVINGS: 4

- 1 lb. boneless skinless chicken breast halves, cut into thin strips
- 2 teaspoons Caribbean jerk seasoning

- 1 package (1 lb.) frozen bell pepper and onion stir-fry
- 1/3 cup orange juice
- 2 teaspoons cornstarch

1 Spray large nonstick skillet with nonstick cooking spray. Heat over medium-high heat until hot. Add chicken and jerk seasoning; cook and stir 5 to 7 minutes or until chicken is no longer pink.

2 Add bell pepper and onion stir-fry; cover and cook 3 to 5 minutes or until vegetables are crisp-tender, stirring occasionally.

3 Meanwhile, in small bowl, combine orange juice and cornstarch; blend until smooth. Add to mixture in skillet; cook and stir until bubbly and thickened.

NUTRITION INFORMATION PER SERVING: Calories 170 • Total Fat 3g • Saturated Fat 1g • Cholesterol 65mg • Sodium 220mg • Total Carbohydrate 10g • Dietary Fiber 3g • Protein 26g. DIETARY EXCHANGES: 2 Vegetable • 3 Very Lean Meat.

**kitchen tip**

*To speed preparation, purchase precut chicken packaged for stir-frying.*

# mediterranean chicken bake

PREP TIME: 20 Minutes ✳ READY IN: 55 Minutes ✳ SERVINGS: 6

1   lb. boneless skinless chicken breasts, cubed
1   medium onion, chopped (1/2 cup)
2   medium zucchini, cut into 1/8-inch slices
1/2 cup uncooked rosamarina or orzo pasta
1/2 cup water
2   medium plum (Roma) tomatoes, chopped

1   jar (26 oz.) roasted tomato and garlic pasta sauce
2   cups shredded mozzarella cheese (8 oz.)
1   teaspoon Italian seasoning
6   sheets frozen phyllo (filo) pastry (14 x 9 inch), thawed (from 1-lb. box)
3   tablespoons butter or margarine, melted

1 Heat oven to 400°F. Coat 3-quart glass casserole with cooking spray. Coat 12-inch nonstick skillet with cooking spray and cook chicken over medium heat 8 to 10 minutes, stirring occasionally, until no longer pink. Stir in onion, zucchini, pasta and water. Cook 5 to 6 minutes, stirring occasionally, until vegetables are crisp-tender.

2 Stir in tomatoes, pasta sauce, cheese and Italian seasoning. Spoon mixture into casserole. Brush top of each phyllo sheet with melted butter. Crumple each phyllo sheet and place on top of chicken mixture in casserole. Bake uncovered 20 to 30 minutes or until phyllo is golden brown.

**HIGH ALTITUDE (3500-6500 FT):** In Step 1, use medium-high heat. Increase water to 3/4 cup. Bake 35 to 45 minutes.

NUTRITION INFORMATION PER SERVING: Calories 490 • Total Fat 21g • Saturated Fat 10g • Cholesterol 80mg • Sodium 930mg • Total Carbohydrate 45g • Dietary Fiber 4g • Protein 32g. DIETARY EXCHANGES: 1-1/2 Starch • 1 Other Carbohydrate • 1 Vegetable • 3-1/2 Very Lean Meat • 3-1/2 Fat • 3 Carb Choices.

## cook's notes

*When working with phyllo dough, keep the remaining sheets covered with a damp cloth until needed to prevent dough from drying out.*

# italian dinner frittata

PREP TIME: 15 Minutes ✳ READY IN: 30 Minutes ✳ SERVINGS: 4

1   tablespoon canola oil
8   medium green onions, sliced (1/2 cup)
1   carton (16 ounces) fat-free egg product or 8 eggs, beaten
1/2 cup shredded mozzarella cheese (2 oz.)
1/2 cup chopped seeded tomato (1 small)

2   tablespoons chopped fresh parsley
1/8 teaspoon pepper
1/3 cup shredded Parmesan cheese
    Additional chopped tomato, if desired
    Additional chopped fresh parsley, if desired

1 In 10-inch nonstick skillet, heat oil over medium heat until hot. Cook onions in oil 2 to 3 minutes, stirring frequently, until tender.

2 Stir in eggs, mozzarella cheese, tomato, parsley and pepper. Reduce heat to medium-low; cover and cook 9 to 11 minutes or until eggs are set around edge and light brown on bottom.

3 Sprinkle Parmesan cheese on top. Cover; remove from heat and let stand 3 to 4 minutes or until cheese is melted. Garnish with additional chopped tomato and parsley.

NUTRITION INFORMATION PER SERVING: Calories 180 • Total Fat 9g • Saturated Fat 3.5g • Cholesterol 15mg • Sodium 440mg • Total Carbohydrate 4g • Dietary Fiber 1g • Protein 19g. DIETARY EXCHANGES: 1/2 Other Carbohydrate • 2-1/2 Lean Meat.

## cook's notes

*To seed a tomato, cut it in half crosswise. Squeeze tomato half gently over a bowl to remove seeds.*

# tomato-basil linguine with chicken

PREP TIME: 20 Minutes ❋ READY IN: 20 Minutes ❋ SERVINGS: 4

5 oz. refrigerated linguine

4 boneless skinless chicken breast halves, cut into 1-inch cubes

2 teaspoons chopped garlic in water (from 4.5-oz. jar)

1 can (14.5 oz.) diced tomatoes with Italian herbs, undrained

1-1/2 teaspoons dried basil leaves

1/4 cup grated Parmesan cheese

1 Cook linguine to desired doneness as directed on package. Drain; cover to keep warm. Meanwhile, spray large nonstick skillet with nonstick cooking spray. Heat over medium-high heat until hot. Add chicken and garlic; cook 5 to 8 minutes or until chicken is no longer pink.

2 Stir in tomatoes and basil. Bring to a boil. Reduce heat; cover and simmer 5 minutes, stirring occasionally. Add cooked linguine; toss gently to mix. Sprinkle with cheese.

NUTRITION INFORMATION PER SERVING: Calories 310 • Total Fat 6g • Saturated Fat 2g • Cholesterol 105mg • Sodium 420mg • Total Carbohydrate 28g • Dietary Fiber 2g • Protein 35g. DIETARY EXCHANGES: 2 Starch • 4 Very Lean Meat.

# sausage ravioli casserole

PREP TIME: 10 Minutes ✳ READY IN: 1 Hour ✳ SERVINGS: 6

- 1 bag (25 oz.) frozen Italian-style sausage-filled ravioli, thawed
- 1 jar (4.5 oz.) Green Giant® sliced mushrooms, drained
- 1 medium zucchini, cut into 1/8-inch slices (about 1 cup)
- 1/2 cup pepperoni slices (2-1/2 oz.)
- 1 jar (26 oz.) roasted tomato and garlic pasta sauce
- 1 cup shredded Swiss cheese (4 oz.)
- 1/8 teaspoon Italian seasoning, if desired

1 Heat oven to 350°F. In large bowl, mix the ravioli, mushrooms, zucchini, pepperoni and pasta sauce. Spoon into ungreased 8-inch square (2-quart) glass baking dish. Sprinkle with cheese and Italian seasoning. Bake 40 to 50 minutes or until hot and bubbly.

**HIGH ALTITUDE (3500-6500 FT):** Bake 50 to 55 minutes.

NUTRITION INFORMATION PER SERVING: Calories 500 • Total Fat 22g • Saturated Fat 9g • Cholesterol 170mg • Sodium 1840mg • Total Carbohydrate 52g • Dietary Fiber 4g • Protein 23g. DIETARY EXCHANGES: 2 Starch • 1-1/2 Other Carbohydrate • 2-1/2 High-Fat Meat • 3-1/2 Carb Choices.

# polka dot meat loaf

PREP TIME: 10 Minutes ✳ READY IN: 1 Hour 55 Minutes ✳ SERVINGS: 6

| | |
|---|---|
| 1-1/2 lb. lean (at least 80%) ground beef | 1 egg |
| 1/2 cup ketchup | 6 sticks (1 oz. each) string cheese |
| 1/4 cup Progresso® plain bread crumbs | 1 teaspoon prepared yellow mustard |
| 2 tablespoons Worcestershire sauce | 1 tablespoon packed brown sugar |
| 1/2 teaspoon salt | |

1 Heat oven to 375°F. In large bowl, mix ground beef, 1/4 cup of the ketchup, the bread crumbs, Worcestershire sauce, salt and egg. Press 1/3 of the mixture in the bottom of ungreased 8 x 4-inch loaf pan.

2 Place 2 pieces of the string cheese lengthwise and evenly spaced over beef mixture, with one end of the cheese about 1/2 inch from one end of pan. Cut 2 pieces of string cheese in half crosswise. Place 2 half pieces on the beef mixture so cheese extends full length of pan. Press cheese into beef mixture.

3 Top with half of remaining beef mixture; pat evenly in place. Top with remaining string cheese in 2 rows; press in. Press remaining beef mixture over cheese. Press ends and edges of beef mixture well to seal in cheese; smooth top.

4 Bake 45 minutes. Meanwhile, in small bowl, mix remaining 1/4 cup ketchup, the mustard and brown sugar. Remove meat loaf from oven. Spoon juices from meat loaf; spoon ketchup mixture evenly over top. Return to oven.

5 Bake 30 to 45 minutes longer or until thermometer inserted in center of meat loaf reads 160°F. Let stand 15 minutes before cutting into slices.

NUTRITION INFORMATION PER SERVING: Calories 340 • Total Fat 20g • Saturated Fat 9g • Cholesterol 120mg • Sodium 750mg • Total Carbohydrate 13g • Dietary Fiber 0g • Protein 29g. DIETARY EXCHANGES: 1 Other Carbohydrate • 4 Medium-Fat Meat • 1 Carb Choice.

*cook's notes*

*Stagger the placement of the cheese on the second layer so it is not directly above the first layer. Press ends and edges of beef mixture well to seal in the cheese.*

# lentil-potato stew

PREP TIME: 45 Minutes ✳ READY IN: 45 Minutes ✳ SERVINGS: 6

| | |
|---|---|
| 1 cup dried lentils, rinsed, sorted | 1/2 teaspoon salt |
| 2 stalks celery, sliced | 1/2 teaspoon dried rosemary leaves, crushed |
| 2 medium russet or baking potatoes, cubed | 1/4 teaspoon dried thyme leaves |
| 1 medium dark-orange sweet potato, peeled, cubed | 1/4 teaspoon pepper |
| 1 medium onion, cut into thin wedges | 1/8 teaspoon garlic powder |
| 2 vegetarian vegetable bouillon cubes | 4-1/2 cups water |

1 In large saucepan or Dutch oven, combine all ingredients; mix well. Bring to a boil. Reduce heat; cover and simmer 15 to 20 minutes or until lentils and vegetables are tender, stirring occasionally.

NUTRITION INFORMATION PER SERVING: Calories 200 • Total Fat 1g • Saturated Fat 0g • Cholesterol 0mg • Sodium 600mg • Total Carbohydrate 36g • Dietary Fiber 12g • Protein 11g. DIETARY EXCHANGES: 2-1/2 Starch • 2-1/2 Other Carbohydrate • 1/2 Very Lean Meat.

*cook's notes*

*This lentil stew thickens in the refrigerator. To reheat, simply thin it with additional broth or water and warm it over medium-low heat, stirring it as little as possible.*

# Holiday Open House

*The simple recipes* in this chapter are perfect for casual get-togethers. Best of all, the delicious dishes are easy, so your soiree can be a memorable yet seamless event!

p. 138

p. 155

p. 161

p. 153

p. 168

lettuce wraps p. 173

# party chicken and pasta salad

PREP TIME: 40 Minutes ✳ READY IN: 40 Minutes ✳ SERVINGS: 12

### SALAD

- 5 cups uncooked rotini pasta (16 oz.)
- 4 cups cubed cooked chicken
- 1 cup thinly sliced celery
- 1/2 cup chopped green onions
- 12 oz. fresh snow pea pods, trimmed, halved crosswise
- 2 cups seedless red and/or green grapes, halved
- 1 can (8 oz.) pineapple tidbits in unsweetened juice, drained, reserving liquid
- 1 cup slivered almonds, toasted if desired
- 6 to 8 leaves leaf lettuce

### DRESSING

- 1 cup mayonnaise or salad dressing
- 2 tablespoons finely chopped fresh gingerroot
- 1 teaspoon garlic salt
- 2 tablespoons reserved pineapple liquid
- 2 tablespoons soy sauce
- 2 tablespoons honey

1 Cook pasta as directed on package. Drain; rinse with cold water to cool. Drain well.

2 Meanwhile, in large bowl, mix remaining salad ingredients except almonds and lettuce. In small bowl, mix dressing ingredients.

3 Add pasta and 1/2 cup of the almonds to salad; stir gently to mix. Add dressing; toss to coat. Line serving bowl or platter with lettuce. Spoon salad over lettuce. Sprinkle with remaining almonds.

NUTRITION INFORMATION PER SERVING: Calories 520 • Total Fat 23g • Saturated Fat 3.5g • Cholesterol 45mg • Sodium 580mg • Total Carbohydrate 54g • Dietary Fiber 5g • Protein 23g. DIETARY EXCHANGES: 2-1/2 Starch • 1 Other Carbohydrate • 2 Lean Meat • 3 Fat • 3-1/2 Carb Choices.

# chicken saté with spicy peanut sauce

PREP TIME: 30 Minutes ✳ READY IN: 50 Minutes ✳ SERVINGS: 24

24 (6-inch) bamboo or wooden skewers

**SAUCE**

1/2 cup chicken broth

1/3 cup reduced-fat creamy peanut butter

2 tablespoons purchased teriyaki marinade and sauce

1 tablespoon fresh lime juice

1 teaspoon grated gingerroot

1/4 teaspoon ground red pepper (cayenne)

**SATÉ**

1-1/4 lb. boneless skinless chicken breast halves

2 medium green bell peppers, cut into 1-inch squares

2 medium red bell peppers, cut into 1-inch squares

1 Soak bamboo skewers in water for 30 minutes. Line 15 x 10 x 1-inch baking pan with foil.

2 Meanwhile, heat oven to 425°F. In small saucepan, combine all sauce ingredients; mix well. Cook about 5 minutes or until blended, stirring frequently.

3 Cut the chicken diagonally into strips, about 3 inches long and 3/4 inch wide. On each bamboo skewer, thread 1 green pepper square, 1 red pepper square and 1 or 2 strips of chicken. Brush chicken mixture with 1/4 cup sauce. Place in foil-lined pan.

4 Bake 15 to 20 minutes or until the chicken is no longer pink in center. Meanwhile, bring the remaining sauce to a boil over medium heat, stirring constantly. Boil 1 minute. Serve chicken saté with warm sauce.

NUTRITION INFORMATION PER SERVING: Calories 55 • Total Fat 2g • Saturated Fat 0g • Cholesterol 15mg • Sodium 110mg • Total Carbohydrate 3g • Dietary Fiber 0g • Protein 6g. DIETARY EXCHANGES: 1 Very Lean Meat • 1/2 Fat.

*cook's notes*

*The sauce can be microwaved on High for 1 to 1-1/2 minutes or until blended and heated through.*

# pita triangles with olive relish

PREP TIME: 30 Minutes ✳ READY IN: 1 Hour 30 Minutes ✳ SERVINGS: 24

### RELISH

- 2 cups mixed olives, pitted, finely chopped
- 1/4 cup chopped green onions
- 2 tablespoons olive oil
- 1 teaspoon lemon juice
- 1/4 teaspoon freshly ground black pepper
- 2 garlic cloves, minced

### PITA TRIANGLES

- 2 (6 to 8-inch) pita (pocket) breads
- 2 tablespoons olive oil

1 In medium bowl, combine all relish ingredients; mix well. Let stand at room temperature for about 1 hour or refrigerate up to 4 hours to blend flavors.

2 Heat oven to 350°F. Line 2 cookie sheets with foil. Cut each pita bread into 6 wedges. Split each wedge to make a total of 24 wedges; place on foil-lined cookie sheets. Brush the wedges with the 2 tablespoons oil.

3 Bake at 350°F. for 5 to 8 minutes or until crisp. Cool 10 minutes. Serve the pita triangles with the olive relish.

NUTRITION INFORMATION PER SERVING: Calories 50 • Total Fat 4g • Saturated Fat 1g • Cholesterol 0mg • Sodium 230mg • Total Carbohydrate 3g • Dietary Fiber 0g • Protein 1g. DIETARY EXCHANGES: 1 Fat.

# pizza in a crescent

PREP TIME: 10 Minutes ✳ READY IN: 30 Minutes ✳ SERVINGS: 4

1 can (8 oz.) Pillsbury® refrigerated crescent dinner rolls

1 package (3.5 oz.) pepperoni slices

4 tablespoons pizza or tomato pasta sauce

1 package (6 oz.) mozzarella cheese slices

1 Heat oven to 375°F. Unroll dough and separate into 4 rectangles; press each into 7 x 5-inch rectangle, firmly pressing perforations to seal.

2 Arrange 9 pepperoni slices crosswise in center 1/3 of each rectangle. Spread 1 tablespoon pizza sauce over pepperoni. Fold each slice of cheese in half; place over pepperoni.

3 Fold short sides of each rectangle over cheese to almost meet in center; firmly pinch edges to seal, leaving middle open. Tuck 4 or 5 pepperoni slices into each middle opening; place on ungreased cookie sheet.

4 Bake 13 to 16 minutes or until golden brown. Immediately remove pizzas from the cookie sheet. Serve warm.

NUTRITION INFORMATION PER SERVING: Calories 450 • Total Fat 27g • Saturated Fat 11g • Cholesterol 45mg • Sodium 1480mg • Total Carbohydrate 30g • Dietary Fiber 1g • Protein 21g. DIETARY EXCHANGES: 2 Starch • 2 Medium-Fat Meat • 3 Fat • 2 Carb Choices.

# polenta rounds with caramelized vegetables

PREP TIME: 25 Minutes ✳ READY IN: 40 Minutes ✳ SERVINGS: 32

2 packages (16 oz.) polenta, cut into 32 round slices

2 tablespoons purchased Italian salad dressing

2 teaspoons butter

1/3 cup chopped onion

1/3 cup diced green bell pepper

1/3 cup diced red bell pepper

1 tablespoon brown sugar

2 teaspoons finely chopped fresh oregano

1/4 teaspoon salt

1 cup finely shredded white Cheddar cheese (4 oz.)

1 Heat oven to 400°F. Line cookie sheet with parchment paper. Place polenta rounds on parchment-lined cookie sheet. Brush each with salad dressing. Set aside.

2 Melt butter in small skillet over medium-high heat. Add onion, bell peppers, brown sugar, oregano and salt. Cook about 5 minutes or until vegetables are tender, stirring occasionally. Top each polenta round with rounded 1/2 teaspoon vegetable mixture.

3 Bake at 400°F. for 10 to 15 minutes or until thoroughly heated. Immediately sprinkle each with Cheddar cheese. Remove from cookie sheet. Serve warm.

NUTRITION INFORMATION PER SERVING: Calories 40 • Total Fat 2g • Saturated Fat 1g • Cholesterol 5mg • Sodium 90mg • Total Carbohydrate 4g • Dietary Fiber 0g • Protein 1g. DIETARY EXCHANGES: 1/2 Fat.

# oven-baked chicken nuggets and french fries

PREP TIME: 25 Minutes ✳ READY IN: 50 Minutes ✳ SERVINGS: 4

4 medium unpeeled baking potatoes (about 5 oz. each)
1 cup Italian dressing
1-1/2 cups Progresso® Italian-style bread crumbs

1/2 teaspoon salt
4 boneless skinless chicken breasts (about 1 lb.), cut into 1-1/2-inch chunks
1/2 cup honey mustard or ketchup

1 Heat oven to 425°F. Spray 15 x 10-inch pan with sides with cooking spray. Cut each potato lengthwise into eight 3/4- to 1-inch-wide wedges; place in large resealable food-storage plastic bag. Add 3/4 cup of the Italian dressing to bag; seal and shake to coat potatoes evenly and set aside bag with potatoes.

2 In another large resealable food-storage plastic bag, place 1 cup of the bread crumbs and the salt. Transfer potatoes to bag with bread crumbs; seal and shake to coat evenly. Arrange potatoes in single layer in pan. Reserve both bags with remaining dressing and crumbs.

3 Bake the potatoes, uncovered, 10 minutes. Turn the potatoes over and bake 10 minutes longer.

4 Meanwhile, place the chicken in bag with dressing; add remaining 1/4 cup Italian dressing and shake to coat. Transfer chicken to bag with crumbs; add remaining 1/2 cup bread crumbs and shake to coat evenly.

5 Turn potatoes and move to one end of pan; place chicken on other end of pan. Bake uncovered 14 to 16 minutes longer or until potatoes are fork-tender and chicken is no longer pink in center. Serve with honey mustard.

NUTRITION INFORMATION PER SERVING: Calories 670 • Total Fat 31g • Saturated Fat 3g • Cholesterol 80mg • Sodium 1600mg • Total Carbohydrate 62g • Dietary Fiber 4g • Protein 35g. DIETARY EXCHANGES: 4 Starch • 3-1/2 Lean Meat • 3-1/2 Fat • 4 Carb Choices.

# taco chicken wraps

PREP TIME: 30 Minutes ✳ READY IN: 30 Minutes ✳ SERVINGS: 4

8 large uncooked chicken breast tenders, not breaded (about 3/4 lb.)
2 tablespoons Old El Paso® taco seasoning mix (from 1-oz. pkg.)

1 can (8 oz.) Pillsbury® refrigerated crescent dinner rolls
1 cup Old El Paso® thick 'n chunky salsa

1 Heat oven to 375°F. Coat each chicken tender with the taco seasoning mix.

2 Separate dough into 8 triangles. Place 1 chicken tender on short side of each triangle. Starting with shortest side of triangle, roll dough around each chicken tender; place point side down on ungreased cookie sheet.

3 Bake 16 to 19 minutes or until the wraps are deep golden brown and the chicken is no longer pink in center. Serve with salsa for dipping.

**HIGH ALTITUDE (3500-6500 FT):** Bake 19 to 22 minutes.

NUTRITION INFORMATION PER SERVING: Calories 350 • Total Fat 15g • Saturated Fat 5g • Cholesterol 50mg • Sodium 1370mg • Total Carbohydrate 31g • Dietary Fiber 0g • Protein 23g. DIETARY EXCHANGES: 2 Starch • 2-1/2 Lean Meat • 1 Fat • 2 Carb Choices.

*cook's notes*

*If you end up with a few extra chicken tenders in the package, you can bake them on the cookie sheet right along with the wraps. Eat them with dinner later in the week, or refrigerate them for fast sandwiches.*

# ham and swiss double pinwheels

PREP TIME: 15 Minutes ✳ READY IN: 35 Minutes ✳ SERVINGS: 16

| | |
|---|---|
| 1/4 lb. cooked ham, cut into pieces (about 1/3 cup) | 2 tablespoons grated Parmesan cheese |
| 1 oz. cream cheese (from 3-oz. pkg.), softened | 1/2 cup shredded Swiss cheese (2 oz.) |
| 1 can (8 oz.) Pillsbury® refrigerated crescent dinner rolls | 2 tablespoons sliced green onions (2 medium) |

1 Heat oven to 350°F. Spray cookie sheet with cooking spray. In food processor bowl with metal blade, process ham and cream cheese until smooth and well blended.

2 Unroll the dough into 1 large rectangle; press into a 13 x 8-inch rectangle, firmly pressing the perforations to seal. Spread ham mixture over rectangle. Sprinkle with Parmesan cheese, Swiss cheese and onions.

3 Starting with both short sides of rectangle, roll up both towards center. With serrated knife, cut into 16 slices; place cut side down on cookie sheet.

4 Bake 13 to 17 minutes or until the edges are golden brown. Immediately remove from cookie sheet. Serve warm.

NUTRITION INFORMATION PER SERVING: Calories 80 • Total Fat 5g • Saturated Fat 2g • Cholesterol 10mg • Sodium 310mg • Total Carbohydrate 7g • Dietary Fiber 0g • Protein 4g. DIETARY EXCHANGES: 1/2 Starch • 1/2 High-Fat Meat • 1/2 Carb Choice.

*Kitchen tip*

*For a later meal, heat the remaining pasta sauce that's left in the jar and serve it over your favorite cooked pasta.*

# cheese mini-wiches

PREP TIME: 20 Minutes ✳ READY IN: 20 Minutes ✳ SERVINGS:18

| | |
|---|---|
| 1/2 cup Old El Paso® thick 'n chunky salsa | 1/3 cup butter or margarine, softened |
| 1/2 cup tomato pasta sauce | 1 package (6 oz.) cracker-cut Cheddar cheese (18 small slices) |
| 36 slices cocktail sourdough or rye bread (from 1 lb. pkg.) | |

1 In a small bowl, mix the salsa and pasta sauce; set aside. Set oven control to broil.

2 Lightly spread one side of each bread slice with 1/2 teaspoon butter. On ungreased cookie sheet, place half of the bread slices, buttered side down. Top each with a slice of cheese. Cover with remaining bread slices, buttered side up.

3 Broil 3 to 4 minutes, turning once, until golden brown and cheese is melted. Serve sandwiches with salsa mixture.

NUTRITION INFORMATION PER SERVING: Calories 150 • Total Fat 9g • Saturated Fat 5g • Cholesterol 25mg • Sodium 290mg • Total Carbohydrate 12g • Dietary Fiber 0g • Protein 4g. DIETARY EXCHANGES: 1 Starch • 1-1/2 Fat • 1 Carb Choice.

ham and swiss
double pinwheels

# individual pastrami braids

PREP TIME: 15 Minutes ✳ READY IN: 35 Minutes ✳ SERVINGS: 4

1 can (8 oz.) Pillsbury® refrigerated crescent dinner rolls

4 teaspoons Dijon mustard

4 oz. thinly sliced pastrami, cut into 1/2-inch-wide strips

1 cup shredded Swiss cheese (4 oz.)

1 egg, beaten

1 teaspoon poppy seeds

1 Heat oven to 375°F. Unroll dough and separate into 4 rectangles; place on ungreased cookie sheet. Press each into 6 x 4-inch rectangle, firmly pressing perforations to seal.

2 Spread mustard lengthwise down center of each rectangle in 1-1/2-inch-wide strip. Top each with pastrami and cheese.

3 On long sides of each rectangle, make 7 cuts at an angle and about 3/4 inch apart almost to edge of filling. For braided appearance, fold strips of dough at an angle halfway across filling with ends of strips slightly overlapping, alternating from side to side. Brush tops with egg; sprinkle with poppy seeds.

4 Bake 11 to 16 minutes or until golden brown. Immediately remove braids from cookie sheet. Serve warm.

NUTRITION INFORMATION PER SERVING: Calories 370 • Total Fat 20g • Saturated Fat 8g • Cholesterol 95mg • Sodium 1280mg • Total Carbohydrate 29g • Dietary Fiber 0g • Protein 19g. DIETARY EXCHANGES: 2 Starch • 2 High-Fat Meat • 1/2 Fat • 2 Carb Choices.

# parmesan rounds with lox

PREP TIME: 25 Minutes ✳ READY IN: 25 Minutes ✳ SERVINGS: 16

4 oz. (1 cup) shredded fresh Parmesan or Asiago cheese

1/4 teaspoon coarsely ground black pepper

3 oz. lox (cold-smoked salmon)

2 tablespoons crème fraîche or sour cream

Fresh dill sprigs

1 Heat oven to 400°F. For each round, spoon 2 teaspoons cheese onto ungreased cookie sheet; pat into 2-inch round. Place rounds 2 inches apart. Sprinkle each with pepper.

2 Bake at 400°F. for 6 to 8 minutes or until edges are light golden brown. Do not overbake. Immediately remove from cookie sheet; place on wire racks. Cool 5 minutes or until completely cooled.

3 To serve, top each round with lox, about 1/4 teaspoon crème fraîche and dill sprig. Serve immediately, or cover and refrigerate until serving time.

NUTRITION INFORMATION PER SERVING: Calories 35 • Total Fat 2g • Saturated Fat 1g • Cholesterol 5mg • Sodium 160mg • Total Carbohydrate 0g • Dietary Fiber 0g • Protein 4g. DIETARY EXCHANGES: 1/2 Lean Meat.

## kitchen tip

*Lox is salmon that is brine-cured, then cold-smoked. Crème fraîche is mature, French cream that is convenient and versatile. Crème fraîche tastes simply wonderful spooned over fruit or warm chocolate cake.*

# italian square meatballs

PREP TIME: 10 Minutes ✳ READY IN: 35 Minutes ✳ SERVINGS: 36

1 egg
1/2 cup finely chopped onion (1 medium)
1/4 cup Progresso® Italian style bread crumbs
1/4 cup ketchup

1/4 teaspoon pepper
1 lb. lean (at least 80%) ground beef
1/2 lb. bulk Italian pork sausage

1 Heat oven to 425°F. Line 15 x 10 x 1-inch pan with foil; spray foil with cooking spray. In large bowl, beat egg. Stir in remaining ingredients.

2 In the foil-lined pan, shape the beef mixture into an 8-inch square. Cut into 36 squares; do not separate the squares.

3 Bake 20 to 25 minutes or until meatballs are thoroughly cooked and no longer pink in center. With sharp knife, cut apart meatballs.

NUTRITION INFORMATION PER SERVING: Calories 350 • Total Fat 22g • Saturated Fat 8g • Cholesterol 145mg • Sodium 550mg • Total Carbohydrate 11g • Dietary Fiber 0g • Protein 28g. DIETARY EXCHANGES: 1/2 Starch • 3-1/2 Medium-Fat Meat • 1 Fat • 1 Carb Choice.

# bourbon cocktail meatballs

PREP TIME: 45 Minutes ✳ READY IN: 45 Minutes ✳ SERVINGS: 24

**MEATBALLS**
1-1/2 lb. meat loaf mixture or lean ground beef
1/2 cup Progresso® plain bread crumbs
1/4 cup finely chopped onion
1 teaspoon salt
1 teaspoon dry mustard
2 tablespoons chili sauce
1 egg

**SAUCE**
1 jar (12 oz.) pineapple preserves
1/3 cup chili sauce
1/4 cup bourbon
1/4 teaspoon hot pepper sauce

1 Heat oven to 400°F. In large bowl, combine all meatball ingredients; mix well. Shape mixture into 1-1/4-inch meatballs. Place in ungreased 15 x 10 x 1-inch baking pan. Bake at 400°F. for 15 to 20 minutes or until thoroughly cooked.

2 Meanwhile, in large saucepan, combine all sauce ingredients; mix well. Cook over low heat until mixture is bubbly, stirring frequently. Add cooked meatballs to sauce; stir gently to coat.

NUTRITION INFORMATION PER SERVING: Calories 100 • Total Fat 3g • Saturated Fat 1g • Cholesterol 20mg • Sodium 190mg • Total Carbohydrate 13g • Dietary Fiber 0g • Protein 4g. DIETARY EXCHANGES: 1 Fruit • 1 Other Carbohydrate • 1/2 Medium-Fat Meat.

# easy buffalo chicken stromboli

PREP TIME: 25 Minutes ✷ READY IN: 1 Hour 5 Minutes ✷ SERVINGS: 6

- 2 cans (8 oz. each) Pillsbury® refrigerated crescent dinner rolls
- 1 package (9 oz.) frozen cooked chicken strips (about 2 cups), thawed, cut into 1/2-inch pieces
- 1/4 cup buffalo wing sauce
- 3/4 cup shredded mozzarella cheese (3 oz.)
- 1/4 cup crumbled blue cheese (1 oz.)
- 1 medium green or red bell pepper, cut into thin bite-size strips (or use strips of both colors)
- 1/4 cup finely chopped red onion

  Blue cheese dressing, if desired

1 Heat oven to 350°F. Spray large cookie sheet with cooking spray. Unroll both cans of dough into 2 large rectangles on cookie sheet. Place rectangles with long sides together, forming 15 x 10-inch rectangle; press edges and perforations to seal.

2 In medium bowl, mix chicken and buffalo wing sauce. Spoon chicken mixture lengthwise in 4-inch-wide strip down center of dough to within 1 inch of short sides. Top with mozzarella and blue cheeses, bell pepper and onion.

3 Bring long sides of dough up over filling, overlapping 1 inch; firmly press center seam and with fork, press ends to seal.

4 Bake 30 to 40 minutes or until deep golden brown. Immediately remove from cookie sheet. Cut crosswise into slices; serve warm with salad dressing.

**HIGH ALTITUDE (3500-6500 FT):** Bake at 350°F. for 33 to 38 minutes.

NUTRITION INFORMATION PER SERVING: Calories 410 • Total Fat 17g • Saturated Fat 6g • Cholesterol 45mg • Sodium 1330mg • Total Carbohydrate 42g • Dietary Fiber 2g • Protein 23g. DIETARY EXCHANGES: 2 Starch • 1 Other Carbohydrate • 2-1/2 Lean Meat • 1-1/2 Fat • 3 Carb Choices.

# chicken cordon bleu sandwich ring

**PREP TIME:** 25 Minutes ✳ **READY IN:** 1 Hour 10 Minutes ✳ **SERVINGS:** 8

2 cans (11 oz. each) Pillsbury® refrigerated crusty French loaf

1 egg white

1 teaspoon water

2 teaspoons Progresso® Italian-style bread crumbs

1/2 lb. thinly sliced cooked chicken (from deli)

1/2 lb. thinly sliced cooked ham (from deli)

2 medium plum (Roma) tomatoes, thinly sliced

6 square slices (3/4 oz. each) process Swiss cheese, cut in half diagonally

6 leaves leaf lettuce

2 tablespoons mayonnaise

1 Heat oven to 350°F. Spray large cookie sheet with cooking spray or grease with shortening. Remove dough from both cans; do not unroll. Place dough, seam side down, on cookie sheet. Join ends of loaf to form ring; pinch ends together firmly to seal.

2 With sharp or serrated knife, cut 12 (1/2-inch-deep) diagonal slashes on top of dough. In small bowl, beat egg white and water with fork; brush over dough. Sprinkle with bread crumbs.

3 Bake 26 to 30 minutes or until deep golden brown. Cool on cookie sheet 15 minutes.

4 Set oven control to broil. Cut bread ring in half horizontally; carefully remove top half and set aside. With bottom half on cookie sheet, top with chicken, ham, tomatoes and Swiss cheese.

5 Broil 4 to 6 inches from heat 1 to 2 minutes or until cheese is melted. Top with lettuce. Spread mayonnaise on cut side of top half of bread ring; place over the lettuce. Cut sandwich ring into sections to serve.

NUTRITION INFORMATION PER SERVING: Calories 360 • Total Fat 13g • Saturated Fat 4.5g • Cholesterol 50mg • Sodium 1070mg • Total Carbohydrate 36g • Dietary Fiber 1g • Protein 25g. DIETARY EXCHANGES: 2-1/2 Starch • 2-1/2 Lean Meat • 1 Fat • 2-1/2 Carb Choices.

# fresh tomato-basil caprese kabobs

PREP TIME: 30 Minutes ✳ READY IN: 1 Hour ✳ SERVINGS: 34

1/4 cup extra-virgin olive oil

2 tablespoons lemon juice

2/3 cup coarsely chopped fresh basil or lemon basil leaves

1/4 teaspoon salt

1/4 teaspoon freshly ground black pepper

1 pint (2 cups) red cherry tomatoes

1 pint (2 cups) yellow cherry tomatoes

2 medium zucchini or yellow squash, cut into cubes

1 lb. fresh mozzarella cheese, cut into cubes

34 bamboo skewers (6 inch)

Additional fresh basil leaves, if desired

1 In large bowl, mix oil, lemon juice, chopped basil, salt and pepper with wire whisk. Gently stir in tomatoes, zucchini and cheese. Cover; refrigerate about 30 minutes.

2 Drain vegetables, reserving oil mixture. On skewers, alternately thread tomatoes, zucchini and cheese; top with basil leaf. Serve kabobs with reserved oil mixture.

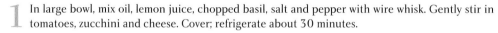

NUTRITION INFORMATION PER SERVING: Calories 60 • Total Fat 4.5g • Saturated Fat 2g • Cholesterol 5mg • Sodium 90mg • Total Carbohydrate 2g • Dietary Fiber 0g • Protein 4g. DIETARY EXCHANGES: 1/2 Medium-Fat Meat • 1/2 Fat.

*special touch*

*Thread the vegetables and the cheese between large leaves of fresh basil for a different look.*

# flaky ham and turkey sandwich slices

PREP TIME: 15 Minutes ✳ READY IN: 40 Minutes ✳ SERVINGS: 8

1 box Pillsbury® refrigerated pie crusts, softened as directed on box

2 teaspoons yellow mustard

1/2 lb. sliced cooked turkey

1 cup shredded Cheddar cheese (4 oz.)

2 small plum (Roma) tomatoes, thinly sliced

1/2 lb. sliced cooked ham

1 Heat oven to 425°F. Remove pie crusts from pouches; place crusts flat on work surface. Brush each crust with 1 teaspoon mustard to within 1/2 inch of edge.

2 Layer turkey, cheese, tomato slices and ham in 4-1/2-inch-wide strip down center of each crust to within 1 inch of top and bottom of edges. Fold top and bottom edges up onto filling. Bring both sides up over filling, meeting in center; press crust edges together forming 1/2-inch-high seam to seal (flute edge if desired). Place on ungreased cookie sheet. Cut 3 or 4 slits in top crust of each to allow steam to escape.

3 Bake 20 to 25 minutes or until golden brown. Cool 5 minutes. Cut each sandwich roll into 8 slices and serve warm.

**HIGH ALTITUDE (3500-6500 FT):** Bake 17 to 22 minutes.

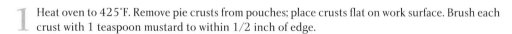

NUTRITION INFORMATION PER SERVING: Calories 400 • Total Fat 23g • Saturated Fat 9g • Cholesterol 65mg • Sodium 770mg • Total Carbohydrate 27g • Dietary Fiber 0g • Protein 20g. DIETARY EXCHANGES: 2 Starch • 2 Lean Meat • 3 Fat • 2 Carb Choices.

# cheese-stuffed pizza

PREP TIME: 15 Minutes ✳ READY IN: 45 Minutes ✳ SERVINGS: 8

| | |
|---|---|
| 1 can (13.8 oz.) Pillsbury® refrigerated classic pizza crust | 1/2 cup pizza sauce |
| 7 sticks (1 oz. each) string cheese | 24 slices pepperoni (from 3.5-oz. pkg.) |
| | 2 cups shredded Italian cheese blend (8 oz.) |

1 Heat oven to 425°F. Spray 12-inch pizza pan with cooking spray. Unroll dough; place in sprayed pan. Starting at center, press out dough to edge of pan, pressing up and extending over edge by at least 1 inch. Place string cheese around inside edge of crust. Fold extended edge of dough over cheese; pinch firmly to seal.

2 Bake 8 to 10 minutes or until crust is set and edges are light golden brown.

3 Remove partially baked crust from oven. Spoon sauce evenly over crust. Top with pepperoni and Italian cheese blend.

4 Bake 12 to 16 minutes longer or until the crust is a deep golden brown and the cheese in the center is melted.

NUTRITION INFORMATION PER SERVING: Calories 370 • Total Fat 20g • Saturated Fat 11g • Cholesterol 60mg • Sodium 1050mg • Total Carbohydrate 27g • Dietary Fiber 0g • Protein 20g. DIETARY EXCHANGES: 2 Starch • 2 High-Fat Meat • 2 Carb Choices.

## *cook's notes*

*Boost the nutrition of this pizza by adding cut mushrooms, bell pepper, tomatoes, broccoli, onion and/or zucchini along with the pepperoni. The pizza might require a longer bake time.*

# pizzazzy sausage crescent sandwiches

PREP TIME: 25 Minutes ✳ READY IN: 45 Minutes ✳ SERVINGS: 8

| | |
|---|---|
| 1 lb. bulk Italian or pork sausage | 1 can (15 oz.) pizza sauce |
| 1/2 cup chopped green bell pepper (1/2 medium) | 2 cans (8 oz. each) Pillsbury® refrigerated crescent dinner rolls |
| 1/3 cup chopped onion | 4 slices (3/4 oz. each) mozzarella cheese, cut in half crosswise, folded |

1 Heat oven to 375°F. In 10-inch skillet, cook sausage, bell pepper and onion over medium-high heat, stirring frequently, until sausage is no longer pink and vegetables are tender; drain. Stir in 3 tablespoons of the pizza sauce.

2 Unroll both cans of the dough and separate into 8 rectangles; firmly press perforations to seal.

3 Place about 1/4 cup sausage mixture and folded 1/2 slice of cheese on one end of each rectangle. Fold dough in half over filling; press edges with fork to seal. Place on ungreased cookie sheet.

4 Bake 15 to 18 minutes or until golden brown. Meanwhile, heat remaining pizza sauce. Immediately remove sandwiches from cookie sheet. Serve warm with warm pizza sauce.

NUTRITION INFORMATION PER SERVING: Calories 400 • Total Fat 23g • Saturated Fat 7g • Cholesterol 40mg • Sodium 1350mg • Total Carbohydrate 33g • Dietary Fiber 2g • Protein 16g. DIETARY EXCHANGES: 2 Starch • 1-1/2 High-Fat Meat • 2 Fat • 2 Carb Choices.

# mini beef and provolone crescents

PREP TIME: 20 Minutes ✳ READY IN: 40 Minutes ✳ SERVINGS: 16

1 can (8 oz.) Pillsbury® refrigerated crescent dinner rolls

1 tablespoon Italian dressing

2 slices (1/2 to 1 oz. each) provolone cheese, each cut into 8 strips

2 tablespoons chopped roasted red bell peppers (from a jar)

3 oz. thinly sliced cooked roast beef (from deli), cut into 16 pieces

1 Heat oven to 350°F. Spray cookie sheet with cooking spray. Unroll dough and separate into 8 triangles; press out each triangle so shortest side measures 4 inches. Cut each triangle in half lengthwise from tip end to short side to make 16 triangles.

2 Brush each triangle with salad dressing. Top each with 1 cheese strip, scant 1/2 teaspoon roasted peppers and 1 slice of beef, folding to fit on triangle. Roll up each, starting at shortest side of triangle and rolling to opposite point; place point side down on cookie sheet.

3 Bake crescents 13 to 18 minutes or until golden brown. Immediately remove from cookie sheet. Serve warm.

NUTRITION INFORMATION PER SERVING: Calories 70 • Total Fat 3g • Saturated Fat 1g • Cholesterol 5mg • Sodium 250mg • Total Carbohydrate 7g • Dietary Fiber 0g • Protein 2g. DIETARY EXCHANGES: 1/2 Starch • 1/2 Fat • 1/2 Carb Choice.

elegant cheese and fruit platter

# elegant cheese and fruit platter

PREP TIME: 15 Minutes ✳ READY IN: 45 Minutes ✳ SERVINGS: 24

- 1 block (8 oz.) white Cheddar cheese
- 1 wedge (8 oz.) blue cheese (such as Stilton or Gorgonzola)
- 1 round (8 oz.) Brie cheese
- 1 large crisp red eating apple, sliced
- 1 medium pear, sliced
- 1 pint (2 cups) strawberries, halved

- 3/4 lb. seedless green grapes, cut into small clusters
- 3/4 lb. seedless red grapes, cut into small clusters
- 1 package (7 oz.) dried apricots
- 1/4 cup dried cherries or sweetened dried cranberries
- Fresh rosemary sprigs, if desired

1 On large serving platter, arrange cheeses in center. Cover; let stand at room temperature about 30 minutes.

2 Arrange fresh fruit in groups around cheeses. Sprinkle dried apricots and cherries over cheeses and fruit. Tuck rosemary sprigs among fruit.

3 To serve, provide cheese planes for harder cheeses and cheese spreaders for soft cheeses. If desired, serve cheeses and fruit with crackers.

NUTRITION INFORMATION PER SERVING: Calories 170 • Total Fat 9g • Saturated Fat 5g • Cholesterol 25mg • Sodium 250mg • Total Carbohydrate 16g • Dietary Fiber 2g • Protein 7g. DIETARY EXCHANGES: 1/2 Fruit • 1/2 Other Carbohydrate • 1 High-Fat Meat • 1 Carb Choice.

cook's notes

*Any of your favorite cheeses or fruits can be substituted for those we've listed here. Use your creativity!*

# chicken caesar sandwich ring

PREP TIME: 15 Minutes ✳ READY IN: 55 Minutes ✳ SERVINGS: 8

- 2 cans (11 oz. each) Pillsbury® refrigerated French loaf
- 1 egg, beaten
- 1 lb. cooked chicken (from deli), cut into 1/8-inch-thick slices

- 4 tablespoons Caesar dressing
- 1/4 cup shredded fresh Parmesan cheese (1 oz.)
- 2 cups torn romaine lettuce (about 6 leaves)
- 1 large tomato, sliced

1 Heat oven to 375°F. Grease large cookie sheet with shortening or cooking spray. Remove dough from both cans. Place dough seam side down and join ends to form large ring; press ends together firmly to seal.

2 Brush dough ring with beaten egg. With kitchen scissors, cut surface of dough every 2 inches to form V's.

3 Bake 20 to 25 minutes or until deep golden brown. Cool 15 minutes.

4 With serrated knife, cut bread ring in half horizontally. Top bottom half of ring with chicken. Drizzle with 2 tablespoons of the dressing. Sprinkle with Parmesan cheese. Top with lettuce, tomato and remaining 2 tablespoons dressing. Cover with top half of ring. Cut into sandwiches.

NUTRITION INFORMATION PER SERVING: Calories 325 • Total Fat 12g • Saturated Fat 3g • Cholesterol 55mg • Sodium 1310mg • Total Carbohydrate 38g • Dietary Fiber 1g • Protein 16g. DIETARY EXCHANGES: 2-1/2 Starch • 1 Lean Meat • 1-1/2 Fat • 2-1/2 Carb Choices.

cook's notes

*Mix things up a bit and try making this change-of-pace sandwich with sliced smoked turkey, ranch dressing and Cheddar cheese.*

## kitchen tip

Ready-made kabobs can be found at meat counters of large supermarkets.

# greek kabob sandwiches

PREP TIME: 35 Minutes ✳ READY IN: 6 Hours 35 Minutes ✳ SERVINGS: 4

| | | | | |
|---|---|---|---|---|
| 1/3 | cup red wine vinegar | | 1 | clove garlic, minced |
| 2 | tablespoons olive oil | | 4 | chicken and vegetable kabobs (5 oz. each) |
| 1/4 | teaspoon dried basil leaves | | 4 | tablespoons cucumber ranch or regular ranch dressing |
| 1/4 | teaspoon dried oregano leaves | | 4 | Greek-style pita flatbreads (6 to 7 inch) |

1  In 1-gallon resealable food-storage plastic bag, mix vinegar, oil, basil, oregano and garlic. Add kabobs; seal bag and turn to coat. Refrigerate at least 6 hours or overnight to marinate, turning bag once or twice.

2  When ready to cook kabobs, heat gas or charcoal grill. When grill is heated, remove kabobs from marinade; discard marinade. Place kabobs on gas grill over medium heat or on charcoal grill over medium coals; cover grill. Cook 12 to 15 minutes, turning once, until the chicken is no longer pink in center.

3  Spread 1 tablespoon dressing on each flatbread. Slide chicken and vegetables from kabobs off skewers and onto breads (if needed, cut chicken and vegetables into smaller pieces). Secure with toothpick, if needed.

NUTRITION INFORMATION PER SERVING: Calories 420 • Total Fat 18g • Saturated Fat 3g • Cholesterol 55mg • Sodium 490mg • Total Carbohydrate 40g • Dietary Fiber 3g • Protein 26g. DIETARY EXCHANGES: 2 Starch • 1/2 Other Carbohydrate • 1 Vegetable • 2-1/2 Very Lean Meat • 3 Fat • 2-1/2 Carb Choices.

## kitchen tip

Originally developed in India, Worcestershire sauce was first bottled in Worcester, England. It includes garlic, soy sauce, onions, molasses, vinegar, anchovies and even a bit of lime.

# sloppy joe biscuit rounds

PREP TIME: 30 Minutes ✳ READY IN: 50 Minutes ✳ SERVINGS: 8

| | | | | |
|---|---|---|---|---|
| 3/4 | lb. lean (at least 80%) ground beef | | 1/8 | teaspoon pepper |
| 1/4 | cup chopped onion | | 1 | can (16.3 oz.) Pillsbury® Grands!® homestyle refrigerated buttermilk biscuits |
| 1/4 | cup chopped green bell pepper | | 1 | egg yolk |
| 1/3 | cup ketchup | | 1/4 | teaspoon water |
| 1 | tablespoon yellow mustard | | 1/2 | cup shredded Monterey Jack or Cheddar cheese (2 oz.) |
| 1 | teaspoon Worcestershire sauce | | | |
| 1/4 | teaspoon salt | | | |

1  Heat oven to 375°F. Spray large cookie sheet with cooking spray. In 10-inch skillet, cook beef, onion and bell pepper over medium-high heat until beef is thoroughly cooked; drain. Stir in ketchup, mustard, Worcestershire sauce, salt and pepper.

2  Separate dough into 8 biscuits. Place 2-1/2 inches apart on cookie sheet. With bottom of flat 2-inch diameter glass or fingers, press out each biscuit to 3-1/2-inch round with 1/4-inch rim around outside edge. In small bowl, beat egg yolk and water with fork. Brush over tops and sides of biscuits.

3  Spoon about 1/3 cup beef mixture into indentation in each biscuit. Sprinkle each biscuit with 1 tablespoon shredded cheese.

4  Bake 12 to 17 minutes or until biscuits are golden brown and cheese is melted.

NUTRITION INFORMATION PER SERVING: Calories 310 • Total Fat 16g • Saturated Fat 6g • Cholesterol 60mg • Sodium 870mg • Total Carbohydrate 28g • Dietary Fiber 0g • Protein 14g. DIETARY EXCHANGES: 1-1/2 Starch • 1/2 Other Carbohydrate • 1-1/2 High-Fat Meat • 1/2 Fat • 2 Carb Choices.

# grilled stuffed pizza burgers

PREP TIME: 35 Minutes ✳ READY IN: 35 Minutes ✳ SERVINGS: 6

2 lb. lean (at least 80%) ground beef
1/2 teaspoon salt
1/4 cup chopped pepperoni (about 1 oz.)
2 tablespoons sliced ripe olives

1/2 cup pizza sauce
6 slices (3/4 oz. each) mozzarella cheese, cut in half diagonally
6 burger buns, split, toasted
6 leaves lettuce

1 Heat gas or charcoal grill. In large bowl, mix ground beef and salt. Shape mixture into 12 thin patties, each about 4 inches in diameter.

2 In small bowl, mix pepperoni, olives and 1/3 cup of the pizza sauce. Spoon rounded tablespoon pepperoni mixture onto center of 6 patties; spread slightly. Top with remaining patties; press edges together firmly to seal.

3 Place the patties on the grill. Cover grill; cook over medium heat 8 to 12 minutes, turning once, until thermometer inserted in center of patties reads 160°F (avoid inserting in filling). During last 1 to 2 minutes of cooking time, top each patty with cheese and rounded teaspoon of remaining pizza sauce, and place buns, cut side down, on grill. Cook until the cheese is melted and the buns are lightly toasted.

4 To serve, place lettuce and patties in bottom halves of buns. Cover with top halves of buns.

*cook's notes*

*To broil the patties, place them on a broiler pan; broil 4 to 6 inches from the heat using times in recipe as a guide, turning once. Top patties with cheese and pizza sauce, and place buns, cut side up, on broiler pan; broil 1 to 2 minutes.*

NUTRITION INFORMATION PER SERVING: Calories 470 • Total Fat 25g • Saturated Fat 10g • Cholesterol 110mg • Sodium 780mg • Total Carbohydrate 24g • Dietary Fiber 1g • Protein 37g. DIETARY EXCHANGES: 1-1/2 Starch • 4-1/2 Medium-Fat Meat • 1/2 Fat • 1-1/2 Carb Choices.

## crescent nacho mini cups

PREP TIME: 20 Minutes ✳ READY IN: 45 Minutes ✳ SERVINGS: 24

1   can (8 oz.) Pillsbury® refrigerated crescent dinner rolls

1/2 cup hot bean dip with jalapeño peppers (from 9-oz. can)

1/4 cup Old El Paso® chopped green chiles (from 4.5-oz. can)

1/4 cup finely chopped red bell pepper (1/4 medium)

1/2 cup finely shredded colby-Monterey Jack cheese (2 oz.)

Guacamole, if desired

Sliced ripe olives, if desired

1   Heat oven to 350°F. Unroll dough and separate into 4 rectangles; firmly press perforations to seal. Cut each into 6 squares. Gently press squares into 24 ungreased miniature muffin cups (dough will not completely cover inside of cup; do not press too much).

2   Spoon about 1 teaspoon bean dip into each cup. Top each with 1/2 teaspoon chiles, 1/2 teaspoon bell pepper and about 1 teaspoon cheese.

3   Bake 15 to 20 minutes or until edges are deep golden brown. Cool in pan on wire rack 5 minutes; remove from muffin cups. Garnish each with guacamole and olives.

NUTRITION INFORMATION PER SERVING: Calories 50 • Total Fat 2g • Saturated Fat 1g • Cholesterol 5mg • Sodium 170mg • Total Carbohydrate 5g • Dietary Fiber 0g • Protein 2g. DIETARY EXCHANGES: 1/2 Starch • 1/2 Fat.

# mexican confetti pinwheels

PREP TIME: 15 Minutes ✳ READY IN: 35 Minutes ✳ SERVINGS: 24

1   can (8 oz.) Pillsbury® refrigerated crescent
    dinner rolls

1/4   cup nacho cheese dip

1/3   cup finely chopped red bell pepper
      (1/4 medium)

1/3   cup chopped green onions (4 medium)

1   Heat the oven to 350°F. Unroll the crescent dough and separate into 4 rectangles; firmly press
    the perforations to seal.

2   Spread the cheese dip over each rectangle to within 1/4 inch of edges. Sprinkle with the bell
    pepper and green onions.

3   Starting with one short side, roll up each rectangle; press edge to seal. With serrated knife, cut
    each roll into 6 slices; place cut side down on ungreased cookie sheet.

4   Bake 13 to 17 minutes or until the edges are golden brown. Immediately remove from cookie
    sheet. Serve warm.

NUTRITION INFORMATION PER SERVING: Calories 40 • Total Fat 2g • Saturated Fat 1g • Cholesterol 0mg • Sodium 150mg •
Total Carbohydrate 5g • Dietary Fiber 0g • Protein 1g. DIETARY EXCHANGES: 1/2 Fat • 0 Carb Choice.

# mini buffalo chicken pastries

PREP TIME: 25 Minutes ✳ READY IN: 40 Minutes ✳ SERVINGS: 16

*kitchen tip*

Red pepper sauce can be substituted for the buffalo wing sauce.

1 tablespoon olive oil

1 boneless skinless chicken breast (4 oz.), cut in half crosswise

2 tablespoons buffalo wing sauce (from 12-oz. jar)

1 tablespoon chopped celery

1 can (8 oz.) Pillsbury® refrigerated crescent dinner rolls

1 tablespoon finely chopped fresh parsley

1/2 cup blue cheese dressing

1 Heat oven to 375°F. In 10-inch skillet, heat 2 teaspoons of the oil over medium-high heat until hot. Cook and stir chicken in oil 3 to 5 minutes or until chicken is no longer pink in center. Remove from heat; place chicken on cutting board. Using a fork, pull chicken into shreds; return to skillet. Stir in sauce and celery.

2 Meanwhile on cutting board, unroll dough and separate into 8 triangles. From center of 1 longest side to opposite point, cut each triangle in half, making 16 triangles. Place rounded tablespoonful chicken mixture on center of each triangle. Bring corners to center over filling, overlapping ends; press gently to seal. Place on ungreased cookie sheets. Brush each lightly with a remaining 1 teaspoon oil. Sprinkle with parsley.

3 Bake 10 to 13 minutes or until golden brown. Serve the pastries warm with blue cheese dressing for dipping.

NUTRITION INFORMATION PER SERVING: Calories 100 • Total Fat 8g • Saturated Fat 1.5g • Cholesterol 5mg • Sodium 260mg • Total Carbohydrate 6g • Dietary Fiber 0g • Protein 3g. DIETARY EXCHANGES: 1/2 Starch • 1-1/2 Fat • 1 Carb Choice.

# mini chicken pot pies

**PREP TIME:** 15 Minutes ✳ **READY IN:** 30 Minutes ✳ **SERVINGS:** 4

1-1/2 cups frozen peas and carrots

1 cup cubed (1/2 inch) cooked chicken

1 cup refrigerated diced cooked potatoes with onions (from 20-oz. bag)

1/4 cup milk

1/2 teaspoon dried thyme leaves

1 can (10-3/4 oz.) condensed cream of chicken soup

1 can (4 oz.) Pillsbury® refrigerated crescent dinner rolls

1 egg

1 tablespoon water

1/8 teaspoon dried thyme leaves

1   Heat the oven to 400°F. In a 2-quart saucepan, mix the peas and carrots, chicken, potatoes, milk, 1/2 teaspoon thyme and the soup. Heat to boiling over medium-high heat, stirring occasionally. Divide mixture evenly among 4 ungreased 10-oz custard cups.

2   Unroll the crescent dough. Place 1 crescent over each custard cup.

3   In small bowl, mix egg and water. Brush mixture over crescent dough. Sprinkle 1/8 teaspoon thyme over dough. Bake 11 to 13 minutes or until crusts are golden brown.

_Kitchen tip_

*If you don't have 10-oz custard cups, use foil tart pans (4-1/2 inches in diameter x 1-1/4 inches tall). Simply look for them in the baking aisle of your grocery store.*

NUTRITION INFORMATION PER SERVING: Calories 330 • Total Fat 15g • Saturated Fat 5g • Cholesterol 90mg • Sodium 920mg • Total Carbohydrate 31g • Dietary Fiber 2g • Protein 18g. DIETARY EXCHANGES: 2 Starch • 1-1/2 Lean Meat • 2 Fat • 2 Carb Choices.

# smoked salmon pinwheels

PREP TIME: 15 Minutes ✴ READY IN: 35 Minutes ✴ SERVINGS: 16

1 can (8 oz.) Pillsbury® refrigerated crescent dinner rolls

1 tablespoon Dijon mustard

2 teaspoons honey

2 oz. smoked salmon, finely chopped (1/2 cup)

2 tablespoons finely chopped red onion

2 teaspoons chopped fresh dill

1 Heat oven to 350°F. Unroll dough and separate into 2 long rectangles; press each into 12 x 4-inch rectangle, firmly pressing perforations to seal.

2 In small bowl, mix mustard and honey; spread over each rectangle. Top each with salmon, onion and chopped dill.

3 Starting with one short side, roll up each rectangle; press edge to seal. With serrated knife, cut each roll into 8 slices; place cut side down on ungreased cookie sheet.

4 Bake 13 to 17 minutes or until the edges are golden brown. Immediately remove from the cookie sheet. Serve warm.

NUTRITION INFORMATION PER SERVING: Calories 60 • Total Fat 2g • Saturated Fat 1g • Cholesterol 0mg • Sodium 220mg • Total Carbohydrate 8g • Dietary Fiber 0g • Protein 2g. DIETARY EXCHANGES: 1/2 Starch • 1/2 Fat • 1/2 Carb Choice.

# grilled spicy chicken sandwiches

PREP TIME: 30 Minutes ✳ READY IN: 30 Minutes ✳ SERVINGS: 4

| | |
|---|---|
| 4 boneless skinless chicken breasts | 1/2 cup peach preserves |
| 1/4 teaspoon salt | 1/4 teaspoon crushed red pepper flakes |
| 1/4 teaspoon pepper | 4 crusty French rolls (6 to 8 inch), split |
| 4 slices (1 oz. each) Havarti or Monterey Jack cheese | |

1 Heat gas or charcoal grill. To flatten each chicken breast, place chicken between 2 pieces of plastic wrap or waxed paper. Working from center, gently pound chicken with flat side of meat mallet or rolling pin until about 1/2 inch thick. Sprinkle chicken with salt and pepper.

2 When grill is heated, place chicken on gas grill over medium heat or on charcoal grill over medium coals; cover grill. Cook 6 to 8 minutes, turning once, until chicken is fork-tender and juices run clear. Top each with slice of cheese; cook 1 minute longer or until cheese is melted.

3 In small bowl, mix peach preserves and red pepper flakes. Place chicken on bottom halves of rolls; top each with 2 tablespoons preserves mixture. Cover with top halves of rolls.

**HIGH ALTITUDE (3500-6500 FT):** Cook chicken on gas grill over medium-low heat or on charcoal grill over medium-low coals. Continue as directed above.

NUTRITION INFORMATION PER SERVING: Calories 490 • Total Fat 16g • Saturated Fat 8g • Cholesterol 105mg • Sodium 700mg • Total Carbohydrate 51g • Dietary Fiber 2g • Protein 37g. DIETARY EXCHANGES: 2-1/2 Starch • 1 Other Carbohydrate • 4 Lean Meat • 1/2 Fat • 3-1/2 Carb Choices.

# terrific turkey burgers

PREP TIME: 25 Minutes ✳ READY IN: 25 Minutes ✳ SERVINGS: 8

| | |
|---|---|
| 2 lb. lean (at least 90%) ground turkey | 4 teaspoons soy sauce |
| 1 cup unseasoned dry bread crumbs | 4 teaspoons Worcestershire sauce |
| 2/3 cup finely chopped onion | 1/4 teaspoon pepper |
| 1/2 cup ketchup or tomato sauce | 8 whole wheat burger buns, split |
| 2 tablespoons lemon juice | Lettuce, if desired |

1 Heat gas or charcoal grill. In large bowl, mix all ingredients except buns and lettuce until well blended. Shape mixture into 8 patties, 1/2 inch thick.

2 Lightly oil grill rack. Place patties on grill over medium heat. Cover grill; cook 10 to 12 minutes, turning once, until meat thermometer inserted in center of patties reads 165°F.

3 Meanwhile, place buns cut sides down on grill. Cook 1 to 2 minutes or until lightly toasted. Place patties in lettuce-lined buns. If desired, serve with additional ketchup and pickle slices.

4 To Broil Patties: Place on sprayed broiler pan; broil 4 to 6 inches from heat using times in the recipe as a guide, turning once. Place buns, cut side up, on broiler pan; broil 1 to 2 minutes.

NUTRITION INFORMATION PER SERVING: Calories 340 • Total Fat 9g • Saturated Fat 2g • Cholesterol 75mg • Sodium 720mg • Total Carbohydrate 34g • Dietary Fiber 4g • Protein 32g. DIETARY EXCHANGES: 2 Starch • 3-1/2 Lean Meat • 2 Carb Choices.

*cook's notes*

*Wet your hands before shaping the ground turkey mixture into patties. The moisture on your hands makes it easier to shape the patties, and it also eliminates some of the sticking.*

# thai appetizer pizza

PREP TIME: 30 Minutes ❋ READY IN: 3 Hours ❋ SERVINGS: 32

2 cans (8 oz. each) Pillsbury® refrigerated crescent dinner rolls

1/2 cup chive-and-onion cream cheese spread (from 8-oz. container)

1/4 cup creamy peanut butter

1/2 teaspoon ground ginger

1/4 teaspoon ground red pepper (cayenne)

1/2 cup shredded carrot (about 1 small)

1/2 cup chopped red bell pepper (1/2 medium)

1/2 cup chopped seeded cucumber (1/2 small)

1/4 cup chopped salted peanuts

1/4 cup chopped fresh cilantro

1 Heat oven to 375°F. Unroll both cans of the dough; separate into 4 long rectangles. Place rectangles in ungreased 15 x 10 x 1-inch pan; press in bottom and up sides to form crust.

2 Bake the pizza 13 to 17 minutes or until golden brown. Cool completely, about 30 minutes.

3 In small bowl, mix cream cheese spread, peanut butter, ginger and ground red pepper. Spread over cooled crust. Top with carrot, bell pepper, cucumber and peanuts. Serve immediately, or cover and refrigerate up to 2 hours before serving.

4 Just before serving, sprinkle with chopped cilantro. Cut into squares.

NUTRITION INFORMATION PER SERVING: Calories 80 • Total Fat 5g • Saturated Fat 2g • Cholesterol 5mg • Sodium 200mg • Total Carbohydrate 8g • Dietary Fiber 0g • Protein 2g. DIETARY EXCHANGES: 1/2 Starch • 1 Fat • 1/2 Carb Choice.

# festive shrimp pinwheels

PREP TIME: 15 Minutes ❋ READY IN: 35 Minutes ❋ SERVINGS: 16

1 can (8 oz.) Pillsbury® refrigerated crescent dinner rolls

1/3 cup garlic-and-herb spreadable cheese (from 5.2- to 6.5-oz. container)

1/2 cup coarsely chopped cooked shrimp

2 tablespoons chopped green onions (2 medium)

1 Heat oven to 350°F. Spray cookie sheet with cooking spray. Unroll dough and separate into 2 long rectangles; press each into 12 x 4-inch rectangle, firmly pressing perforations to seal.

2 Spread the cheese over each rectangle. Sprinkle each with shrimp and onions; press in lightly.

3 Starting with one short side, roll up each rectangle; press edge to seal. With serrated knife, cut each roll into 8 slices; place cut side down on cookie sheet.

4 Bake 15 to 20 minutes or until the edges are golden brown. Immediately remove from cookie sheet. Serve warm.

NUTRITION INFORMATION PER SERVING: Calories 70 • Total Fat 3g • Saturated Fat 1g • Cholesterol 15mg • Sodium 190mg • Total Carbohydrate 7g • Dietary Fiber 0g • Protein 2g. DIETARY EXCHANGES: 1/2 Starch • 1/2 Fat • 1/2 Carb Choice.

thai appetizer pizza

# crescent-wrapped brie

PREP TIME: 10 Minutes ✳ READY IN: 50 Minutes ✳ SERVINGS: 12

| | |
|---|---|
| 1 can (8 oz.) Pillsbury® refrigerated crescent dinner rolls | 1 egg, beaten |
| 1 round (8 oz.) natural Brie cheese | 48 water crackers or baguette French bread slices |

1 Heat oven to 350°F. Unroll the dough and separate crosswise into 2 sections; press the dough into 2 squares, firmly pressing perforations to seal. Place cheese round on center of 1 dough square.

2 With small cookie or canapé cutter, cut 1 shape from each corner of remaining dough square; set cutouts aside. Place dough square on top of cheese round. Press dough evenly around cheese, folding bottom edges over top edges; press to seal completely. Place on ungreased cookie sheet.

3 Brush the dough with egg. Arrange dough cutouts on top, then brush with the beaten egg.

4 Bake 20 to 24 minutes or until golden brown. Remove from cookie sheet; place on serving plate. Cool 15 minutes. Serve warm with crackers.

NUTRITION INFORMATION PER SERVING: Calories 190 • Total Fat 9g • Saturated Fat 4g • Cholesterol 35mg • Sodium 440mg • Total Carbohydrate 19g • Dietary Fiber 0g • Protein 8g. DIETARY EXCHANGES: 1 Starch • 1/2 High-Fat Meat • 1 Fat • 1 Carb Choice.

# bacon-cheddar pinwheels

PREP TIME: 15 Minutes ✳ READY IN: 35 Minutes ✳ SERVINGS: 16

1 can (8 oz.) Pillsbury® refrigerated crescent dinner rolls

2 tablespoons ranch dressing

1/4 cup real bacon pieces or 4 slices bacon, crisply cooked, crumbled

1/2 cup finely shredded Cheddar cheese (2 oz.)

1/4 cup chopped green onions (4 medium)

1 Heat oven to 350°F. Unroll dough and separate into 2 long rectangles; press each into 12 x 4-inch rectangle, firmly pressing perforations to seal.

2 Spread the dressing over each rectangle to edges. Sprinkle each with bacon, Cheddar cheese and the green onions.

3 Starting with one short side, roll up each rectangle; press edge to seal. With serrated knife, cut each roll into 8 slices; place cut side down on ungreased cookie sheet.

4 Bake 12 to 17 minutes or until the edges are golden brown. Immediately remove from cookie sheet. Serve warm.

NUTRITION INFORMATION PER SERVING: Calories 80 • Total Fat 5g • Saturated Fat 2g • Cholesterol 5mg • Sodium 230mg • Total Carbohydrate 7g • Dietary Fiber 0g • Protein 2g. DIETARY EXCHANGES: 1/2 Starch • 1 Fat • 1/2 Carb Choice.

# bagel nachos

PREP TIME: 5 Minutes ✳ READY IN: 5 Minutes ✳ SERVINGS: 2

2 oz. bagel chips (from 6-oz. pkg.)

2 oz. (1/2 cup) shredded Mexican taco cheese blend

2 tablespoons Old El Paso® thick 'n chunky salsa

2 tablespoons sour cream

1 Place bagel chips in single layer on microwave-safe plate. (Broken pieces work fine.) Sprinkle evenly with cheese.

2 Microwave on High for 30 to 45 seconds or until the cheese is melted and bubbly. Top nachos with salsa and sour cream.

NUTRITION INFORMATION PER SERVING: Calories 250 • Total Fat 15g • Saturated Fat 8g • Cholesterol 40mg • Sodium 400mg • Total Carbohydrate 23g • Dietary Fiber 1g • Protein 9g. DIETARY EXCHANGES: 1-1/2 Starch • 1-1/2 Other Carbohydrate • 1/2 High-Fat Meat • 2 Fat.

# cheesy chicken and artichoke bites

**PREP TIME:** 30 Minutes ✳ **READY IN:** 50 Minutes ✳ **SERVINGS:** 48

2 cans (8 oz. each) Pillsbury® refrigerated crescent dinner rolls (8 rolls each)

6 slices fully cooked bacon (from 2.1-oz. pkg.)

1 package (6 oz.) refrigerated cooked chicken breast strips, cubed

1 box (9 oz.) Green Giant® frozen spinach, thawed, squeezed to drain and thoroughly chopped

1 can (13.75 oz.) quartered artichoke hearts, drained, coarsely chopped

2 medium cloves garlic, finely chopped

1/2 cup mayonnaise or salad dressing

1/4 cup sour cream

1/2 cup shredded Asiago cheese (2 oz.)

1/4 cup grated Parmesan cheese

1 Heat oven to 375°F. Separate dough from both cans into 8 rectangles; press perforations to seal. Cut each rectangle into 6 (2-inch) squares. Press 1 square in bottom and up side of each of 48 ungreased mini muffin cups.

2 Heat bacon as directed on package; crumble. In large bowl, mix bacon and remaining ingredients. Place 1 tablespoon chicken filling in each cup.

3 Bake 12 to 20 minutes or until edges are golden brown. Immediately remove from pans to serving platter. Serve warm.

NUTRITION INFORMATION PER SERVING: Calories 80 • Total Fat 5g • Saturated Fat 1.5g • Cholesterol 10mg • Sodium 160mg • Total Carbohydrate 5g • Dietary Fiber 0g • Protein 3g. DIETARY EXCHANGES: 1/2 Starch • 1 Fat • 1/2 Carb Choice.

# basil and havarti cheese pinwheels

PREP TIME: 20 Minutes * READY IN: 40 Minutes * SERVINGS: 16

1 can (8 oz.) Pillsbury® refrigerated crescent dinner rolls

2 tablespoons drained finely chopped marinated sun-dried tomatoes (from 8-oz. jar)

1 package (2/3 oz.) fresh basil leaves (30 to 35 leaves)

1/2 cup shredded Havarti cheese (2 oz.)

1 Heat oven to 350°F. Spray cookie sheet with cooking spray. Unroll dough and separate into 2 long rectangles; press each into 12 x 4-inch rectangle, firmly pressing perforations to seal.

2 Sprinkle the sun-dried tomatoes over each rectangle, spreading evenly. Sprinkle each with basil and cheese.

3 Starting with one short side, roll up each rectangle; press edge to seal. With serrated knife, cut each roll into 8 slices; place cut side down on cookie sheet.

4 Bake 15 to 20 minutes or until the edges are golden brown. Immediately remove from cookie sheet. Serve warm.

**HIGH ALTITUDE (3500-6500 FT):** Bake at 350°F. 13 to 18 minutes.

NUTRITION INFORMATION PER SERVING: Calories 70 • Total Fat 4g • Saturated Fat 1g • Cholesterol 5mg • Sodium 200mg • Total Carbohydrate 7g • Dietary Fiber 0g • Protein 2g. DIETARY EXCHANGES: 1/2 Starch • 1/2 Fat • 1/2 Carb Choice.

## cook's notes

*Havarti is a popular and versatile Danish cheese that is often used for sandwiches and omelets. Its mild flavor and soft texture add creamy contrast to the sun-dried tomatoes and basil in this recipe.*

## kitchen tip

*For easy cleanup, roast the*

*potatoes on parchment paper*

*cut to fit the cookie sheet.*

# california beef crostini

PREP TIME: 20 Minutes ✳ READY IN: 1 Hour ✳ SERVINGS: 30

| | |
|---|---|
| 10 small (about 2-inch) Yukon gold or red potatoes | 1/4 teaspoon minced garlic<br>Dash white pepper |
| 1 tablespoon olive oil | 1/4 lb. shaved London-broil roast beef (from deli) |
| 1/2 teaspoon garlic salt | 30 slices pimiento-stuffed green olives |
| 1/4 cup mayonnaise | |
| 1 teaspoon wasabi powder or prepared horseradish | |

1 Heat oven to 400°F. Cut off ends of each potato; discard ends. Cut potatoes into 3/8-inch-thick slices (about 3 per potato). Place slices on ungreased cookie sheet. Brush slices with oil; sprinkle each with garlic salt.

2 Bake at 400°F. for 15 to 20 minutes or until tender and golden brown. Cool 20 minutes or until completely cooled.

3 Meanwhile, in small bowl, combine mayonnaise, wasabi powder, garlic and pepper; mix well.

4 To serve, place potato slices on serving platter. Top each with about 1/2 teaspoon mayonnaise mixture. Top with roast beef. Garnish each with an olive slice.

**HIGH ALTITUDE (3500-6500 FT):** Bake at 425°F. for 15 to 20 minutes.

NUTRITION INFORMATION PER SERVING: Calories 55 • Total Fat 2g • Saturated Fat 0g • Cholesterol 5mg • Sodium 100mg • Total Carbohydrate 8g • Dietary Fiber 0g • Protein 1g. DIETARY EXCHANGES: 1/2 Starch • 1/2 Fat • 1/2 Carb Choice.

# mexican ham and cheese

PREP TIME: 10 Minutes ✳ READY IN: 40 Minutes ✳ SERVINGS: 4

1 can (11 oz.) Pillsbury® refrigerated crusty French loaf

1 cup refried beans (black or pinto)

8 oz. thinly sliced baked ham

4 oz. sliced mozzarella or provolone cheese

5 tomato slices

3 romaine lettuce leaves

3 white onion slices

1 can (7 oz.) pickled sliced jalapeño peppers, if desired

1 Heat oven to 350°F.

2 Bake loaf as directed on package directions; cool 5 minutes. Carefully cut in half lengthwise.

3 Spread 1/2 cup refried beans on cut side of each half. Place remaining ingredients on bottom half. Top with other half to make sandwich. To serve, cut into fourths.

NUTRITION INFORMATION PER SERVING: Calories 410 • Total Fat 12g • Saturated Fat 6g • Cholesterol 50mg • Sodium 1490mg • Total Carbohydrate 48g • Dietary Fiber 5g • Protein 29g. DIETARY EXCHANGES: 3 Starch • 3 Lean Meat • 3 Carb Choices.

*special touch*

*If desired, peel and cut 1 avocado into slices and layer it in the sandwich.*

# cheesy hot beef sandwiches

PREP TIME: 20 Minutes ✳ READY IN: 45 Minutes ✳ SERVINGS: 8

1-1/2 lb. extra-lean (at least 90%) ground beef

1 envelope dry French onion soup mix (from 2.6-oz. pkg.)

1/4 cup water

1/2 red bell pepper, chopped (about 1/2 cup)

2 tablespoons chopped fresh parsley

2 cups shredded Cheddar-Monterey Jack cheese blend (8 oz.)

1 loaf (1 lb.) French bread, about 24 inches long

1 Heat oven to 350°F. Cut 26 x 18-inch piece of heavy duty foil. In 12-inch nonstick skillet, cook ground beef over medium-high heat 5 to 7 minutes, stirring occasionally, until thoroughly cooked; drain. Add soup mix, water, bell pepper and parsley. Cook 2 to 3 minutes or until thoroughly heated. Stir in cheese until melted.

2 Cut 1/2 inch lengthwise slice from top of French bread; set aside. With fork, remove inside of bread, leaving 1/2 inch around edges. Place loaf on foil. If desired, reserve bread pieces for another use. Fill indentation in bread with ground beef mixture. Place top of bread over ground beef. Wrap loaf in foil. Place on cookie sheet.

3 Bake the loaf 20 to 25 minutes or until thoroughly heated. For sandwiches, cut the loaf into 8 crosswise sections.

**HIGH ALTITUDE (3500-6500 FT):** Bake 30 to 35 minutes.

NUTRITION INFORMATION PER SERVING: Calories 410 • Total Fat 18g • Saturated Fat 9g • Cholesterol 80mg • Sodium 940mg • Total Carbohydrate 32g • Dietary Fiber 2g • Protein 29g. DIETARY EXCHANGES: 2 Starch • 3 Medium-Fat Meat • 1/2 Fat • 2 Carb Choices.

*cook's notes*

*Use a fork to remove the bread inside the loaf to form a bread shell.*

cook's notes

If you do not have roasted

red bell peppers, fresh red bell

pepper can be used instead.

# garlic and herb beef appetizers

PREP TIME: 20 Minutes ✻ READY IN: 35 Minutes ✻ SERVINGS: 24

| | | | |
|---|---|---|---|
| 2 | oz. thinly sliced cooked roast beef (from deli), finely chopped | 2 | tablespoons finely chopped roasted red bell peppers (from a jar) |
| 1/2 | cup crumbled Boursin cheese with garlic and herbs | 1 | can (8 oz.) Pillsbury® refrigerated crescent dinner rolls |
| 2 | tablespoons finely chopped onion | 1 | egg yolk, slightly beaten |

1 Heat oven to 375°F. In small bowl, mix the beef, Boursin cheese, onion and roasted red peppers until well combined.

2 Remove half of dough from can in rolled section; refrigerate remaining half of dough in can. On lightly floured surface, unroll dough; separate into 2 rectangles. Firmly press perforations to seal. Press each rectangle into 7-1/2 x 6-inch rectangle. Cut each rectangle into 6 (3 x 2-1/2-inch) rectangles.

3 Place 1 teaspoon beef mixture in center of each rectangle. Brush edges of dough with water. Take short sides of dough and bring to center of filling, slightly overlapping. Press edges with fork. Place on ungreased cookie sheet. Make 2 small slits on top of each appetizer; brush with egg yolk. Repeat with remaining half of dough and beef mixture.

4 Bake 11 to 13 minutes or until golden brown. Serve warm.

NUTRITION INFORMATION PER SERVING: Calories 60 • Total Fat 4g • Saturated Fat 1.5g • Cholesterol 15mg • Sodium 85mg • Total Carbohydrate 4g • Dietary Fiber 0g • Protein 2g. DIETARY EXCHANGES: 1/2 Starch • 1/2 Fat.

cook's notes

To reduce the fat in each

serving by about 6 grams,

substitute turkey sausage

for the Italian sausage and

use Grands!® reduced-fat

buttermilk biscuits instead of

the regular ones.

# cheesy sausage calzones

PREP TIME: 30 Minutes ✻ READY IN: 45 Minutes ✻ SERVINGS: 5

| | | | |
|---|---|---|---|
| 1/2 | lb. bulk Italian pork sausage | 1 | can (10.2 oz.) Pillsbury® Grands!® refrigerated buttermilk biscuits (5 biscuits) |
| 1/3 | cup chopped onion | 1/2 | cup shredded mozzarella cheese (2 oz.) |
| 1/4 | cup chopped red bell pepper | 1-1/2 | cups tomato pasta sauce, heated |

1 Heat oven to 375°F. In 8-inch skillet, cook sausage, onion and bell pepper over medium heat 10 minutes, stirring frequently, until sausage is no longer pink; drain. Cool 10 minutes.

2 Separate dough into 5 biscuits. On ungreased large cookie sheet, press each biscuit into 6-inch round. Top half of each round with sausage mixture and cheese to within 1/2 inch of edge. Fold dough over filling; press edges firmly with fork to seal.

3 Bake 12 to 15 minutes or until golden brown. Serve the warm calzones with warm pasta sauce for dipping.

NUTRITION INFORMATION PER SERVING: Calories 360 • Total Fat 19g • Saturated Fat 7g • Cholesterol 30mg • Sodium 1350mg • Total Carbohydrate 32g • Dietary Fiber 1g • Protein 15g. DIETARY EXCHANGES: 1-1/2 Starch • 1/2 Other Carbohydrate • 1-1/2 High-Fat Meat • 1-1/2 Fat • 2 Carb Choices.

# lettuce wraps

PREP TIME: 30 Minutes ✳ READY IN: 1 Hour ✳ SERVINGS: 16

### SAUCE
- 1/2 cup apricot preserves
- 1/3 cup fresh lime juice
- 2 tablespoons lite soy sauce
- 2 garlic cloves, minced
- 1 teaspoon cornstarch

### WRAPS
- 1 tablespoon dark sesame oil or vegetable oil
- 2 boneless skinless chicken breast halves, finely chopped

- 1/2 cup chopped seeded cucumber
- 1/2 cup grated carrot
- 2 tablespoons chopped peanuts
- 1 teaspoon grated gingerroot
- 1 teaspoon chopped garlic
- 16 leaves (about 2 heads) butterhead (Bibb or Boston) lettuce

1 In small bowl, combine preserves, lime juice, soy sauce and garlic; mix well. Spoon 1/4 cup sauce into 1-cup measuring cup. Stir in cornstarch until smooth; set aside. Refrigerate remaining sauce in bowl until serving time.

2 Heat oil in medium skillet over medium-high heat until hot. Add chicken; cook 5 to 7 minutes or until browned, stirring frequently. Stir in cucumber, carrot, peanuts, gingerroot and garlic. Stir in reserved sauce with cornstarch. Cook 2 to 3 minutes or until bubbly and thickened, stirring constantly. Spoon mixture into shallow dish. Cover; refrigerate 30 minutes or until cooled.

3 Spoon 2 tablespoons chicken mixture onto center of each lettuce leaf. Fold sides of lettuce in toward center; roll up like burrito. Secure with toothpicks. Place seam side down on serving platter. Serve immediately, or cover and refrigerate until serving time. Serve wraps with sauce.

NUTRITION INFORMATION PER SERVING: Calories 70 • Total Fat 2g • Saturated Fat 0g • Cholesterol 10mg • Sodium 90mg • Total Carbohydrate 9g • Dietary Fiber 0g • Protein 4g. DIETARY EXCHANGES: 1/2 Other Carbohydrate • 1/2 Very Lean Meat • 1/2 Fat • 1/2 Carb Choice.

# Cozy Christmas Breakfast

*Start your Christmas* right with hearty egg casseroles, fresh-baked quick breads and tempting breakfast goodies. What a wonderful way to welcome the Yuletide!

p. 176

p. 178

p. 185

p. 178

p. 185

apple-cream cheese
muffins p. 188

# banana-walnut brunch squares

PREP TIME: 15 Minutes ❋ READY IN: 1 Hour ❋ SERVINGS: 9

**DEBBIE BRACKER**
Car Junction, Missouri
Bake-Off® Contest 41, 2004

3   eggs
1   cup mashed ripe bananas (2 to 3 medium)
3   tablespoons granulated sugar
1   can (17.5 oz.) Pillsbury® Grands!® refrigerated cinnamon rolls with cream cheese icing
1/2   cup all-purpose flour

1/3   cup packed light brown sugar
1/4   cup butter or margarine, softened
3/4   cup coarsely chopped walnuts
1/4   cup maple syrup
      Banana slices, if desired

1   Heat oven to 350°F. Spray 8-inch square (2-quart) glass baking dish with cooking spray. In large bowl, beat eggs, bananas and granulated sugar with wire whisk until well blended.

2   Separate dough into 5 rolls; set icing aside. Cut each roll into 8 equal pie-shaped wedges. Gently stir the dough pieces into the egg mixture until well coated. Spoon mixture into sprayed dish; spread evenly.

3   In medium bowl, mix flour and brown sugar. With fork, cut in butter until mixture resembles coarse crumbs. Stir in walnuts. Sprinkle mixture over dough mixture in dish.

4   Bake at 350°F. for 35 to 40 minutes or until center is puffed and set and edges are deep golden brown. Cool 10 minutes. Meanwhile, in small bowl, mix icing and syrup until blended.

5   To serve, cut into squares; place on individual serving plates. Drizzle the icing mixture over each serving; garnish with banana slices.

**HIGH ALTITUDE (3500-6500 FT):** Bake at 375°F. for 35 to 40 minutes.

NUTRITION INFORMATION PER SERVING: Calories 440 • Total Fat 21g • Saturated Fat 6g • Cholesterol 95mg • Sodium 510mg • Total Carbohydrate 58g • Dietary Fiber 2g • Protein 8g. DIETARY EXCHANGES: 2 Starch • 2 Other Carbohydrate • 4 Fat • 4 Carb Choices.

# poppin' fresh® citrus-glazed crullers

PREP TIME: 15 Minutes ✱ READY IN: 40 Minutes ✱ SERVINGS: 12

## ROLLS
- 1/4 cup butter or margarine, melted
- 1/2 cup granulated sugar
- 1 can (11 oz.) Pillsbury® refrigerated original breadsticks

## GLAZE
- 2/3 cup powdered sugar
- 1/4 teaspoon grated orange peel
- 1/4 teaspoon grated lemon peel
- 1 tablespoon orange juice
- 1 teaspoon lemon juice

ERIKA COUCH
Ballston Spa, New York
Bake-Off® Contest 39, 2000

1 Heat oven to 375°F. Line the cookie sheet with parchment paper, or spray with cooking spray. In shallow dish, place melted butter; in another shallow dish, place granulated sugar.

2 Unroll dough; separate into breadsticks. Dip both sides of each breadstick in butter; coat with sugar. Twist each breadstick; place on cookie sheet, pressing ends down firmly.

3 Bake 13 to 17 minutes or until golden brown. Meanwhile, in small bowl, blend all glaze ingredients until smooth.

4 Immediately drizzle the glaze over the hot rolls. Remove from cookie sheet and cool 5 minutes before serving.

NUTRITION INFORMATION PER SERVING: Calories 160 • Total Fat 5g • Saturated Fat 3g • Cholesterol 10mg • Sodium 210mg • Total Carbohydrate 28g • Dietary Fiber 0g • Protein 2g. DIETARY EXCHANGES: 1 Starch • 1/2 Other Carbohydrate • 1 Fat • 2 Carb Choices.

# onion-cheese custard tartlets

PREP TIME: 20 Minutes ✳ READY IN: 45 Minutes ✳ SERVINGS: 12

1 can (8 oz.) Pillsbury® refrigerated crescent dinner rolls or 1 can (8 oz.) Pillsbury® Crescent Recipe Creations™ refrigerated seamless dough sheet

1/3 cup shredded Gruyère cheese (about 1-1/2 oz.)

4 green onions, sliced (1/4 cup)

1 tablespoon diced pimientos

1 egg

3 tablespoons whipping cream

1 Heat oven to 375°F.

2 If using crescent rolls: Unroll dough into 1 large rectangle on work surface. Press into 12 x 9-inch rectangle, firmly pressing perforations to seal. If using dough sheet: Unroll dough on work surface. Press into 12 x 9-inch rectangle.

3 Cut dough into 12 squares. Gently press squares into 12 ungreased mini muffin cups, shaping edges to form rims 1/4 inch high. Spoon cheese evenly into dough-lined cups. Top each with onions and pimientos. In small bowl, beat egg and whipping cream with wire whisk or fork until blended. Spoon slightly less than 1 tablespoon mixture into each cup.

4 Bake 15 to 20 minutes or until edges are golden brown and filling is set. Cool 5 minutes. Remove from muffin cups.

NUTRITION INFORMATION PER SERVING: Calories 100 • Total Fat 7g • Saturated Fat 3g • Cholesterol 25mg • Sodium 170mg • Total Carbohydrate 8g • Dietary Fiber 0g • Protein 3g. DIETARY EXCHANGES: 1/2 Starch • 1-1/2 Fat • 1/2 Carb Choice.

# leek quiche

PREP TIME: 25 Minutes ✳ READY IN: 1 Hour 15 Minutes ✳ SERVINGS: 6

1 Pillsbury® refrigerated pie crust, softened as directed on box

2 tablespoons butter or margarine

2 medium leeks, rinsed, cut in half lengthwise and then cut into 1/2-inch slices (about 4 cups)

3 eggs

1 cup milk

1 cup shredded Swiss cheese (4 oz.)

1/2 teaspoon salt

1/4 teaspoon pepper

1/8 teaspoon ground nutmeg

1 Heat oven to 400°F. Place pie crust in 9-inch glass pie plate as directed on box for One-Crust Filled Pie. Partially bake crust about 8 minutes or until very lightly browned.

2 Meanwhile, in 12-inch skillet, melt butter over medium heat. Cook leeks in butter 7 to 9 minutes, stirring frequently, until tender but not brown. Remove from heat; set aside.

3 In medium bowl, beat eggs with wire whisk. Stir in milk, cheese, salt, pepper and nutmeg until blended. Stir in leeks. Pour mixture into partially baked crust.

4 Bake 10 minutes. Cover crust edge with foil to prevent excessive browning. Reduce the oven temperature to 300°F. and bake 20 to 25 minutes longer or until knife inserted in center comes out clean. Let stand 15 minutes before cutting.

NUTRITION INFORMATION PER SERVING: Calories 320 • Total Fat 20g • Saturated Fat 10g • Cholesterol 140mg • Sodium 490mg • Total Carbohydrate 23g • Dietary Fiber 0g • Protein 11g. DIETARY EXCHANGES: 1-1/2 Starch • 1/2 Vegetable • 1/2 Medium-Fat Meat • 1/2 High-Fat Meat • 2-1/2 Fat • 1-1/2 Carb Choices.

onion-cheese custard tartlets

# pineapple-orange blossoms

PREP TIME: 15 Minutes ✳ READY IN: 45 Minutes ✳ SERVINGS: 8

**SHARON HENDERSON**
Ellettsville, Indiana
Bake-Off® Contest 41, 2004

1  can (12.4 oz.) Pillsbury® refrigerated cinnamon rolls with icing

1/2  cup crushed pineapple (from 8-oz. can), well drained on paper towels

1/3  cup orange marmalade

4  oz. cream cheese (from 8-oz. pkg.), softened

1  Heat oven to 350°F. Spray 8 (2-3/4 x 1-1/4-inch) muffin cups with cooking spray. Separate dough into 8 rolls; set icing aside. Cut each roll into quarters; place 4 quarters, points up and separated slightly, in each sprayed muffin cup.

2  In small bowl, mix pineapple, marmalade and cream cheese. Place 2 tablespoons mixture into center of dough in each cup.

3  Bake at 350°F. for 17 to 22 minutes or until light golden brown. Cool in pan on wire rack 5 minutes. Run knife around edge of muffin cups; remove rolls from cups and place on serving plate.

4  Remove cover from icing; microwave on Medium (50%) for 10 to 15 seconds or until drizzling consistency. Drizzle icing over warm rolls. Serve warm.

**HIGH ALTITUDE (3500-6500 FT):** Bake at 375°F. for 20 to 23 minutes.

NUTRITION INFORMATION PER SERVING: Calories 240 • Total Fat 11g • Saturated Fat 5g • Cholesterol 25mg • Sodium 410mg • Total Carbohydrate 34g • Dietary Fiber 0g • Protein 4g. DIETARY EXCHANGES: 1 Starch • 1 Other Carbohydrate • 2 Fat • 2 Carb Choices.

# cinnamon twisties

PREP TIME: 30 Minutes ✳ READY IN: 30 Minutes ✳ SERVINGS: 6

1 can (8 oz.) refrigerated Pillsbury® refrigerated crescent dinner rolls

1 tablespoon butter or margarine, melted

2 teaspoons cinnamon-sugar blend

1 Heat oven to 375°F. Lightly spray cookie sheet with cooking spray.

2 Remove dough from can; unroll into 1 large rectangle. Seal perforations in dough. Press out dough to 12 x 7-inch rectangle. Brush dough with melted butter.

3 Sprinkle the cinnamon-sugar evenly over dough. Cut the dough crosswise into 12 strips that are 7 x 1-inch. Cut each strip in half to make 24 (3-1/2-inch) strips. Twist each strip and put it on the cookie sheet.

4 Bake the twisted strips for 8 to 10 minutes or until they are deep golden brown. Remove pan from oven; remove twisties from cookie sheet and place on cooling rack. Cool for about 5 minutes before serving.

NUTRITION INFORMATION PER SERVING: Calories 150 • Total Fat 7g • Saturated Fat 2.5g. • Cholesterol 5mg • Sodium 470mg • Total Carbohydrate 19g • Dietary Fiber 0g • Protein 3g. DIETARY EXCHANGES: 1 Starch • 1 Carb Choice.

*special touch*

*These Cinnamon Twisties taste even better when you dip them in yogurt or pudding.*

# italian egg bake

PREP TIME: 15 Minutes ✳ READY IN: 1 Hour 35 Minutes ✳ SERVINGS: 6

1 lb. bulk Italian pork sausage

4 cups frozen diced or shredded hash brown potatoes (from 30- or 32-oz. bag), thawed

1 cup shredded Cheddar cheese (4 oz.)

1 cup frozen cut leaf spinach, thawed, drained

1/4 cup julienne-cut sun-dried tomatoes in oil and herbs (from 8-oz. jar)

1 cup shredded mozzarella cheese (4 oz.)

4 eggs

3/4 cup milk

1/4 teaspoon salt

1/8 teaspoon pepper

2 tablespoons shredded Parmesan cheese

1 Heat oven to 350°F. Spray 8-inch square (2-quart) glass baking dish with cooking spray.

2 In 10-inch nonstick skillet, cook sausage over medium-high heat, stirring occasionally, until no longer pink; drain.

3 In medium bowl, mix potatoes and Cheddar cheese. In baking dish, layer half of the potato mixture, the sausage, spinach and tomatoes, remaining potato mixture and mozzarella cheese. In medium bowl, beat eggs slightly with wire whisk. Add milk, salt and pepper; beat well. Pour evenly over potato mixture.

4 Cover with foil; bake 1 hour. Uncover; sprinkle with Parmesan cheese. Bake 15 minutes longer or until knife inserted in center comes out clean. Let stand 5 minutes. Cut into 6 squares.

NUTRITION INFORMATION PER SERVING: Calories 560 • Total Fat 37g • Saturated Fat 14g • Cholesterol 205mg • Sodium 1080mg • Total Carbohydrate 32g • Dietary Fiber 3g • Protein 25g. DIETARY EXCHANGES: 1-1/2 Starch • 1-1/2 Vegetable • 1 Medium-Fat Meat • 1-1/2 High-Fat Meat • 4 Fat • 2 Carb Choices.

*kitchen tip*

*Mozzarella cheese freezes well, so purchase a block of it when it's on sale, shred it and freeze in resealable freezer plastic bags. Simply take out what you need for a recipe and return the rest to the freezer.*

**KAREN GULKIN**
Greeley, Colorado
Bake-Off® Contest 41, 2004

# sausage and apple bake

PREP TIME: 40 Minutes ✹ READY IN: 1 Hour 25 Minutes ✹ SERVINGS: 12

- 2 cans (8 oz. each) Pillsbury® refrigerated crescent dinner rolls or 2 cans (8 oz. each) Pillsbury® Crescent Recipe Creations™ refrigerated seamless dough sheets
- 2 lb. bulk pork or turkey breakfast sausage
- 2 cups chopped peeled apples (2 medium)
- 1 medium onion, chopped (1/2 cup)

- 1-1/2 tablespoons grated orange peel (from 1 medium orange)
- 4 eggs
- 1/2 cup milk
- 1 teaspoon fennel seed
- 1-1/2 cups shredded Cheddar cheese (6 oz.)
- 1-1/2 cups shredded fontina cheese (6 oz.)

1 Heat oven to 350°F. Spray 13 x 9-inch (3-quart) glass baking dish with cooking spray.

2 If using crescent rolls: Unroll 1 can of dough into dish and firmly press perforations to seal. If using dough sheets: Unroll 1 can of dough into dish.

3 Bake 10 to 15 minutes or until light golden brown. Cool while cooking sausage. In 12-inch skillet, cook sausage over medium-high heat 8 to 10 minutes, stirring frequently, until browned. Drain well; remove sausage from skillet.

4 In same skillet, cook apples, onion and orange peel over medium heat about 5 minutes, stirring occasionally, until onion is translucent. Meanwhile, in small bowl, lightly beat eggs and milk.

5 Stir cooked sausage and fennel seed into apple mixture. Remove from heat. Stir egg mixture into sausage mixture. Sprinkle Cheddar cheese over partially baked crust. Spread sausage mixture evenly over cheese. Sprinkle fontina cheese over top.

6 If using crescent rolls: Unroll second can of dough onto work surface; press to form 13 x 9-inch rectangle, firmly pressing perforations to seal. Place dough rectangle over cheese; press edges to side of dish.

7 If using dough sheets: Unroll second can of dough onto work surface; press to form 13 x 9-inch rectangle. Place dough rectangle over cheese; press edges to side of dish.

8 Bake 25 to 35 minutes or until golden brown. Let stand 10 minutes before serving. Cut into squares.

NUTRITION INFORMATION PER SERVING: Calories 420 • Total Fat 29g • Saturated Fat 12g • Cholesterol 135mg • Sodium 790mg • Total Carbohydrate 19g • Dietary Fiber 0g • Protein 19g. DIETARY EXCHANGES: 1 Starch • 1/2 Other Carbohydrate • 2 High-Fat Meat • 2-1/2 Fat • 1 Carb Choice.

# ham 'n cheese omelet bake

PREP TIME: 15 Minutes ✳ READY IN: 1 Hour 15 Minutes ✳ SERVINGS: 8

1 box (10 oz.) Green Giant® frozen broccoli & cheese flavored sauce

1 can (10.2 oz.) Pillsbury® Grands!® flaky layers refrigerated original biscuits (5 biscuits)

10 eggs

1-1/2 cups milk

1 teaspoon ground mustard

Salt and pepper, if desired

2 cups diced cooked ham

1/3 cup chopped onion

1 cup shredded Cheddar cheese (4 oz.)

1 cup shredded Swiss cheese (4 oz.)

1 jar (4.5 oz.) Green Giant® sliced mushrooms, drained

JULIE AMBERSON
Browns Point, Washington
Bake-Off® Contest 41, 2004

1 Heat oven to 350°F. Cut small slit in center of broccoli and cheese sauce pouch. Microwave on High 3 to 4 minutes, rotating pouch 1/4 turn once halfway through microwaving. Set aside to cool slightly.

2 Meanwhile, spray bottom of 13 x 9-inch (3-quart) glass baking dish with cooking spray. Separate dough into 5 biscuits. Cut each biscuit into 8 pieces; arrange evenly in baking dish.

3 In large bowl, beat eggs, milk, mustard, salt and pepper with wire whisk until well blended. Stir in ham, onion, both cheeses, mushrooms and cooked broccoli and cheese sauce. Pour mixture over biscuit pieces in dish. Press down with back of spoon, making sure all biscuit pieces are covered with egg mixture.

4 Bake 40 to 50 minutes or until the edges are deep golden brown and center is set. Let stand 10 minutes before serving. Cut into squares.

**HIGH ALTITUDE (3500-6500 FT):** Bake at 375°F.

NUTRITION INFORMATION PER SERVING: Calories 450 • Total Fat 27g • Saturated Fat 12g • Cholesterol 320mg • Sodium 1360mg • Total Carbohydrate 24g • Dietary Fiber 2g • Protein 30g. DIETARY EXCHANGES: 1-1/2 Starch • 3-1/2 Medium-Fat Meat • 1-1/2 Fat • 1-1/2 Carb Choices.

spinach sausage brunch casserole

# spinach sausage brunch casserole

PREP TIME: 15 Minutes ✳ READY IN: 50 Minutes ✳ SERVINGS: 8

- 1 lb. bulk Italian sausage
- 1 cup chopped onions
- 1 jar (7.25 oz.) mild roasted red bell peppers, drained, chopped
- 1 package (9 oz.) Green Giant® frozen chopped spinach, thawed, well drained
- 1 cup all-purpose flour

- 1/4 cup grated Parmesan cheese
- 1 tablespoon chopped fresh basil or 1 teaspoon dried basil leaves
- 1/2 teaspoon salt
- 2 cups milk
- 8 eggs
- 1 cup shredded Provolone cheese (4 oz.)

1. Heat oven to 425°F. Grease 13 x 9-inch pan. In 10-inch skillet, brown sausage and onions. Remove from skillet; drain on paper towels. Arrange sausage mixture in greased pan. Sprinkle chopped red peppers over sausage mixture; top with spinach.

2. In large bowl, combine flour, Parmesan cheese, basil and salt. In another large bowl, combine milk and eggs; beat until smooth. Add egg mixture to flour mixture; beat until well blended. Pour over the spinach.

3. Bake 20 to 25 minutes or until knife inserted in center comes out clean. Sprinkle casserole with Provolone cheese. Bake an additional 1 to 2 minutes or until cheese is melted.

4. Let stand 5 minutes. Cut into squares.

NUTRITION INFORMATION PER SERVING: Calories 380 • Total Fat 22g • Saturated Fat 9g • Cholesterol 260mg • Sodium 810mg • Total Carbohydrate 21g • Dietary Fiber 2g • Protein 24g. DIETARY EXCHANGES: 1/2 Starch • 1 Other Carbohydrate • 3 Medium-Fat Meat • 1-1/2 Fat • 1-1/2 Carb Choices.

# fresh fruit orange fizz

PREP TIME: 10 Minutes ✳ READY IN: 10 Minutes ✳ SERVINGS: 12

- 2 cups cubed cantaloupe
- 2 cups cubed honeydew melon
- 1 cup halved fresh strawberries
- 1 large banana, cut in half lengthwise, sliced

- 1/2 cup frozen (thawed) orange juice concentrate
- 3/4 cup orange carbonated beverage, chilled

1. In large bowl, gently mix the melon, berries, banana and orange juice concentrate. Stir in carbonated beverage.

2. Serve in small dessert bowls with toothpicks.

NUTRITION INFORMATION PER SERVING: Calories 60 • Total Fat 0g • Saturated Fat 0g • Cholesterol 0mg • Sodium 10mg • Total Carbohydrate 15g • Dietary Fiber 1g • Protein 1g. DIETARY EXCHANGES: 1 Fruit • 1 Carb Choice.

*cook's notes*

*You can cut up all of the fruit except the banana ahead of time. Add the orange juice and carbonated beverage just before serving.*

REBECCA NURSE
Waterford, Pennsylvania
Bake-Off® Contest 42, 2006

# cinnamon-fruit snack mix

PREP TIME: 20 Minutes ✳ READY IN: 1 Hour 50 Minutes ✳ SERVINGS: 32

| | |
|---|---|
| 2 cups Cinnamon Toast Crunch® cereal | 1 teaspoon ground cinnamon |
| 1 cup Fiber One® cereal | 1/4 cup vegetable oil |
| 1-1/2 cups flaked coconut | 1 can (14 oz.) fat-free sweetened condensed milk (not evaporated) |
| 1 cup pecan halves | 1 cup chopped dried apricots |
| 1 cup blanched whole almonds | 1 cup banana chips |
| 1/2 cup sunflower nuts | 1 cup sweetened dried cranberries |
| 1/2 cup wheat germ | 1/2 cup dried cherries |
| 1/2 cup ground flax seed | 1/2 cup golden raisins |
| 1 teaspoon salt | |

1 Heat oven to 300°F. Spray 15 x 10 x 1-inch pan with cooking spray. In large bowl, mix both the cereals, coconut, pecans, almonds, sunflower nuts, wheat germ, flax seed, salt and cinnamon. In small bowl, mix oil and condensed milk. Pour over cereal mixture; toss until well coated. Spread evenly in pan.

2 Bake 50 to 60 minutes, stirring every 15 minutes to break up any large clumps, until light golden brown. Cool 30 minutes.

3 In large bowl, mix cereal mixture, apricots, banana chips, cranberries, cherries and raisins. Store in tightly covered container.

NUTRITION INFORMATION PER SERVING: Calories 230 • Total Fat 11g • Saturated Fat 2.5g • Cholesterol 0mg • Sodium 120mg • Total Carbohydrate 28g • Dietary Fiber 3g • Protein 4g. DIETARY EXCHANGES: 1 Starch • 1 Other Carbohydrate • 2 Fat • 2 Carb Choices.

## kitchen tip

To freeze the foldovers, place on a cookie sheet and freeze until firm, then transfer to resealable freezer bags and label. Bake according to the recipe, adding 5 minutes.

# flaky sausage foldovers

PREP TIME: 25 Minutes ✳ READY IN: 40 Minutes ✳ SERVINGS: 22

| | |
|---|---|
| 6 oz. bulk hot pork sausage | 1 box Pillsbury® refrigerated pie crusts, softened as directed on box |
| 1/4 teaspoon garlic powder | 1 egg, beaten |
| 1 can (15 oz.) pizza sauce | |

1 Heat oven to 425°F. In 8-inch skillet, cook the sausage over medium-high heat 6 to 8 minutes, stirring occasionally until thoroughly cooked; drain well. Stir in garlic powder and 1/4 cup of the pizza sauce.

2 Remove 1 crust from pouch. On work surface, roll into 13-inch round. With 3-inch round cutter, cut 11 rounds. Repeat with second crust.

3 Spoon about 1 teaspoon sausage mixture onto each round. Fold each in half; seal edges with fork. Cut small slit in top of each with sharp knife. Place on ungreased large cookie sheet. Brush each foldover with beaten egg. If desired, cut decorative shapes from remaining dough and attach with beaten egg.

4 Bake 9 to 11 minutes or until golden brown. Meanwhile, in 1-quart saucepan, heat remaining pizza sauce until hot. Serve warm appetizers with warm pizza sauce for dipping.

NUTRITION INFORMATION PER SERVING: Calories 80 • Total Fat 4.5g • Saturated Fat 1.5g • Cholesterol 15mg • Sodium 170mg • Total Carbohydrate 8g • Dietary Fiber 0g • Protein 1g. DIETARY EXCHANGES: 1/2 Starch • 1 Fat • 1/2 Carb Choice.

# scrambled egg-parmesan soft crust pizza

PREP TIME: 25 Minutes ✳ READY IN: 35 Minutes ✳ SERVINGS: 6

4  slices bacon

1  can (8 oz.) Pillsbury® refrigerated garlic breadsticks

8  eggs

1/4  cup milk

1/2  teaspoon salt

Dash pepper

2  cups shredded pizza cheese blend (8 oz.)

1  small tomato, very thinly sliced

Old El Paso® thick 'n chunky salsa, if desired

*cook's notes*

*Because the eggs will continue to cook in the oven, scramble them just until they are set and a bit shiny.*

1  In 10-inch skillet, cook bacon until crisp. Remove the bacon from skillet; drain on paper towels. Crumble the bacon; set aside. Drain all but 2 teaspoons drippings from skillet. Set skillet aside.

2  Heat oven to 375°F. Unroll dough; separate into 8 breadsticks. Starting in center of ungreased 12-inch pizza pan or large cookie sheet, shape 1 breadstick into a coil. Add remaining breadsticks in coil pattern. Press dough to form 12-inch round.

3  Bake 10 to 12 minutes or until light golden brown. Meanwhile, in large bowl, beat eggs, milk, salt and pepper with wire whisk until well blended. Add to drippings in skillet; cook over medium heat about 5 minutes, stirring occasionally, until set but still moist. Stir in 1 cup of the cheese. Remove from heat. Let stand 1 to 2 minutes or until cheese is melted.

4  Remove partially baked crust from oven. Sprinkle 1/2 cup cheese evenly over crust. Top evenly with eggs, crumbled bacon and remaining 1/2 cup cheese. Arrange tomato slices over top.

5  Bake 5 to 7 minutes longer or until the pizza is thoroughly heated and the cheese is melted. Serve with salsa.

NUTRITION INFORMATION PER SERVING: Calories 330 • Total Fat 18g • Saturated Fat 6g • Cholesterol 295mg • Sodium 1070mg • Total Carbohydrate 18g • Dietary Fiber 0g • Protein 24g. DIETARY EXCHANGES: 1 Starch • 2-1/2 High-Fat Meat • 1 Carb Choice.

# apple-cream cheese muffins

PREP TIME: 30 Minutes ✳ READY IN: 1 Hour 10 Minutes ✳ SERVINGS: 15

### MUFFINS
3/4 cup packed brown sugar
1-3/4 cups all-purpose flour
1 teaspoon baking powder
1/2 teaspoon ground cinnamon
1/2 teaspoon salt
2 eggs, beaten
2/3 cup oil

1/4 cup applesauce
1 teaspoon vanilla
1 large apple, peeled, shredded (about 1 cup)
1/3 cup cream cheese (from 8-oz. package)

### STREUSEL
3 tablespoons packed brown sugar
2 tablespoons all-purpose flour
1 tablespoon butter or margarine, softened

1 Heat oven to 350°F. Line 15 muffin cups with paper baking cups. Reserve 1 tablespoon of the brown sugar in the muffins for filling.

2 In large bowl with electric mixer, mix remaining brown sugar for muffins, 1-3/4 cups flour, the baking powder, cinnamon and salt on low speed until mixed. Reserve 1 tablespoon of the beaten egg for filling. Add oil, applesauce, vanilla and remaining egg to flour mixture. Beat on medium speed until mixed. With spoon, stir in apple.

3 In small bowl, mix cream cheese, the reserved 1 tablespoon brown sugar and reserved 1 tablespoon egg. Fill muffin cups slightly less than half full of batter. Top each with 1 teaspoon cream cheese mixture. Top with spoonful of remaining batter to fill cups 2/3 full. In small bowl, mix all streusel ingredients; sprinkle over batter.

4 Bake 22 to 26 minutes or until toothpick inserted in center comes out clean. Remove from pan. Cool slightly, about 10 minutes.

**HIGH ALTITUDE (3500-6500 FT):** Decrease baking powder to 3/4 teaspoon. Bake at 375°F.

NUTRITION INFORMATION PER SERVING: Calories 240 • Total Fat 13g • Saturated Fat 3g • Cholesterol 35mg • Sodium 150mg • Total Carbohydrate 28g • Dietary Fiber 0g • Protein 3g. DIETARY EXCHANGES: 1 Starch • 1 Other Carbohydrate • 2-1/2 Fat • 2 Carb Choices.

# granola fruit kabobs

PREP TIME: 10 Minutes ✳ READY IN: 10 Minutes ✳ SERVINGS: 8

2 cups granola

2 medium apples, unpeeled, cut into chunks

2 small bananas, peeled, cut into chunks

1 cup fresh pineapple chunks

1 cup Yoplait® original fruit-flavored yogurt

1 Place the granola in a shallow bowl. Insert a toothpick into each piece of fruit.

2 To serve, dip the fruit into yogurt, coating all sides. Roll in granola, coating completely.

NUTRITION INFORMATION PER SERVING: Calories 200 • Total Fat 5g • Saturated Fat 2g • Cholesterol 0mg • Sodium 30mg • Total Carbohydrate 35g • Dietary Fiber 4g • Protein 4g. DIETARY EXCHANGES: 1 Starch • 1/2 Fruit • 1 Other Carbohydrate • 1 Fat • 2 Carb Choices.

*cook's notes*

*To prevent cut fruits such as bananas and apples from browning, toss the pieces with a small amount of lemon or orange juice.*

# spinach, strawberry and grapefruit toss

PREP TIME: 25 Minutes ✳ READY IN: 25 Minutes ✳ SERVINGS: 12

**ALMONDS AND DRESSING**

1/3 cup vegetable oil

1/2 cup sliced almonds

3 tablespoons honey

Dash ground cinnamon

1/2 teaspoon grated lime peel

3 tablespoons fresh lime juice

1 teaspoon Dijon mustard

1/4 teaspoon salt

**SALAD**

1 package (10 oz.) fresh spinach, stems removed, torn

2 cups fresh strawberries, sliced

1 grapefruit, peeled, sectioned

1 Line cookie sheet with foil; spray foil with cooking spray. In 7-inch skillet, heat 2 teaspoons of the oil over medium heat. Cook and stir almonds in oil until lightly browned. Add 1 tablespoon of the honey and the cinnamon; cook and stir 1 to 2 minutes longer or until almonds are glazed and golden brown. Transfer to cookie sheet; cool.

2 Meanwhile, in jar with tight-fitting lid, place remaining oil and honey, the lime peel, lime juice, mustard and salt; shake until well blended.

3 In large serving bowl, combine spinach, strawberries and grapefruit. Just before serving, drizzle dressing over salad; toss lightly to coat. Sprinkle with toasted almonds.

NUTRITION INFORMATION PER SERVING: Calories 130 • Total Fat 8g • Saturated Fat 1g • Cholesterol 0mg • Sodium 80mg • Total Carbohydrate 11g • Dietary Fiber 2g • Protein 2g. DIETARY EXCHANGES: 1/2 Fruit • 1 Vegetable • 1-1/2 Fat • 1 Carb Choices.

*cook's notes*

*To section a grapefruit, use a sharp serrated knife to remove its peel and outer membrane. Then, cut along 1 side of each section next to the dividing membrane, using the knife to help release the fruit from the membrane on the other side of the section.*

# provolone and pesto quiche

PREP TIME: 15 Minutes ✳ READY IN: 1 Hour 10 Minutes ✳ SERVINGS: 8

- 1 box Pillsbury® refrigerated pie crusts, softened as directed on box
- 2 cups shredded Provolone cheese (8 oz.)
- 3 tablespoons refrigerated pesto
- 1/4 cup grated Parmesan cheese
- 1/2 cup chopped red bell pepper
- 5 eggs
- 1-1/2 cups milk
- 1/4 teaspoon salt

1 Heat oven to 425°F. Make pie crust as directed on box for One-Crust Filled Pie using 9-inch glass pie plate. Bake 7 minutes.

2 Remove crust from oven; sprinkle 1 cup of the Provolone cheese over bottom of crust.

3 In small bowl, mix pesto and Parmesan cheese until smooth. Carefully spread over Provolone cheese. Sprinkle with bell pepper and remaining Provolone cheese.

4 In large bowl, with wire whisk, beat eggs, milk and salt until well blended. Pour over cheese.

5 Bake 7 minutes. Reduce oven temperature to 325°F. and bake 15 minutes. Cover edge of crust with foil. Bake 23 to 28 minutes longer or until set and knife inserted in center comes out clean. Let stand for 5 minutes before serving.

NUTRITION INFORMATION PER SERVING: Calories 320 • Total Fat 22g • Saturated Fat 10g • Cholesterol 160mg • Sodium 610mg • Total Carbohydrate 16g • Dietary Fiber 0g • Protein 15g. DIETARY EXCHANGES: 1 Starch • 1-1/2 High-Fat Meat • 2 Fat • 1 Carb Choice.

# ham frittata

PREP TIME: 20 Minutes ✳ READY IN: 20 Minutes ✳ SERVINGS: 4

- 1-1/2 cups frozen southern-style cubed hash brown potatoes (from 32-oz. pkg.)
- 1 medium zucchini, quartered lengthwise, then sliced (1 cup)
- 1-1/2 cups cubed cooked ham
- 4 eggs
- 1/4 cup milk
- 1/4 teaspoon salt
- 1 cup shredded Cheddar cheese (4 oz.)

1 Spray 10-inch skillet with cooking spray; heat over medium-high heat. Add potatoes, zucchini and ham; cook 5 to 8 minutes, stirring frequently, until zucchini is crisp-tender and potatoes are thoroughly cooked.

2 Meanwhile, in medium bowl, beat eggs with wire whisk. Add milk and salt; beat well.

3 Pour egg mixture over mixture in skillet. Reduce heat to medium-low. Cover; cook 5 to 7 minutes, lifting the edges occasionally to allow the uncooked egg mixture to flow to bottom of skillet, until center is set.

4 Sprinkle cheese over frittata. Cover; cook 2 to 3 minutes or until cheese is melted. To serve, cut into wedges.

NUTRITION INFORMATION PER SERVING: Calories 350 • Total Fat 18g • Saturated Fat 9g • Cholesterol 265mg • Sodium 1170mg • Total Carbohydrate 22g • Dietary Fiber 2g • Protein 25g. DIETARY EXCHANGES: 1 Starch • 1/2 Other Carbohydrate • 3 Very Lean Meat • 3 Fat • 1-1/2 Carb Choices.

provolone and pesto quiche

### cook's notes

*A microwavable slow cooker insert is one that removes from the cooking unit and is made of microwavable material such as pottery or ceramic glass. Never microwave the cooking unit part of a slow cooker.*

# southwestern brunch eggs

**PREP TIME:** 40 Minutes ✳ **READY IN:** 3 Hours 40 Minutes ✳ **SERVINGS:** 12

| | |
|---|---|
| 5 cups frozen shredded hash-brown potatoes (from 30-oz. bag) | 1/4 teaspoon pepper |
| 1 can (15 oz.) Progresso® black beans, drained, rinsed | 2 tablespoons butter or margarine |
| 16 eggs | 1 can (10-3/4 oz.) condensed cream of mushroom soup |
| 1 cup half-and-half | 2 cups shredded Colby-Monterey Jack cheese blend (8 oz.) |
| 1/2 teaspoon salt | 1 cup Old El Paso® thick 'n chunky salsa |

1 In microwavable 3- to 4-quart slow cooker insert or medium bowl, microwave potatoes on High 3 minutes 30 seconds to 4 minutes, stirring once, until thawed. Stir in beans. With back of spoon, press mixture in bottom and 2 to 3 inches up side of slow cooker; set aside.

2 In large bowl, beat eggs, half-and-half, salt and pepper with wire whisk until well blended. In 10-inch nonstick skillet, melt butter over medium heat. Add egg mixture; cook, stirring occasionally, until eggs are almost set.

3 Spoon half of egg mixture into slow cooker; top with half each of the soup, cheese and salsa. Layer with remaining egg mixture, soup, cheese and salsa.

4 Cover and cook on Low heat setting 3 to 4 hours.

NUTRITION INFORMATION PER SERVING: Calories 360 • Total Fat 19g • Saturated Fat 9g • Cholesterol 315mg • Sodium 660mg • Total Carbohydrate 29g • Dietary Fiber 4g • Protein 17g. DIETARY EXCHANGES: 2 Starch • 1-1/2 High-Fat Meat • 1 Fat • 2 Carb Choices.

# three-pepper galette

PREP TIME: 15 Minutes ✳ READY IN: 50 Minutes ✳ SERVINGS: 6

1 Pillsbury® refrigerated pie crust, softened as directed on box

1/4 medium green bell pepper, cut into 2 x 1/4-inch strips (about 1/2 cup)

1/4 medium red bell pepper, cut into 2 x 1/4-inch strips (about 1/2 cup)

1/4 medium yellow bell pepper, cut into 2 x 1/4-inch strips (about 1/2 cup)

1/3 cup milk

2 eggs

1 container (4 oz.) garlic-and-herbs spreadable cheese

1/4 cup shredded Italian cheese blend (1 oz.)

Fresh basil leaves, if desired

1 Heat oven to 400°F. Place the pie crust in a 9-inch glass pie plate. Arrange half the peppers in pie plate.

2 In small bowl, beat milk, eggs and spreadable cheese with electric mixer on low speed until well blended. Pour egg mixture over peppers in pie plate. Place remaining peppers over top of egg mixture. Fold edge of crust over filling, pleating crust slightly as necessary.

3 Bake 20 to 30 minutes or until crust is golden brown and center is set. Sprinkle with cheese blend. Bake 3 to 5 minutes longer or until cheese is melted. Sprinkle with basil. Serve immediately.

**HIGH ALTITUDE (3500-6500 FT):** Increase first bake time to 25 to 30 minutes.

NUTRITION INFORMATION PER SERVING: Calories 280 • Total Fat 12g • Saturated Fat 6g • Cholesterol 95mg • Sodium 590mg • Total Carbohydrate 33g • Dietary Fiber 0g • Protein 10g. DIETARY EXCHANGES: 1 Starch • 1 Other Carbohydrate • 1 Medium-Fat Meat • 1-1/2 Fat • 2 Carb Choices.

*cook's notes*

*Like spicy food? Chop up a jalapeño chile and add it to the filling.*

# piglets in blankets

PREP TIME: 15 Minutes ✽ READY IN: 30 Minutes ✽ SERVINGS: 8

| | |
|---|---|
| 1 can (8 oz.) Pillsbury® refrigerated crescent dinner rolls | 24 fully cooked cocktail wieners<br>Ketchup or sweet-and-sour sauce |

1 Heat oven to 375°F. Grease cookie sheet. Unroll dough; separate into 8 triangles. Cut each triangle into 3 smaller triangles.

2 Place 1 wiener on shortest side of each triangle; roll up to opposite point. Place point side down cookie sheet.

3 Bake 11 to 15 minutes or until deep golden brown. Immediately remove from cookie sheet. Serve with ketchup.

NUTRITION INFORMATION PER SERVING: Calories 200 • Total Fat 15g • Saturated Fat 5g • Cholesterol 15mg • Sodium 570mg • Total Carbohydrate 12g • Dietary Fiber 0g • Protein 5g. DIETARY EXCHANGES: 1/2 Starch • 1/2 Other Carbohydrate • 1/2 High-Fat Meat • 2 Fat • 1 Carb Choice.

# spinach-tomato frittata

PREP TIME: 20 Minutes ✽ READY IN: 35 Minutes ✽ SERVINGS: 4

| | |
|---|---|
| 6 eggs | 1/8 teaspoon ground nutmeg |
| 1/3 cup grated Parmesan cheese | 2 teaspoons olive oil |
| 1/2 teaspoon garlic powder | 6 oz. fresh spinach, stems removed, torn into bite-size pieces (about 6 cups loosely packed) |
| 1/2 teaspoon dried basil leaves | |
| 1/4 teaspoon salt | 5 to 6 cherry tomatoes, quartered |
| 1/4 teaspoon pepper | |

1 In small bowl with wire whisk or fork, beat eggs. Stir in cheese, garlic powder, basil, salt, pepper and nutmeg; set aside.

2 In 9- or 10-inch nonstick skillet with sloping sides (omelet or crepe pan), heat oil over medium heat. Add spinach; cover and cook 2 to 3 minutes, stirring once or twice and watching carefully to prevent burning, until spinach is slightly wilted (if necessary, add 2 tablespoons water if spinach becomes dry).

3 Reduce heat to low. Spread spinach evenly in skillet; top evenly with tomatoes. Pour egg mixture over top. Cover; cook 12 to 15 minutes or until bottom is lightly browned and top is set, lifting edges occasionally to allow uncooked egg mixture to flow to bottom of skillet. Cut into wedges.

NUTRITION INFORMATION PER SERVING: Calories 190 • Total Fat 13g • Saturated Fat 4.5g • Cholesterol 325mg • Sodium 430mg • Total Carbohydrate 4g • Dietary Fiber 2g • Protein 14g. DIETARY EXCHANGES: 1 Vegetable • 1-1/2 Medium-Fat Meat • 1 Fat.

# topped mini quiches

PREP TIME: 25 Minutes ✹ READY IN: 1 Hour ✹ SERVINGS: 48

### QUICHES

- 1 package (33.6 oz.) frozen Florentine or Lorraine mini quiches (48)

### CREAMY PESTO TOPPER

- 2 tablespoons cream cheese spread (from 8-oz. container)
- 2 tablespoons basil pesto
- 1 tablespoon finely chopped red bell pepper or pimiento

### RED AND GREEN TOPPER

- 3 tablespoons cream cheese spread (from 8-oz. container)
- 4 grape tomatoes, each cut into quarters
- 1 tablespoon chopped fresh parsley

### DILL-SHRIMP TOPPER

- 2 tablespoons dill dip
- 16 ready-to-eat cooked tiny shrimp (from 8-oz. bag)

1 Bake quiches as directed on package. Meanwhile, prepare ingredients for toppers.

2 For Creamy Pesto Topper, mix cream cheese and pesto; spoon about 3/4 teaspoon onto each of 16 quiches. Garnish each with bell pepper.

3 For Red and Green Topper, spoon about 1/2 teaspoon cream cheese spread onto each of 16 quiches; place 1 tomato quarter in center of each. Garnish each with parsley.

4 For Dill-Shrimp Topper, spread about 1 teaspoon dill dip on each of 16 quiches; place shrimp with tail end facing upward in center of each. Sprinkle with dill, if desired.

NUTRITION INFORMATION PER SERVING: Calories 70 • Total Fat 5g • Saturated Fat 2g • Cholesterol 25mg • Sodium 115mg • Total Carbohydrate 5g • Dietary Fiber 0g • Protein 3g. DIETARY EXCHANGES: 1/2 Starch • 1 Fat • 1/2 Carb Choice.

## kitchen tip

*If you don't want to make all three toppers, simply choose any topper and double or triple the ingredient amounts depending on how many you plan to make.*

kiwi-pineapple yogurt parfaits

# kiwi-pineapple yogurt parfaits

PREP TIME: 15 Minutes ✳ READY IN: 15 Minutes ✳ SERVINGS: 2

### GRANOLA MIXTURE

4 oats 'n honey crunchy granola bars
(2 pouches from 8.9-oz. box), broken
into pieces

12 to 14 whole macadamia nuts

### YOGURT MIXTURE

1 container (6 oz.) vanilla nonfat yogurt

1/2 cup frozen (thawed) reduced-fat whipped
topping

1 tablespoon shredded coconut

1 tablespoon finely grated white chocolate
baking bar

### FRUIT MIXTURE

1/2 cup coarsely chopped peeled kiwifruit
(1-1/2 medium)

1/2 cup drained coarsely chopped fresh
pineapple or well-drained canned pineapple
tidbits

1-1/2 teaspoons honey

### GARNISH, IF DESIRED

White chocolate baking bar curls or shavings

2 kiwifruit slices

**SHERRI KING-RODRIGUES**
Warren, Rhode Island
Bake-Off® Contest 41, 2004

1 In food processor or gallon-size resealable food-storage plastic bag, place granola bars and nuts; process or crush with meat mallet until chopped.

2 In small bowl, mix yogurt mixture ingredients; set aside. In another small bowl, gently toss fruit mixture ingredients until coated; set aside.

3 In each of 2 (12- to 14-oz) tulip-shaped parfait glasses, alternately spoon about 3 tablespoons granola mixture, 1/4 cup yogurt mixture and 1/4 cup fruit mixture; repeat layers. Top each parfait with a sprinkle of remaining granola mixture. Garnish each with white chocolate curls and kiwifruit slice if desired. Serve immediately.

NUTRITION INFORMATION PER SERVING: Calories 550 • Total Fat 24g • Saturated Fat 7g • Cholesterol 0mg • Sodium 230mg • Total Carbohydrate 72g • Dietary Fiber 6g • Protein 11g. DIETARY EXCHANGES: 3 Starch • 1 Fruit • 1 Other Carbohydrate • 4 Fat • 5 Carb Choices.

# cheesy apple chunk bagels

PREP TIME: 20 Minutes ✳ READY IN: 20 Minutes ✳ SERVINGS: 4

1/4 cup strawberry cream cheese spread

1/4 cup diced unpeeled apple

1 banana, peeled, sliced

2 whole wheat bagels, halved

1 In medium bowl, beat the cream cheese until creamy. Add the apple and the banana pieces; mix well.

2 Toast bagel halves. Spoon cream cheese mixture on each bagel half.

NUTRITION INFORMATION PER SERVING: Calories 160 • Total Fat 5g • Saturated Fat 3g • Cholesterol 15mg • Sodium 250mg • Total Carbohydrate 24g • Dietary Fiber 2g • Protein 4g. DIETARY EXCHANGES: 1 Starch • 1 Fat • 1-1/2 Carb Choices.

# Festive Cookies & Bars

*Fill your holiday* cookie platter and pack those pretty gift tins with the fun and yummy bite-size sweets in this chapter. These Christmasy goodies are irresistible!

p. 226

p. 214

p. 213

p. 221

p. 221

gingerbread
pinwheels p. 229

# almond holly wreaths

**PREP TIME:** 40 Minutes ❋ **READY IN:** 50 Minutes ❋ **SERVINGS:** 2-1/2 dozen

| | |
|---|---|
| 1 roll (16.5 oz.) Pillsbury® refrigerated sugar cookies | Granulated sugar |
| 1/4 cup all-purpose flour | 15 red gumdrops (1/2 inch) |
| 3/4 teaspoon almond extract | 8 green gumdrops (1/2 inch) |
| | Blue and green colored sugar |

1 Heat oven to 350°F. In large bowl, break up cookie dough. Stir or knead in flour and almond extract until well blended. Work with half of dough at a time; refrigerate remaining dough until needed. In cookie press fitted with 1/2-inch star template, place dough. On ungreased cookie sheets, press dough into 7-inch strips. Shape each strip into 2-inch ring, crossing ends slightly.

2 Sprinkle small amount of sugar onto flat surface. Flatten green gumdrops with thumb. Using a paring knife, cut out shapes that resemble holly leaves, two for each cookie. Sprinkle more sugar onto flat surface and flatten red gumdrops; use paring knife to cut out shapes that resemble small berries, three for each cookie. Arrange 3 red gumdrop "berries" on top of each wreath where ends cross; arrange 2 green gumdrop "leaves" next to and touching "berries" on each cookie. Press firmly into dough. Repeat with remaining dough and gumdrop pieces. Sprinkle "wreath" with colored sugar.

3 Bake 7 to 9 minutes or until edges just begin to brown. Cool 1 minute; remove from cookie sheets. Cool completely, about 10 minutes. Store in tightly covered container.

**HIGH ALTITUDE (3500-6500 FT):** Increase flour to 1/2 cup. Bake 8 to 10 minutes.

NUTRITION INFORMATION PER SERVING: Calories 100 • Total Fat 3g • Saturated Fat 1g • Cholesterol 5mg • Sodium 50mg • Total Carbohydrate 17g • Dietary Fiber 0g • Protein 0g. DIETARY EXCHANGES: 1 Other Carbohydrate • 1 Fat • 1 Carb Choice.

# macaroon-topped sugar cookies

PREP TIME: 45 Minutes ✹ READY IN: 1 Hour 15 Minutes ✹ SERVINGS: 32 cookies

1 roll (16.5 oz.) Pillsbury® refrigerated sugar cookies

1-1/2 cups coconut

1/3 cup sugar

1 tablespoon all-purpose flour

1/4 teaspoon almond extract

1 egg white

16 red or green maraschino cherries, halved, drained on paper towel

1 Place cookie dough in freezer for 30 minutes. Meanwhile, heat oven to 350°F. In medium bowl, mix coconut, sugar, flour, almond extract and egg white.

2 Cut cookie dough into 32 slices; place 2 inches apart on ungreased cookie sheets. Spoon 1 rounded teaspoon coconut mixture onto each slice, spreading slightly. Press 1 cherry half, cut-side down, on each.

3 Bake 12 to 15 minutes or until the edges are light golden brown. Cool 1 minute; remove from cookie sheets. Cool completely, about 30 minutes. Store between sheets of waxed paper in tightly covered container.

NUTRITION INFORMATION PER SERVING: Calories 100 • Total Fat 4.5g • Saturated Fat 2g • Cholesterol 10mg • Sodium 55mg • Total Carbohydrate 15g • Dietary Fiber 0g • Protein 0g. DIETARY EXCHANGES: 1 Other Carbohydrate • 1 Fat • 1 Carb Choice.

*special touch*

*Top half of the cookies with red cherries and half with green cherries for a colorful cookie tray.*

# heavenly layered bars

PREP TIME: 10 Minutes ✽ READY IN: 2 Hours 50 Minutes ✽ SERVINGS: 36 bars

1 roll (16.5 oz.) Pillsbury® refrigerated chocolate chip cookies

1/2 cup chocolate cookie crumbs

1 package (11 oz.) butterscotch chips

1-1/2 cups flaked coconut

1/2 cup chopped walnuts

1 can (14 oz.) sweetened condensed milk (not evaporated)

1 Heat oven to 350°F. Line 13 x 9-inch pan with heavy-duty foil, extending foil over sides of pan. Spray bottom and sides of foil with nonstick cooking spray or grease foil. Break up cookie dough into sprayed foil-lined pan. With floured fingers, press dough evenly in bottom of pan to form crust.

2 Sprinkle cookie crumbs evenly over crust. Top evenly with butterscotch chips, coconut and walnuts. Drizzle sweetened condensed milk over top.

3 Bake 30 to 40 minutes or until edges are golden brown. (Center will not be set.) Cool about 2 hours or until completely cooled. Use foil to lift bars from pan. Cut into bars.

NUTRITION INFORMATION PER SERVING: Calories 190 • Total Fat 9g • Saturated Fat 5g • Cholesterol 5mg • Sodium 95mg • Total Carbohydrate 24g • Dietary Fiber 0g • Protein 3g. DIETARY EXCHANGES: 1 Starch • 1/2 Other Carbohydrate • 2 Fat • 1-1/2 Carb Choices.

## Kitchen tip

*An offset spatula works great for frosting cookies and cakes. It has a long, thin blade with a slight bend in it. This inexpensive tool would make a great gift or stocking stuffer for a friend who likes to bake.*

# ginger sandwich cookies

PREP TIME: 1 Hour 20 Minutes ✽ READY IN: 2 Hours 20 Minutes ✽ SERVINGS: 3 dozen

### COOKIES

1/2 cup molasses

3/4 cup granulated sugar

1/2 cup butter, softened

2 cups all-purpose flour

2 teaspoons pumpkin pie spice

1/2 teaspoon baking soda

1/4 teaspoon salt

1 egg

### FROSTING

1/4 cup butter, softened

2 cups powdered sugar

2 to 3 tablespoons milk

1 In 2-quart saucepan, heat molasses to boiling over medium heat, stirring frequently. Remove from heat. With wooden spoon, stir in granulated sugar and 1/2 cup butter. Stir in flour, pumpkin pie spice, baking soda, salt and egg until well mixed. Remove dough from saucepan; wrap tightly in plastic wrap. Refrigerate dough 1 hour for easier handling.

2 Heat oven to 350°F. Lightly grease cookie sheets. On floured surface, roll half of dough at a time to 1/8-inch thickness. (Keep remaining dough refrigerated.) Cut with 2-1/2 to 3-inch cookie cutters in desired shapes. Cut an equal number of corresponding 1-inch cookies with canapé cutter or small cookie cutter. Place large and small cookies 1-inch apart on cookie sheets.

3 Bake 8 to 12 minutes or until set and edges start to brown. Remove from cookie sheets to cooling racks. Cool completely, about 15 minutes.

4 In small bowl with wooden spoon, beat all frosting ingredients, adding enough milk for desired spreading consistency. Frost large cookies. Place a small cookie in center over frosting; gently press together.

**HIGH ALTITUDE (3500-6500 FT):** Bake 8 to 10 minutes.

NUTRITION INFORMATION PER SERVING: Calories 120 • Total Fat 4g • Saturated Fat 2.5g • Cholesterol 15mg • Sodium 65mg • Total Carbohydrate 20g • Dietary Fiber 0g • Protein 0g. DIETARY EXCHANGES: 1 Other Carbohydrate • 1 Fat • 1 Carb Choice.

heavenly layered bars

**SITA WILLIAMS**
Blacksburg, Virginia
Bake-Off® Contest 41, 2004

*cook's notes*

*This sweet cookie recipe*

*starts with convenient*

*Pillsbury® refrigerated sugar*

*cookies and finishes with*

*luscious frosting, crunchy*

*granola and holiday-colored*

*gumdrops. Change the*

*gumdrop colors to suit*

*another holiday or*

*your mood!*

# monkey cereal bars

**PREP TIME:** 15 Minutes ✳ **READY IN:** 45 Minutes ✳ **SERVINGS:** 12

| | |
|---|---|
| 1 cup coarsely chopped walnuts | 2 tablespoons unsweetened baking cocoa |
| 1/4 cup flaked coconut | 6 cups Cocoa Puffs® cereal |
| 1/4 cup butter or margarine | 1 cup coarsely crushed dried banana chips |
| 1 bag (10 oz.) marshmallows | |

1 Heat oven to 350°F. Spray 13 x 9-inch pan with cooking spray. On ungreased cookie sheet with sides, bake walnuts 5 minutes.

2 Remove cookie sheet from oven. Stir coconut into walnuts. Return to oven; bake 4 to 6 minutes or until coconut is light golden brown, stirring twice during baking. Set aside to cool.

3 In 4-quart saucepan or Dutch oven, melt butter over medium heat. Add marshmallows and cook 4 to 6 minutes, stirring constantly, until melted. Stir in cocoa until well blended. Remove from heat.

4 Stir in cereal, banana chips, toasted walnuts and coconut until evenly coated; pour into pan. Spread mixture evenly, pressing down slightly. Cool 30 minutes. Cut into bars.

NUTRITION INFORMATION PER SERVING: Calories 295 • Total Fat 14g • Saturated Fat 5g • Cholesterol 10mg • Sodium 130mg • Total Carbohydrate 39g • Dietary Fiber 2g • Protein 3g. DIETARY EXCHANGES:1 Starch • 1-1/2 Other Carbohydrate • 3 Fat • 2-1/2 Carb Choices.

# tropical cheesecake bars

PREP TIME: 15 Minutes ✳ READY IN: 2 Hours 35 Minutes ✳ SERVINGS: 36 bars

**CRUST**
1 roll (16.5 oz.) Pillsbury® refrigerated sugar cookies

**FILLING**
1 package (8 oz.) cream cheese, softened
1/2 cup sugar

1 teaspoon grated lemon peel
1 tablespoon lemon juice

**TOPPING**
1/2 cup pineapple ice cream topping
1/4 cup shredded coconut
2 tablespoons chopped pecans

1 Heat oven to 350°F. Cut cookie dough into 1/2-inch-thick slices; arrange in bottom of ungreased 13 x 9-inch pan. Press dough evenly in pan to form crust.

2 Bake 14 to 19 minutes or until cookie dough is golden brown. Cool completely on wire rack, about 1 hour.

3 In small bowl with electric mixer, beat all filling ingredients on medium speed until smooth. Spread over cooled crust.

4 Spoon and gently spread pineapple topping over filling. Sprinkle evenly with coconut and pecans. Refrigerate until firm, about 1 hour. Cut into bars.

NUTRITION INFORMATION PER SERVING: Calories 115 • Total Fat 5g • Saturated Fat 2g • Cholesterol 5mg • Sodium 70mg • Total Carbohydrate 16g • Dietary Fiber 0g • Protein 1g. DIETARY EXCHANGES: 1 Other Carbohydrate • 1 Fat • 1 Carb Choice.

## *kitchen tip*

*Want to soften the cream cheese quickly? Do it in the microwave. Unwrap the cream cheese and place it in a microwavable dish. Microwave on Low for 30 to 60 seconds just until softened. Check with a spoon or rubber spatula every 15 seconds so the cheese doesn't start to cook.*

# candy bar-frosted chippers

PREP TIME: 45 Minutes ✳ READY IN: 45 Minutes ✳ SERVINGS: 20 cookies

1 roll (16.5 oz.) Pillsbury® refrigerated chocolate chip cookies
3 Milky Way® original candy bars (2.05 oz. each), unwrapped, chopped

1/4 cup margarine or butter
1 tablespoon milk
1 cup powdered sugar

1 Heat oven to 350°F. Shape cookie dough into 20 (1-1/4 inch) balls; place 2 inches apart on ungreased cookie sheets.

2 Bake 10 to 15 minutes or until light golden brown. Cool 2 minutes; remove from cookie sheets. Cool 15 minutes or until completely cooled.

3 Meanwhile, in small saucepan, combine 2 of the chopped candy bars and margarine. Cook over low heat for 2 to 3 minutes or until melted and smooth, stirring frequently. Remove from heat. Add milk and powdered sugar; beat until smooth.

4 Frost cooled cookies with warm frosting. Immediately sprinkle remaining chopped candy bar over frosted cookies; press lightly into frosting.

NUTRITION INFORMATION PER SERVING: Calories 200 • Total Fat 10g • Saturated Fat 4g • Cholesterol 10mg • Sodium 110mg • Total Carbohydrate 26g • Dietary Fiber 0g • Protein 1g. DIETARY EXCHANGES: 1/2 Starch • 1 Other Carbohydrate • 2 Carb Choices.

JENNIFER MEYER
Elmwood Park, Illinois
Bake-Off® Contest 39, 2000

# cinnamon-toffee pecan cookies

PREP TIME: 50 Minutes ✹ READY IN: 50 Minutes ✹ SERVINGS: 24 cookies

1 roll (16.5 oz.) Pillsbury® refrigerated sugar cookies
2 teaspoons ground cinnamon
1/2 teaspoon ground nutmeg

2 teaspoons vanilla
3/4 cup chopped pecans
1/2 cup toffee bits

1 Heat oven to 350°F. Spray cookie sheets with nonstick cooking spray. Break up cookie dough into large bowl. Add cinnamon, nutmeg and vanilla; mix well. Stir in pecans and toffee bits.

2 Drop dough by heaping teaspoonfuls 3 inches apart onto sprayed cookie sheets.

3 Bake 11 to 14 minutes or until the edges are golden brown. Cool 3 minutes; remove from the cookie sheets.

NUTRITION INFORMATION PER SERVING: Calories 180 • Total Fat 9g • Saturated Fat 3g • Cholesterol 10mg • Sodium 90mg • Total Carbohydrate 21g • Dietary Fiber 0g • Protein 1g. DIETARY EXCHANGES: 1/2 Starch • 1 Other Carbohydrate • 2 Fat • 1-1/2 Carb Choices.

# sugar cookie shortcake

PREP TIME: 25 Minutes ✳ READY IN: 2 Hours 10 Minutes ✳ SERVINGS: 10

1  roll (16.5 oz.) Pillsbury® refrigerated sugar cookies, well chilled

2  tablespoons sugar

1  lb. fresh strawberries

1  box (4-serving size) vanilla instant pudding and pie filling mix

1  cup cold milk

3/4  cup whipping cream

10  whole strawberries, if desired

1  Heat oven to 350°F. Line 2 (9-inch) round cake pans with foil so edges extend over sides of pans. Cut cookie dough in half. Press half of dough in bottom of each pan. Sprinkle each cookie layer with 1 tablespoon sugar. Bake about 20 minutes or until light golden brown. Cool in pans on cooling racks 10 minutes.

2  Use the foil to lift the cookie layers from the pans; place on cooling racks. Cool completely, about 20 minutes.

3  Meanwhile, slice 1 lb. strawberries; set aside. In small bowl, beat pudding mix and milk with wire whisk about 2 minutes or until thickened. In another small bowl with electric mixer, beat the whipping cream until stiff peaks form. Fold the whipped cream into the pudding mixture. Reserve 1/2 cup mixture for garnish.

4  Remove foil from cookie layers. Place 1 layer on serving plate. Spread with half of the pudding mixture; top with half of the sliced strawberries. Place second cookie layer on strawberries; top with remaining pudding mixture and sliced strawberries.

5  Spoon reserved pudding mixture onto center of shortcake. Arrange whole strawberries on top. Refrigerate at least 1 hour before serving. Cut into wedges to serve.

NUTRITION INFORMATION PER SERVING: Calories 350 • Total Fat 17g • Saturated Fat 7g • Cholesterol 40mg • Sodium 300mg • Total Carbohydrate 47g • Dietary Fiber 1g • Protein 3g. DIETARY EXCHANGES: 1 Starch • 2 Other Carbohydrate • 3 Fat • 3 Carb Choices.

*cook's notes*

*This recipe could easily use multiple varieties of berries. Use 2 cups sliced strawberries, 1 cup blueberries and 1 cup raspberries for the 1 pound of strawberries.*

chocolate chip-almond-cherry cups

# chocolate chip-almond-cherry cups

PREP TIME: 45 Minutes ❋ READY IN: 1 Hour 45 Minutes ❋ SERVINGS: 48 cookies

1 roll (16.5 oz.) Pillsbury® refrigerated chocolate chip cookies
1/2 cup almond paste, crumbled
1/2 cup dried cherries
1/2 cup cherry preserves

**ICING**
1 cup powdered sugar
1/4 teaspoon almond extract
4 to 5 teaspoons milk
Powdered sugar, if desired

1 Heat oven to 350°F. Grease 48 miniature muffin cups with shortening; lightly flour. In large bowl, break up cookie dough. With hands, knead in almond paste and cherries.

2 Divide dough into 48 pieces. Shape each piece into ball; place in muffin cup. With thumb, make indentation in center of each.

3 Bake 6 to 8 minutes or until edges are golden brown. Cool in pan on cooling rack 5 minutes. Run knife around edge of cookie to loosen; cool 1 to 2 minutes longer. Remove from muffin cups; place on cooling rack to cool. Spoon 1/2 teaspoon preserves into each cooled cup.

4 In small bowl, mix the powdered sugar, almond extract and enough milk for a desired drizzling consistency; blend until smooth. Drizzle over cookies; let stand until set, about 30 minutes. Sprinkle with powdered sugar.

**HIGH ALTITUDE (3500-6500 FT):** Bake 10 to 12 minutes.

NUTRITION INFORMATION PER SERVING: Calories 80 • Total Fat 2.5g • Saturated Fat 0.5g • Cholesterol 0mg • Sodium 30mg • Total Carbohydrate 13g • Dietary Fiber 0g • Protein 0g. DIETARY EXCHANGES: 1 Other Carbohydrate • 1/2 Fat • 1 Carb Choice.

*special touch*

*For extra appeal, simply tint the glaze with a few drops of red food color. When set, drizzle with a little additional white glaze.*

# brickle bars

PREP TIME: 10 Minutes ❋ READY IN: 1 Hour 20 Minutes ❋ SERVINGS: 36

**BARS**
1/2 cup granulated sugar
1/2 cup packed brown sugar
1/2 cup butter or margarine, softened
2 teaspoons vanilla
2 eggs
1-1/2 cups all-purpose flour
2 teaspoons baking powder
1/4 teaspoon salt
1/2 cup toffee bits

**TOPPING**
3/4 cup semisweet chocolate chips
1/3 cup toffee bits

1 Heat oven to 350°F. Grease 13 x 9-inch pan with shortening. In large bowl with electric mixer, beat granulated sugar, brown sugar and butter on medium speed until well blended. Beat in vanilla and eggs until light and fluffy. On low speed, beat in flour, baking powder and salt until dough forms. With spoon, stir in 1/2 cup toffee bits. Spread in pan.

2 Bake 20 to 25 minutes or until golden brown and toothpick inserted in center comes out clean.

3 Remove pan from oven. Immediately sprinkle with chocolate chips; let stand 1 minute. Spread melted chips over bars. Sprinkle 1/3 cup toffee bits evenly over the top. Cool completely, about 45 minutes. Cut into bars. Store bars, in a single layer, in an airtight container.

NUTRITION INFORMATION PER SERVING: Calories 110 • Total Fat 5g • Saturated Fat 3g • Cholesterol 20mg • Sodium 70mg • Total Carbohydrate 15g • Dietary Fiber 0g • Protein 1g. DIETARY EXCHANGES: 1 Other Carbohydrate • 1 Fat • 1 Carb Choice.

# thumbprint heart sugar cookies

PREP TIME: 1 Hour ✳ READY IN: 1 Hour 30 Minutes ✳ SERVINGS: 32 cookies

1 roll (16.5 oz.) Pillsbury® refrigerated sugar cookies

1 egg yolk

10 drops red food color

1/4 cup sugar

Red decorating icing (from a tube)

1 Freeze cookie dough for 30 minutes. Heat oven to 350°F.

2 Beat the egg yolk with a fork. Add 10 drops of red food color to the beaten yolk; mix well.

3 Remove cookie dough from freezer; remove wrapper. Cut dough into 1/4-inch-thick slices; place on ungreased cookie sheets about 2 inches apart.

4 Dip your thumb or finger into egg mixture. Press thumb with red color onto each cookie at an angle twice to make a heart shape. Sprinkle a little sugar on each cookie.

5 Bake 7 to 11 minutes or until the edges are light golden brown. Cool 1 minute; remove from cookie sheets. With icing, write names or messages on cookies.

NUTRITION INFORMATION PER SERVING: Calories 110 • Total Fat 3.5g • Saturated Fat 2g • Cholesterol 5mg • Sodium 55mg • Total Carbohydrate 19g • Dietary Fiber 0g • Protein 0g. DIETARY EXCHANGES: 1 Starch • 1/2 Fat • 1 Carb Choice.

## kitchen tip

For easy removal and cutting, line the pan with foil, extending the foil over the sides of the pan.

# no-bake cereal bars

PREP TIME: 25 Minutes ✳ READY IN: 55 Minutes ✳ SERVINGS: 36

1 cup light corn syrup

1 cup sugar

1-1/4 cups creamy peanut butter

6 cups Cheerios® cereal

1 bag (12 oz.) semisweet chocolate chips (2 cups)

1 Lightly butter 13 x 9-inch pan. In 4- to 5-quart Dutch oven, heat corn syrup and sugar to boiling over medium-high heat, stirring constantly. Cook until sugar is dissolved; remove from heat. Add 1 cup of peanut butter; stir until smooth. Add cereal; mix well. Immediately press in buttered pan.

2 In 2-quart saucepan over low heat, melt chocolate chips with remaining 1/4 cup peanut butter, stirring constantly. Spread evenly over bars. Refrigerate about 30 minutes or cool completely at room temperature until chocolate is set. Cut into 9 rows by 4 rows.

NUTRITION INFORMATION PER SERVING: Calories 180 • Total Fat 8g • Saturated Fat 2.5g • Cholesterol 0mg • Sodium 85mg • Total Carbohydrate 24g • Dietary Fiber 1g • Protein 3g. DIETARY EXCHANGES: 1 Starch • 1/2 Other Carbohydrate • 1-1/2 Fat • 1-1/2 Carb Choices.

# lemon-ginger thumbprints

PREP TIME: 45 Minutes ✷ READY IN: 45 Minutes ✷ SERVINGS: 3 dozen cookies

1  roll (16.5 oz.) Pillsbury® refrigerated
   gingerbread cookies

3  tablespoons graham cracker crumbs

1/2  cup lemon curd or lemon pie filling

1   Heat oven to 350°F. Cut cookie dough into 3 equal pieces. Work with 1 piece of dough at a time; refrigerate remaining dough until ready to use.

2   Place graham cracker crumbs in shallow dish. Shape each piece of dough into 12 (1-inch) balls; roll in crumbs to coat. Place 1 inch apart on ungreased large cookie sheet.

3   Bake at 350°F. for 8 to 11 minutes or until cookies are almost set. Cool 2 minutes on cookie sheet. With thumb or handle of wooden spoon, make slight indentation in center of each cookie. Remove cookies from cookie sheet. Cool 15 minutes or until completely cooled.

4   Place lemon curd in small resealable food storage plastic bag; partially seal bag. Cut small hole in bottom corner of bag. Squeeze bag to pipe small dollop of lemon curd into indentation in each cookie. Store cookies in refrigerator.

NUTRITION INFORMATION PER SERVING: Calories 65 • Total Fat 3g • Saturated Fat 1g • Cholesterol 5mg • Sodium 60mg • Total Carbohydrate 11g • Dietary Fiber 1g • Protein 1g. DIETARY EXCHANGES: 1/2 Starch • 1/2 Fat • 1 Carb Choice.

*special touch*

*For an elegant presentation, cut the brownies into squares, arrange on a pretty doily-lined platter and garnish with fresh strawberries.*

# double chocolate-caramel-fudge brownies

PREP TIME: 30 Minutes ✳ READY IN: 3 Hours ✳ SERVINGS: 24

**FILLING**
- 1 package (14 oz.) caramels, unwrapped
- 1/2 cup evaporated milk

**BROWNIES**
- 1 cup butter
- 2 cups sugar
- 2 teaspoons vanilla
- 4 eggs, slightly beaten

- 1-1/4 cups all-purpose flour
- 3/4 cup unsweetened baking cocoa
- 1/4 teaspoon salt
- 1 package (11.5 or 12 oz.) semisweet chocolate chunks (2 cups)
- 1-1/2 cups chopped pecans
- 1 teaspoon oil

1 Heat oven to 350°F. Grease 13 x 9-inch pan. In small saucepan, cook caramels and milk over low heat until caramels are melted and smooth, stirring frequently.

2 In medium saucepan, melt butter over low heat. Remove from heat. Stir in sugar, vanilla and eggs. Stir in the flour, cocoa and salt until well blended. Stir in 1-1/2 cups of the chocolate chunks and 1 cup of the pecans. Spoon and spread batter in pan.

3 Gently and evenly drizzle caramel filling over batter to prevent large pockets of caramel and to prevent caramel from reaching bottom of bars. (Caramel can cover entire surface of batter.)

4 Bake 35 to 40 minutes or until set.

5 In small saucepan, melt remaining 1/2 cup chocolate chunks with oil over low heat, stirring until smooth. Drizzle over warm brownies. Sprinkle with remaining 1/2 cup pecans; press in lightly. Cool 20 minutes. Refrigerate 1 hour 30 minutes or until the chocolate is set. Cut into squares. If refrigerated longer, let stand at room temperature for 20 minutes before serving.

NUTRITION INFORMATION PER SERVING: Calories 395 • Total Fat 21g • Saturated Fat 10g • Cholesterol 60mg • Sodium 130mg • Total Carbohydrate 47g • Dietary Fiber 3g • Protein 5g. DIETARY EXCHANGES: 1 Starch • 2 Fruit • 3 Other Carbohydrate • 4 Fat • 3 Carb Choices.

# polvorones cookies

PREP TIME: 10 Minutes ✳ READY IN: 21 Minutes ✳ SERVINGS: 22

- 1 roll (16.5 oz.) Pillsbury® refrigerated sugar cookies
- 1/2 cup all-purpose flour
- 1/2 cup powdered sugar or 2 tablespoons colored sugar

1 Heat the oven to 350°F. Meanwhile, in large bowl, stir together cookie dough and flour. Shape dough by rounded tablespoonfuls into balls; roll balls in sugar.

2 On ungreased cookie sheet, place balls 2 inches apart. Press bottom of drinking glass on each ball until about 1/4 inch thick.

3 Bake 9 to 11 minutes or until light golden brown. Immediately sprinkle with additional sugar. Cool 1 minute; remove from cookie sheet to wire rack. Store loosely covered. Do not stack cookies.

**HIGH ALTITUDE (3500-6500 FT):** Bake 10-12 min.

NUTRITION INFORMATION PER SERVING: Calories 120 • Total Fat 4.5g • Saturated Fat 1g • Cholesterol 5mg • Sodium 60mg • Total Carbohydrate 19g • Dietary Fiber 0g • Protein 1g. DIETARY EXCHANGES: 1/2 Starch • 1/2 Other Carbohydrate • 1 Fat • 1 Carb Choice.

# cherry chocolate blossoms

PREP TIME: 45 Minutes ✳ READY IN: 45 Minutes ✳ SERVINGS: 48 cookies

- 1 cup powdered sugar
- 1 cup butter or margarine, softened
- 2 teaspoons maraschino cherry liquid
- 1/2 teaspoon almond extract
- 3 to 4 drops red food color
- 2-1/4 cups all-purpose flour
- 1/2 teaspoon salt
- 1/2 cup maraschino cherries, drained, chopped
- 48 milk chocolate cone-shaped candies, unwrapped

1 Heat oven to 350°F. In large bowl, combine powdered sugar, butter, cherry liquid, almond extract and food color; blend well. Add flour and salt; mix well. Stir in cherries.

2 Shape dough into 1-inch balls. Place 2 inches apart on ungreased cookie sheets.

3 Bake at 350°F. for 8 to 10 minutes or until edges are light golden brown. Immediately top each cookie with one candy, pressing down firmly. Remove from cookie sheets.

NUTRITION INFORMATION PER SERVING: Calories 90 • Total Fat 5g • Saturated Fat 3g • Cholesterol 10mg • Sodium 65mg • Total Carbohydrate 11g • Dietary Fiber 0g • Protein 1g. DIETARY EXCHANGES: 1/2 Starch • 1/2 Other Carbohydrate • 1 Fat .

# marshmallow peanut blossoms

**PREP TIME:** 20 Minutes ✳ **READY IN:** 35 Minutes ✳ **SERVINGS:** 36

| | |
|---|---|
| 1 roll (16.5 oz.) Pillsbury® refrigerated peanut butter cookies | 18 large marshmallows |
| 3 tablespoons sugar | 1 tablespoon Christmas candy decors |

1 Heat oven to 375°F. Shape dough into 36 (1-inch) balls; roll in sugar. On ungreased cookie sheets, place balls 2 inches apart.

2 Bake 7 to 9 minutes or until edges are golden brown. Meanwhile, using serrated knife, cut the marshmallows in half; dip uncut edge of each into water, then in candy decors. Immediately top each hot cookie with 1 marshmallow, candy decors-side up, pressing down firmly.

3 Remove from cookie sheets to cooling racks. Cool completely before storing.

**HIGH ALTITUDE (3500-6500 FT):** In large bowl, break up cookie dough. Stir or knead 2 tablespoons all-purpose flour into dough until well blended.

NUTRITION INFORMATION PER SERVING: Calories 70 • Total Fat 2.5g • Saturated Fat 0.5g • Cholesterol 0mg • Sodium 65mg • Total Carbohydrate 11g • Dietary Fiber 0g • Protein 0g. DIETARY EXCHANGES: 1 Other Carbohydrate • 1/2 Fat • 1 Carb Choices.

# chocolate-almond layered hearts

**PREP TIME:** 1 Hour ✳ **READY IN:** 1 Hour 40 Minutes ✳ **SERVINGS:** 2-1/2 dozen

| | |
|---|---|
| 1 roll (16.5 oz.) Pillsbury® refrigerated sugar cookies | 1/2 teaspoon almond extract |
| 2 tablespoons all-purpose flour | 2 tablespoons unsweetened baking cocoa |
| 1/4 cup finely chopped almonds | 1/2 cup semisweet chocolate chips |
| | 1/2 teaspoon vegetable oil |

1 Heat oven to 350°F. Remove 2/3 of the cookie dough from wrapper and place in medium bowl; refrigerate remaining dough until needed. Stir or knead flour, almonds and almond extract into dough in bowl until well blended.

2 On floured surface with rolling pin, roll dough to 1/4-inch thickness (about 12-inch round). Cut with floured 2-1/2-inch heart-shaped cookie cutter; place on ungreased cookie sheets.

3 Bake 7 to 9 minutes or until the edges are light golden brown. Cool 1 minute and remove from the cookie sheet.

4 Meanwhile, in small bowl, place remaining 1/3 of dough. Stir or knead in cocoa until well blended. On floured surface, roll dough to 1/4-inch thickness (about 8-inch round). Cut with floured 1-inch heart-shaped cookie cutter; place on ungreased large cookie sheet.

5 Bake 5 to 6 minutes or just until set. Cool 1 minute; remove from cookie sheet.

6 In small microwavable bowl, microwave chocolate chips and oil on High 30 seconds; stir. Microwave 10 to 15 seconds longer until smooth. Place melted chocolate in small resealable food-storage plastic bag; seal bag. Cut 1/8-inch hole in bottom corner of bag.

7 Squeeze the bag to pipe a small amount of chocolate on the center of each large heart cookie. Top each with 1 small heart cookie. Drizzle remaining melted chocolate over layered cookies. Let stand until the chocolate is set, about 40 minutes. Store between sheets of waxed paper in a tightly covered container.

**HIGH ALTITUDE (3500-6500 FT):** In Step 3, bake 8 to 10 minutes.

NUTRITION INFORMATION PER SERVING: Calories 100 • Total Fat 4.5g • Saturated Fat 1.5g • Cholesterol 5mg • Sodium 45mg • Total Carbohydrate 13g • Dietary Fiber 0g • Protein 1g. DIETARY EXCHANGES: 1 Other Carbohydrate • 1 Fat • 1 Carb Choice.

marshmallow peanut blossoms

### cook's notes

*In this recipe, butter is necessary to obtain the browned butter flavor. Margarine will not provide the same flavor and will burn quickly.*

# quick cashew cookies
# with brown butter icing

PREP TIME: 40 Minutes ✻ READY IN: 40 Minutes ✻ SERVINGS: 2-1/2 dozen

### COOKIES

- 1 roll (16.5 oz.) Pillsbury® refrigerated sugar cookies
- 3/4 cup coarsely chopped cashews
- 1/2 cup white chocolate chunks or white vanilla baking chips

### ICING

- 1/3 cup butter (do not use margarine)
- 1-1/2 cups powdered sugar
- 1/4 teaspoon vanilla
- 2 tablespoons milk

1 Heat oven to 350°F. In large bowl, break up cookie dough. Stir in cashews and white chocolate chunks. Drop dough by heaping teaspoonfuls onto ungreased cookie sheets.

2 Bake 9 to 12 minutes or until golden brown. Immediately remove from cookie sheets; place on wire racks.

3 While cookies are baking, in 1-quart saucepan, cook butter over medium heat, stirring constantly, until light golden brown. Remove from heat. Stir in remaining icing ingredients until smooth.

4 On top of warm cookies, immediately spoon about 1 teaspoon icing (if icing becomes too thick, reheat over low heat).

**HIGH ALTITUDE (3500-6500 FT):** Bake 10 to 13 minutes.

NUTRITION INFORMATION PER SERVING: Calories 160 • Total Fat 8g • Saturated Fat 3g • Cholesterol 10mg • Sodium 65mg • Total Carbohydrate 20g • Dietary Fiber 0g • Protein 1g. DIETARY EXCHANGES: 1/2 Starch • 1 Other Carbohydrate • 1-1/2 Fat • 1 Carb Choice.

# lemon-glazed pistachio bars

PREP TIME: 20 Minutes ❋ READY IN: 1 Hour 20 Minutes ❋ SERVINGS: 36 bars

**BARS**

- 1 roll (16.5 oz.) Pillsbury® refrigerated sugar cookies
- 1/4 cup finely chopped pistachio nuts
- 1 tablespoon grated lemon peel
- 1 tablespoon fresh lemon juice
- 2 tablespoons all-purpose flour

**GLAZE AND GARNISH**

- 1 cup powdered sugar
- 2 to 3 tablespoons fresh lemon juice
- 1 tablespoon finely chopped pistachio nuts, if desired

1 Heat oven to 350°F. (325°F. for dark pan). Line 13 x 9-inch pan with foil, extending foil over sides of pan; spray foil with cooking spray.

2 In large bowl, break up cookie dough. Stir or knead in 1/4 cup nuts, the lemon peel, 1 tablespoon lemon juice and the flour until well blended. Place dough in pan; with floured fingers, press dough evenly in pan.

3 Bake 17 to 21 minutes or until light golden brown. Cool completely, about 30 minutes.

4 In small bowl, mix powdered sugar and 2 to 3 tablespoons lemon juice until smooth and desired consistency. Spread glaze evenly over bars. Sprinkle with 1 tablespoon nuts. Let stand until glaze is set, about 10 minutes.

5 Use foil to lift bars from pan. Cut into 6 rows by 6 rows. Store in tightly covered container.

**HIGH ALTITUDE (3500-6500 FT):** Heat oven to 375°F.

NUTRITION INFORMATION PER SERVING: Calories 80 • Total Fat 3g • Saturated Fat 0.5g • Cholesterol 0mg • Sodium 40mg • Total Carbohydrate 12g • Dietary Fiber 0g • Protein 0g. DIETARY EXCHANGES: 1 Other Carbohydrate • 1/2 Fat • 1 Carb Choice.

*special touch*

*For a special occasion, cut these lemony bars into small squares and serve them in foil or paper candy cups.*

# hidden marshmallow chippers

PREP TIME: 45 Minutes ✳ READY IN: 45 Minutes ✳ SERVINGS: 32 cookies

1 roll (16.5 oz.) Pillsbury® refrigerated chocolate chip cookies

16 regular marshmallows

8 oz. chocolate-flavored candy coating, chopped

1. Heat oven to 350°F. Shape cookie dough into 32 (1-inch) balls; place 2 inches apart on ungreased cookie sheets.

2. Bake 9 to 13 minutes or until edges are light golden brown. Meanwhile, cut each marshmallow in half crosswise with kitchen scissors.

3. Remove partially baked cookies from oven. Immediately place 1 half marshmallow, cut side down, on top of each hot cookie. Return to oven; bake an additional 1 to 2 minutes or just until the marshmallows begin to puff. Cool 2 minutes; remove from the cookie sheets. With fingers, gently flatten marshmallows.

4. Melt the candy coating as directed on package. Spoon about 1 teaspoon candy coating over the marshmallow on each cookie, swirling with back of spoon to nearly cover marshmallow.

NUTRITION INFORMATION PER SERVING: Calories 135 • Total Fat 6g • Saturated Fat 2g • Cholesterol 0mg • Sodium 65mg • Total Carbohydrate 18g • Dietary Fiber 0g • Protein 2g. DIETARY EXCHANGES: 1 Starch • 1 Fat • 1 Carb Choice.

# cherry-chocolate chip cookies

PREP TIME: 50 Minutes ✳ READY IN: 1 Hour 10 Minutes ✳ SERVINGS: 32 cookies

1 roll (16.5 oz.) Pillsbury® refrigerated chocolate chip cookies

3 tablespoons all-purpose flour

8 oz. chocolate-flavored candy coating, chopped

1 aerosol can (6.4 oz.) white decorating icing

2 jars (10 oz. each) maraschino cherries with stems, drained on paper towels

1. Heat oven to 350°F. In large bowl, break up cookie dough. Stir or knead in flour until well blended. Work with half of dough at a time; refrigerate remaining dough until needed.

2. Shape dough into 16 (1-inch) balls; place 2 inches apart on ungreased cookie sheets. Repeat with remaining dough.

3. Bake 8 to 12 minutes or until light golden brown. Cool 1 minute; remove from cookie sheets. Cool completely, about 15 minutes.

4. Meanwhile, in small microwavable bowl, microwave candy coating on High 30 seconds. Stir and microwave in 15-second increments until melted and smooth. Set aside.

5. With can of decorating icing fitted with star tip, pipe 1-inch star of icing (about 1 teaspoon) on center of each cookie. Dip cherries into melted chocolate; place on white icing on cookies. Let stand until icing is set and chocolate is firm, about 20 minutes. Store between sheets of waxed paper in tightly covered container.

**HIGH ALTITUDE (3500-6500 FT):** Bake 9 to 13 minutes.

NUTRITION INFORMATION PER SERVING: Calories 140 • Total Fat 5g • Saturated Fat 2.5g • Cholesterol 5mg • Sodium 45mg • Total Carbohydrate 23g • Dietary Fiber 0g • Protein 0g. DIETARY EXCHANGES: 1-1/2 Other Carbohydrate • 1 Fat • 1-1/2 Carb Choices.

*cook's notes*

*Maraschino cherries without stems can be used in place of the cherries with stems.*

# caramel and nut diamond delights

PREP TIME: 25 Minutes ✳ READY IN: 1 Hour 15 Minutes ✳ Servings: 20

## BASE
- 1 cup all purpose flour
- 1/2 cup firmly packed brown sugar
- 4 teaspoons cornstarch
- 1/2 cup margarine or butter, chilled
- 1/3 cup finely chopped toasted hazelnuts (filberts)
- 1/2 teaspoon vanilla

## TOPPING
- 1 oz. semisweet chocolate
- 20 pecan halves (about 1/2 cup)
- 8 vanilla caramels, unwrapped
- 1-1/2 teaspoons water

1 Heat oven to 350°F. Line 8-inch square pan with foil so edges extend over pan.

2 Lightly spoon flour into measuring cup; level off. In medium bowl, combine flour, brown sugar and cornstarch; mix well. With pastry blender or fork, cut in margarine until mixture resembles coarse crumbs. Stir in hazelnuts and vanilla. Press evenly in bottom of foil-lined pan.

3 Bake at 20 to 25 minutes or until golden brown. Cool in pan 2 minutes.

4 Remove bars from pan by lifting foil. Immediately cut into 6 strips. Cut once diagonally from 1 corner to opposite corner. Make 3 parallel cuts on each side of diagonal cut, forming diamond shapes. (Some end pieces will be incomplete diamonds.) Cool on foil for 20 minutes or until completely cooled.

5 Meanwhile, in small saucepan, melt chocolate over low heat, stirring constantly until smooth. Dip half of each pecan half in melted chocolate; place on waxed paper-lined cookie sheet. Refrigerate 5 minutes or until chocolate is set.

6 In another small saucepan, combine caramels and water; cook over low heat until caramels are melted and mixture is smooth, stirring constantly.

7 To assemble bars, remove cooled bars from foil; place on waxed paper-lined cookie sheet. Spoon 1/2 teaspoon melted caramel in center of each bar. (If melted caramel runs off first bar, wait 1 to 2 minutes for caramel to thicken before continuing.) Top with 1 chocolate-coated pecan half.

*Kitchen tip*

To melt the chocolate, microwave in a small microwave-safe bowl on High for 30 seconds; stir, then microwave again for 30 seconds. Stir until melted and smooth. To melt the caramels, place in a small microwave-safe bowl with the water and microwave on High for 25 seconds; stir, then microwave again 20 seconds. Stir until smooth.

NUTRITION INFORMATION PER SERVING: Calories 130 • Total Fat 7g • Saturated Fat 1g • Cholesterol 0mg • Sodium 65mg • Total Carbohydrate 15g • Dietary Fiber 0g • Protein 1g. DIETARY EXCHANGES: 1 Fruit • 1 Other Carbohydrate • 1-1/2 Fat.

quick cookie bars

# quick cookie bars

PREP TIME: 5 Minutes ✳ READY IN: 1 Hour 20 Minutes ✳ SERVINGS: 16

| | |
|---|---|
| 1 roll (16.5 oz.) Pillsbury® refrigerated chocolate chip, sugar or peanut butter cookies | Ready-to-spread frosting<br>Assorted sprinkles |

1 Heat oven to 350°F. In 8- or 9-inch square pan, break up cookie dough. With floured fingers, press dough evenly in pan.

2 Bake 25 to 30 minutes or until golden brown. Cool completely, about 45 minutes. If desired, frost or decorate using ready-to-spread frosting and sprinkles. Cut into 4 rows by 4 rows. Store tightly covered.

**HIGH ALTITUDE (3500-6500 FT):** Use 9-inch pan. In Step 1, in large bowl, break up cookie dough. If using chocolate chip cookie dough, stir or knead in 2 tablespoons all-purpose flour. If using sugar cookie dough, stir or knead in 1/4 cup flour. If using peanut butter cookie dough, stir or knead in 3 tablespoons flour. Press dough evenly in pan.

NUTRITION INFORMATION PER SERVING: Calories 150 • Total Fat 8g • Saturated Fat 2.5g • Cholesterol 0mg • Sodium 100mg • Total Carbohydrate 19g • Dietary Fiber 0g • Protein 1g. DIETARY EXCHANGES: 1/2 Starch • 1/2 Other Carbohydrate • 1-1/2 Fat • 1 Carb Choice.

# cookie pizza

PREP TIME: 20 Minutes ✳ READY IN: 1 Hour 5 Minutes ✳ SERVINGS: 16

| | |
|---|---|
| 1 roll (16.5 oz.) Pillsbury® refrigerated sugar or peanut butter cookies | 6 large red gumdrops |
| 1/2 cup chocolate ready-to-spread frosting (from 16-oz. container) | 2 large green gumdrops |
| 2 Nature Valley® peanut butter crunchy granola bars (1 pouch from 8.9-oz. box), coarsely crushed | 2 to 4 tablespoons vanilla ready-to-spread frosting (from 16-oz. container), melted |

1 Heat oven to 350°F. Grease 12-inch pizza pan with shortening. Cut cookie dough into 1/4-inch-thick slices. With lightly floured fingers, press slices in bottom of pan to form crust.

2 Bake 18 to 22 minutes or until deep golden brown. Cool completely, about 20 minutes.

3 Spread baked crust with chocolate frosting to within 1/2 inch of edge. To decorate, sprinkle pizza with crushed granola bars to resemble sausage. Slice red gumdrops into thirds to resemble pepperoni. Cut green gumdrops into small pieces to resemble green bell peppers. Arrange gumdrop pieces on pizza.

4 Drizzle melted vanilla frosting over pizza to resemble mozzarella cheese. Cut into wedges or squares to serve.

**HIGH ALTITUDE (3500-6500 FT):** In Step 1, in large bowl, break up cookie dough. If using sugar cookie dough, stir or knead in 1/4 cup all-purpose flour; if using peanut butter dough, stir or knead in 2 tablespoons flour. Press dough in pan to within 1/2 inch of edge.

NUTRITION INFORMATION PER SERVING: Calories 220 • Total Fat 9g • Saturated Fat 3.5g • Cholesterol 10mg • Sodium 100mg • Total Carbohydrate 34g • Dietary Fiber 0g • Protein 1g. DIETARY EXCHANGES: 2 Other Carbohydrate • 2 Fat • 2 Carb Choices.

CAROL HAPPLEY
Jordan, Minnesota
Bake-Off® Contest 33, 1988

# easy baklava bars

PREP TIME: 25 Minutes ✳ READY IN: 1 Hour 45 Minutes ✳ SERVINGS: 48 bars

**CRUST**
- 1 can (8 oz.) Pillsbury® refrigerated crescent dinner rolls
- 2 tablespoons butter or margarine, melted

**FILLING**
- 2 cups finely chopped walnuts
- 1 cup coconut
- 1 cup quick-cooking oats
- 2 tablespoons packed brown sugar
- 1/2 cup butter or margarine, melted
- 1/2 teaspoon ground cinnamon
- 1/8 teaspoon ground allspice
- 1/8 teaspoon ground cloves

**GLAZE**
- 1/2 cup granulated sugar
- 1/4 cup water
- 1/4 cup butter or margarine
- 2 tablespoons honey
- 1 tablespoon brandy, if desired
- 1 teaspoon lemon juice
- 1/4 teaspoon ground cinnamon
- 3 whole cloves

1 Heat oven to 350°F. Grease 15 x 10 x 1-inch baking pan with shortening or cooking spray. Unroll dough into 2 long rectangles. Place in pan; press over bottom to form crust. Firmly press perforations to seal. Brush with 2 tablespoons melted butter. Bake 5 minutes. Remove from oven.

2 In large bowl, mix all filling ingredients. Spoon evenly over partially baked crust; gently press down. Bake 15 to 20 minutes longer or until golden brown.

3 In 1-quart saucepan, heat all glaze ingredients to boiling. Reduce heat; simmer 2 to 3 minutes, stirring constantly. Remove whole cloves. Drizzle glaze evenly over warm bars. Cool completely, about 1 hour. For bars, cut into 8 rows by 6 rows.

**HIGH ALTITUDE (3500-6500 FT):** Bake 20 to 25 minutes.

NUTRITION INFORMATION PER SERVING: Calories 110 • Total Fat 8g • Saturated Fat 3.5g • Cholesterol 10mg • Sodium 65mg • Total Carbohydrate 8g • Dietary Fiber 0g • Protein 1g. DIETARY EXCHANGES: 1/2 Starch • 1-1/2 Fat • 1/2 Carb Choice.

# oh-so-easy chocolate-peanut-caramel bars

PREP TIME: 10 Minutes ✳ READY IN: 1 Hour 45 Minutes ✳ SERVINGS: 36

- 1 roll (16.5 oz.) Pillsbury® refrigerated sugar cookies
- 1-1/2 cups salted peanuts
- 1 cup semisweet chocolate chips
- 1/2 cup caramel ice cream topping
- 2 tablespoons all-purpose flour

1 Heat oven to 350°F (325°F for dark pan). In ungreased 13 x 9-inch pan, break up cookie dough. With floured fingers, press the dough evenly in pan. Bake 13 to 17 minutes or until light golden brown.

2 Remove partially baked bars from oven. Sprinkle peanuts and chocolate chips evenly over warm bars. In small bowl, mix caramel topping and flour until well blended. Drizzle evenly over top.

3 Return to oven; bake 15 to 18 minutes longer or until center just begins to bubble. Cool completely, about 1 hour. Cut into 6 rows by 6 rows. Store tightly covered.

NUTRITION INFORMATION PER SERVING: Calories 140 • Total Fat 7g • Saturated Fat 2g • Cholesterol 0mg • Sodium 80mg • Total Carbohydrate 16g • Dietary Fiber 1g • Protein 2g. DIETARY EXCHANGES: 1/2 Starch • 1/2 Other Carbohydrate • 1-1/2 Fat • 1 Carb Choice.

# poppin' fresh® double-decker cookies

PREP TIME: 1 Hour 15 Minutes ✳ READY IN: 1 Hour 15 Minutes ✳ SERVINGS: 3 dozen

- 2 rolls (16.5 oz. each) Pillsbury® refrigerated chocolate chip cookies
- 1 can (16 oz.) chocolate ready-to-spread frosting
- 1/2 cup creamy peanut butter

1 Heat oven to 350°F. Work with 1 roll of cookie dough at a time; refrigerate the remaining dough until ready to use.

2 Shape each roll of dough into 36 (1-inch) balls; place 2 inches apart on ungreased cookie sheets.

3 Bake at 350°F. for 8 to 11 minutes or until light golden brown. Cool 1 minute; remove from cookie sheets. Cool 10 minutes or until completely cooled.

4 In small bowl, combine frosting and peanut butter; blend well. For each sandwich cookie, spread scant tablespoon frosting mixture on bottom of 1 cookie. Top with second cookie, bottom side down; press together gently. Store cookies in refrigerator.

NUTRITION INFORMATION PER SERVING: Calories 225 • Total Fat 11g • Saturated Fat 4g • Cholesterol 0mg • Sodium 130mg • Total Carbohydrate 27g • Dietary Fiber 1g • Protein 4g. DIETARY EXCHANGES: 1 Starch • 1 Other Carbohydrate • 2 Fat • 2 Carb Choices.

**BETTY EDER**
Las Vegas, Nevada
Bake-Off® Contest 38, 1998

# orangeburst cookie bars

PREP TIME: 15 Minutes ✳ READY IN: 1 Hour 45 Minutes ✳ SERVINGS: 24

**CRUST**
- 1 roll (16.5 oz.) Pillsbury® refrigerated sugar cookies
- 1/2 cup chopped hazelnuts (filberts) or almonds

**FILLING**
- 1/2 cup granulated sugar
- 5 teaspoons all-purpose flour
- 1/3 cup light corn syrup
- 2 to 3 teaspoons grated orange peel
- 1/4 cup orange juice
- 1 tablespoon butter or margarine, melted
- 1 egg
- 1/2 cup chopped hazelnuts (filberts) or almonds

**GARNISH**
- 1 to 3 tablespoons powdered sugar, if desired

1 Heat oven to 350°F. Cut cookie dough into 1/2-inch-thick slices; arrange in bottom of ungreased 13 x 9-inch pan. Press dough evenly in pan to form crust. Sprinkle with 1/2 cup hazelnuts; press in firmly. Bake 12 to 15 minutes or until dough is puffed.

2 Meanwhile, in medium bowl, mix granulated sugar and flour. With wire whisk, stir in corn syrup, orange peel, orange juice, butter and egg until smooth. Stir in 1/2 cup hazelnuts.

3 Remove partially baked crust from oven. Carefully pour filling over crust.

4 Return to oven; bake 18 to 23 minutes longer or until edges are golden brown and filling is set. Cool on wire rack 10 minutes. Sprinkle with powdered sugar. Cool completely, about 45 minutes. Cut into bars.

**HIGH ALTITUDE (3500-6500 FT):** Heat oven to 375°F. Continue and bake as directed above.

NUTRITION INFORMATION PER SERVING: Calories 165 • Total Fat 7g • Saturated Fat 1g • Cholesterol 10mg • Sodium 85mg • Total Carbohydrate 24g • Dietary Fiber 0g • Protein 2g. DIETARY EXCHANGES: 1-1/2 Other Carbohydrate • 1-1/2 Fat • 1-1/2 Carb Choices.

# glazed peanut butter cups

PREP TIME: 1 Hour 30 Minutes ✳ READY IN: 2 Hours 15 Minutes ✳ SERVINGS: 4 dozen

### COOKIES
2 cups Easy Cookie Mix (recipe at right)
1/2 cup creamy peanut butter
1/3 cup butter, softened
1 egg
1 to 2 tablespoons milk, if needed

48 miniature milk chocolate-covered peanut butter cups, unwrapped

### GLAZE
1/2 cup semisweet chocolate chips
2 teaspoons shortening

1 Heat oven to 350°F. Grease 48 mini muffin cups with shortening or cooking spray. Stir cookie mix before measuring. In large bowl, beat cookie mix, peanut butter, butter and egg with electric mixer on medium speed, scraping bowl occasionally, until dough forms; if needed, add 1 to 2 tablespoons milk.

2 Shape dough into 1-inch balls; place in muffin cups. Press 1 peanut butter cup into each ball. Bake 13 to 18 minutes or until dough is set and golden brown around edges of candy. Cool 5 minutes; remove from pan. Cool completely, about 30 minutes.

3 In small microwavable bowl, microwave glaze ingredients on High 45 to 60 seconds, stirring once halfway through microwaving, until melted. If necessary, continue to microwave on High in 15-second increments, stirring until smooth. Drizzle glaze evenly over cooled cookies.

NUTRITION INFORMATION PER SERVING: Calories 90 • Total Fat 5g • Saturated Fat 2g • Cholesterol 10mg • Sodium 55mg • Total Carbohydrate 10g • Dietary Fiber 0g • Protein 2g. DIETARY EXCHANGES: 1/2 Starch • 1 Fat • 1/2 Carb Choice.

*easy cookie mix*

*In a 4-quart bowl, mix 3-3/4 cups all-purpose flour, 2-1/2 cups granulated sugar, 2 cups powdered sugar, 4 teaspoons baking power and 1 teaspoon salt. Stir in 4 cups of all-purpose flour. Makes 12 cups. Store in an airtight container up to 3 months.*

# christmas ornament cookies

PREP TIME: 1 Hour  ✳  READY IN: 1 Hour 30 Minutes  ✳  SERVINGS: 2 dozen

| | |
|---|---|
| 1 roll (16.5 oz.) Pillsbury® refrigerated sugar cookies | 1 tablespoon red sugar |
| 1/4 cup all-purpose flour | 1 tablespoon green sugar |
| 1 egg white, beaten | 12 small gumdrops, cut in half |

1 In large bowl, break up cookie dough. Stir or knead in flour until well blended. Reshape into log. Cut cookie dough lengthwise into 3 long slices. On work surface, separate slices with rounded sides down. Lightly brush all cut surfaces with beaten egg white.

2 Sprinkle egg white area of 1 rounded slice with red sugar. Place middle slice on top; sprinkle with green sugar. Place the remaining rounded slice, egg white side down, on top; press firmly and if necessary, reshape into roll. Wrap roll in plastic wrap; freeze 30 minutes.

3 Heat oven to 350°F. Cut roll into 24 slices; place 1 inch apart on ungreased cookie sheets. Bake 9 to 11 minutes or until edges are light golden brown. Immediately press gumdrop half onto outer edge of each cookie to look like ornament hanger; remove from cookie sheets to cooling racks.

**HIGH ALTITUDE (3500-6500 FT):** Bake 12 to 14 minutes.

NUTRITION INFORMATION PER SERVING: Calories 100 • Total Fat 4g • Saturated Fat 1g • Cholesterol 5mg • Sodium 55mg • Total Carbohydrate 15g • Dietary Fiber 0g • Protein 0g. DIETARY EXCHANGES: 1 Other Carbohydrate • 1 Fat • 1 Carb Choice.

**BETTY BOYLE**
Monroeville, Pennsylvania
Bake-Off® Contest 41, 2004

# granola-almond macaroons

PREP TIME: 1 Hour  ✳  READY IN: 1 Hour  ✳  SERVINGS: 3 dozen cookies

| | |
|---|---|
| 1 roll (16.5 oz.) Pillsbury® refrigerated sugar cookies | 2-1/2 cups coconut |
| 1 package (7 oz.) almond paste | 1 teaspoon almond extract |
| 4 Nature Valley® oats 'n honey crunchy granola bars (2 pouches from 8.9-oz. box), coarsely crushed | 1/2 cup coarse or granulated sugar (for rolling) |

1 Heat oven to 350°F. Spray cookie sheets with cooking spray. In large bowl, break up cookie dough and almond paste; with hands, knead mixture until well combined. Stir in crushed granola bars, coconut and almond extract.

2 Shape mixture into 1-1/4-inch balls; roll in the sugar and place 2 inches apart on the sprayed cookie sheets.

3 Bake 12 to 14 minutes or until the edges are light golden brown. Cool 1 minute; remove from cookie sheets.

**HIGH ALTITUDE (3500-6500 FT):** Bake at 350°F. for 13 to 15 minutes.

NUTRITION INFORMATION PER SERVING: Calories 130 • Total Fat 5g • Saturated Fat 2g • Cholesterol 0mg • Sodium 70mg • Total Carbohydrate 20g • Dietary Fiber 0g • Protein 2g. DIETARY EXCHANGES: 1/2 Starch • 1/2 Other Carbohydrate • 1 Fat • 1 Carb Choice.

christmas ornament cookies

# so-easy lemon bars

PREP TIME: 15 Minutes ✳ READY IN: 1 Hour 35 Minutes ✳ SERVINGS: 36

1 roll (16.5 oz.) Pillsbury® refrigerated
   sugar cookies

4 eggs

1-1/2 cups sugar

2 tablespoons all-purpose flour

2 tablespoons butter or margarine, melted

2 tablespoons grated lemon peel (2 medium)

1/3 cup fresh lemon juice (2 medium)

1 to 2 tablespoons powdered sugar

1 Heat oven to 350°F. Break up cookie dough into ungreased 13 x 9-inch pan. With floured fingers, press dough evenly in bottom of pan to form crust.

2 Bake 15 to 20 minutes or until light golden brown. Meanwhile, beat eggs in large bowl until well blended. Add sugar, flour and margarine; beat with wire whisk or fork until well blended. Stir in lemon peel and lemon juice.

3 Remove partially baked crust from oven. Pour the egg mixture over the warm crust. Return to oven. Bake an additional 20 to 30 minutes or until edges are light golden brown. Cool 30 minutes or until completely cooled. Sprinkle with powdered sugar. With knife dipped in hot water, cut into bars.

**HIGH ALTITUDE (3500-6500 FT):** Bake crust at 350°F. for 18 to 21 minutes. After pouring the egg mixture into crust, bake 25 to 30 minutes.

NUTRITION INFORMATION PER SERVING: Calories 105 • Total Fat 3g • Saturated Fat 1g • Cholesterol 25mg • Sodium 65mg • Total Carbohydrate 19g • Dietary Fiber 0g • Protein 1g. DIETARY EXCHANGES: 1/2 Starch • 1/2 Other Carbohydrate • 1/2 Fat • 1 Carb Choice.

# flip-flop fun cookies

PREP TIME: 35 Minutes ✳ READY IN: 35 Minutes ✳ SERVINGS: 12 cookies

4 rectangles (1-1/2 x 1 inch each)
vanilla-flavored candy coating (almond bark)
(from 20-oz. pkg.)

1 roll Fruit by the Foot® chewy fruit snack
(from 6-roll box)

12 peanut butter sandwich cookies
(from 1-lb. pkg.)

12 miniature candy-coated chocolate
baking bits

Brown sugar, if desired

1 In 1-quart saucepan, melt candy coating over low heat, stirring occasionally.

2 Meanwhile, unroll fruit snack roll. Using kitchen scissors, cut 12 (4-1/2 x 1/4-inch) strips from fruit snack roll. Remove paper. Fold each strip in half, forming a V shape.

3 Dip tops and sides of cookies into melted candy coating; lift out with fork or tongs, letting excess drip off. Place cookies, coated side up, on cookie sheets. Before coating sets, carefully attach fruit snack pieces to make tops of flip-flop sandals, placing point of V shape near one end of cookie, and ends at other end of cookie. Place one baking bit at the tip of V shape. Let stand until set, about 10 minutes.

4 Spoon brown sugar onto tray to look like sand; arrange cookies on brown sugar.

NUTRITION INFORMATION PER SERVING: Calories 130 • Total Fat 6g • Saturated Fat 3g • Cholesterol 0mg • Sodium 60mg • Total Carbohydrate 16g • Dietary Fiber 0g • Protein 1g. DIETARY EXCHANGES: 1/2 Starch • 1/2 Other Carbohydrate • 1 Fat • 1 Carb Choice.

*special touch*

Add a few drops of food color to the vanilla-flavored candy coating to tint the flip-flops to your liking.

# gingerbread pinwheels

PREP TIME: 1 Hour ✳ READY IN: 2 Hours ✳ SERVINGS: 5 dozen

1 roll (16.5 oz.) Pillsbury® refrigerated
gingerbread cookies

1 roll (16.5 oz.) Pillsbury® refrigerated
sugar cookies

1 tablespoon sugar

1 Place 17 x 12-inch sheet of waxed paper on cookie sheet. Cut gingerbread cookie dough in half lengthwise. Arrange halves, side by side, on waxed paper-lined cookie sheet. Top with second sheet of waxed paper. Roll dough to form 15 x 9-inch rectangle.

2 Repeat on work surface with sheets of waxed paper and sugar cookie dough. Remove top sheet of waxed paper. Lifting dough with waxed paper, invert sugar cookie rectangle onto gingerbread rectangle. Gently pat doughs together. Refrigerate 15 minutes.

3 Remove and discard waxed paper from top of dough. Using remaining waxed paper and starting with 1 long side, roll up stacked dough jelly-roll fashion, without rolling paper into roll. Wrap roll of dough securely with waxed paper. Freeze 45 minutes or until very firm.

4 Heat oven to 350°F. Unwrap dough; cut into 4 equal rolls. Work with 1 roll at a time; keep remaining 3 rolls in freezer until ready to slice. Cut each roll into 1/4-inch-thick slices; place 2 inches apart on ungreased cookie sheets, reshaping into rounds as necessary. Sprinkle each cookie with sugar.

5 Bake 10 to 12 minutes or until the edges are golden brown. Cool 2 minutes and remove from the cookie sheets.

NUTRITION INFORMATION PER SERVING: Calories 75 • Total Fat 3g • Saturated Fat 1g • Cholesterol 5mg • Sodium 55mg • Total Carbohydrate 11g • Dietary Fiber 0g • Protein 1g. DIETARY EXCHANGES: 1 Other Carbohydrate • 1/2 Fat • 1 Carb Choice.

# peanut butter cup cookies

PREP TIME: 40 Minutes ✻ READY IN: 40 Minutes ✻ SERVINGS: 2 dozen

1 roll (16.5 oz.) Pillsbury® refrigerated peanut butter cookies

1 cup miniature candy-coated chocolate baking bits, fall colored (yellow, orange, brown, green, red)

24 miniature chocolate-covered peanut butter cup candies, unwrapped

1 Heat oven to 350°F. In large bowl, break up cookie dough. Stir or knead in the baking bits until well mixed.

2 Onto ungreased cookie sheets, drop dough by heaping tablespoonfuls 2 inches apart; flatten each slightly with fingers.

3 Bake 10 to 14 minutes or until light golden brown. Immediately top each cookie with 1 peanut butter cup; press lightly into cookie. Cool 2 minutes; remove from cookie sheets. Let cookies stand until peanut butter cups are set before storing, about 3 hours.

NUTRITION INFORMATION PER SERVING: Calories 160 • Total Fat 8g • Saturated Fat 2.5g • Cholesterol 0mg • Sodium 115mg • Total Carbohydrate 20g • Dietary Fiber 0g • Protein 2g. DIETARY EXCHANGES: 1/2 Starch • 1 Other Carbohydrate • 1-1/2 Fat • 1 Carb Choice.

# fresh orange cookies

PREP TIME: 1 Hour 15 Minutes ✻ READY IN: 1 Hour 15 Minutes ✻ SERVINGS: 6 dozen

**COOKIES**
1-1/2 cups sugar
1 cup margarine or butter, softened
1 cup sour cream
2 eggs
4 cups all-purpose flour
1 teaspoon baking powder
1 teaspoon baking soda
1/2 teaspoon salt
2/3 cup orange juice
3 tablespoons grated orange peel

**FROSTING**
1/4 cup margarine or butter, melted
2 cups powdered sugar
1 tablespoon grated orange peel
2 to 3 tablespoons orange juice

1 Heat oven to 375°F. In large bowl, combine sugar and 1 cup margarine; beat until light and fluffy. Add sour cream and eggs; blend well. Add all remaining cookie ingredients; mix well. Drop dough by rounded tablespoonfuls onto ungreased cookie sheets.

2 Bake at 375°F. for 8 to 11 minutes or until edges are light golden brown. Immediately remove from cookie sheets.

3 Meanwhile, in small bowl, blend all frosting ingredients until smooth, adding enough orange juice for desired spreading consistency. Frost warm cookies.

NUTRITION INFORMATION PER SERVING: Calories 90 • Total Fat 4g • Saturated Fat 1g • Cholesterol 10mg • Sodium 80mg • Total Carbohydrate 13g • Dietary Fiber 0g • Protein 1g. DIETARY EXCHANGES: 1 Starch • 1 Other Carbohydrate • 1 Fat.

# sweet 'n salty crunch bars

PREP TIME: 15 Minutes ✳ READY IN: 1 Hour 50 Minutes ✳ SERVINGS: 20 bars

1 roll (16.5 oz.) Pillsbury® refrigerated peanut butter cookies

1 cup butterscotch chips

1/4 cup semisweet chocolate chips

1/4 cup peanut butter

1-1/4 cups shoestring potatoes (from 1-3/4-oz. can)

1/4 cup lightly salted peanuts

1/2 cup flaked or shredded coconut

1 Heat oven to 350°F. Spray 9 or 8-inch square pan with cooking spray. Remove half of cookie dough from wrapper; refrigerate remaining dough until needed. Break up half of dough into pan; press evenly to form crust. Bake 6 to 12 minutes or until edges are light golden brown.

2 Remove partially baked crust from oven; cool on wire rack 10 minutes. Meanwhile, in medium microwavable bowl, microwave butterscotch chips, chocolate chips and peanut butter on Medium (50%) 1 to 1-1/2 minutes or until mixture is melted, stirring every 30 seconds until smooth. Gently stir in shoestring potatoes and peanuts until coated.

3 Spoon and carefully spread mixture over crust. Crumble remaining half of dough evenly over top. Sprinkle with coconut.

4 Return to oven. Bake 12 to 22 minutes longer or until top is golden brown. Cool on wire rack until firm, about 1 hour. Cut into bars.

**HIGH ALTITUDE (3500-6500 FT):** After breaking up half of cookie dough into pan, stir or knead 2 tablespoons all-purpose flour into dough until well blended. Increase first bake time to 10 to 14 minutes at 350°F. Before crumbling remaining half of dough, stir or knead in 2 tablespoons all-purpose flour until well blended. Increase second bake time to 18 to 23 minutes.

NUTRITION INFORMATION PER SERVING: Calories 230 • Total Fat 12g • Saturated Fat 5g • Cholesterol 0mg • Sodium 125mg • Total Carbohydrate 27g • Dietary Fiber 1g • Protein 3g. DIETARY EXCHANGES: 1 Starch • 1 Other Carbohydrate • 2 Fat • 2 Carb Choices.

**CHERYL SCOTT**
Shaker Heights, Ohio
Bake-Off® Contest 40, 2002

*kitchen tip*

*Shoestring potatoes can be found near the salty snacks at the grocery store.*

## cook's notes

*Use your fingers to crumble the soft macaroons into crumbs for the filling in these rich bars.*

# cherry-macaroon bars

PREP TIME: 25 Minutes ✻ READY IN: 2 Hours 20 Minutes ✻ SERVINGS: 48 bars

1 roll (16.5 oz.) Pillsbury® refrigerated chocolate chip cookies

1-1/2 cups chopped slivered almonds

1 egg

1 can (14 oz.) sweetened condensed milk (not evaporated)

1/2 teaspoon almond extract

1-1/2 cups soft coconut macaroon cookie crumbs (about six 1-3/4-inch cookies)

1 jar (10 oz.) maraschino cherries, drained, chopped (about 3/4 cup)

1/4 cup semisweet chocolate chips

1 Heat oven to 350°F. (325°F. for dark pan). In ungreased 13 x 9-inch pan, break up cookie dough; press evenly in pan to form crust. Sprinkle with 1 cup of the almonds; firmly press into dough. Bake 11 to 16 minutes or until light golden brown.

2 Meanwhile, in medium bowl, beat egg. Stir in condensed milk and almond extract until smooth. Stir in cookie crumbs.

3 Remove partially baked crust from oven. Carefully spread crumb macaroon mixture over crust to edges. Sprinkle with cherries and remaining 1/2 cup almonds; press into crumb mixture. Return to oven. Bake 18 to 23 minutes longer or until edges are golden brown and filling is set.

4 In small microwavable dish, microwave chocolate chips on High 15 to 30 seconds or until melted and can be stirred smooth. Drizzle over warm bars. Cool completely on wire rack, about 1-1/2 hours. Cut into bars.

**HIGH ALTITUDE (3500-6500 FT):** Heat oven to 375°F. Continue and bake as directed above.

NUTRITION INFORMATION PER SERVING: Calories 155 • Total Fat 7g • Saturated Fat 2g • Cholesterol 10mg • Sodium 90mg • Total Carbohydrate 20g • Dietary Fiber 1g • Protein 3g. DIETARY EXCHANGES: 1 Starch • 1-1/2 Fat • 1 Carb Choice.

# quick snickerdoodles

PREP TIME: 1 Hour ✳ READY IN: 1 Hour ✳ SERVINGS: 32

3 tablespoons sugar
1/2 teaspoon ground cinnamon

1 roll (18 oz.) Pillsbury® refrigerated sugar cookies

1 Heat oven to 350°F. In small bowl, mix sugar and cinnamon.

2 Cut cookie dough into 32 (1/4-inch-thick) slices. Shape each into ball and roll in sugar-cinnamon mixture; place 2 inches apart on ungreased cookie sheets.

3 Bake 10 to 14 minutes or until the edges are golden brown. Cool 1 minute and remove from cookie sheets.

NUTRITION INFORMATION PER SERVING: Calories 70 • Total Fat 2g • Saturated Fat 1g • Cholesterol 0mg • Sodium 55mg • Total Carbohydrate 12g • Dietary Fiber 0g • Protein 1g. DIETARY EXCHANGES: 1 Other Carbohydrate • 1/2 Fat • 1 Carb Choice.

# coffee shop cookies

PREP TIME: 45 Minutes ✳ READY IN: 45 Minutes ✳ SERVINGS: 9 large cookies

1 roll (16.5 oz.) Pillsbury® refrigerated sugar cookies
1/3 cup firmly packed brown sugar
1 teaspoon vanilla

3/4 cup old-fashioned rolled oats
1/2 cup butterscotch chips
2 milk chocolate candy bars (1.55 oz. each), unwrapped, chopped

1 Heat oven to 350°F. Spray 1 large or 2 small cookie sheets with nonstick cooking spray. Break up cookie dough into large bowl. Add brown sugar and vanilla; mix well. Stir in oats, butterscotch chips and chocolate. (Dough will be stiff.)

2 Drop dough by rounded 1/4 cupfuls 2 inches apart onto sprayed cookie sheets. Flatten each with fingers to 1/2-inch thickness.

3 Bake 13 to 18 minutes or until cookies are slightly puffed and edges are golden brown. Cool 1 minute; remove from cookie sheets.

NUTRITION INFORMATION PER SERVING: Calories 395 • Total Fat 14g • Saturated Fat 6g • Cholesterol 5mg • Sodium 210mg • Total Carbohydrate 63g • Dietary Fiber 1g • Protein 4g. DIETARY EXCHANGES: 1 Starch • 3 Other Carbohydrate • 3 Fat • 4 Carb Choices.

**CINDY SCHMUELLING**
Fort Mitchell, Kentucky
Bake-Off® Contest 40, 2002

# mint-in-the-middle brownies

PREP TIME: 15 Minutes ✳ READY IN: 1 Hour 30 Minutes ✳ SERVINGS: 24 bars

1 box (19.5 oz.) fudge brownie mix
1/2 cup oil
1/4 cup water

2 eggs
1/2 cup quartered unwrapped chocolate-covered peppermint patties

1 Heat oven to 350°F. Grease bottom only of 13 x 9-inch pan or coat with nonstick cooking spray.

2 In large bowl, combine brownie mix, oil, water and eggs; beat 50 strokes with spoon until all dry mix is moistened. Spread half of batter in greased pan. Sprinkle quartered patties in single layer over batter; press lightly into place. Spoon remaining batter over patties; spread gently to cover.

3 Bake 28 to 30 minutes. Do not overbake. Cool 45 minutes or until completely cooled. Cut into bars and serve.

NUTRITION INFORMATION PER SERVING: Calories 170 • Total Fat 7g • Saturated Fat 2g • Cholesterol 20mg • Sodium 70mg • Total Carbohydrate 25g • Dietary Fiber 1g • Protein 2g. DIETARY EXCHANGES: 1 Starch • 1/2 Fruit • 1-1/2 Other Carbohydrate • 1-1/2 Fat.

# Wintry Desserts

*This heavenly assortment* of rich dinner finales will dazzle your guests, deck out your dinner menu and be the sparkling jewel on any buffet table.

p. 265

p. 240

p. 255

p. 264

p. 258

peppermint mousse cups p. 248

## cook's notes

*White chocolate is sensitive to heat and can scorch and clump easily when melted. By melting the white chocolate with milk, scorching and clumping are prevented.*

# white chocolate bread pudding with red berry sauce

PREP TIME: 30 Minutes ✳ READY IN: 1 Hour 55 Minutes ✳ SERVINGS: 8

**BREAD PUDDING**

- 1 box (6 oz.) white chocolate baking bar (6 bars), coarsely chopped
- 3 cups milk
- 6 cups cubed (1-inch) French bread (about 6 oz.)
- 2 eggs
- 1/4 cup sugar
- 1 teaspoon ground cinnamon
- 1 teaspoon vanilla

**SAUCE**

- 1 package (10 oz.) frozen sweetened raspberries in syrup, thawed
- 3/4 cup cranberry juice cocktail
- 2 tablespoons sugar
- 2 tablespoons cornstarch

1 Heat oven to 350°F. Grease 2-quart casserole with shortening or spray with cooking spray. In 3-quart saucepan, cook white chocolate and milk over medium heat about 5 minutes, stirring frequently, until white chocolate is melted (do not boil). Stir in bread cubes; set aside.

2 In large bowl, beat eggs. Stir in all remaining bread pudding ingredients until well blended. Stir in bread mixture. Pour into casserole.

3 Bake 45 to 55 minutes or until knife inserted in center comes out clean. Cool on wire rack 30 minutes.

4 Meanwhile, in 2-quart saucepan, combine all sauce ingredients. Cook over medium heat about 4 minutes, stirring constantly, until mixture comes to a boil and thickens.

5 Place strainer over 2-cup serving bowl; pour raspberry mixture into strainer. Press mixture with back of spoon through strainer to remove seeds; discard seeds. Serve warm bread pudding with sauce.

NUTRITION INFORMATION PER SERVING: Calories 345 • Total Fat 11g • Saturated Fat 6g • Cholesterol 65mg • Sodium 240mg • Total Carbohydrate 54g • Dietary Fiber 2g • Protein 8g, DIETARY EXCHANGES: 3 Starch • 1/2 Other Carbohydrate • 2 Fat • 3-1/2 Carb Choices.

# grands!® strawberry shortcakes

**PREP TIME:** 30 Minutes ✳ **READY IN:** 30 Minutes ✳ **SERVINGS:** 5

1 can (10.2 oz.) Pillsbury® Grands!® homestyle refrigerated buttermilk biscuits (5 biscuits)

2 tablespoons butter or margarine, melted

1/4 cup sugar

1-1/2 pints (3 cups) fresh strawberries, sliced

1/3 cup sugar

1/2 cup whipping cream

2 tablespoons sugar

1/4 teaspoon vanilla, if desired

1 Heat oven to 375°F. Separate dough into 5 biscuits. Dip top and side of each in melted butter, then in 1/4 cup sugar. On ungreased cookie sheet, place 2 inches apart. Bake 13 to 17 minutes or until golden brown. Cool 5 minutes.

2 Meanwhile, in medium bowl, stir together strawberries and 1/3 cup sugar. In small bowl, beat whipping cream until soft peaks form. Beat in 2 tablespoons sugar and the vanilla.

3 To serve, split the biscuits and place on 5 dessert plates. Layer each with whipped cream and strawberry mixture.

NUTRITION INFORMATION PER SERVING: Calories 460 • Total Fat 22g • Saturated Fat 9g • Cholesterol 35mg • Sodium 660mg • Total Carbohydrate 60g • Dietary Fiber 3g • Protein 5g. DIETARY EXCHANGES: 2 Starch • 2 Fruit • 4 Other Carbohydrate • 4 Fat.

*cook's notes*

*One 8-oz container of frozen whipped topping, thawed, can be used in place of the whipped cream mixture.*

# cranberry cornmeal torte

PREP TIME: 15 Minutes ✳ READY IN: 2 Hours 15 Minutes ✳ SERVINGS: 12

### CAKE
- 3/4 cup sugar
- 3/4 cup margarine or butter, softened
- 1 tablespoon vanilla
- 1 egg
- 1 cup all purpose flour
- 1/2 cup yellow cornmeal
- 1-1/4 teaspoons baking powder
- 3/4 cup fresh or frozen cranberries

### TOPPING
- 1/2 cup whipping cream
- 2 tablespoons powdered sugar

**1** Heat oven to 350°F. Grease and flour 8 or 9-inch springform pan. In large bowl, combine sugar, margarine, vanilla and egg; beat until well blended.

**2** Lightly spoon flour into measuring cup; level off. Stir in flour, cornmeal and baking powder until well mixed. Spoon into greased and floured pan. Sprinkle with cranberries; press in slightly.

**3** Bake at 350°F. for 40 to 45 minutes or until edges are golden brown. Cool at least 1 hour 15 minutes or until completely cooled.

**4** In small bowl, combine whipping cream and powdered sugar; beat until stiff peaks form. Garnish torte with whipped cream. Store in refrigerator.

**HIGH ALTITUDE (3500-6500 FT):** Decrease sugar to 2/3 cup. Bake as directed above.

NUTRITION INFORMATION PER SERVING: Calories 260 • Total Fat 16g • Saturated Fat 5g • Cholesterol 30mg • Sodium 200mg • Total Carbohydrate 27g • Dietary Fiber 1g • Protein 2g. DIETARY EXCHANGES: 1 Starch • 1 Fruit • 2 Other Carbohydrate • 3 Fat.

# lemon-pineapple dessert squares

PREP TIME: 15 Minutes ✷ READY IN: 2 Hours ✷ SERVINGS: 18

2 boxes (4-serving size each) lemon-flavored gelatin

1-1/2 cups boiling water

1 can (20 oz.) crushed pineapple in juice, well drained, liquid reserved

1 container (12 oz.) frozen whipped topping, thawed

1 round angel food cake (9 or 10 inch)

2 cups sliced fresh strawberries

1 In large bowl, mix the gelatin and boiling water until gelatin is completely dissolved. In 2-cup measuring cup, mix reserved pineapple liquid and enough cold water to make 2 cups. Stir into gelatin mixture. Refrigerate until thickened but not set, about 45 minutes.

2 Stir pineapple into thickened gelatin mixture. With rubber spatula, fold in 3 cups of the whipped topping.

3 Tear the angel food cake into 1-inch pieces, placing half of the pieces in ungreased 13 x 9-inch (3-quart) glass baking dish. Spoon half of gelatin mixture evenly over cake pieces. Repeat layers. Cover tightly with plastic wrap; refrigerate until set, about 1 hour.

4 Cut dessert into serving pieces and place on dessert plates. Top each with about 2 tablespoons strawberries and about 1 tablespoon remaining whipped topping.

NUTRITION INFORMATION PER SERVING: Calories 190 • Total Fat 3.5g • Saturated Fat 3g • Cholesterol 0mg • Sodium 250mg • Total Carbohydrate 37g • Dietary Fiber 1g • Protein 3g. DIETARY EXCHANGES: 1/2 Starch • 2 Other Carbohydrate • 1/2 Fat • 2-1/2 Carb Choices.

*cook's notes*

*For a "lighter" version of this tasty recipe, use sugar-free gelatin and reduced-fat whipped topping.*

*special touch*

Garnish these tangy,

creamy desserts with fresh

raspberries, blueberries or a

sprig of fresh mint.

# lemon cheesecake tarts

**PREP TIME:** 10 Minutes ✷ **READY IN:** 1 Hour 55 Minutes ✷ **SERVINGS:** 2 tarts

1/3 cup Yoplait® thick & creamy lemon supreme lowfat yogurt

2 tablespoons whipped cream cheese spread (from 8-oz. container)

2 tablespoons fat-free egg product

2 teaspoons sugar

1 teaspoon grated lemon peel

2 single-serve graham cracker crusts (from 4-oz. pkg.)

Sweetened whipped cream, if desired

Fresh raspberries, if desired

**1** Heat oven to 350°F. In small bowl, beat yogurt, cream cheese spread, egg product and sugar with electric mixer on medium speed until light, fluffy and smooth. Stir in lemon peel with spoon. Divide mixture evenly between crusts.

**2** Place tarts on ungreased cookie sheet. Bake 22 to 24 minutes or until filling is set. Cool 20 minutes. Refrigerate at least 1 hour until serving time. Serve topped with whipped cream and raspberries.

NUTRITION INFORMATION PER SERVING: Calories 260 • Total Fat 14g • Saturated Fat 5g • Cholesterol 15mg • Sodium 170mg • Total Carbohydrate 29g • Dietary Fiber 0g • Protein 5g. DIETARY EXCHANGES: 1/2 Starch • 1 Other Carbohydrate • 1/2 Skim Milk • 2 1/2 Fat • 2 Carb Choices.

# holly and eggnog pie

PREP TIME: 1 Hour ✳ READY IN: 5 Hours 15 Minutes ✳ SERVINGS: 10

## CRUST

- 1 package Pillsbury® refrigerated pie crusts, softened as directed on package
- 1 egg, separated
- 6 drops red food color
- 6 drops green food color

## FILLING

- 1-1/2 cups eggnog
- 1 envelope unflavored gelatin
- 1 cup powdered sugar
- 1/4 cup butter or margarine, softened
- 2 packages (8 oz. each) cream cheese, softened
- 1/4 teaspoon nutmeg
- 1/2 teaspoon rum extract

1 Heat oven to 450°F. Prepare pie crust as directed on package for one-crust baked shell using 9-inch glass pie pan. Bake at 450°F. for 9 to 11 minutes or until light golden brown.

2 To make holly and berries, use 2-inch holly leaf-shaped cutter or sharp knife and leaf pattern. Cut 20 leaves from remaining pie crust. From dough scraps, make 30 (1/4-inch) balls. Beat egg white in small bowl until foamy. On ungreased cookie sheet, make 10 arrangements, using 2 leaves and 3 berries for each and attaching dough pieces together using small brush and egg white.

3 Place half of egg yolk in each of 2 custard cups. Add red food color to one and green food color to the other; mix well. With small brush, paint green mixture on leaves; paint red mixture on berries. Bake at 450°F. for 2 to 3 minutes or until very lightly browned. Immediately remove from cookie sheet; cool 5 minutes or until completely cooled.

4 Place 1 cup of the eggnog in small saucepan. Evenly sprinkle gelatin over eggnog; let stand 1 minute to soften. Cook over medium heat, stirring constantly until gelatin is dissolved. Remove from heat; set aside.

5 In large bowl, combine powdered sugar, margarine and cream cheese; beat with electric mixer at low speed until light and fluffy. Gradually beat in the nutmeg, rum extract, gelatin mixture and remaining 1/2 cup eggnog. Beat at high speed until smooth. Refrigerate 15 minutes or until mixture mounds slightly when stirred.

6 Pour filling into cooled baked shell. Refrigerate pie until firm, about 4 hours. If desired, sprinkle filling with additional nutmeg.

7 Just before serving, arrange holly and berries on top of pie, one arrangement for each serving. Store in refrigerator.

NUTRITION INFORMATION PER SERVING: Calories 505 • Total Fat 35g • Saturated Fat 18g • Cholesterol 100mg • Sodium 390mg • Total Carbohydrate 39g • Dietary Fiber 0g • Protein 8g. DIETARY EXCHANGES: 2-1/2 Starch • 7 Fat • 2-1/2 Carb Choices.

# dipped cream cheese strawberries

**PREP TIME:** 25 Minutes ✳ **READY IN:** 1 Hour 25 Minutes ✳ **SERVINGS:** 12

| | |
|---|---|
| 1 package (1 lb.) fresh strawberries | 1 bag (12 oz.) semisweet chocolate chips (2 cups) |
| 6 oz. cream cheese (from 8-oz pkg.), softened | 2 oz. bittersweet baking chocolate, chopped |
| 24 vanilla wafer cookies, finely crushed (3/4 cup) | 1/2 cup white vanilla baking chips |
| 3 tablespoons powdered sugar | 1 teaspoon vegetable oil |
| 1 teaspoon grated orange peel | |

1 Rinse strawberries; pat dry with paper towels. Line cookie sheet with waxed paper. In medium bowl, beat cream cheese, cookie crumbs, powdered sugar and orange peel with electric mixer on medium speed until mixed. Press about 1 rounded tablespoon cream cheese mixture over bottom half of each strawberry, molding to fit the strawberry. Place on cookie sheet. Refrigerate 30 minutes.

2 In 1-quart saucepan, melt semisweet chocolate chips and bittersweet chocolate over low heat, stirring frequently. Holding strawberry by the leaves, dip each strawberry into chocolate mixture, covering cheese mixture. Place on cookie sheet. Refrigerate about 30 minutes or until chocolate is completely set.

3 In small microwavable bowl, microwave vanilla baking chips and oil uncovered on High 1 minute, stirring every 30 seconds, until melted. Continue to microwave at 15-second intervals if necessary to melt chips. Drizzle melted vanilla chips over dark chocolate on strawberries. Place each in paper baking cup. Store in tightly covered container in refrigerator no longer than 24 hours.

NUTRITION INFORMATION PER SERVING: Calories 330 • Total Fat 20g • Saturated Fat 12g • Cholesterol 15mg • Sodium 90mg • Total Carbohydrate 34g • Dietary Fiber 3g • Protein 4g. DIETARY EXCHANGES: 1 Starch • 1 Other Carbohydrate • 4 Fat • 2 Carb Choices.

# frozen raspberry dessert

**PREP TIME:** 15 Minutes ✳ **READY IN:** 3 Hours 10 Minutes ✳ **SERVINGS:** 12

**CRUST**

| | |
|---|---|
| 1 cup crushed vanilla wafers (28 wafers) | 3 tablespoons orange-flavored liqueur or orange juice |
| 1/2 cup finely chopped blanched almonds or macadamia nuts | 1 package (10 oz.) frozen raspberries with syrup, thawed |
| 1/4 cup butter or margarine, melted | 1 cup whipping cream, whipped |

**FILLING**

| | |
|---|---|
| 1 can (14 oz.) sweetened condensed milk (not evaporated) | 2 drops red food color |
| 3 tablespoons lemon juice | Sweetened whipped cream, if desired |
| | Chocolate hearts, if desired |

1 Heat oven to 375°F. In small bowl, mix crust ingredients. Press firmly in bottom of ungreased 8-inch springform pan. Bake 8 to 10 minutes. Cool completely, about 30 minutes.

2 In large bowl, beat sweetened condensed milk, lemon juice and liqueur with electric mixer on medium speed until smooth. Add raspberries; beat on low speed until well blended. Fold in whipped cream and red food color. Pour over crust. Freeze at least 2 hours or until firm.

3 Just before serving, let stand at room temperature about 15 minutes. Garnish with sweetened whipped cream and chocolate hearts. Store dessert in freezer.

**HIGH ALTITUDE (3500-6500 FT):** Heat oven to 400°F.

NUTRITION INFORMATION PER SERVING: Calories 300 • Total Fat 18g • Saturated Fat 9g • Cholesterol 45mg • Sodium 110mg • Total Carbohydrate 32g • Dietary Fiber 2g • Protein 4g. DIETARY EXCHANGES: 1 Starch • 1 Other Carbohydrate • 3 1/2 Fat • 2 Carb Choices.

dipped cream cheese strawberries

# royal marble cheesecake

PREP TIME: 35 Minutes ✳ READY IN: 12 Hours ✳ SERVINGS: 16

**ISAAC FEINSTEIN**
Atlantic City, New Jersey
Bake-Off® Contest 16, 1964

### cook's notes

*For the best results, beat*

*eggs just until blended.*

*Overbeating the eggs*

*can cause cracks in the*

*cheesecake.*

### CRUST

| | |
|---|---|
| 3/4 | cup Pillsbury Best® all-purpose flour |
| 2 | tablespoons sugar |
| | Dash salt |
| 1/4 | cup butter or margarine |
| 1 | cup semisweet chocolate chips, melted |

### FILLING

| | |
|---|---|
| 3 | packages (8 oz. each) cream cheese, softened |
| 1 | cup sugar |
| 1/4 | cup all-purpose flour |
| 2 | teaspoons vanilla |
| 6 | eggs |
| 1 | cup sour cream |

1 Heat oven to 400°F. Combine 3/4 cup flour, 2 tablespoons sugar and salt. With pastry blender or fork, cut in butter until mixture resembles coarse crumbs. Stir in 2 tablespoons of melted chocolate. Reserve remaining chocolate for filling. Press crumb mixture in bottom of ungreased 9-inch springform pan. Bake crust 10 minutes or until very light brown. Remove pan from the oven. Reduce the oven temperature to 325°F.

2 Meanwhile, in large bowl, beat cream cheese and 1 cup sugar with electric mixer on medium speed until light and fluffy. Beat in 1/4 cup flour and vanilla until well blended. On low speed, add eggs 1 at a time, beating just until blended after each addition. Add sour cream; blend well. Place 1-3/4 cups filling mixture in medium bowl; stir in reserved melted chocolate.

3 Pour half of plain filling over crust. Top with spoonfuls of half of the chocolate filling. Cover with remaining plain filling, then with spoonfuls of remaining chocolate filling. With table knife, swirl chocolate filling through plain filling. Place cheesecake in center of oven. Place shallow pan half full of water on bottom oven rack under cheesecake.

4 Bake 1 hour to 1 hour 15 minutes or until set but center of cheesecake still jiggles when moved. Cool on wire rack 10 minutes. Run knife around the edge of pan to loosen cheesecake. Cool at least 2 hours. Refrigerate 8 hours or overnight before serving. Carefully remove side of pan. Store in refrigerator.

NUTRITION INFORMATION PER SERVING: Calories 370 • Total Fat 26g • Saturated Fat 14g • Cholesterol 135mg • Sodium 200mg • Total Carbohydrate 29g • Dietary Fiber 0g • Protein 7g. DIETARY EXCHANGES: 2 Other Carbohydrate • 1 Medium-Fat Meat • 4 Fat • 2 Carb Choices.

# pumpkin pie cream cups

PREP TIME: 35 Minutes ✳ READY IN: 1 Hour 5 Minutes ✳ SERVINGS: 32 cookie cups

| | |
|---|---|
| 1 roll (18 oz.) Pillsbury® refrigerated gingerbread cookies | 3 tablespoons sugar |
| 1-1/2 cups frozen (thawed) whipped topping | 1 teaspoon pumpkin pie spice |
| 3/4 cup canned pumpkin (not pumpkin pie mix) | 4 teaspoons chocolate decors |

1 Heat oven to 350°F. (325°F. for dark pan). Grease 32 mini muffin cups with shortening or coat with cooking spray. Work with half of the cookie dough at a time; refrigerate remaining dough until needed.

2 Cut dough into 16 equal pieces. Press each piece in bottom and up side of mini muffin cup. Bake 9 to 12 minutes or until centers appear dry and edges begin to turn light golden brown.

3 Remove from oven. With handle of wooden spoon, make shallow indentation in center of each baked cookie cup. Cool 10 minutes. Run tip of knife around edge of each muffin cup; remove cookie cups from pan. Cool completely, about 10 minutes. Repeat with remaining half of cookie dough.

4 Meanwhile, in medium bowl, mix whipped topping, pumpkin, sugar and pumpkin pie spice. Cover; refrigerate until needed.

5 Up to 2 hours before serving, spoon 1 measuring tablespoonful pumpkin mixture into each cooled cookie cup. Sprinkle each with 1/8 teaspoon decors. Store in refrigerator.

**HIGH ALTITUDE (3500-6500 FT):** In Step 1, in large bowl, break up cookie dough; stir or knead in 1/4 cup all-purpose flour. Work with half of dough at a time; refrigerate remaining dough until needed. Cut dough into 18 pieces; press into cups. Bake 10 to 13 minutes. If shallow indentations have not formed during baking, gently form as directed in Step 3. Repeat with remaining dough.

NUTRITION INFORMATION PER SERVING: Calories 90 • Total Fat 4.5g • Saturated Fat 1.5g • Cholesterol 10mg • Sodium 55mg • Total Carbohydrate 12g • Dietary Fiber 0g • Protein 0g. DIETARY EXCHANGES: 1 Other Carbohydrate • 1 Fat • 1 Carb Choice.

*kitchen tip*

*Real whipped cream can be used in place of the whipped topping. Whip 3/4 cup whipping cream or use 1-1/2 cups of whipped cream from an aerosol can.*

# rhubarb and strawberry cornbread cobbler

PREP TIME: 15 Minutes ✳ READY IN: 1 Hour 30 Minutes ✳ SERVINGS: 8

| | |
|---|---|
| 1 package (16 oz.) frozen unsweetened sliced rhubarb | 1 package (6.5 oz.) golden corn muffin and bread mix |
| 1 package (16 oz.) frozen unsweetened whole strawberries | 1-1/4 cups rolled oats |
| 1 cup sugar | 1/4 cup margarine or butter, melted |
| 1/4 cup cornstarch | 2 tablespoons brown sugar |
| 1 egg | 1/3 cup milk |
| | 1 pint (2 cups) vanilla ice cream |

1 Heat oven to 350°F. In ungreased 13 x 9-inch (3-quart) glass baking dish, combine the rhubarb and strawberries.

2 In small bowl, combine sugar and cornstarch; mix well. Sprinkle the sugar mixture over the fruit; toss to coat.

3 Beat egg in medium bowl. Add all remaining ingredients except ice cream; mix well. Drop batter by teaspoonfuls evenly over fruit mixture.

4 Bake 1 hour 5 minutes to 1 hour 15 minutes or until fruit mixture is bubbly in center and topping is golden brown. Serve warm with ice cream.

NUTRITION INFORMATION PER SERVING: Calories 435 • Total Fat 14g • Saturated Fat 5g • Cholesterol 45mg • Sodium 310mg • Total Carbohydrate 71g • Dietary Fiber 4g • Protein 6g. DIETARY EXCHANGES: 2 Starch • 3 Fruit • 5 Other Carbohydrate • 3 Fat.

# cookie dough ice cream dessert

PREP TIME: 15 Minutes ✳ READY IN: 2 Hours 5 Minutes ✳ SERVINGS: 12

| | |
|---|---|
| 1 roll (18 oz.) Pillsbury® refrigerated chocolate chip cookies | 2 cups Cookie Crisp® cereal |
| 1 container (1/2 gallon) cookie dough ice cream | 2/3 cup hot fudge ice cream topping |

1 Heat oven to 350°F. Line 13 x 9-inch pan with heavy-duty foil, extending foil over sides of pan. Break up cookie dough into foil-lined pan. With floured fingers, press dough evenly in bottom of pan to form crust.

2 Bake at 350°F. for 15 to 18 minutes or until golden brown. Meanwhile, remove ice cream from freezer; place in refrigerator to soften.

3 Remove crust from oven. Cool 30 minutes or until completely cooled. Spread softened ice cream evenly over cooled crust. Top evenly with cereal; press lightly into ice cream.

4 Place ice cream topping in small resealable food storage plastic bag; partially seal bag. Cut small hole in bottom corner of bag. Squeeze bag to drizzle topping over dessert. Freeze at least 1 hour or until firm before serving. Use foil to lift dessert from pan. Cut into squares.

**HIGH ALTITUDE (3500-6500 FT):** Bake crust at 350°F. for 17 to 20 minutes.

NUTRITION INFORMATION PER SERVING: Calories 475 • Total Fat 21g • Saturated Fat 9g • Cholesterol 40mg • Sodium 310mg • Total Carbohydrate 64g • Dietary Fiber 1g • Protein 8g. DIETARY EXCHANGES: 3 Starch • 1 Other Carbohydrate • 4 Fat • 4 Carb Choices.

# turtle cheesecake tartlets

**PREP TIME:** 35 Minutes ✳ **READY IN:** 2 Hours 35 Minutes ✳ **SERVINGS:** 24 tartlets

1 box Pillsbury® refrigerated pie crusts, softened as directed on box

1/2 cup milk chocolate chips

4 oz. cream cheese (from 8-oz. pkg.), softened

1/4 cup packed brown sugar

2 tablespoons caramel topping

1 egg

1/2 teaspoon vegetable oil

2 tablespoons finely chopped pecans

1 Heat oven to 450°F. Remove 1 crust from pouch; unroll on work surface. Roll lightly with rolling pin. Cut 12 rounds from crust with 2-1/2- to 2-3/4-inch cookie cutter. Press rounds in bottom and up sides of 12 mini muffin cups, with edges extending above cups about 1/8 inch. Repeat with remaining pie crust. Place about 5 of the chocolate chips in each crust. Bake 6 minutes. Leave crusts in pan. Reduce oven temperature to 375°F.

2 Meanwhile, in medium bowl, beat cream cheese, brown sugar, caramel topping and egg with electric mixer on medium speed until creamy. Spoon evenly over chocolate chips, about 1-1/2 teaspoons for each tartlet.

3 Bake at 375°F. 10 to 12 minutes or until cheesecake is set. Cool in pan on cooling rack 10 minutes; remove from pan.

4 In small custard cup or other small microwavable bowl, place remaining chocolate chips and the oil. Microwave uncovered on High 30 seconds; stir. Microwave about 30 seconds longer or until melted; stir. Drizzle over each cheesecake; immediately sprinkle with pecans. Refrigerate at least 2 hours before serving. Cover and refrigerate any remaining tartlets.

**HIGH ALTITUDE (3500-6500 FT):** Bake 12 to 14 minutes.

NUTRITION INFORMATION PER SERVING: Calories 110 • Total Fat 7g • Saturated Fat 3g • Cholesterol 15mg • Sodium 80mg • Total Carbohydrate 12g • Dietary Fiber 0g • Protein 0g. DIETARY EXCHANGES: 1 Other Carbohydrate • 1 1/2 Fat • 1 Carb Choice.

*cook's notes*

*If you prefer your chocolate less sweet, use semisweet chocolate chips instead of the milk chocolate.*

# peppermint mousse cups

PREP TIME: 35 Minutes ✳ READY IN: 35 Minutes ✳ SERVINGS: 24

| | |
|---|---|
| 1-1/2 cups semisweet chocolate chips | 1/2 teaspoon peppermint extract |
| 1/2 cup white vanilla baking chips | 2 drops red food color |
| 1 cup whipping cream | 2 tablespoons crushed candy canes (about 6 miniature candy canes) |

1 Line 24 mini muffin cups with petit four paper cups. In 1-quart saucepan, melt semisweet chocolate chips over low heat, stirring frequently. Spoon about 2 teaspoons of the chocolate into each paper cup. With back of small measuring spoon, spread chocolate up sides to within 1/8 inch of the top. Chocolate should be warm enough to spread. Refrigerate about 20 minutes or until completely set.

2 Meanwhile, in small microwavable bowl, microwave vanilla baking chips uncovered on High 1 minute. Stir in 3 tablespoons of the whipping cream; microwave about 30 seconds longer or until chips are melted. Stir in the peppermint extract and food color. Cool slightly, about 5 minutes. Carefully remove paper cups from chocolate cups.

3 In medium bowl, beat remaining whipping cream with electric mixer on high speed until stiff peaks form. Fold melted vanilla chip mixture into whipped cream. Spoon or pipe whipped cream mixture into chocolate cups. Refrigerate until serving. Just before serving, sprinkle with candy.

*Kitchen tip*

Make the chocolate cups a day or two ahead of time. Cover loosely and store in a cool place. These festive desserts keep in the refrigerator up to 2 days. Sprinkle with the crushed candy just before you serve them.

NUTRITION INFORMATION PER SERVING: Calories 110 • Total Fat 8g • Saturated Fat 5g • Cholesterol 10mg • Sodium 15mg • Total Carbohydrate 11g • Dietary Fiber 0g • Protein 0g. DIETARY EXCHANGES:1/2 Other Carbohydrate • 1-1/2 Fat • 1 Carb Choice.

# easy-as-peach-pie wedges

PREP TIME: 10 Minutes ✳ READY IN: 1 Hour ✳ SERVINGS: 8

1 box Pillsbury® refrigerated pie crusts,
softened as directed on box

1 can (21 oz.) peach pie filling with more fruit

1/8 teaspoon ground nutmeg

2 teaspoons sugar

1 Heat oven to 450°F. Coat large cookie sheet with cooking spray. Remove crusts from pouches; unroll crusts onto opposite ends of cookie sheet (edges of crusts may hang over sides of cookie sheet).

2 Spoon half of pie filling onto one half of each crust to within 1 inch of edge. Sprinkle with nutmeg. Fold other half of each crust over filling; press 1/2-inch edge with fork to seal. Cut several slits in top crust of each. Sprinkle with sugar.

3 Bake 10 minutes. Cover edges of crusts with strips of foil. Bake 5 to 8 minutes longer or until crusts are golden brown. Cool at least 30 minutes. Cut into wedges to serve.

NUTRITION INFORMATION PER SERVING: Calories 310 • Total Fat 14g • Saturated Fat 5g • Cholesterol 5mg • Sodium 220mg • Total Carbohydrate 45g • Dietary Fiber 1g • Protein 1g. DIETARY EXCHANGES: 1 Starch • 2 Other Carbohydrate • 2-1/2 Fat • 3 Carb Choices.

## cook's notes

*For a small family, it's easy to prepare half of this recipe for 4 servings. Keep the second pie crust in the refrigerator for another 1-crust pie at a later date. Use the other half of the pie filling as a topping for ice cream or cake.*

# chocolate mousse cones

PREP TIME: 2 Hours ✳ READY IN: 3 Hours ✳ SERVINGS: 8

1 bag (12 oz.) semisweet chocolate chips
(2 cups)

1 tablespoon vegetable oil

8 sugar-style ice cream cones with pointed ends

2 eggs

2 tablespoons sugar

2 cups whipping cream

2 cups raspberry sorbet

8 fresh raspberries

1 To make a holder to hold the cones upright, turn an egg carton upside down. Punch holes in 8 of the egg cases to hold the cones. If you don't have an egg carton, use 8 heavy, narrow-rimmed drinking glasses.

2 Place chocolate chips and oil in top of double boiler over simmering water or in medium bowl over saucepan of simmering water. Melt chocolate, stirring as chocolate starts to soften. Dip and twirl top 2 inches of each cone into melted chocolate; quickly remove and place in holder. Refrigerate or freeze until chocolate is hardened, about 1 hour.

3 In small bowl, beat eggs with electric mixer on high speed 3 minutes. Gradually beat in sugar; beat 1 minute longer.

4 In 2-quart saucepan, heat 1 cup of the whipping cream over medium heat just until hot. Gradually stir at least half of the hot cream into eggs, then stir back into hot cream in saucepan. Cook over medium-low heat about 10 minutes, stirring constantly, until mixture thickens (do not boil).

5 Stir in remaining melted chocolate from dipping cones. Cover; refrigerate about 1 hour, stirring occasionally, just until chilled.

6 In chilled medium bowl, beat remaining 1 cup whipping cream on high speed until stiff. Fold the chocolate mixture into whipped cream; refrigerate up to 1 hour before serving time. Spoon the chocolate mixture into cones, place 1 small scoop of sorbet on top of each. Garnish each with a fresh raspberry.

NUTRITION INFORMATION PER SERVING: Calories 570 • Total Fat 35g • Saturated Fat 20g • Cholesterol 120mg • Sodium 60mg • Total Carbohydrate 57g • Dietary Fiber 3g • Protein 6g. DIETARY EXCHANGES: 2 Starch • 2 Other Carbohydrate • 6-1/2 Fat • 4 Carb Choices.

## kitchen tip

*Decorate the outsides of the cones with colored sprinkles before the chocolate hardens. Drop a specialty candy into each cone before adding mousse for a surprise treat!*

# cherry christmas trifle

PREP TIME: 25 Minutes ✴ READY IN: 2 Hours 25 Minutes ✴ SERVINGS: 16

| | |
|---|---|
| 1 box (4-serving size) white chocolate instant pudding and pie filling mix | 1/4 cup orange liqueur or orange juice |
| 2 cups milk | 1 can (21 oz.) cherry pie filling |
| 1 frozen pound cake (10.75 oz.), thawed, cut into 1-inch cubes | 1 cup frozen whipped topping, thawed |
| | Real chocolate dessert decorations (leaves), if desired |

1 In medium bowl, with wire whisk, beat pudding mix and milk 2 minutes. Let stand 1 to 2 minutes until thickened.

2 Place half of the pound cake cubes in glass trifle bowl or 3-quart glass bowl. Sprinkle with half of the liqueur. Reserve 2 tablespoons of the pie filling for garnish. Spoon half of the remaining pie filling over the cake cubes. Top with half of the pudding. Repeat layers. Refrigerate for at least 2 hours before serving.

3 Just before serving, pipe or spoon whipped topping around outer edge of trifle; garnish with reserved 2 tablespoons pie filling and dessert decorations.

NUTRITION INFORMATION PER SERVING: Calories 190 • Total Fat 7g • Saturated Fat 3.5g • Cholesterol 25mg • Sodium 120mg • Total Carbohydrate 27g • Dietary Fiber 1g • Protein 3g. DIETARY EXCHANGES: 1 Starch • 1 Other Carbohydrate • 1 Fat • 2 Carb Choices.

# lemon mini tarts

PREP TIME: 15 Minutes ✴ READY IN: 25 Minutes ✴ SERVINGS: 16 tarts

| | |
|---|---|
| 1 cup milk | 1 Pillsbury® refrigerated pie crust, softened as directed on package |
| 1 box (4-serving size) lemon instant pudding and pie filling mix | Strawberry halves, lemon slices or other fresh fruit |
| 1 teaspoon grated lemon peel | Fresh mint leaves |

1 In medium bowl, beat milk and pudding mix 2 minutes with electric mixer at medium speed or 2 to 3 minutes with wire whisk until well blended. Stir in lemon peel. Refrigerate.

2 Heat oven to 450°F. Allow 1 pie crust pouch to stand at room temperature 15 to 20 minutes. (Refrigerate remaining crust for another use.)

3 Using rolling pin, roll crust to 15-inch diameter. With lightly floured 3-inch round cutter, cut 16 rounds from crust; discard scraps. Fit rounds into 16 (2-3/4-inch) ungreased muffin cups, pressing in gently. Generously prick crusts with fork. Bake 5 to 7 minutes or until very light golden brown. Remove from pan; cool completely.

4 Spoon lemon filling into tart shells. Garnish with sliced fruit and mint leaves. If desired, sprinkle with powdered sugar.

NUTRITION INFORMATION PER SERVING: Calories 90 • Total Fat 3.5g • Saturated Fat 1.5g • Cholesterol 0mg • Sodium 140mg • Total Carbohydrate 14g • Dietary Fiber 0g • Protein 0g. DIETARY EXCHANGES: 1 Other Carbohydrate • 1/2 Fat • 1 Carb Choice.

# honeyed pumpkin pie
# with broiled praline topping

**PREP TIME:** 20 Minutes ✳ **READY IN:** 2 Hours 35 Minutes ✳ **SERVINGS:** 10

**CRUST AND FILLING**
- 1 Pillsbury® refrigerated pie crust, softened as directed on box
- 1 can (15 oz.) pumpkin (not pumpkin pie mix)
- 1 cup honey
- 3/4 teaspoon salt
- 3/4 teaspoon ground nutmeg
- 1/4 teaspoon ground allspice
- 4 eggs
- 3/4 cup evaporated milk

**TOPPING**
- 1/3 cup chopped pecans
- 1/4 cup packed brown sugar
- 2 tablespoons butter or margarine, melted

1 Heat oven to 375°F. On lightly floured surface, roll crust into 13-inch round. Place in ungreased 10-inch deep dish glass pie plate as directed on box for One-Crust Filled Pie.

2 In large bowl, beat pumpkin, honey, salt, nutmeg and allspice with electric mixer on low speed 1 to 2 minutes or until smooth. Beat in eggs until well blended. On low speed, gradually add milk, beating until well blended. Pour into crust-lined pie plate. Bake 45 to 55 minutes or until edges are set. Cool completely, about 1 hour.

3 In small bowl, mix all topping ingredients; sprinkle over top of cooled pie. Broil 4 to 6 inches from heat 2 to 3 minutes or until topping is bubbly. Store pie in refrigerator.

**HIGH ALTITUDE (3500-6500 FT):** Bake 50 to 60 minutes, covering edge of crust with foil during last 30 minutes of baking to prevent overbrowning.

NUTRITION INFORMATION PER SERVING: Calories 340 • Total Fat 14g • Saturated Fat 5g • Cholesterol 95mg • Sodium 330mg • Total Carbohydrate 50g • Dietary Fiber 2g • Protein 5g. DIETARY EXCHANGES: 1 Starch • 2-1/2 Other Carbohydrate • 2-1/2 Fat • 3 Carb Choices.

*cook's notes*

*Firmly press the dough against the sides and bottom of the pan without stretching it. If the dough is stretched, the crust will shrink when it bakes.*

lime-kiwi cloud with strawberry sauce

# lime-kiwi cloud with strawberry sauce

PREP TIME: 30 Minutes ✳ READY IN: 3 Hours 30 Minutes ✳ SERVINGS: 15

### DESSERT
- 1 large angel food cake, cut into 1-inch cubes (about 12 cups)
- 2 containers (6 oz. each) Yoplait® Custard Style® lowfat vanilla yogurt
- 2 teaspoons grated lime peel
- 1/4 cup lime juice

- 1 container (8 oz.) frozen light whipped topping, thawed
- 6 kiwifruit, peeled, sliced

### SAUCE
- 2 packages (10 oz. each) frozen strawberries in syrup, thawed
- 2 teaspoons cornstarch

1 In ungreased 13 x 9-inch (3-quart) glass baking dish, arrange half of cake cubes. In large bowl, mix yogurt, lime peel and lime juice until well blended. Fold in whipped topping.

2 Spoon half of mixture over cake cubes in baking dish; press down to smooth layer. Arrange kiwifruit slices over mixture. Repeat cake and yogurt layers; press down. Cover; refrigerate 3 hours or until set.

3 Meanwhile, drain strawberries, reserving liquid in 2-quart saucepan; set strawberries aside. Stir cornstarch into liquid until well blended. Heat to boiling over medium heat, stirring constantly. Remove from heat; cool 15 minutes. Stir in strawberries. Refrigerate until chilled, about 30 minutes.

4 To serve, cut dessert into squares; place on individual dessert plates. Spoon the sauce over each serving. Store dessert and sauce in refrigerator.

**HIGH ALTITUDE (3500-6500 FT):** In Step 3, boil 2 to 3 minutes after adding cornstarch.

NUTRITION INFORMATION PER SERVING: Calories 240 • Total Fat 3.5g • Saturated Fat 2.5g • Cholesterol 0mg • Sodium 320mg • Total Carbohydrate 47g • Dietary Fiber 2g • Protein 5g. DIETARY EXCHANGES: 1 Starch • 2 Other Carbohydrate • 1/2 Fat • 3 Carb Choices.

*cook's notes*

*For a more intense lime flavor, substitute Key lime pie yogurt for the vanilla yogurt. Be sure to use custard-style yogurt in 6 ounce containers.*

# apple-raspberry cookie cobbler

PREP TIME: 10 Minutes ✳ READY IN: 1 Hour 55 Minutes ✳ SERVINGS: 10

- 2 cans (21 oz. each) apple pie filling
- 1 package (14 oz.) frozen unsweetened whole raspberries (3-1/2 cups)
- 1/4 cup sugar

- 1 roll (18 oz.) Pillsbury® refrigerated sugar cookies
- 1 cup quick-cooking rolled oats
- 2 tablespoons sugar

1 Heat oven to 350°F. In ungreased 13 x 9-inch (3-quart) glass baking dish, combine pie filling, raspberries and 1/4 cup sugar; mix well.

2 Break up cookie dough into medium bowl. Add oats; mix well. Crumble mixture evenly over fruit mixture. Sprinkle 2 tablespoons sugar over top.

3 Bake 50 to 60 minutes or until topping is golden brown. Cool about 45 minutes or until slightly cooled before serving. If desired, serve with ice cream.

NUTRITION INFORMATION PER SERVING: Calories 410 • Total Fat 8g • Saturated Fat 2g • DIETARY EXCHANGES: 1-1/2 Starch • 4 Other Carbohydrate • 1-1/2 Fat • 5-1/2 Carb Choices.

*cook's notes*

*Cookie dough isn't only for cookies; it makes a great topping for your cobblers or crisps!*

# creamy chocolate-mint pie

PREP TIME: 25 Minutes ✳ READY IN: 2 Hours 25 Minutes ✳ SERVINGS: 8

1 Pillsbury® Pet-Ritz® frozen deep dish pie crust (from 12-oz. pkg.)

1-1/4 cups milk

1 package (4-serving size) chocolate pudding and pie filling mix (not instant)

1 cup semisweet chocolate chips

4 oz. cream cheese, softened

1/2 cup powdered sugar

1/4 teaspoon peppermint extract

3 to 5 drops green food color

2 cups frozen (thawed) whipped topping

2 thin rectangular chocolate and green mints, unwrapped

1 Heat oven to 400°F. Bake pie crust as directed on package for a One-Crust Baked Shell. Cool completely, about 30 minutes.

2 Meanwhile, in 2-quart saucepan, stir together milk and pudding mix; cook as directed on package. Continue cooking over low heat while adding chocolate chips, stirring until melted. Set aside.

3 In medium bowl, beat cream cheese, powdered sugar, peppermint extract and 1 to 2 drops of the green food color until smooth. Gently fold in 1 cup of the whipped topping.

4 Spread cream cheese mixture in shell. Top with chocolate mixture. Refrigerate at least 2 hours until set. To color remaining 1 cup whipped topping, in small bowl, stir together whipped topping and remaining 2 drops food color. Garnish pie with whipped topping. Chop mints and sprinkle over whipped topping. Store in refrigerator.

NUTRITION INFORMATION PER SERVING: Calories 360 • Total Fat 21g • Saturated Fat 11g • Cholesterol 20mg • Sodium 200mg • Total Carbohydrate 39g • Dietary Fiber 2g • Protein 5g. DIETARY EXCHANGES: 1 Starch • 1-1/2 Other Carbohydrate • 4 Fat • 2-1/2 Carb Choices.

# tiramisu bites

PREP TIME: 1 Hour ✳ READY IN: 5 Hours ✳ SERVINGS: 24

| | |
|---|---|
| 12 slices (1/4 inch thick) frozen (thawed) pound cake (from 10-oz. pkg.) | 1 container (8 oz.) mascarpone cheese |
| 1/4 cup water | 1/4 cup powdered sugar |
| 1-1/2 teaspoons instant coffee granules | 1/2 cup whipping cream |
| 1-1/2 teaspoons rum extract | 1/2 oz. semisweet baking chocolate |
| | 24 espresso coffee beans, if desired |

1 Line 24 mini muffin cups with petit four paper cups. Cut 2 (1-1/4-inch) rounds from each cake slice. Place 1 cake round in bottom of each cup.

2 In small bowl, mix water, coffee granules and 1/2 teaspoon of the rum extract. Drizzle about 1/2 teaspoon of the coffee mixture over cake in each muffin cup. Set aside.

3 In medium bowl, beat cheese, powdered sugar and remaining 1 teaspoon rum extract with electric mixer on medium speed until creamy. In another medium bowl, beat whipping cream on high speed until soft peaks form. On low speed, beat cheese mixture into whipped cream. Spoon or pipe a rounded tablespoon whipped cream mixture into each cup, covering cake.

4 Grate semisweet chocolate over each cup. Top each with coffee bean. Refrigerate at least 4 hours to blend flavors. Store covered in refrigerator.

NUTRITION INFORMATION PER SERVING: Calories 110 • Total Fat 8g • Saturated Fat 4.5g • Cholesterol 25mg • Sodium 15mg • Total Carbohydrate 9g • Dietary Fiber 0g • Protein 1g. DIETARY EXCHANGES: 1/2 Starch • 1-1/2 Fat • 1/2 Carb Choice.

## cook's notes

Although these yummy little bites are ready to serve in 5 hours, the flavor and texture actually improve with longer standing. Make a day ahead, and let them mellow in the refrigerator.

# mascarpone-filled fresh strawberries

PREP TIME: 20 Minutes ✳ READY IN: 20 Minutes ✳ SERVINGS: 20

1 quart fresh strawberries
1 container (8 oz.) mascarpone cheese
3 tablespoons powdered sugar

1 teaspoon milk
1/2 teaspoon almond extract
Sliced almonds

1 Using larger strawberries, trim tops and bottoms of strawberries to level. Using small melon baller, scoop out center of each strawberry.

2 In medium bowl, mix cheese, powdered sugar, milk and extract until smooth. Spoon cheese mixture into small resealable food freezer plastic bag or pastry bag fitted with star tip; seal bag. Cut small hole in bottom corner of plastic bag. Squeeze bag to pipe cheese mixture into strawberries; top with almonds.

NUTRITION INFORMATION PER SERVING: Calories 60 • Total Fat 3.5g • Saturated Fat 2.5g • Cholesterol 10mg • Sodium 0mg • Total Carbohydrate 6g • Dietary Fiber 0g • Protein 0g. DIETARY EXCHANGES: 1/2 Other Carbohydrate • 1/2 Fat • 1/2 Carb Choice.

# raspberry mousse in chocolate cups

PREP TIME: 25 Minutes ✳ READY IN: 2 Hours 25 Minutes ✳ SERVINGS: 8

1-1/2  cups semi-sweet chocolate chips
1-1/2  teaspoons shortening
    1  tablespoon water
    1  teaspoon unflavored gelatin
1-1/2  cups fresh raspberries

    1  cup whipping cream
  1/4  cup powdered sugar
       Fresh raspberries, if desired
       Fresh mint leaves, if desired

1  In small saucepan, combine chocolate chips and shortening; cook over low heat until melted, stirring frequently. Line 8 muffin cups with paper baking cups. With pastry brush, coat sides and bottom of each cup thickly and evenly with chocolate. Refrigerate 10 minutes or until set. Brush any thin spots with additional chocolate. Cover; refrigerate at least 2 hours or until firm.

2  Place water in small microwave-safe bowl; sprinkle gelatin over water. Let stand 5 minutes to soften. Meanwhile, place 1-1/2 cups raspberries in blender container or food processor bowl with metal blade. Cover; blend until pureed. Microwave gelatin on High for 30 to 40 seconds or until gelatin is dissolved. Add to raspberry mixture; mix well.

3  In small bowl, beat whipping cream and sugar until medium-stiff peaks form. Do not overbeat. Gently fold in raspberry mixture. Cover; refrigerate until serving time.

4  Fifteen minutes before serving, carefully peel paper from chocolate cups. Spoon raspberry mixture into cups. Garnish with raspberries and mint. Store in refrigerator.

NUTRITION INFORMATION PER SERVING: Calories 310 • Total Fat 21g • Saturated Fat 13g • Cholesterol 40mg • Sodium 15mg • Total Carbohydrate 28g • Dietary Fiber 3g • Protein 2g. DIETARY EXCHANGES: 2 Fruit • 2 Other Carbohydrate • 4 Fat.

*kitchen tip*

*Instead of preparing chocolate cups, purchase ready-made cups to hold the raspberry mousse. Try individual shortcakes, sponge cake cups or tartlet shells.*

# cream cheese brownie cups

PREP TIME: 20 Minutes ✳ READY IN: 1 Hour 5 Minutes ✳ SERVINGS: 36 brownie cups

1/2 cup butter or margarine, softened
1 package (3 oz.) cream cheese, softened
1 cup granulated sugar
1 teaspoon vanilla
2 eggs
3/4 cup all-purpose flour
1/3 cup unsweetened baking cocoa
1/4 teaspoon baking powder

1/4 teaspoon salt
8 rectangular green crème de menthe chocolate candies, unwrapped, chopped (1/4 cup)

**FROSTING**
1/2 cup powdered sugar
2 to 3 teaspoons milk
18 rectangular green crème de menthe chocolate candies, unwrapped, cut in half diagonally

1 Heat oven to 350°F. Line 36 miniature muffin cups with paper baking cups. In large bowl, beat butter, cream cheese and granulated sugar with electric mixer on medium speed 1 minute or until creamy.

2 On medium speed, beat in vanilla and eggs until smooth. On low speed, beat in flour, cocoa, baking powder and salt until blended. With spoon, stir in chopped candies. Spoon batter evenly into muffin cups (cups will be almost full).

3 Bake 15 to 20 minutes, or until firm to touch and set. Do not overbake. Remove from muffin cups to cooling rack. Cool completely, about 25 minutes.

4 In small bowl with wooden spoon, beat powdered sugar and enough milk for desired drizzling consistency until smooth. With fork, drizzle over each brownie cup. Top each with a mint candy triangle.

NUTRITION INFORMATION PER SERVING: Calories 100 • Total Fat 5g • Saturated Fat 3g • Cholesterol 20mg • Sodium 50mg • Total Carbohydrate 12g • Dietary Fiber 0g • Protein 1g. DIETARY EXCHANGES: 1 Other Carbohydrate • 1 Fat • 1 Carb Choice.

# chocolate chip cheesecake bars

PREP TIME: 10 Minutes ✳ READY IN: 3 Hours 20 Minutes ✳ SERVINGS: 16

1 package (8 oz.) cream cheese, softened
1/2 cup sugar
1 egg

1/2 cup coconut, if desired
1 roll (18 oz.) Pillsbury® refrigerated chocolate chip cookies

1 Heat oven to 350°F. In small bowl, combine cream cheese, sugar and egg; beat until smooth. Stir in coconut.

2 Break up half of cookie dough into ungreased 9 or 8-inch square pan. With floured fingers, press dough evenly in bottom of pan to form crust. Spread cream cheese mixture over dough. Crumble and sprinkle remaining half of dough over cream cheese mixture.

3 Bake at 350°F. for 35 to 40 minutes or until golden brown and firm to the touch. Cool 30 minutes. Refrigerate at least 2 hours or until chilled. Cut into bars. Store in refrigerator.

NUTRITION INFORMATION PER SERVING: Calories 235 • Total Fat 12g • Saturated Fat 5g • Cholesterol 30mg • Sodium 170mg • Total Carbohydrate 28g • Dietary Fiber 0g • Protein 4g. DIETARY EXCHANGES: 1 Starch • 1 Other Carbohydrate • 2-1/2 Fat • 2 Carb Choices.

# oats 'n honey granola pie

PREP TIME: 15 Minutes ✳ READY IN: 1 Hour 35 Minutes ✳ SERVINGS: 8

### CRUST
- 1 Pillsbury® refrigerated pie crust, softened as directed on box

### FILLING
- 1/2 cup butter or margarine
- 1/2 cup packed light brown sugar
- 3/4 cup corn syrup
- 1/8 teaspoon salt
- 1 teaspoon vanilla
- 3 eggs, slightly beaten
- 4 Nature Valley® oats 'n honey crunchy granola bars (2 pouches from 8.9-oz. box), crushed (3/4 cup)
- 1/2 cup chopped walnuts
- 1/4 cup quick-cooking or old-fashioned oats
- 1/4 cup chocolate chips
  Whipped cream or ice cream, if desired

SUZANNE CONRAD
Findlay, Ohio
Bake-Off® Contest 41, 2004

*cook's notes*

*Use the flat side of a meat mallet to crush the granola bars while they're still in their packages.*

1 Heat oven to 350°F. Place pie crust in 9-inch glass pie plate as directed on box for One-Crust Filled Pie.

2 In large microwavable bowl, microwave butter uncovered on High 50 to 60 seconds or until melted. Stir in brown sugar and corn syrup until blended. Beat in salt, vanilla and eggs. Stir in remaining filling ingredients. Pour into crust-lined pie plate. Cover crust edge with 2- to 3-inch-wide strips of foil to prevent excessive browning; remove foil during last 15 minutes of bake time.

3 Bake 40 to 50 minutes or until filling is set and crust is golden brown. Cool at least 30 minutes before serving. Serve warm, at room temperature or chilled, with whipped cream or ice cream. Cover and refrigerate any remaining pie.

NUTRITION INFORMATION PER SERVING: Calories 540 • Total Fat 29g • Saturated Fat 12g • Cholesterol 115mg • Sodium 320mg • Total Carbohydrate 64g • Dietary Fiber 1g • Protein 5g. DIETARY EXCHANGES: 1 1/2 Starch • 3 Other Carbohydrate • 5 Fat • 4 Carb Choices.

# lime angel food cake roll

PREP TIME: 30 Minutes ✳ READY IN: 1 Hour 30 Minutes ✳ SERVINGS: 12

### CAKE

- 1  package (16 oz.) angel food cake mix
- 1-1/4  cups water
- 2  tablespoons powdered sugar

### FILLING AND TOPPING

- 1  can (14 oz.) sweetened condensed milk (not evaporated)
- 1/2  cup lime juice
- 1-1/2  teaspoons grated lime peel
- 1  cup whipping cream

1 Heat oven to 350°F. Grease 15 x 10 x 1-inch baking pan. Line bottom of pan with waxed paper. Prepare cake batter as directed on package using water. Spoon batter into lined pan. Bake at 350°F. for 17 to 22 minutes or until golden brown and cracks in cake appear dry.

2 Meanwhile, place clean towel on work surface. With strainer or sifter, lightly sprinkle powdered sugar evenly onto towel.

3 Loosen edges of warm cake with spatula; immediately invert cake onto sugared towel. Remove pan and waxed paper. Starting with short side, roll up cake in towel; cool on wire rack for 45 minutes or until completely cool.

4 Meanwhile, in small bowl, combine condensed milk, lime juice and lime peel; mix well. In large bowl, beat whipping cream until stiff peaks form. Fold condensed milk mixture into whipped cream just until blended. Reserve 1 cup lime mixture for topping. Refrigerate while cake is cooling or until thickened.

5 To assemble cake, unroll cooled cake, removing towel. Spread remaining lime mixture evenly over cake. Using towel, reroll cake; do not roll towel into cake. If desired, trim ends of roll. Use towel to lift cake roll onto serving platter. Spoon reserved 1 cup lime mixture on top of cake. If desired, garnish with additional whipped cream and lime twists. Store in refrigerator.

**HIGH ALTITUDE (3500-6500 FT):** Add 2 tablespoons flour to dry cake mix; increase water to 1-1/2 cups. Place 3 cups of the batter in greased 9 x 5-inch loaf pan; bake at 375°F. for 20 to 30 minutes. Pour remaining batter into greased 15 x 10 x 1-inch baking pan; bake at 375°F. for 14 to 19 minutes.

NUTRITION INFORMATION PER SERVING: Calories 320 • Total Fat 10g • Saturated Fat 6g • Cholesterol 40mg • Sodium 390mg • Total Carbohydrate 51g • Dietary Fiber 0g • Protein 6g. DIETARY EXCHANGES: 2 Starch • 1-1/2 Fruit • 3-1/2 Other Carbohydrate • 1-1/2 Fat.

# banana-chocolate-caramel cake

PREP TIME: 20 Minutes ✳ READY IN: 2 Hours 20 Minutes ✳ SERVINGS: 12

1 round angel food cake (8 to 10 inch)

2 cups (4 oz. each) refrigerated chocolate pudding snacks (from 24-oz. pkg.)

3 medium bananas

1/2 cup caramel ice cream topping, room temperature

1 aerosol can (7 oz.) whipped cream

2 tablespoons chocolate candy sprinkles

1 Cut angel food cake in half horizontally; separate layers. Spread 1 pudding snack on top of bottom cake layer.

2 Slice 2 of the bananas into 1/8-inch-thick slices; arrange slices on top of pudding. Place top cake layer on bottom layer, cut side down. Top with second pudding snack. Refrigerate at least 2 hours or overnight before serving.

3 To serve, cut cake into 12 slices; place on individual dessert plates. Drizzle each with caramel topping. Slice remaining banana into 12 slices. Top each serving with whipped cream and 1 banana slice. Sprinkle each with 1/2 teaspoon candy sprinkles.

NUTRITION INFORMATION PER SERVING: Calories 250 • Total Fat 2.5g • Saturated Fat 1.5g • Cholesterol 0mg • Sodium 450mg • Total Carbohydrate 54g • Dietary Fiber 1g • Protein 5g. DIETARY EXCHANGES: 1 Starch • 1/2 Fruit • 2 Other Carbohydrate • 1/2 Fat • 3-1/2 Carb Choices.

*cook's notes*

To cut the cake, measure the height and divide in half. Insert toothpicks at halfway point around entire cake, and slice with serrated knife above toothpicks.

# maple-walnut-pumpkin pie

PREP TIME: 20 Minutes ✳ READY IN: 3 Hours ✳ SERVINGS: 8

**CRUST**

1 Pillsbury® refrigerated pie crust, softened as directed on box

**FILLING**

1 can (15 oz.) pumpkin (not pumpkin pie mix)

1 can (14 oz.) sweetened condensed milk (not evaporated)

2 tablespoons real maple syrup or maple-flavored syrup

1-1/2 teaspoons pumpkin pie spice

2 eggs

**STREUSEL**

1/4 cup packed brown sugar

2 tablespoons all-purpose flour

2 tablespoons cold butter or margarine

1/4 cup finely chopped walnuts

**TOPPING**

1 cup whipping cream

2 tablespoons packed brown sugar

Chopped walnuts, if desired

1 Heat oven to 425°F. Place pie crust in 9-inch glass pie plate as directed on box for One-Crust Filled Pie. In large bowl, beat filling ingredients with electric mixer until smooth. Pour into crust-lined pie plate. Bake 10 minutes.

2 Meanwhile, in small bowl, mix 1/4 cup brown sugar and the flour. Cut in butter with pastry blender or fork until mixture looks like coarse crumbs. Stir in nuts; set aside.

3 Remove pie from oven. Reduce oven temperature to 350°F. Sprinkle streusel over pie. Cover crust edge with foil to prevent excessive browning. Return to oven. Bake 30 to 35 minutes longer or until knife inserted 1 inch from edge comes out clean. Cool completely on cooling rack, about 2 hours. Serve or refrigerate until serving time.

4 When ready to serve, in medium bowl, beat whipping cream and 2 tablespoons brown sugar with electric mixer on medium-high speed until soft peaks form. Serve pie with whipped cream and chopped walnuts. Cover and refrigerate any remaining pie.

**HIGH ALTITUDE (3500-6500 FT):** In Step 3, bake 40 to 45 minutes.

NUTRITION INFORMATION PER SERVING: Calories 520 • Total Fat 27g • Saturated Fat 13g • Cholesterol 115mg • Sodium 230mg • Total Carbohydrate 61g • Dietary Fiber 2g • Protein 8g. DIETARY EXCHANGES: 2 Starch • 2 Other Carbohydrate • 5 Fat • 4 Carb Choices.

*kitchen tip*

Be sure to purchase plain pumpkin, not pumpkin pie mix, which includes seasonings...and canned sweetened condensed milk, which is thick and sweet, rather than canned evaporated milk, which is usually used when making pumpkin pie.

# cookie ice cream-a-rounds

PREP TIME: 1 Hour ✳ READY IN: 4 Hours ✳ SERVINGS: 9

1 roll (18 oz.) Pillsbury® refrigerated chocolate chip cookies

1/2 cup miniature semisweet chocolate chips or candy sprinkles

2-1/4 cups any flavor ice cream, slightly softened

1 Heat oven to 350°F. Shape cookie dough into 18 balls; place 3 inches apart on ungreased cookie sheets. Bake at 350°F. for 10 to 15 minutes or until light golden brown. Cool 1 minute; remove from cookie sheets. Cool 15 minutes or until completely cooled.

2 Cut nine 12 x 9-inch sheets of plastic wrap or waxed paper. Place the chocolate chips in a small shallow bowl.

3 For each sandwich, spoon about 1/4 cup ice cream onto bottom of 1 cookie. Top with second cookie, bottom side down; press together gently. Roll outer edge of ice cream in chocolate chips. Quickly wrap each sandwich in plastic wrap. Freeze 3 hours or until firm. For longer storage, place wrapped sandwiches in resealable freezer plastic bag. Let stand 10 minutes before serving.

NUTRITION INFORMATION PER SERVING: Calories 405 • Total Fat 19g • Saturated Fat 7g • Cholesterol 20mg • Sodium 250mg • Total Carbohydrate 52g • Dietary Fiber 2g • Protein 7g. DIETARY EXCHANGES: 2-1/2 Starch • 1 Other Carbohydrate • 3-1/2 Fat • 3-1/2 Carb Choices.

**SHARON RICHARDSON**
Dallas, Texas
Bake-Off® Contest 34, 1999

# country french apple crescent casserole

PREP TIME: 25 Minutes ✳ READY IN: 1 Hour 5 Minutes ✳ SERVINGS: 8

**WRAPPED APPLES**

2 tablespoons sugar

1/2 to 1 teaspoon ground cinnamon

1 can (8 oz.) Pillsbury® refrigerated crescent dinner rolls

1 large apple, peeled, cut into 8 slices

**SAUCE**

1/2 cup sugar

1/2 cup whipping cream

1 tablespoon almond extract or amaretto

1 egg

**TOPPING**

1/2 cup sliced almonds

Ground cinnamon

1 Heat oven to 375°F. In small bowl, mix 2 tablespoons sugar and 1/2 to 1 teaspoon cinnamon. Unroll dough; separate into 8 triangles. Sprinkle sugar mixture evenly over each; gently press in, flattening each triangle slightly.

2 Place apple slice on shortest side of each triangle; tuck in dough edges around apple slice. Roll up, starting at shortest side of triangle and rolling to opposite point; seal all seams.

3 In ungreased 9-inch round glass baking dish or pie pan, place long side of seven filled rolls, point side down, around the outside edge of dish; place one in center. Bake 15 to 20 minutes or until golden brown.

4 Remove partially baked rolls from oven. In small bowl, mix all sauce ingredients with wire whisk until well blended; spoon evenly over rolls. Sprinkle with almonds and cinnamon.

5 Return to oven. Bake 13 to 18 minutes longer or until deep golden brown, covering with foil during last 5 minutes of baking if necessary to prevent excessive browning. Serve warm. Store in refrigerator.

**HIGH ALTITUDE (3500-6500 FT):** Bake rolls at 375°F. 15 to 20 minutes. After spooning sauce over rolls, return to oven; bake 16 to 21 minutes longer, covering with foil during last 5 minutes of baking if necessary to prevent excessive browning.

NUTRITION INFORMATION PER SERVING: Calories 270 • Total Fat 13g • Saturated Fat 4g • Cholesterol 45mg • Sodium 350mg • Total Carbohydrate 35g • Dietary Fiber 2g • Protein 4g. DIETARY EXCHANGES: 1 Starch • 1 Other Carbohydrate • 2-1/2 Fat • 2 Carb Choices.

cookie ice cream-a-rounds

# peppermint-fudge pie

PREP TIME: 25 Minutes ✳ READY IN: 2 Hours 10 Minutes ✳ SERVINGS: 8

**CRUST**

1 Pillsbury® refrigerated pie crust, softened as directed on box

**FILLING**

2 cups milk

1 box (4-serving size) chocolate pudding and pie filling mix (not instant)

1/2 cup semisweet chocolate chips

1 package (8 oz.) cream cheese, softened

1/2 cup powdered sugar

1 teaspoon peppermint extract

2 drops green or red food color

2 cups frozen (thawed) whipped topping
Shaved chocolate, if desired

1 Heat oven to 450°F. Make pie crust as directed on box for One-Crust Baked Shell, using 9-inch glass pie plate. Bake 9 to 11 minutes or until light golden brown. Cool completely, about 30 minutes.

2 Meanwhile, in 2-quart saucepan, heat milk and pudding mix to a full boil over medium heat, stirring constantly. Remove from heat. Stir in chocolate chips until melted. Place plastic wrap directly over surface of pudding. Refrigerate 45 minutes or just until cooled.

3 In small bowl, beat cream cheese, powdered sugar, peppermint extract and food color with electric mixer on medium speed until smooth. On low speed, gradually beat in 1 cup of whipped topping until blended. Spread in cooled baked shell.

4 Stir cooled pudding mixture; spread over cream cheese layer. Carefully spread remaining 1 cup whipped topping over pudding layer. Garnish with chocolate shavings. Refrigerate 1 hour or until chilled before serving. Cover; refrigerate any remaining pie.

NUTRITION INFORMATION PER SERVING: Calories 430 • Total Fat 25g • Saturated Fat 13g • Cholesterol 40mg • Sodium 280mg • Total Carbohydrate 45g • Dietary Fiber 1g • Protein 6g. DIETARY EXCHANGES: 2 Starch • 1 Other Carbohydrate • 5 Fat • 3 Carb Choices.

# chocolate supreme fondue

PREP TIME: 10 Minutes ✳ READY IN: 10 Minutes ✳ SERVINGS: 8

**FONDUE**
1 cup milk chocolate frosting
  (from 16-oz. can)

**DIPPERS**
1 large apple, cut into 16 slices

2 medium bananas, cut into 16 chunks

16 strawberries

16 regular marshmallows

1 Melt frosting in medium saucepan over low heat for 2 to 3 minutes, stirring occasionally. Pour into small fondue pot or heatproof bowl. Serve immediately.

2 To serve, arrange the dippers on a serving platter or tray. Spear dippers with fondue forks or long skewers; dip into fondue.

NUTRITION INFORMATION PER SERVING: Calories 210 • Total Fat 5g • Saturated Fat 1g • Cholesterol 0mg • Sodium 55mg • Total Carbohydrate 40g • Dietary Fiber 2g • Protein 1g. DIETARY EXCHANGES: 3 Fruit • 3 Other Carbohydrate • 1 Fat.

# cupcake strawberries

PREP TIME: 45 Minutes ❅ READY IN: 1 Hour 35 Minutes ❅ SERVINGS: 24

| | |
|---|---|
| 1 box (18.25) white cake mix with pudding | 1/4 teaspoon red gel or paste food color |
| Water | 1 (16-oz.) can vanilla frosting |
| Oil | Green chewy fruit snack in 3-foot rolls |
| Eggs | 2 tablespoons miniature semisweet chocolate chips |

1 Heat oven to 350°F. Line 24 muffin cups with paper baking cups. To make strawberry-shaped cupcakes, pinch in one side of each paper baking cup. Insert 1-inch ball of foil between liner and muffin cup to hold in place.

2 Prepare, bake and cool cake mix as directed on package for cupcakes, using water, oil and eggs.

3 Stir food color into frosting until well blended. Frost cooled cupcakes with frosting to resemble strawberries. Cut chewy fruit snack into leaf shapes; press into top of cupcakes. Arrange chocolate chips on frosting to resemble seeds.

NUTRITION INFORMATION PER SERVING: Calories 215 • Total Fat 9g • Saturated Fat 4g • Cholesterol 25mg • Sodium 160mg • Total Carbohydrate 32g • Dietary Fiber 0g • Protein 2g. DIETARY EXCHANGES: 1 Starch • 1 Fruit • 2 Other Carbohydrate • 2 Fat.

## cook's notes

*Cover and refrigerate any leftover dumplings. To reheat, microwave each dumpling on High for 10 to 15 seconds.*

# cranberry-glazed apple dumplings

PREP TIME: 20 Minutes ❅ READY IN: 2 Hours 15 Minutes ❅ SERVINGS: 4

| | |
|---|---|
| 1 Pillsbury® refrigerated pie crust, softened as directed on box | 1 tablespoon sugar |
| 4 medium baking apples, peeled, cored | 1/4 teaspoon ground cinnamon |
| 2 tablespoons cream cheese | 1-1/2 cups raspberry-cranberry juice drink |
| 2 tablespoons sweetened dried cranberries | 2/3 cup sugar |

1 Heat oven to 400°F. Remove crust from pouch; place on work surface. With kitchen scissors or knife, cut crust into 8 wedges.

2 For each dumpling, place 2 crust wedges together at points, overlapping points about 1/2 inch; press to seal. Center 1 apple on overlapped points. Spoon about 1/2 tablespoon each of the cream cheese and cranberries into center of each apple.

3 In small bowl, mix 1 tablespoon sugar and the cinnamon; sprinkle each apple with 1/4 teaspoon sugar-cinnamon mixture. (Reserve remaining mixture.) Make 1 cut in each crust wedge from apple to edge to make 4 strips per apple. Separate strips enough to space evenly around apple. Bring strips up around apple, overlapping and sealing at top. Place wrapped apples in ungreased 8-inch square (2-quart) glass baking dish.

4 In 1-quart saucepan, mix juice drink and 2/3 cup sugar. Heat to boiling, stirring well to dissolve sugar. Pour over wrapped apples in the baking dish. Sprinkle the apples with remaining sugar-cinnamon mixture. Bake 35 to 45 minutes or until the apples are almost tender and the crust is deep golden brown.

5 Spoon sauce mixture from baking dish over each apple; bake 5 to 10 minutes longer or until apples are fork-tender. Cool at least 1 hour before serving. Serve sauce over dumplings.

**HIGH ALTITUDE (3500-6500 FT):** In Step 4, bake dumplings 45 to 55 minutes. In Step 5, bake 10 to 15 minutes longer. If pastry is overbrowning, cover dumplings loosely with foil during last 20 minutes of baking.

NUTRITION INFORMATION PER SERVING: Calories 550 • Total Fat 17g • Saturated Fat 7g • Cholesterol 15mg • Sodium 250mg • Total Carbohydrate 99g • Dietary Fiber 2g • Protein 0g. DIETARY EXCHANGES: 1/2 Starch • 1 Fruit • 5 Other Carbohydrate • 3-1/2 Fat • 6-1/2 Carb Choices.

# black-bottom banana cream pie

PREP TIME: 30 Minutes ❄ READY IN: 4 Hours 30 Minutes ❄ SERVINGS: 8

1 box (4-serving size) vanilla pudding and pie filling mix (not instant)

2 cups milk

1 Pillsbury® refrigerated pie crust, softened as directed on box

2/3 cup hot fudge topping

2 cups sliced ripe bananas (about 2 large bananas)

1 cup whipping cream, whipped

Chocolate curls, if desired

1 Make pudding mix with milk as directed on box for pie. Cool 30 minutes, stirring 2 or 3 times. Meanwhile, heat oven to 450°F. Bake pie crust as directed on box for One-Crust Baked Shell, using 9-inch glass pie plate. Cool on cooling rack 10 minutes.

2 Spread fudge topping in bottom of shell. Top with bananas, pudding and whipped cream. Refrigerate at least 4 hours until serving time. Garnish with chocolate curls. Cover and refrigerate any remaining pie.

NUTRITION INFORMATION PER SERVING: Calories 400 • Total Fat 20g • Saturated Fat 10g • Cholesterol 40mg • Sodium 300mg • Total Carbohydrate 51g • Dietary Fiber 1g • Protein 4g. DIETARY EXCHANGES: 1 Starch • 1/2 Fruit • 2 Other Carbohydrate • 4 Fat • 3-1/2 Carb Choices..

## cook's notes

To make chocolate curls, warm a chocolate bar by holding it in your hands for several minutes. Run a vegetable peeler across the bar to create the curls.

# Jolly Kitchen Creations

*Deck the halls* with this cute collection of shaped cookies, creative confections and other whimsical bites. Each adorable idea is sure to delight the child in everyone.

p. 276

p. 284

p. 279

p. 287

p. 281

white chocolate
gingerbread bears p. 285

marshmallow santas

# marshmallow santas

PREP TIME: 1 Hour 10 Minutes ✻ READY IN: 1 Hour 10 Minutes ✻ SERVINGS:10

cook's notes

As the coating cools and
hardens, microwave at
10-second intervals and
stir to keep smooth for use.

| | |
|---|---|
| 10 small pretzel twists | 1/2 cup shredded coconut |
| 5 oz. vanilla-flavored candy coating (almond bark) from 16- or 20-oz. package, chopped (slightly less than 1 cup) | 1/4 teaspoon pink sugar |
| | 10 red cinnamon candies |
| 20 large marshmallows | 10 red or green foil-wrapped milk chocolate candy bells |
| 1/4 cup red sugar | 5 large green gumdrops, cut in half |
| 40 miniature chocolate chips | 20 candy-coated chocolate candies |

1 Place cooking parchment paper or waxed paper on cookie sheet; place pretzels on paper for feet of Santas.

2 In 1-cup microwavable measuring cup, microwave candy coating uncovered on High 35 seconds, stir. Continue heating 10 seconds at a time until smooth after stirring.

3 Using wooden skewer inserted into 1 flat end of marshmallow, dip marshmallow into melted coating. Allow excess to drip off; sprinkle with red sugar and place on top of pretzel. Place 2 miniature chocolate chips on front for buttons (where feet extend). Insert another marshmallow on skewer; dip again, allow excess to drip off. Sprinkle with coconut; sprinkle with small amount of pink sugar for face; add eyes (miniature chocolate chips) and nose (red cinnamon candy). Place on top of other marshmallow. Set aside to cool, or refrigerate. Repeat with remaining marshmallows.

4 When coating is firm, attach hats (foil-wrapped chocolate candy bells) tassels (miniature marshmallows) and bags (gumdrop halves) with small amount of melted coating. Use toothpick to make small opening for arms (candy-coated chocolate candies); insert arms into marshmallows with small amount of melted coating.

NUTRITION INFORMATION PER SERVING: Calories 230 • Total Fat 8g • Saturated Fat 5g • Cholesterol 0mg • Sodium 60mg • Total Carbohydrate 39g • Dietary Fiber 0g • Protein 2g. DIETARY EXCHANGES: 1/2 Starch • 2 Other Carbohydrate • 1-1/2 Fat • 2-1/2 Carb Choices.

# brownie sundae pizza

PREP TIME: 10 Minutes ✻ READY IN: 2 Hours ✻ SERVINGS: 12

| | |
|---|---|
| 1 box (15.1 oz.) fudge brownie mix with hot fudge swirl | 1 pint (2 cups) vanilla ice cream |
| | 1/4 cup chopped peanuts |
| 1/4 cup oil | 1-1/2 cups whipped cream (from aerosol can) |
| 3 tablespoons water | 12 maraschino cherries with stems |
| 1 egg | |

1 Heat oven to 350°F. Grease 12-inch pizza pan. Reserve fudge packet from brownie mix package. In medium bowl, combine brownie mix, oil, water and egg; mix well. Spread batter in greased pan. Bake 17 minutes. Do not overbake. Cool 30 minutes or until completely cooled.

2 Meanwhile, place ice cream in refrigerator for 30 minutes to soften. Place reserved fudge packet in cup of hot water to soften fudge.

3 Spread softened ice cream over cooled brownie crust. Cut small hole in one corner of fudge packet. Drizzle fudge over ice cream. Sprinkle with peanuts.

4 Freeze at least 1 hour before serving. To serve, make 12 mounds of whipped cream evenly around edge of pizza. Top each with cherry.

**HIGH ALTITUDE (3500-6500 FT):** Add 2 tablespoons flour to dry brownie mix. Bake as directed above.

NUTRITION INFORMATION PER SERVING: Calories 280 • Total Fat 14g • Saturated Fat 5g • Trans Fat 0g • Cholesterol 35mg • Sodium 150mg • Total Carbohydrate 35g • Dietary Fiber 1g • Protein 4g. DIETARY EXCHANGES: 1 Starch • 1 1/2 Fruit • 2-1/2 Other Carbohydrate • 2-1/2 Fat.

# sweetheart cookie bouquet

PREP TIME: 1 Hour ✳ READY IN: 2 Hours ✳ SERVINGS: 4 cookie bouquets, 24 cookies

1 roll (16.5 oz.) Pillsbury® refrigerated chocolate chip cookies

24 craft sticks of various lengths

24 dark or milk chocolate heart candies, unwrapped

Decorative container

Plastic foam

Tissue paper

1 Heat oven to 350°F. Divide cookie dough into 24 (1-1/2-inch) balls. Place each cookie dough ball over one end of a craft stick; press gently to adhere dough to stick. Place 2 inches apart on ungreased cookie sheets, overlapping craft sticks as needed.

2 Bake at 350°F. for 10 to 12 minutes or until edges are light golden brown. Press 1 candy in center of each cookie. Cool on cookie sheets for 5 minutes. Remove from cookie sheets; cool 1 hour or until completely cooled. (Do no pick up cookie pops using stick until completely cooled.)

3 To assemble each cookie bouquet, place plastic foam in decorative container. Arrange six cookies in container as desired. Tuck tissue paper in between sticks to fill out bouquet.

NUTRITION INFORMATION PER SERVING: Calories 150 • Total Fat 7g • Saturated Fat 3g • Cholesterol 2mg • Sodium 85mg • Total Carbohydrate 20g • Dietary Fiber 1g • Protein 2g. DIETARY EXCHANGES: 1 Starch • 1-1/2 Fat • 1 Carb Choice.

# nutty little mice

PREP TIME: 1 Hour ✳ READY IN: 1 Hour 15 Minutes ✳ SERVINGS: 24 cookies

1 roll (16.5 oz.) Pillsbury® refrigerated peanut butter cookies

1/4 cup chopped salted peanuts

3 tablespoons all-purpose flour

2 tablespoons sugar

24 pieces (2 inch) red string candy or licorice

1 tube (0.68 oz.) white decorating gel

48 red cinnamon candies

24 semisweet chocolate chips

48 sliced almonds

1 Heat oven to 350°F. In large bowl, break up cookie dough. Stir or knead in chopped peanuts and flour until well blended. Work with half of the dough at a time; refrigerate the remaining dough until needed.

2 Place sugar in shallow dish. For each cookie, shape dough into 1-inch ball, then shape ball into 1-1/2-inch-long egg shape. Roll in sugar to coat. Place cookies 2 inches apart on ungreased cookie sheets. Repeat with remaining dough.

3 Bake 8 to 11 minutes or until light golden brown. Cool 1 minute; remove from cookie sheets. Immediately insert a string candy piece in one end of each cookie for tail. Cool completely, about 15 minutes.

4 On each cookie, use decorating gel to attach 2 cinnamon candies for eyes and 1 chocolate chip for nose. With sharp knife, make 2 small slits in each cookie above eyes; insert almond slices for ears. Store in tightly covered container.

NUTRITION INFORMATION PER SERVING: Calories 130 • Total Fat 6g • Saturated Fat 2g • Cholesterol 0mg • Sodium 110mg • Total Carbohydrate 17g • Dietary Fiber 0g • Protein 2g. DIETARY EXCHANGES: 1/2 Starch • 1/2 Other Carbohydrate • 1 Fat • 1 Carb Choice.

# mrs. claus' mittens

PREP TIME: 50 Minutes ✳ READY IN: 1 Hour 20 Minutes ✳ SERVINGS: 16 cookies

1 roll (16.5 oz.) Pillsbury® refrigerated gingerbread cookies

1 container (12 oz.) fluffy white whipped ready-to-spread frosting

1/2 to 1 teaspoon red paste icing color or 3 teaspoons red liquid food color

4 teaspoons white nonpareils

cook's notes

*For fun, make half of the mittens with the thumbs on the opposite sides. Arrange them on your cookie plate in pairs.*

1 Heat oven to 350°F. Work with half of cookie dough at a time; refrigerate remaining dough until needed. Cut dough into 8 (1/2-inch) slices.

2 For each cookie, cut off 1/3 of 1 slice of dough. Place larger piece of dough lengthwise on ungreased cookie sheet. Place smaller piece of dough slightly at a diagonal next to larger piece; press dough into 4-inch mitten shape. Repeat with remaining dough, placing the cookies 1 inch apart on cookie sheets.

3 Bake 7 to 10 minutes or until light golden brown and set. Cool 2 minutes; remove from cookie sheets. Cool completely, about 10 minutes.

4 In small bowl, place 1 cup of the frosting. Stir in red icing color until well blended. Frost mittens with red frosting.

5 Place remaining frosting in small resealable food-storage plastic bag; seal bag. Cut 1/8-inch hole in bottom corner of bag. Pipe white frosting at bottom of each mitten. Sprinkle each with 1/4 teaspoon nonpareils. Let stand until frosting is set, about 30 minutes. Store between sheets of waxed paper in tightly covered container.

NUTRITION INFORMATION PER SERVING: Calories 240 • Total Fat 11g • Saturated Fat 4.5g • Cholesterol 15mg • Sodium 105mg • Total Carbohydrate 34g • Dietary Fiber 0g • Protein 2g. DIETARY EXCHANGES: 1/2 Starch • 2 Other Carbohydrate • 2 Fat • 2 Carb Choices.

# confetti snowman cake

PREP TIME: 30 Minutes ✸ READY IN: 2 Hours 5 Minutes ✸ SERVINGS: 12

### CAKE

1 box (18.25 oz.) white cake mix with pudding in the mix (not butter recipe)

1-1/4 cups water

1/3 cup vegetable oil

3 egg whites

2 tablespoons red and green holiday decors

### FROSTING

1 container (1 lb.) creamy white ready-to-spread frosting

4 drops blue food color

### DECORATIONS

1 cup coconut

Red and green candy-coated chocolate-covered peanut candies or gumdrops

2 raisins

1 candy corn

1 brown licorice twist (6 inch), cut in half crosswise, or pretzel stick

1 red or green chewy fruit snack roll (from 4.5-oz. box)

1/2 round oatmeal cookie

1 pretzel rod half or licorice twist half

Snowflake sprinkles, if desired

1 Heat oven to 350°F. Grease bottom only of 13 x 9-inch pan with shortening. Make cake as directed on box with water, oil and egg whites. Stir in holiday decors. Pour batter into pan.

2 Bake 28 to 33 minutes or until cake springs back when touched lightly in center. Cool completely, about 1 hour.

3 With small plate or top of jar for pattern, cut 1 (4-inch) round and 1 (5-1/2- to 6-inch) round from waxed paper. Spread frosting over cake. Place waxed paper rounds on frosted cake to make snowman shape with larger round at bottom.

4 On each side of snowman pattern, carefully drop 2 drops of food color; swirl with knife around snowman to resemble sky. Remove and discard waxed paper.

5 Sprinkle coconut on snowman, filling in round shapes completely. Decorate with peanut candies for buttons, raisins for eyes, candy corn for nose, licorice for arms and fruit snack roll for scarf. Add cookie half for hat and pretzel rod for hat brim. Top blue area with snowflake sprinkles.

**HIGH ALTITUDE (3500-6500 FT):** Follow High Altitude cake mix directions for 13 x 9-inch pan.

NUTRITION INFORMATION PER SERVING: Calories 450 • Total Fat 18g • Saturated Fat 9g • Cholesterol 0mg • Sodium 330mg • Total Carbohydrate 69g • Dietary Fiber 0g • Protein 3g. DIETARY EXCHANGES: 1 Starch • 3-1/2 Other Carbohydrate • 3-1/2 Fat • 4-1/2 Carb Choices.

# carousel cupcakes

PREP TIME: 30 Minutes ✸ READY IN: 30 Minutes ✸ SERVINGS: 6 cupcakes

6 pretzel sticks

1 tablespoons semisweet chocolate chips, melted

6 animal crackers

1 container (1 lb.) strawberry whipped ready-to-spread frosting

6 unfrosted cupcakes, paper baking cups removed

Candy sprinkles

6 small paper beverage umbrellas

1 Dip 1 inch of one end of each pretzel into melted chocolate chips; press on back of 1 animal cracker. Place on sheet of waxed paper; let stand until chocolate is set.

2 Meanwhile, spread frosting on sides and bottom of cupcakes. Sprinkle with candy sprinkles. Insert 1 animal cracker on pretzel into each cupcake. Place umbrellas in center of cupcake.

NUTRITION INFORMATION PER SERVING: Calories 480 • Total Fat 17g • Saturated Fat 12g • Cholesterol 20mg • Sodium 170mg • Total Carbohydrate 80g • Dietary Fiber 0g • Protein 2g. DIETARY EXCHANGES: 1/2 Starch • 5 Other Carbohydrate • 3 Fat • 5 Carb Choices.

confetti snowman cake

# candy cane cookie box

PREP TIME: 1 Hour ✳ READY IN: 15 Hours 35 Minutes

1 half-gallon empty milk or juice carton, washed and dried

2/3 roll (16.5 oz. size) Pillsbury® refrigerated sugar cookies

1/2 cup all-purpose flour

**ROYAL ICING**

3 teaspoons meringue powder

1-1/2 cups powdered sugar

2 tablespoons water

Miniature candy canes and peppermint candies

**GLAZE**

1 cup powdered sugar

3 to 4 teaspoons milk

Sparkling sanding sugar, if desired

Snowflake candy sprinkles, if desired

1 Heat oven to 350°F. Draw a line around all sides of carton 3-3/4 inches from the bottom. Cut carton, discarding top half.

2 In large bowl, break up cookie dough (refrigerate 1/3 roll for another use). Stir or knead in flour until well blended. Sprinkle additional flour on work surface. Roll cookie dough 3/8 inch thick; cut into 4 (3-1/2-inch) squares.

3 Carefully place squares 2 inches apart on ungreased cookie sheets. Bake 12 to 14 minutes or until edges are light golden brown. Cool 2 minutes on cookie sheet; trim sides of each cookie to 3-3/4-inch square, using straight edge knife. Remove from cookie sheet to cooling rack. Cool completely, about 10 minutes.

4 Move cookies to waxed paper. In medium bowl, beat meringue powder, 1-1/2 cups powdered sugar and the water with electric mixer on low speed until blended; increase to high speed. Beat 5 to 10 minutes or until peaks form. If frosting is too stiff, beat in additional teaspoon water. Place icing in decorating bag fitted with writing tip #5. Using icing to attach candy canes; pipe icing around candy canes.

5 In small bowl, stir 1 cup powdered sugar and enough milk for desired spreading consistency. For Snowflake Cookie Box, spread or brush glaze on bottom half of 2 cookies to look like snow-covered hills. Immediately sprinkle with sanding sugar. Pipe icicles dripping from top of cookie. Use a dot of icing to attach each candy snowflake.

6 Spread 1 rounded tablespoon icing on 1 side of carton. Attach 1 cookie to icing; gently press. Repeat with remaining sides. Allow to dry until hardened, 4 to 6 hours or overnight, or use hot glue gun for cookies to hold immediately. (Cover and refrigerate icing if drying overnight.)

7 Using decorating bag fit with tip #3, pipe icing along sides and corners of box. Allow to dry completely, 4 to 6 hours or overnight. **(For decoration only; not edible.)**

# happy face cookie pops

PREP TIME: 45 Minutes ✳ READY IN: 1 Hour 45 Minutes ✳ SERVINGS: 24 cookie pops

24 flat wooden sticks with round ends
1 roll (16.5 oz.) Pillsbury® refrigerated sugar cookies
1 container(16 oz.) vanilla ready-to-spread frosting

Food color
Assorted small candies

1 Heat oven to 350°F. Cut cookie dough into 24 equal pieces. Roll each piece into ball; flatten each slightly in hand. Insert wooden stick into side of each ball. Place 2 inches apart on ungreased cookie sheets, overlapping wooden sticks as necessary.

2 Bake at 350°F. for 10 to 12 minutes or until edges are light golden brown. Cool on cookie sheets for 5 minutes. Remove from cookie sheets; place on wire racks. Cool 1 hour or until completely cooled. (Do not pick up cookie pops using stick until completely cooled.)

3 Divide frosting into small bowls or cups; add food color as desired. Frost cookies and decorate with candies to make faces.

**HIGH ALTITUDE (3500-6500 FT):** Bake at 350°F. for 12 to 14 minutes.

NUTRITION INFORMATION PER SERVING: Calories 190 • Total Fat 9g • Saturated Fat 1g • Cholesterol 0mg • Sodium 95mg • Total Carbohydrate 26g • Dietary Fiber 0g • Protein 1g. DIETARY EXCHANGES: 1-1/2 Other Carbohydrate • 1 Fat • 2 Carb Choice.

# christmas cookie meringues

PREP TIME: 30 Minutes ✳ READY IN: 1 Hour 15 Minutes ✳ SERVINGS: 7 dozen cookies

**COOKIES**
3 egg whites
1/4 teaspoon cream of tartar
1/2 cup sugar

**FILLING**
1 cup semisweet chocolate chips, melted
1/4 cup sugar
1 tablespoon coffee-flavored liqueur
1 egg, beaten
1/4 cup finely chopped walnuts

1 Heat oven to 275°F. Line cookie sheets with parchment paper or grease and flour cookie sheets. In small bowl, beat egg whites and cream of tartar at medium speed until soft peaks form. Gradually add 1/2 cup sugar, beating at high speed until stiff peaks form. Drop mixture by scant teaspoonfuls onto paper-lined cookie sheets.

2 In medium bowl, combine all filling ingredients except walnuts; mix well. Stir in walnuts. Drop 1/2 teaspoon filling onto each cookie.

3 Bake at 275°F. for 30 minutes. Do not open oven. Turn oven off; leave cookies in oven with door closed for 10 minutes. Remove from oven; cool completely. Remove cookies from paper.

NUTRITION INFORMATION PER SERVING: Calories 20 • Total Fat 1g • Saturated Fat 0g • Cholesterol 3mg • Sodium 0mg • Total Carbohydrate 3g • Dietary Fiber 0g • Protein 0g. DIETARY EXCHANGES: Free.

*cook's notes*

To make cocoa cookies meringues, add 2 teaspoons of unsweetened cocoa with the 1/2 cup of sugar.

chocolate-covered cheesecake trees

# chocolate-covered cheesecake trees

**PREP TIME:** 1 Hour 10 Minutes ✳ **READY IN:** 5 Hours 15 Minutes ✳ **SERVINGS:** 28

| | |
|---|---|
| 1 cup chocolate wafer crumbs | 28 paper lollipop sticks or flat wooden sticks with round ends |
| 1/4 cup butter or margarine, melted | |
| 2 packages (8 oz. each) cream cheese, softened | 3-1/2 cups semisweet chocolate chips (from 24-oz. bag) |
| 1/2 cup sugar | 3 tablespoons shortening |
| 1/4 cup sour cream | 2 oz. vanilla-flavored candy coating (almond bark), chopped |
| 1 teaspoon vanilla | 1/2 teaspoon vegetable oil |
| 2 eggs | 1 to 2 drops green paste food color, if desired |

1 Heat oven to 300°F. Line 8-inch square pan with heavy-duty foil so foil extends over sides of pan. In small bowl, mix wafer crumbs and butter. Press in bottom of pan.

2 In large bowl, beat cream cheese and sugar with electric mixer on medium speed until smooth. Beat in sour cream, vanilla and eggs. Pour over crust.

3 Bake 30 to 40 minutes or until edges are set (center will be soft but will set when cool). Cool in pan on cooling rack 30 minutes. Cover; freeze 2 hours.

4 Cover large cookie sheet with waxed paper. Remove cheesecake from pan by lifting foil; remove foil. Cut cheesecake lengthwise into 4 long pieces.

5 Working with 1 long piece at a time, cut each piece into 7 triangles (save corner pieces for snacking). Insert sticks into bottoms of triangles. Place on cookie sheet; freeze 30 minutes.

6 In 2-quart saucepan, melt chocolate chips and shortening over medium-low heat, stirring frequently, until smooth. Place in medium bowl.

7 Working in 2 batches of 14 (keep remaining trees in freezer until ready to coat), dip each tree quickly into melted chocolate to coat, letting excess drip off. Use knife or spatula to spread chocolate around stick entrance. Place crust side down on waxed paper.

8 In small microwavable bowl, microwave candy coating and oil uncovered on High 1 minute, stirring every 15 seconds, until melted. Stir in food color.

9 Spoon into 1-quart resealable food-storage plastic bag. Seal bag; cut off tiny corner of bag. Squeeze bag to pipe melted coating over trees to look like garland. Store covered in freezer.

NUTRITION INFORMATION PER SERVING: Calories 250 • Total Fat 17g • Saturated Fat 10g • Cholesterol 40mg • Sodium 90mg • Total Carbohydrate 21g • Dietary Fiber 1g • Protein 3g. DIETARY EXCHANGES: 1-1/2 Other Carbohydrate • 1/2 High-Fat Meat • 2-1/2 Fat • 1-1/2 Carb Choices.

# star puzzle decorations

PREP TIME: 20 Minutes  ✳  READY IN: 30 Minutes  ✳  SERVINGS: 6 (1 decoration per serving)

1   box Pillsbury® refrigerated pie crusts, softened as directed on box

Assorted small candy sprinkles, edible glitter or decorating sugars

1   Heat oven to 425°F. Grease cookie sheets or line with parchment paper. Remove crusts from pouches. Place on work surface. Using 3-inch, 3-1/2-inch and 4-inch star cookie cutters, cut 4 small (3-inch) stars, 4 medium (3-1/2-inch) stars and 4 large (4-inch) stars from crusts. Place on cookie sheet.

2   Using small sharp knife, cut out a thin wedge, about 1/4 inch past the center of each star, and about 1/4 inch at widest end of each wedge. Prick stars several times with fork. Decorate with desired sprinkles.

3   Bake 6 to 10 minutes or until light golden brown. Cool completely on cookie sheet, about 20 minutes. Remove from cookie sheet to cooling rack.

4   Attach same size baked stars by interlocking cut-out wedges, like a puzzle, making 3 dimensional standing stars. Use as table decorations.

NUTRITION INFORMATION PER SERVING: Calories 220 • Total Fat 13g • Saturated Fat 5g • Cholesterol 5mg • Sodium 210mg • Total Carbohydrate 25g • Dietary Fiber 0g • Protein 0g. DIETARY EXCHANGES: 1/2 Starch • 1 Other Carbohydrate • 2 1/2 Fat • 1-1/2 Carb Choices.

# family tree cake

PREP TIME: 25 Minutes  ✳  READY IN: 1 Hour 35 Minutes  ✳  SERVINGS: 20

1     box (1 lb. 2.25 oz.) yellow cake mix with pudding

1-1/4 cups water

1/3   cup vegetable oil

3     eggs

1     container (1 lb.) vanilla ready-to-spread frosting

1/2   cup chocolate ready-to-spread frosting (from 1-lb. container)

6     spearmint candy leaves, cut in half (from 13-oz. pkg.)

8     small red gumdrops, cut in half

Green paper leaves with guest names

1   Heat oven to 350°F. Grease bottom only of 15 x 10 x 1-inch pan with shortening. Make cake mix as directed on box using water, oil and eggs. Spread batter in pan.

2   Bake 20 to 25 minutes or until toothpick inserted in center comes out clean. Cool completely on cooling rack, about 45 minutes.

3   Spread vanilla frosting on top of cake. With toothpick, draw tree trunk on bottom 1/3 of cake. With chocolate frosting, fill in trunk and branches, using tines of fork to create bark on tree. Place candy leaves over top 2/3 of cake, leaving space between leaves.

4   With sharp knife, cut small slit in side of each gumdrop half. Insert one end of paper leaf in slit; place on cake.

NUTRITION INFORMATION PER SERVING: Calories 290 • Total Fat 11g • Saturated Fat 6g • Cholesterol 35mg • Sodium 180mg • Total Carbohydrate 45g • Dietary Fiber 0g • Protein 2g. DIETARY EXCHANGES: 1/2 Starch • 2-1/2 Other Carbohydrate • 2 Fat • 3 Carb Choices.

## cook's notes

Use a toothpick to outline the shape of the tree before frosting it with the canned chocolate frosting.

# marzipan snow people

PREP TIME: 45 Minutes ✳ READY IN: 45 Minutes ✳ SERVINGS: 8

1 package (7 or 8 oz.) marzipan or almond paste

56 slivered almonds (about 2 tablespoons)

8 round chocolate-covered peppermint candies (1-1/2 inches each), unwrapped

Multi-colored oblong candy sprinkles

2 packages (0.75 oz. each) fruit snacks in 3-foot rolls (any flavor)

8 small gumdrops

1 Roll marzipan into log shape; divide into 8 portions. Divide each portion into large (1-1/4-inch) ball, medium (1-inch) ball and small (3/4-inch) ball.

2 For each snow person, poke 1 slivered almond into center of chocolate-covered peppermint candy. Place large ball over almond, gently pushing downward to attach. Gently push 2 almonds in center of large ball; attach medium ball, gently pushing down. Gently push 1 almond in center of medium ball; place small ball over almond, gently pushing down to attach.

3 Using toothpick, make holes in face of snowman for eyes and nose. Place 2 brown oblong sprinkles into holes to look like eyes. Place 1 oblong sprinkle in hole to look like nose. If desired, make holes for buttons and add colored oblong sprinkles. Place 2 slivered almonds in center of middle ball to look like arms.

4 Unroll fruit snacks. For scarf; cut eight 5 x 1/2-inch strips. Fold each strip in half horizontally, leaving 1 inch on each end unfolded; make small cuts at ends for fringe. Wrap around neck, slightly overlapping at shoulder. To make base of hats, cut eight 3/4-inch diameter circles of fruit snack. Place fruit snack round on snowman's head. Insert slivered almond halfway down into center. Cut off and discard 1/8 inch off bottom of gumdrop; flatten bottom slightly. Attach onto slivered almond to finish hat.

NUTRITION INFORMATION PER SERVING: Calories 220 • Total Fat 9g • Saturated Fat 1.5g • Cholesterol 0mg • Sodium 15mg • Total Carbohydrate 33g • Dietary Fiber 2g • Protein 3g. DIETARY EXCHANGES: 2 Other Carbohydrate • 1/2 High-Fat Meat • 1 Fat • 2 Carb Choices.

## cook's notes

*If the marzipan is hard or crumbly, gently knead in a small amount of corn syrup, 1 teaspoon at a time, until desired softness.*

# layered christmas cake

PREP TIME: 45 Minutes  ✳  READY IN: 1 Hour 40 Minutes  ✳  SERVINGS: 12

**CAKE**
- 1 box white cake mix
- 1-1/4 cups water
- 1/4 cup oil
- 2 eggs

**FROSTING**
- 2/3 cup butter, softened
- 4 cups powdered sugar

- 3 to 5 tablespoons half-and-half or milk
- 1 teaspoon vanilla

**FILLING**
- 1-1/3 cups raspberry pie filling

**BOW**
- Red food color
- 1 package (7 oz.) marzipan

**1** Heat oven to 350°F. Grease and flour 15 x 10 x 1-inch baking pan. In large bowl, combine all cake ingredients; beat at low speed until moistened. Beat 2 minutes at high speed. Pour batter into greased and floured pan.

**2** Bake 15 to 20 minutes or until toothpick inserted in center comes out clean. Cool in pan on wire rack for 10 minutes. Remove from pan; cool completely.

**3** In large bowl, beat butter until light and fluffy. Gradually add powdered sugar and 2 tablespoons of the half-and-half, beating well after each addition. Add vanilla and additional half-and-half one tablespoon at a time, beating until of desired spreading consistency.

**4** To assemble cake, cut cake crosswise into thirds, forming three 10 x 5-inch layers. Place 1 cake layer on serving plate; pipe or spread small amount of frosting around top edge. Spread 2/3 cup raspberry pie filling on cake. Top with second cake layer; repeat with frosting and pie filling. Top with remaining cake layer. Frost cake with remaining frosting.

**5** Knead a few drops of red food color into marzipan until of desired color. Place between 2 sheets of parchment or waxed paper; roll to 1/4-inch thickness. With knife or pastry wheel, cut into 3/4-inch-wide strips. Place strips on cake to resemble ribbon on package; fold additional strips to form bow.

**HIGH ALTITUDE (3500-6500 FT):** Add 1/4 cup flour to dry cake mix. Bake as directed above.

NUTRITION INFORMATION PER SERVING: Calories 610 • Total Fat 25g • Saturated Fat 9g • Cholesterol 65mg • Sodium 400mg • Total Carbohydrate 90g • Dietary Fiber 2g • Protein 5g. DIETARY EXCHANGES: 2 Starch • 4 Fruit • 6 Other Carbohydrate • 5 Fat.

# mint meringue parfaits

PREP TIME: 15 Minutes  ✳  READY IN: 15 Minutes  ✳  SERVINGS: 4

- 1 cup frozen (thawed) whipped topping
- 1/8 teaspoon mint extract
- 1 pint (2 cups) chocolate ice cream

- 1/2 cup chocolate topping
- 8 mint meringue cookies (from 4.25-oz. pkg.), coarsely crushed

**1** In medium bowl, gently stir whipped topping and mint extract to blend.

**2** In each of four tall glasses, layer 1/4 cup ice cream, 1 tablespoon chocolate topping, 1 heaping tablespoon crushed cookies and 2 tablespoons mint whipped topping. Repeat layers. Sprinkle with remaining crushed cookies. Serve immediately.

NUTRITION INFORMATION PER SERVING: Calories 350 • Total Fat 11g • Saturated Fat 8g • Trans Fat 0g • Cholesterol 20mg • Sodium 90mg • Total Carbohydrate 57g • Dietary Fiber 2g • Protein 4g. DIETARY EXCHANGES: 1 Starch • 3 Other Carbohydrate • 2 Fat • 4 Carb Choices.

layered christmas cake

# secret santa trees

**PREP TIME:** 20 Minutes • **READY IN:** 25 Minutes ✳ **SERVINGS:** 8

1 container (12 oz.) fluffy white or vanilla whipped ready-to-spread frosting

16 small foil-wrapped milk chocolate Santa candies

8 fudge-striped cookies

8 sugar-style ice cream cones with pointed ends

2 to 3 drops green food color

Sugar sequins, sugar crystals or assorted decors

1 For each tree, place small amount of frosting between backs of 2 wrapped Santa candies; attach to bottom of cookie with small amount of frosting.

2 Spread rim of cone with small amount of vanilla frosting. Attach over Santa to 1 cookie, chocolate side to cone. Stand upright on tray. Let stand 5 minutes.

3 Stir food color into remaining frosting; frost each tree with 3 tablespoons green frosting. Decorate with sugar sequins, crystals or decors as desired. For frosting to be firm to touch, prepare the day before serving.

NUTRITION INFORMATION PER SERVING: Calories 400 • Total Fat 19g • Saturated Fat 8g • Cholesterol 0mg • Sodium 110mg • Total Carbohydrate 54g • Dietary Fiber 1g • Protein 3g. DIETARY EXCHANGES: 1 Starch • 2 1/2 Other Carbohydrate • 3-1/2 Fat • 3-1/2 Carb Choices.

# white chocolate gingerbread bears

**PREP TIME:** 1 Hour 45 Minutes • **READY IN:** 2 Hours 45 Minutes **SERVINGS:** About 8 dozen cookies

| | |
|---|---|
| 1-1/2 cups sugar | 2 teaspoons baking soda |
| 1 cup butter or margarine, softened | 2 teaspoons ground ginger |
| 1/3 cup molasses | 2 teaspoons ground cinnamon |
| 1 egg | 1/2 teaspoon salt |
| 2 cups all-purpose or unbleached flour | 3 oz. (1/2 cup) white vanilla baking chips or vanilla-flavored candy coating, melted |
| 1 cup whole wheat flour | Decorating icing, if desired |

1. In large bowl, beat sugar and butter until light and fluffy. Add molasses and egg; blend well. Stir in all-purpose flour, whole wheat flour, baking soda, ginger, cinnamon and salt; mix well. Cover with plastic wrap; refrigerate 1 hour for easier handling.

2. Heat oven to 350°F. On lightly floured surface, roll out dough, 1/4 at a time, to 1/8-inch thickness. Refrigerate remaining dough until ready to roll. Cut dough with floured 4-1/2-inch bear-shaped cookie cutter. Place 1 inch apart on ungreased cookie sheets. Using small heart-shaped canapé cutter, cut design from center of each bear.

3. Bake heart shapes on separate cookie sheet 5 to 7 minutes or until set. Bake bears 6 to 9 minutes or until set. Cool 1 minute; remove from cookie sheets. Cool completely. Line large cookie sheet with sides with waxed paper. Spread backs of cooled cookies with melted vanilla chips; place on cookie sheet. Refrigerate to set. Dip gingerbread hearts into melted vanilla chips and press to bear's paw. Add facial features with decorating icing. Allow frosting to set. Store between sheets of waxed paper in loosely covered container.

**cook's notes**

*Don't let even a drop of water come into contact with the chips when you melt them. Water will cause the melted chips to harden and to streak.*

NUTRITION INFORMATION PER SERVING: Calories 50 • Total Fat 2.5g • Saturated Fat 1.5g • Cholesterol 5mg • Sodium 55mg • Total Carbohydrate 8g • Dietary Fiber 0g • Protein 0g. DIETARY EXCHANGES: 1/2 Other Carbohydrate • 1/2 Fat • 1/2 Carb Choice.

chocolate candy cupcakes

# chocolate candy cupcakes

PREP TIME: 25 Minutes ✳ READY IN: 1 Hour 40 Minutes ✳ SERVINGS: 18

### CUPCAKES

- 2 packages (3 oz. each) cream cheese, softened
- 2 tablespoons powdered sugar
- 1 egg
- 2 chocolate-covered nougat, caramel and peanut candy bars (2.07 oz. each), unwrapped, finely chopped
- 1-1/2 cups all-purpose flour
- 1 cup granulated sugar
- 1/3 cup unsweetened baking cocoa
- 1 teaspoon baking soda
- 1/2 teaspoon salt
- 1 cup buttermilk
- 1/3 cup vegetable oil
- 1 teaspoon vanilla

### FROSTING

- 1/3 cup packed brown sugar
- 1/3 cup butter or margarine
- 3 tablespoons milk
- 1-1/2 cups powdered sugar
- 1 chocolate-covered nougat, caramel and peanut candy bar (2.07 oz.), unwrapped, finely chopped, if desired

**1** Heat oven to 350°F. Place paper baking cups in each of 18 regular-size muffin cups. In small bowl, beat cream cheese, 2 tablespoons powdered sugar and the egg with electric mixer on medium speed until smooth. With spoon, stir in 2 chopped candy bars; set aside.

**2** In large bowl, mix flour, granulated sugar, cocoa, baking soda and salt. Add buttermilk, oil and vanilla; beat 2 minutes with mixer on medium speed. Divide batter evenly among muffin cups, filling each half full. Spoon 1 tablespoon cream cheese mixture in center of batter in each cup.

**3** Bake 23 to 30 minutes or until the cream cheese mixture is light golden brown. Cool in pans about 15 minutes. (Cupcakes will sink slightly in center.) Remove cupcakes from muffin cups. Cool completely, about 30 minutes.

**4** Meanwhile, in 1-1/2-quart saucepan, cook brown sugar and butter over medium heat just until mixture boils, stirring frequently. Remove from heat. Stir in milk. Cool 30 minutes. With spoon, beat 1-1/2 cups powdered sugar into brown sugar mixture until spreading consistency, adding 1 tablespoon additional powdered sugar at a time if necessary.

**5** Frost cooled cupcakes. Sprinkle with chopped candy bar.

**HIGH ALTITUDE (3500-6500 FT):** Heat oven to 375°F. Bake 16 to 23 minutes.

NUTRITION INFORMATION PER SERVING: Calories 290 • Total Fat 13g • Saturated Fat 6g • Cholesterol 35mg • Sodium 220mg • Total Carbohydrate 40g • Dietary Fiber 1g • Protein 4g. DIETARY EXCHANGES: 1 Starch • 1-1/2 Other Carbohydrate • 2-1/2 Fat • 2-1/2 Carb Choices.

---

# seaside pudding cups

PREP TIME: 20 Minutes ✳ READY IN: 20 Minutes ✳ SERVINGS: 12

- 6 cinnamon shortbread cookies
- 2 packages (24 oz. each) refrigerated strawberries and creme swirled pudding snacks (12 cups)
- 1 roll chewy fruit snacks in 3-foot rolls (any flavor from 4.5-oz. box)
- 24 teddy graham snacks
- 12 drink umbrellas
- 12 ring-shaped hard candies

**1** Place cookies in small resealable food-storage plastic bag. With hand or rolling pin, crush cookies. Sprinkle about 1 tablespoon crushed cookies on top of each cup of pudding.

**2** Cut chewy fruit snack into 12 (1-inch) pieces. Peel each piece of fruit snack from plastic backing; place over crushed cookies on pudding for "beach towel." Top each "towel" with teddy bear and umbrella. Place 1 hard candy around each remaining teddy bear for "inner tube;" place 1 on each pudding cup.

NUTRITION INFORMATION PER SERVING: Calories 180 • Total Fat 4.5g • Saturated Fat 2.5g • Cholesterol 10mg • Sodium 120mg • Total Carbohydrate 33g • Dietary Fiber 0g • Protein 2g. DIETARY EXCHANGES: 1 Starch • 1 Other Carbohydrate • 1 Fat • 2 Carb Choices.

---

## cook's notes

*To substitute for buttermilk, combine 1 tablespoon vinegar or lemon juice plus milk to make 1 cup.*

## kitchen tip

*In place of the cinnamon shortbread cookies, you can use vanilla wafer cookies.*

## cook's notes

The cookie bark can be cut

into bars after refrigerating

for 1 hour.

# peanut butter cookie bark

**PREP TIME:** 35 Minutes ✳ **READY IN:** 5 Hours 20 Minutes ✳ **SERVINGS:** 40 pieces

| | |
|---|---|
| 4 cups Golden Grahams® Cereal | 1 bag (12 oz.) semisweet chocolate chips |
| 1 cup unsalted butter or butter | 1 cup peanut butter chips |
| 1 cup packed light brown sugar | 1/2 cup chopped peanuts |
| 1 roll (16.5 oz.) Pillsbury® refrigerated peanut butter cookies | |

1 Heat oven to 350°F. Line 15 x 10 x 3/4-inch pan with heavy-duty foil, extending foil over sides of pan. In blender or food processor, blend or process cereal until fine crumbs form.

2 In 2-quart saucepan, melt butter and brown sugar over medium-high heat 3 to 5 minutes, stirring frequently, until mixture boils and coats back of spoon. Remove from heat. Add cereal crumbs; stir until well combined. Spread and press evenly in foil-lined pan. Bake at 350°F. for 7 minutes. Meanwhile, cut cookie dough into 16 slices.

3 Remove pan from oven. With hands, flatten cookie slices slightly; arrange on hot cereal mixture in 4 rows of 4 slices each. Let stand 2 to 3 minutes to soften dough (heat from cereal mixture will allow unbaked cookies to become warm and easier to spread). With spatula, press and carefully spread dough evenly over cereal mixture. Return to oven; bake 12 to 14 minutes or until puffed and golden brown.

4 Remove pan from oven. Sprinkle chocolate chips evenly over top. Return to oven; bake an additional minute. Remove pan from oven; spread softened chocolate chips over cookie layer. Sprinkle peanut butter chips evenly over chocolate. Return to oven; bake an additional minute.

5 Remove pan from oven. With small metal spatula or knife, lightly swirl melted peanut butter chips over chocolate. Sprinkle peanuts over top; press in lightly. Cool 30 minutes. Refrigerate 4 hours. With foil, lift bark from pan; break into 2-inch pieces. Store in refrigerator.

**HIGH ALTITUDE (3500-6500 FT):** After pressing and spreading cookie dough slices over the cereal mixture, bake at 350°F. for 14 to 16 minutes. Continue as directed above.

NUTRITION INFORMATION PER SERVING: Calories 190 • Total Fat 12g • Saturated Fat 5g • Cholesterol 15mg • Sodium 100mg • Total Carbohydrate 20g • Dietary Fiber 1g • Protein 2g. DIETARY EXCHANGES: 1 Starch • 2-1/2 Fat • 1 Carb Choice.

# easy gumdrop whirligigs

PREP TIME: 50 Minutes ✳ READY IN: 50 Minutes ✳ SERVINGS: 18 large cookies

1 roll (16.5 oz.) Pillsbury® refrigerated sugar cookies

18 flat wooden sticks with rounded ends

9 small gumdrops (cut in half crosswise)
Red and/or green sugar

1 Heat oven to 350°F. Remove half of cookie dough from wrapper; refrigerate remaining dough until needed. On lightly floured surface with rolling pin, roll half of dough into 9-inch square (make edges square with side of ruler). Cut into 9 (3-inch) squares; place on ungreased large cookie sheet.

2 With sharp knife or fluted pastry wheel, cut each square from each corner almost to the center, leaving about 1 inch uncut in center. Place wooden stick on each square with one end in center. Fold alternate corners of square over, pressing in center. Place gumdrop half in center to resemble button. Sprinkle whirligigs with red and/or green sugar. Repeat with remaining half of dough.

3 Bake 9 to 11 minutes or until golden brown. Cool 1 minute; remove from cookie sheet and place on wire racks. Cool completely, about 15 minutes.

NUTRITION INFORMATION PER SERVING: Calories 130 • Total Fat 5g • Saturated Fat 1.5g • Cholesterol 10mg • Sodium 75mg • Total Carbohydrate 20g • Dietary Fiber 0g • Protein 0g. DIETARY EXCHANGES: 1-1/2 Other Carbohydrate • 1 Fat • 1 Carb Choice.

*cook's notes*

*To cut the gumdrops easily,*

*use a sharp knife or scissors*

*coated with cooking spray.*

*Another idea: Dip the scissor*

*blades or the knife in a glass*

*of water as you work.*

# strawberry-rhubarb meringue clouds

PREP TIME: 35 Minutes ✳ READY IN: 2 Hours 35 Minutes ✳ SERVINGS: 8

**MERINGUE SHELLS**

3 egg whites

1/4 teaspoon cream of tartar

1/2 cup sugar

**FILLING**

2 cups sliced fresh or frozen rhubarb

2/3 cup sugar

2 tablespoons cornstarch

1/2 cup water

1 cup halved fresh strawberries

1 Heat oven to 225°F. Grease 2 cookie sheets with shortening or cooking spray. In large bowl, beat egg whites and cream of tartar with electric mixer on medium speed until soft peaks form. On high speed, gradually beat in 1/2 cup sugar until stiff glossy peaks form and sugar is almost dissolved. Spoon meringue into 8 (4- to 5-inch) rounds on cookie sheets, hollowing center slightly with back of spoon to form shells.

2 Bake 1 hour. Do not open oven. Turn oven off; let meringue shells stand in the oven with door closed 1 hour.

3 Meanwhile, in 2-quart saucepan, mix all filling ingredients except strawberries. Cook over medium-low heat 15 to 20 minutes, stirring frequently, until filling is slightly thickened and rhubarb is soft. Stir in strawberries. Cool completely, about 1 hour. Store filling in refrigerator.

4 Spoon about 1/4 cup filling into each meringue shell. Serve immediately.

NUTRITION INFORMATION PER SERVING: Calories 140 • Total Fat 0g • Saturated Fat 0g • Cholesterol 0mg • Sodium 20mg • Total Carbohydrate 33g • Dietary Fiber 0g • Protein 2g. DIETARY EXCHANGES: 1/2 Starch • 1-1/2 Other Carbohydrate • 2 Carb Choices.

# Gifts of Good Taste

*You'll put smiles* on loved ones' faces after giving them delightful homemade treats. These cookies, specialty breads and candies make gift giving extra-special.

p. 294

p. 299

p. 307

p. 293

p. 302

cranberry-orange
biscotti p. 299

# puffy pink popcorn hearts

PREP TIME: 20 Minutes ✶ READY IN: 25 Minutes ✶ SERVINGS: 8

 1  bag (10 oz.) large marshmallows
1/4  cup butter or margarine
 4  drops red food color

8  cups popped light butter flavor microwave popcorn (from 3.5-oz. bag)

1 In 3-quart saucepan, cook marshmallows and butter over medium heat, stirring constantly, just until marshmallows are melted. Remove from heat. Stir in food color.

2 Stir in popped popcorn until evenly coated. Cool 5 minutes.

3 With buttered hands, shape 1 cup mixture into heart shape. Repeat with remaining mixture. Wrap each heart in plastic wrap.

NUTRITION INFORMATION PER SERVING: Calories 220 • Total Fat 9g • Saturated Fat 3.5g • Cholesterol 15mg • Sodium 130mg • Total Carbohydrate 33g • Dietary Fiber 0g • Protein 1g. DIETARY EXCHANGES: 2 Other Carbohydrate • 2 Fat • 2 Carb Choices.

# cookie crumb truffle mice

PREP TIME: 45 Minutes ✻ READY IN: 45 Minutes ✻ SERVINGS: 24

| | |
|---|---|
| 25 creme-filled chocolate sandwich cookies | 1 can (1 lb.) vanilla ready-to-spread frosting |
| 1 package (3 oz.) cream cheese, softened | 1 to 2 tablespoons chocolate ready-to-spread frosting (from 1-lb. can) |
| 48 almond slices | |

1 Line shallow baking pan with waxed paper. Place cookies in large plastic bag and seal, or in food processor bowl with metal blade. Crush cookies with rolling pin or process until crumbs form.

2 Add cream cheese to bag or processor bowl; squeeze bag or process until well combined. Shape mixture into 24 (1-inch) balls. Pinch one side of each ball to form teardrop shape. Insert 2 almond slices about 1/2 inch from pointed end for ears. Place in waxed paper-lined pan.

3 Remove lid and foil from can of vanilla frosting. Microwave on High for 15 seconds. Stir; microwave on High in 5 second increments until smooth and pourable, stirring after heating.

4 Place 1 truffle on fork; dip in melted frosting, allowing excess to drip off. Return to waxed paper-lined pan. Repeat with remaining truffles, reheating frosting in microwave as necessary.

5 Place chocolate frosting in resealable small plastic bag; seal bag. Cut tiny hole in bottom corner of bag. Squeeze bag to pipe "eyes," "nose" and "tail" on each truffle. Refrigerate 15 minutes or until frosting is set.

NUTRITION INFORMATION PER SERVING: Calories 150 • Total Fat 7g • Saturated Fat 4g • Cholesterol 5mg • Sodium 80mg • Total Carbohydrate 22g • Dietary Fiber 1g • Protein 1g. DIETARY EXCHANGES: 1/2 Starch • 1 Fruit • 1-1/2 Other Carbohydrate • 1 Fat.

# chocolate swirl almond toffee

PREP TIME: 30 Minutes ✳ READY IN: 1 Hour ✳ SERVINGS: 42

**TOFFEE**
- 1 cup butter or margarine
- 2 tablespoons light corn syrup
- 2 tablespoons water
- 1 cup sugar
- 1 cup chopped almonds

**TOPPING**
- 1/2 cup semisweet chocolate chips
- 1/2 cup white vanilla baking chips

1 Line 15 x 10 x 1-inch pan with foil. Butter foil. In 2-quart saucepan, mix butter, corn syrup, water and sugar. Cook over medium heat until sugar dissolves and mixture boils, stirring constantly. Cook until candy thermometer reaches soft-crack stage (290°F.). Remove saucepan from heat. Quickly stir in almonds. Pour mixture into buttered foil-lined pan. Let stand 2 to 3 minutes to harden.

2 Sprinkle chips over hot toffee; let stand 1 to 1-1/2 minutes to soften. With knife, swirl softened chips over toffee. Refrigerate about 30 minutes or until chocolate is set. Break toffee into serving-size pieces.

**HIGH ALTITUDE (3500-6500 FT):** Cook until candy thermometer reaches high altitude soft-crack stage (260°F. to 286°F.).

NUTRITION INFORMATION PER SERVING: Calories 110 • Total Fat 7g • Saturated Fat 4g • Cholesterol 10mg • Sodium 40mg • Total Carbohydrate 9g • Dietary Fiber 0g • Protein 0g. DIETARY EXCHANGES: 1/2 Other Carbohydrate • 1-1/2 Fat • 1/2 Carb Choice.

# christmas fruitcake braid

PREP TIME: 25 Minutes ✳ READY IN: 50 Minutes ✳ SERVINGS: 8

- 1 can (8 oz.) Pillsbury® refrigerated crescent dinner rolls
- 1/3 cup apricot or peach preserves
- 1/4 cup finely chopped dried apricots
- 1/4 cup finely chopped sweetened dried pineapple
- 1/4 cup sweetened dried cherries or cranberries
- 1 egg white, beaten
- 2 tablespoons sliced almonds

1 Heat oven to 375°F. Grease cookie sheet. On cookie sheet, unroll dough into 2 long rectangles. Overlap long sides 1/4 inch; press edges firmly to seal. Press into 12 x 8-inch rectangle, pressing perforations to seal.

2 Spoon and spread preserves down center 1/3 of rectangle. Sprinkle evenly with apricots, pineapple and cherries. On each long side of rectangle, make cuts 1 inch apart to edge of filling. Fold opposite strips of dough over filling, twisting strips once, to form a braided appearance; seal ends.

3 Brush top with beaten egg white; sprinkle with almonds. Bake 18 to 22 minutes or until deep golden brown.

NUTRITION INFORMATION PER SERVING: Calories 190 • Total Fat 7g • Saturated Fat 2g • Cholesterol 0mg • Sodium 230mg • Total Carbohydrate 29g • Dietary Fiber 1g • Protein 3g. DIETARY EXCHANGES: 1 Starch • 1 Other Carbohydrate • 1 Fat • 2 Carb Choices.

chocolate swirl almond toffee

# orange-pecan cookies

PREP TIME: 1 Hour 30 Minutes ✳ READY IN: 1 Hour 30 Minutes ✳ SERVINGS: 60

1 cup sugar
1 cup margarine or butter, softened
2 eggs
3 cups all purpose flour
1 teaspoon baking soda
1/2 teaspoon salt

1 can (6 oz.) frozen orange juice concentrate, thawed, reserving 3 tablespoons
1/2 cup chopped pecans
1/2 cup golden raisins
1 tablespoon water
Sugar

1 Heat oven to 375°F. In large bowl, combine 1 cup sugar, margarine and eggs; blend well.

2 Lightly spoon flour into measuring cup; level off. In small bowl, combine flour, baking soda and salt. Alternately add dry ingredients and orange juice concentrate to sugar mixture, mixing well after each addition. Stir in pecans and raisins. Drop by teaspoonfuls 2 inches apart onto ungreased cookie sheets.

3 Bake 7 to 11 minutes or until light golden brown. Immediately remove from cookie sheets; place on wire racks.

4 In small bowl, combine reserved orange juice concentrate and water; brush over tops of cookies. Sprinkle with sugar.

**HIGH ALTITUDE (3500-6500 FT):** Increase flour to 3-1/4 cups. Bake as directed above.

NUTRITION INFORMATION PER SERVING: Calories 90 • Total Fat 4g • Saturated Fat 1g • Cholesterol 5mg • Sodium 75mg • Total Carbohydrate 12g • Dietary Fiber 0g • Protein 1g. DIETARY EXCHANGES: 1/2 Starch • 1/2 Fruit • 1 Other Carbohydrate • 1/2 Fat.

# two-in-one holiday bars

PREP TIME: 20 Minutes ✳ READY IN: 1 Hour 50 Minutes ✳ SERVINGS: 48

**BASE**

- 1 cup granulated sugar
- 3/4 cup butter or margarine, softened
- 1 teaspoon vanilla
- 1 egg
- 2 cups all-purpose flour

- 1 cup diced mixed candied fruit
- 1/2 cup semisweet chocolate chips
- 1/2 cup chopped pecans

**GLAZE**

- 1 cup powdered sugar
- 1 to 2 tablespoons milk

1 Heat oven to 350°F. In large bowl, beat granulated sugar and butter with electric mixer on medium speed until light and fluffy. On low speed, beat in vanilla and egg. Beat in flour until well blended. Spread dough in ungreased 15 x 10 x 1-inch pan.

2 Sprinkle half of dough with candied fruit; sprinkle other half with chocolate chips and pecans. Press lightly into dough.

3 Bake 25 to 30 minutes or until edges are light golden brown. Cool completely, about 1 hour.

4 In small bowl, mix powdered sugar and enough milk until smooth for desired drizzling consistency. Drizzle over cooled bars. Let stand until glaze is set. For bars, cut into 8 rows by 6 rows.

**HIGH ALTITUDE (3500-6500 FT):** Increase flour to 2-1/4 cups.

NUTRITION INFORMATION PER SERVING: Calories 100 • Total Fat 3g • Saturated Fat 2g • Cholesterol 10mg • Sodium 30mg • Total Carbohydrate 17g • Dietary Fiber 0g • Protein 0g. DIETARY EXCHANGES: 1 Other Carbohydrate • 1/2 Fat • 1 Carb Choice.

*cook's notes*

*To avoid mingling flavors, store each of the two types of bars separately. Before storing, allow the glaze to set, then layer the bars in an airtight container between sheets of waxed paper.*

cranberry-orange biscotti

# cranberry-orange biscotti

PREP TIME: 1 Hour 5 Minutes ✳ READY IN: 1 Hour 45 Minutes ✳ SERVINGS: 48

1/2 cup sugar

1/2 cup firmly packed brown sugar

1/4 cup butter or margarine, softened

2 teaspoons grated orange peel

3 eggs

3 cups all-purpose flour

3 teaspoons baking powder

3/4 cup sweetened dried cranberries, chopped

1/4 cup chopped almonds

**GLAZE**

8 oz. white chocolate baking bar, chopped

1 cup dark chocolate chips

1 teaspoon grated orange peel

1 Heat oven to 350°F. Spray 1 large or 2 small cookie sheets with cooking spray. In 4-quart bowl, beat sugar, brown sugar and butter with electric mixer on medium speed until well blended. Add 2 teaspoons orange peel and the eggs; beat well. Stir in flour and baking powder; mix well. Stir in cranberries and almonds.

2 Shape dough into 3 rolls, each about 7 inches long. Place rolls at least 3 inches apart on cookie sheet; flatten each to form 3/4-inch-thick rectangle, about 3 inches wide and 7 inches long.

3 Bake 20 to 25 minutes or until rectangles are light golden brown and centers are firm to the touch. Place rectangles on cooling racks; cool 5 minutes.

4 Wipe cookie sheet clean. With serrated knife, cut each rectangle into 1/2-inch slices; place, cut side up, on cookie sheet.

5 Bake 6 to 8 minutes or until top surface is slightly dry. Turn cookies over; bake 6 to 8 minutes longer or until top surface is slightly dry. Remove cookies from cookie sheets; cool completely on cooling racks.

6 Melt white chocolate in 2-quart heavy saucepan over low heat, stirring until smooth. Remove from heat; dip 1 long side of each of 24 cookies into chocolate. Place on waxed paper until chocolate is set. In another 2-quart heavy saucepan, melt dark chocolate over low heat, stirring until smooth. Remove from heat; dip 1 long side of remaining 24 cookies into chocolate. Place on waxed paper until chocolate is set. Store tightly covered.

NUTRITION INFORMATION PER SERVING: Calories 110 • Total Fat 4.5g • Saturated Fat 2.5g • Cholesterol 15mg • Sodium 45mg • Total Carbohydrate 17g • Dietary Fiber 0g • Protein 2g. DIETARY EXCHANGES: 1 Other Carbohydrate • 1 Fat • 1 Carb Choice.

# marshmallow melties

PREP TIME: 15 Minutes ✳ READY IN: 15 Minutes ✳ SERVINGS: 24

3 tablespoons butter or margarine

1 bag (10-1/2 oz.) miniature marshmallows (6 cups)

5 cups Cheerios® cereal

1 Butter 13 x 9-inch pan. Microwave the butter and marshmallows in a large microwavable bowl uncovered on High about 2 minutes, stirring after every minute, until smooth. Immediately stir in cereal until evenly coated.

2 Press mixture in pan; cool. For bars, cut into 6 rows by 4 rows. Store loosely covered.

NUTRITION INFORMATION PER SERVING: Calories 80 • Total Fat 2g • Saturated Fat 0.5g • Cholesterol 0mg • Sodium 60mg • Total Carbohydrate 15g • Dietary Fiber 0g • Protein 0g. DIETARY EXCHANGES: 1/2 Starch • 1/2 Other Carbohydrate • 1/2 Fat • 1 Carb Choice.

*cook's notes*

*You can easily substitute Banana Nut Cheerios® for regular Cheerios.*

# cherry chocolate biscotti

PREP TIME: 40 Minutes ✳ READY IN: 1 Hour 10 Minutes ✳ SERVINGS: 36 biscotti

| | |
|---|---|
| 3/4 cup sugar | 1/2 cup chopped candied cherries |
| 1/2 cup butter or margarine, softened | 1/2 cup miniature semisweet chocolate chips |
| 2 teaspoons almond extract | 3 tablespoons semisweet chocolate chips, melted, if desired |
| 3 eggs | |
| 3 cups all-purpose flour | 3 tablespoons white vanilla baking chips, melted, if desired |
| 2 teaspoons baking powder | |

1 Heat oven to 350°F. Lightly grease cookie sheet. In large bowl, beat sugar and butter with electric mixer on medium speed until well blended. Beat in almond extract and eggs until smooth.

2 On low speed, beat in flour and baking powder until well blended. With spoon, stir in cherries and miniature chocolate chips. Shape dough into two 10-inch rolls. Place rolls 5 inches apart on cookie sheet; flatten each to 3-inch width.

3 Bake 20 to 25 minutes or until set and light golden brown. Remove from cookie sheet; place on cooling racks. Cool 10 minutes. With serrated knife, cut rolls diagonally into 1/2-inch slices. Arrange slices, cut side down, on same cookie sheets.

4 Bake 8 to 10 minutes or until bottoms begin to brown. Turn cookies over; bake 5 minutes longer or until browned and crisp. Remove from cookie sheets. Cool completely, about 15 minutes. Drizzle cookies with melted chocolate and vanilla chips. Store in tightly covered container.

NUTRITION INFORMATION PER SERVING: Calories 100 • Total Fat 4g • Saturated Fat 2g • Cholesterol 25mg • Sodium 55mg • Total Carbohydrate 16g • Dietary Fiber 0g • Protein 2g. DIETARY EXCHANGES: 1/2 Starch • 1/2 Other Carbohydrate • 1 Fat • 1 Carb Choice.

# festive fruitcake treats

PREP TIME: 45 Minutes ✳ READY IN: 1 Hour 45 Minutes ✳ SERVINGS: 48

**COOKIES**
- 1 roll (16.5oz.) Pillsbury® refrigerated sugar cookies
- 1 package (7 oz.) diced dried fruits and raisins
- 1/2 cup chopped walnuts
- 1/2 teaspoon ground cinnamon
- 1/4 cup apple jelly

**CUPS**
- 48 miniature paper or foil baking cups (1-1/4-inch diameter)

**ICING**
- 10 vanilla caramels, unwrapped
- 1 tablespoon milk

**GARNISH**
- 48 sweetened dried cranberries, if desired

1 Heat oven to 350°F. In large bowl, break up cookie dough. Stir in dried fruits, walnuts, cinnamon and apple jelly. Cover; freeze dough 30 minutes for easier handling.

2 Place paper cups on ungreased large cookie sheet. Spoon the dough by heaping teaspoons into paper cups.

3 Bake 9 to 12 minutes or until light golden brown. Immediately remove cookies in cups from cookie sheet; place on wire racks. Cool completely, about 30 minutes.

4 In 1-quart saucepan, heat caramels and milk over medium-low heat, stirring occasionally, until caramels are melted and smooth. Drizzle icing over cooled cookies. Garnish each with cranberry.

**HIGH ALTITUDE (3500-6500 FT):** After breaking up the cookie dough in a bowl, stir or knead 3 tablespoons all-purpose flour into dough until well blended. Decrease apple jelly to 2 tablespoons. Bake at 350°F. 13 to 16 minutes. Continue as directed above.

NUTRITION INFORMATION PER SERVING: Calories 75 • Total Fat 2g • Saturated Fat 1g • Cholesterol 0mg • Sodium 45mg • Total Carbohydrate 13g • Dietary Fiber 0g • Protein 1g. DIETARY EXCHANGES: 1 Other Carbohydrate • 1/2 Fat • 1 Carb Choice.

# fire-it-up snack mix

PREP TIME: 10 Minutes ✳ READY IN: 1 Hour 10 Minutes ✳ SERVINGS: 40 (1/4 cup each)

| | |
|---|---|
| 2 cups corn chips | 1/4 cup butter or margarine, melted |
| 2 cups small pretzel twists | 1/4 cup packed brown sugar |
| 2 cups oyster crackers | 1 teaspoon chili powder |
| 2 cups honey-roasted peanuts | 2 teaspoons Worcestershire sauce |
| 2 cups pumpkin seeds | 1 teaspoon red pepper sauce |

1 Heat oven to 300°F. In large bowl, mix corn chips, pretzel twists, oyster crackers, peanuts and pumpkin seeds.

2 In small bowl, mix remaining ingredients. Pour butter mixture over corn chip mixture; toss to coat. Spread in 2 ungreased 15 x 10 x 1-inch pans or large roasting pans.

3 Bake 25 to 30 minutes, stirring every 10 minutes, until peanuts are golden brown. Cool completely, about 30 minutes. (Mixture becomes crisp as it cools.)

NUTRITION INFORMATION PER SERVING: Calories 160 • Total Fat 11g • Saturated Fat 2.5g • Cholesterol 0mg • Sodium 180mg • Total Carbohydrate 9g • Dietary Fiber 1g • Protein 6g. DIETARY EXCHANGES: 1/2 Starch • 1/2 High-Fat Meat • 1-1/2 Fat • 1/2 Carb Choice.

*kitchen tip*

*For an anytime snack,*

*prepare this tasty mix up to*

*1 week before serving. Store*

*in an airtight container.*

ANITA HUNTER
Stilwell, Kansas
Bake-Off® Contest 42, 2006

# great day granola

PREP TIME: 15 Minutes ✳ READY IN: 2 Hours 15 Minutes ✳ SERVINGS: 32

| | |
|---|---|
| 4 cups oats | 1 cup packed brown sugar |
| 3 cups Golden Grahams® cereal | 1/2 cup canola or vegetable oil |
| 3 cups Fiber One® cereal | 1/2 cup honey |
| 1 cup chopped walnuts | 1/2 cup water |
| 1 cup sliced almonds | 1/2 teaspoon vanilla |
| 1 cup sunflower nuts | 1/2 teaspoon almond extract |

1 Heat oven to 250°F. Spray two 15 x 10 x 1-inch pans with cooking spray. In 6-quart bowl, mix oats, both cereals, the walnuts, almonds and sunflower nuts.

2 In 2-quart saucepan, cook the brown sugar, oil, honey and water over medium-high heat 3 to 5 minutes, stirring constantly, until brown sugar is melted. Remove from heat. Stir in vanilla and almond extract. Pour over cereal mixture; stir until well coated. Spread mixture evenly in pans.

3 Bake 1 hour, rearranging pans once halfway through baking. Cool completely in pan, about 1 hour. Break into pieces. Store in tightly covered container. Serve as breakfast cereal, snack or as topping for ice cream, yogurt or fresh fruit.

NUTRITION INFORMATION PER SERVING: Calories 220 • Total Fat 10g • Saturated Fat 1g • Cholesterol 0mg • Sodium 65mg • Total Carbohydrate 27g • Dietary Fiber 5g • Protein 4g. DIETARY EXCHANGES: 1 Starch • 1 Other Carbohydrate • 2 Fat • 2 Carb Choices.

# banana peanut butter bread

PREP TIME: 20 Minutes ✳ READY IN: 3 Hours 40 Minutes ✳ SERVINGS: 12

| | |
|---|---|
| 3/4 cup sugar | 2 cups all-purpose flour |
| 1/2 cup butter or margarine, softened | 1-1/2 teaspoons baking powder |
| 2 eggs | 1/2 teaspoon baking soda |
| 2 tablespoons milk | 1/2 teaspoon salt |
| 2 teaspoons vanilla | 4 packages (1.5 oz. each) chocolate-covered peanut butter candy cups, cut into small pieces |
| 1 cup mashed ripe bananas (2 large) | |

1 Heat oven to 350°F. (325°F. for dark pan). Grease and flour bottom only of 9 x 5-inch loaf pan. In large bowl with electric mixer, beat sugar and butter on medium speed until creamy.

2 Add the eggs, milk, vanilla and bananas. Beat about 30 seconds or until well blended. Add all remaining ingredients except candy. Mix just until moistened. Reserve 2 tablespoons cut up candy. With spoon, fold in remaining candy. Pour into pan.

3 Bake 1 hour to 1 hour 10 minutes or until toothpick inserted near center comes out clean. Cool in pan 10 minutes. Remove from pan to cooling rack. Finely chop the reserved 2 tablespoons candy; sprinkle on warm bread. Cool completely, about 2 hours.

**HIGH ALTITUDE (3500-6500 FT):** Decrease baking powder to 1 teaspoon.

NUTRITION INFORMATION PER SERVING: Calories 300 • Total Fat 13g • Saturated Fat 7g • Cholesterol 55mg • Sodium 320mg • Total Carbohydrate 41g • Dietary Fiber 2g • Protein 5g. DIETARY EXCHANGES: 1-1/2 Starch • 1 Other Carbohydrate • 2-1/2 Fat • 3 Carb Choices.

*kitchen tip*

*For the best flavor, use bananas that have lots of brown specks on the skin and are slightly soft.*

great day granola

# soft and chewy chocolate chip cookies

PREP TIME: 55 Minutes ✳ READY IN: 55 Minutes ✳ SERVINGS: 6 dozen cookies

1-1/4 cups granulated sugar

1-1/4 cups packed brown sugar

1-1/2 cups butter or margarine, softened

2 teaspoons vanilla

3 eggs

4-1/4 cups all-purpose flour

2 teaspoons baking soda

1/2 teaspoon salt

1 to 2 bags (12 oz. each) semisweet chocolate chips (2 to 4 cups)

1 Heat oven to 375°F. In large bowl with electric mixer, beat granulated sugar, brown sugar and butter until light and fluffy. Beat in vanilla and eggs until well blended. Beat in flour, baking soda and salt. Stir in chocolate chips.

2 On ungreased cookie sheets, drop dough by rounded tablespoonfuls 2 inches apart.

3 Bake 8 to 10 minutes or until light golden brown. Cool 1 minute; remove from cookie sheets to cooling racks.

**HIGH ALTITUDE (3500-6500 FT):** Bake 9 to 11 minutes.

NUTRITION INFORMATION PER SERVING: Calories 120 • Total Fat 6g • Saturated Fat 3.5g • Cholesterol 20mg • Sodium 85mg • Total Carbohydrate 16g • Dietary Fiber 0g • Protein 1g. DIETARY EXCHANGES: 1/2 Starch • 1/2 Other Carbohydrate • 1 Fat • 1 Carb Choice.

## kitchen tip

*Since this is a big-batch recipe, freeze half of the dough. Drop the dough by spoonfuls on a cookie sheet and freeze. Once the mounds of dough are frozen, place them in an airtight container and freeze. When it's time to bake the cookies, add about 5 minutes to compensate for the frozen dough.*

# strawberry-almond crumble bars

PREP TIME: 20 Minutes ✳ READY IN: 2 Hours 25 Minutes ✳ SERVINGS: 24

*cook's notes*

*If preserves contain large strawberry pieces, break them apart with a spoon for more even coverage.*

### FILLING

- 2 cups frozen whole unsweetened strawberries, slightly thawed, finely chopped (about 2/3 of a 16-oz. pkg.)
- 3/4 cup strawberry preserves
- 4 teaspoons cornstarch

### BASE AND TOPPING

- 1 cup slivered almonds
- 2 cups all-purpose flour
- 1 cup powdered sugar
- 1/2 teaspoon baking powder
- 1 cup butter, cut into 1-inch pieces, slightly softened

1. Heat oven to 350°F. Line 13 x 9-inch pan with 18 x 18-inch piece of heavy-duty foil so foil extends over long sides of pan. Spray foil with cooking spray. In 1-quart saucepan, place the strawberries, preserves and cornstarch. Heat to boiling over medium heat, stirring frequently. Cook 1 to 2 minutes or until slightly thickened, stirring constantly. Set aside to cool.

2. Meanwhile, place almonds on ungreased cookie sheet. Bake 7 to 9 minutes or until golden brown, stirring once. Cool completely, about 10 minutes.

3. In food processor, process 3/4 cup of the almonds 5 to 10 seconds or until finely chopped. Add flour, powdered sugar and baking powder; process 10 seconds or until well-mixed. Add butter; process with on/off pulses until mixture is crumbly. Reserve 2 cups of the mixture for topping. Press remaining mixture in pan. Spoon and spread strawberry mixture over base. Crumble reserved flour mixture over filling. Sprinkle with remaining almonds; press gently.

4. Bake 32 to 40 minutes or until light golden brown. Cool completely, about 1 hour 15 minutes. Lift foil with bars from pan. For bars, cut into 6 rows by 4 rows. Store bars in refrigerator.

   **HIGH ALTITUDE (3500-6500 FT):** After pressing base mixture in pan, bake 10 minutes. Continue as directed.

NUTRITION INFORMATION PER SERVING: Calories 190 • Total Fat 10g • Saturated Fat 5g • Cholesterol 20mg • Sodium 70mg • Total Carbohydrate 23g • Dietary Fiber 1g • Protein 2g. DIETARY EXCHANGES: 1/2 Starch • 1 Other Carbohydrate • 2 Fat • 1-1/2 Carb Choices.

# gingerbread teddies

PREP TIME: 1 Hour ✳ READY IN: 1 Hour ✳ SERVINGS: 24

- 1 roll (16.5 oz.) Pillsbury® refrigerated gingerbread cookies
- Purchased colored decorator icing in tubes

1. Heat oven to 350°F. Cut cookie dough into 4 equal pieces. Work with 1 piece at a time; refrigerate remaining dough until ready to use.

2. Cut each piece of dough into 6 equal portions. Using 1 portion for each cookie, shape dough into 1-inch ball for body, 1/2-inch ball for head, four 1/4-inch balls for arms and legs, and 2 smaller balls for ears. On ungreased cookie sheet, arrange balls to resemble teddy bear shape. Repeat with remaining portions of dough, arranging cookies 2 inches apart on ungreased cookie sheets.

3. Bake 10 to 13 minutes or until set. Cool 2 minutes and remove from cookie sheets. Decorate with icing as desired.

NUTRITION INFORMATION PER SERVING: Calories 95 • Total Fat 5g • Saturated Fat 1g • Cholesterol 10mg • Sodium 70mg • Total Carbohydrate 12g • Dietary Fiber 0g • Protein 1g. DIETARY EXCHANGES: 1 Other Carbohydrate • 1 Fat.

glazed pecans

# glazed pecans

PREP TIME: 20 Minutes ✳ READY IN: 50 Minutes ✳ SERVINGS: 16

2 tablespoons butter

2 tablespoons packed dark brown sugar

2 tablespoons maple-flavored syrup or real maple syrup

2 cups pecan halves (8 oz.)

1 Heat oven to 350°F. Line cookie sheet with cooking parchment paper. In 12-inch skillet, melt butter over medium heat. Add brown sugar and syrup; mix well. Cook until bubbly, stirring constantly.

2 Add pecans; cook 2 to 3 minutes, stirring constantly, until coated. Spread mixture onto parchment-lined cookie sheet.

3 Bake 6 to 8 minutes or until golden brown. Cool completely, about 30 minutes. Store in tightly covered container up to 2 weeks.

NUTRITION INFORMATION PER SERVING: Calories 130 • Total Fat 12g • Saturated Fat 2g • Cholesterol 0mg • Sodium 10mg • Total Carbohydrate 6g • Dietary Fiber 1g • Protein 1g. DIETARY EXCHANGES: 1/2 Other Carbohydrate • 2-1/2 Fat • 1/2 Carb Choice.

*kitchen tip*

*Pecans can become rancid easily. Store any shelled pecans in an airtight container in the refrigerator for up to 3 months.*

# chocolate-caramel oatmeal thumbprints

PREP TIME: 1 Hour 10 Minutes • READY IN: 1 Hour 10 Minutes ✳ SERVINGS: 48

1 cup butter, softened

1/2 cup packed brown sugar

2 teaspoons vanilla

1 egg

1-1/2 cups all-purpose flour

1-1/4 cups quick-cooking oats

1/4 teaspoon salt

48 chewy caramel candies in milk chocolate, unwrapped

2 oz. vanilla-flavored candy coating (almond bark), chopped

1 teaspoon oil

1 Heat oven to 325°F. In large bowl, beat butter and brown sugar with electric mixer on medium speed 1 to 2 minutes or until light and fluffy. Beat in vanilla and egg until well blended.

2 On low speed, beat in flour, oats and salt until mixed. Shape dough into 1-inch balls. Place 2 inches apart on ungreased cookie sheets. With floured thumb, make indentation in center of each cookie.

3 Bake 10 to 15 minutes or until set and golden brown on bottom. Press caramel candy in center of each cookie. Cool on cookie sheets 1 minute. Remove from cookie sheets to cooling rack. Let stand 10 minutes. With tip of knife, flatten and swirl melted candy to fill indentation. Cool completely, about 15 minutes.

4 In small microwavable bowl, microwave candy coating and oil on High 30 seconds; stir. If necessary, microwave in 10 second increments, stirring each time until melted. With fork, drizzle melted coating over cooled cookies.

**HIGH ALTITUDE (3500-6500 FT):** Bake 15 to 20 minutes.

NUTRITION INFORMATION PER SERVING: Calories 100 • Total Fat 6g • Saturated Fat 3.5g • Cholesterol 15mg • Sodium 55mg • Total Carbohydrate 11g • Dietary Fiber 0g • Protein 1g. DIETARY EXCHANGES: 1 Other Carbohydrate • 1 Fat • 1 Carb Choice.

*kitchen tip*

*When the vanilla coating is set, store these cookies in airtight containers with waxed paper between the layers. You can freeze them for up to 4 weeks.*

# sugar and spice candied walnuts

PREP TIME: 25 Minutes ✳ READY IN: 25 Minutes ✳ SERVINGS: 32 servings (2 cups total)

| | |
|---|---|
| 1 cup packed brown sugar | 1 package (8 oz.) walnut halves or pieces (2 cups) |
| 1/3 cup boiling water | 1/4 teaspoon maple flavor |
| 1 teaspoon pumpkin pie spice | |

1 Lightly butter a 15 x 10 x 1-inch pan.

2 In 3-quart heavy saucepan, heat brown sugar, water and pumpkin pie spice to boiling over medium-high heat, stirring occasionally. Boil without stirring 5 minutes; remove from heat. Add nuts and maple flavor. Stir until coating on nuts begins to sugar, about 2-1/2 to 3 minutes.

3 Pour into pan and quickly separate nuts. Cool completely. Store in airtight container in a cool dry place.

**HIGH ALTITUDE (3500-6500 FT):** Boil 5 minutes on medium heat.

NUTRITION INFORMATION PER SERVING: Calories 80 • Total Fat 4.5g • Saturated Fat 0g • Cholesterol 0mg • Sodium 0mg • Total Carbohydrate 8g • Dietary Fiber 0g • Protein 1g. DIETARY EXCHANGES: 1/2 Other Carbohydrate • 1 Fat • 1/2 Carb Choice.

# charming cheerios® necklace

PREP TIME: 35 Minutes ✳ READY IN: 35 Minutes ✳ SERVINGS: 1

| | |
|---|---|
| 4 piece red shoestring licorice (about 32 inches each) | 1 cup fruit-flavored gummi, ring-shaped candy |
| 1 cup Cheerios® cereal | 1/2 cup pieces pastel-colored tube-shaped licorice candies (from 5.5-oz. bag) |

1 Working from each end of the piece of licorice, string an arrangement of cereal and candies to create desired pattern on the necklace.

2 Tie the ends of the licorice together in a double knot to secure the necklace.

NUTRITION INFORMATION PER SERVING: Calories 160 • Total Fat 0.5g • Saturated Fat 0g • Cholesterol 0mg • Sodium 100mg • Total Carbohydrate 39g • Dietary Fiber 0g • Protein 1g. DIETARY EXCHANGES: 1/2 Starch • 2 Other Carbohydrate • 2-1/2 Carb Choices.

# mocha mix

PREP TIME: 5 Minutes • READY IN: 5 Minutes ✳ SERVINGS: 21

| | |
|---|---|
| 2-1/4 cups nondairy creamer | 3/4 cup instant coffee granules or crystals |
| 1-1/2 cups sugar | 3/4 cup unsweetened cocoa |

1 In large bowl, mix all ingredients until well blended. Spoon mix into decorative jars or food storage containers; cover tightly.

2 To serve, spoon 1/4 cup mix into mug; fill with 1 cup boiling water. Stir to blend.

NUTRITION INFORMATION PER SERVING: Calories 130 • Total Fat 4g • Saturated Fat 3.5g • Cholesterol 0mg • Sodium 20mg • Total Carbohydrate 23g • Dietary Fiber 1g • Protein 1g. DIETARY EXCHANGES: 1-1/2 Other Carbohydrate • 1 Fat • 1-1/2 Carb Choices.

# molasses raisin cookies

PREP TIME: 1 Hour ✳ READY IN: 1 Hour ✳ SERVINGS: 3 dozen

| | |
|---|---|
| 1/2 cup sugar | 1 teaspoon ginger |
| 1/2 cup firmly packed brown sugar | 1 teaspoon cinnamon |
| 3/4 cup margarine or butter, softened | 1/2 teaspoon cloves |
| 1/4 cup molasses | 1/4 teaspoon salt |
| 1 egg | 1-1/2 cups raisins |
| 2-1/2 cups all purpose flour | 3 tablespoons sugar |
| 1 teaspoon baking soda | |

1 Heat oven to 325°F. In large bowl, combine 1/2 cup sugar, brown sugar and margarine; beat until light and fluffy. Add molasses and egg; blend well.

2 Lightly spoon flour into measuring cup; level off. Add flour, baking soda, ginger, cinnamon, cloves and salt; mix well. Stir in raisins. Shape into 1-inch balls. Place 2 inches apart on ungreased cookie sheets. Flatten to 1/8-inch thickness with bottom of glass dipped in 3 tablespoons sugar.

3 Bake 6 to 9 minutes or just until edges begin to brown. Immediately remove from cookie sheets.

**HIGH ALTITUDE (3500-6500 FT):** Increase flour to 2-3/4 cups. Bake as directed above.

NUTRITION INFORMATION PER SERVING: Calories 120 • Total Fat 4g • Saturated Fat 1g • Cholesterol 5mg • Sodium 100mg • Total Carbohydrate 20g • Dietary Fiber 1g • Protein 1g. DIETARY EXCHANGES: 1/2 Starch • 1 Fruit • 1-1/2 Other Carbohydrate • 1/2 Fat.

## *cook's notes*

*The cookie dough can be wrapped tightly and refrigerated for up to 24 hours before baking. If the dough becomes too firm, let it stand at room temperature for 15 minutes. For longer storage, freeze the wrapped dough in an airtight container for up to 9 months. Thaw the dough just until it's soft enough to handle, then bake.*

**ENNY WILLIAMS**
Honolulu, Hawaii
Bake-Off® Contest 42, 2006

# cereal-almond brittle

PREP TIME: 15 Minutes ✳ READY IN: 1 Hour 10 Minutes ✳ SERVINGS: 14

2 cups Cheerios® cereal
2 cups Cinnamon Toast Crunch® cereal
2 cups oats
1 cup sliced almonds

1/2 cup butter or margarine
1/4 cup packed brown sugar
1/3 cup real maple or maple-flavored syrup

1 Heat oven to 300°F. Line 1 large (17 x 14-inch) cookie sheet or 2 (15 x 10 x 1-inch) pans with foil; spray foil with cooking spray. In large bowl, mix both cereals, the oats and almonds; set aside.

2 In 1-quart saucepan, heat butter, brown sugar and syrup over medium heat, stirring frequently, until butter is melted and mixture boils. Pour over cereal mixture; stir until well coated. Spread mixture evenly on cookie sheet with rubber spatula until about 1/2 inch thick.

3 Bake 35 to 40 minutes or until almonds are golden brown. Cool completely, about 15 minutes. Break into pieces with fingers. Store in tightly covered container.

NUTRITION INFORMATION PER SERVING: Calories 220 • Total Fat 12g • Saturated Fat 4.5g • Cholesterol 15mg • Sodium 120mg • Total Carbohydrate 26g • Dietary Fiber 3g • Protein 4g. DIETARY EXCHANGES: 1/2 Starch • 1 Other Carbohydrate • 1/2 High-Fat Meat, 1-1/2 Fat • 2 Carb Choices.

# chipotle pico de gallo

PREP TIME: 20 Minutes ✳ READY IN: 20 Minutes ✳ SERVINGS: 12

- 1 cup coarsely chopped unpeeled seedless cucumber
- 1/2 cup chopped peeled jicama
- 1/2 cup chopped red bell pepper
- 1 tablespoon lime juice
- 1 tablespoon honey

- 1/4 teaspoon salt
- 2 seedless oranges, peeled, coarsely chopped
- 2 chipotle chiles in adobo sauce (from 7-oz. can), chopped

  Whole grain tortilla chips, if desired

1 In medium bowl, mix all ingredients except chips. Serve immediately with chips, or cover and refrigerate until serving time.

NUTRITION INFORMATION PER SERVING: Calories 25 • Total Fat 0g • Saturated Fat 0g • Cholesterol 0mg • Sodium 75mg • Total Carbohydrate 6g • Dietary Fiber 1g • Protein 0g. DIETARY EXCHANGES: 1/2 Other Carbohydrate • 1/2 Carb Choice.

## cook's notes

*Adobo sauce is rather potent, so to turn up the heat of this relish, add more adobo. To make this relish less spicy, use just one chipotle chile.*

# general recipe index

## appetizers & snacks
*(also see snack mixes)*

Apple Snack Stacks, 21

Asparagus Melts with Horseradish Sauce, 29

Bacon-Cheddar Pinwheels, 16

Bacon-Cheeseburger Calzones, 8

Bacon-Crab Dip, 35

Bagel Nachos, 167

Basil and Havarti Cheese Pinwheels, 169

Bourbon Cocktail Meatballs, 148

Bratwurst Braids, 37

Buffalo Chicken Pinwheels, 13

California Beef Crostini, 170

Cheesy Chicken and Artichoke Bites, 168

Cheesy Fish Stick Taco Dogs, 18

Chicken and Blue Cheese Bundles, 28

Chicken Crescent Pot Stickers, 16

Chicken Saté with Spicy Peanut Sauce, 139

Chile-Lime Shrimp with Creamy Chipotle Dip, 21

Chili Con Crescent Snacks, 9

Citrus Gazpacho with Honey-Lime Cream, 27

Crescent Nacho Mini Cups, 158

Crescent Sloppy Joes, 26

Crescent-Wrapped Brie, 166

Cucumber-Hummus Stacks, 24

Easy Crescent Dogs™, 9

Elegant Cheese and Fruit Platter, 155

Festive Shrimp Pinwheels, 164

Festive Spinach Dip, 30

Fresh Tomato-Basil Caprese Kabobs, 151

Garlic and Herb Beef Appetizers, 172

Ham and Cheese Crescent Sandwiches, 30

Honey-Mustard Sweet Onion Blossoms, 29

Individual Beef Wellingtons with Madeira Sauce, 10

Layered Italian Dip with Crisp Wontons, 22

Mango-Mint Fruit Dip, 19

Mexican Confetti Pinwheels, 159

Mini Beef and Provolone Crescents, 153

Mini Buffalo Chicken Pastries, 160

Mini Soft Pretzels and Dip, 40

Parmesan Rounds with Lox, 147

Peanutty Rice Cake Rounds, 23

Picadillo Empanadas, 34

Pita Triangles with Olive Relish, 140

Pizza Crisps, 36

Polenta Rounds with Caramelized Vegetables, 142

Pretzel Butterflies, 25

Ranch Deviled Eggs, 17

Roast Beef Rolls, 37

Rudolph Nibblers with Cinnamon-Orange Dip, 25

Slow Cooker Spicy Cheeseburger Nachos, 33

Smoked Salmon Pinwheels, 162

Spanish Salsa with Crispy French Bread, 32

Spicy Chicken Mini Burritos, 12

Strawberry-Orange Fruit Dip, 33

Stuffed Cucumber Snacks, 14

Thai Appetizer Pizza, 164

## apples

Apple-Cream Cheese Muffins, 188

Apple-Raspberry Cookie Cobbler, 253

Apple Snack Stacks, 21

Cheesy Apple Chunk Bagels, 197

Cornish Hens with Apple-Raisin Stuffing, 122

Country French Apple Crescent Casserole, 262

Cranberry-Glazed Apple Dumplings, 266

Sausage and Apple Bake, 182

## artichokes

Artichoke-Cheese Braids, 45

Cheesy Chicken and Artichoke Bites, 168

Spanish Salsa with Crispy French Bread, 32

## asparagus

Asparagus Melts with Horseradish Sauce, 29

Chicken Phyllo Bundles, 100

Grilled Chicken-Asparagus Bundles, 117

Ham and Asparagus Chowder, 79

Seafood and Asparagus Manicotti, 120

## bacon & canadian bacon

Bacon-Cheddar Pinwheels, 167

Bacon-Cheeseburger Calzones, 8

Bacon-Crab Dip, 35

## bananas

Banana-Chocolate-Caramel Cake, 261

Banana Peanut Butter Bread, 302

Banana-Strawberry Muffins, 60

Banana-Walnut Brunch Squares, 176

Black-Bottom Banana Cream Pie, 267

Cheesy Apple Chunk Bagels, 197

## bars & brownies

Brickle Bars, 209

Caramel and Nut Diamond Delights, 219

Cherry-Macaroon Bars, 232

Chocolate Chip Cheesecake Bars, 258

Double Chocolate-Caramel-Fudge Brownies, 212

Easy Baklava Bars, 222

Heavenly Layered Bars, 202

Lemon-Glazed Pistachio Bars, 217

Mint-in-the-Middle Brownies, 233

Monkey Cereal Bars, 204

No-Bake Cereal Bars, 210

Oh-So-Easy Chocolate-Peanut-Caramel Bars, 222

Orangeburst Cookie Bars, 224

Quick Cookie Bars, 221

So-Easy Lemon Bars, 228

Strawberry-Almond Crumble Bars, 305

Sweet 'n Salty Crunch Bars, 231

Tropical Cheesecake Bars, 205

Two-in-One Holiday Bars, 297

## beans

Baja Pie, 108

Bean and Barley Vegetable Soup, 66

Chicken-Chile Casserole, 124

Crispy-Topped Meatballs and Baked Beans, 86

Hearty Multi-Bean Chili, 127

Layered Italian Dip with Crisp Wontons, 22

Lentil-Potato Stew, 135

White Chicken Chili, 79

## beef *(also see ground beef)*

appetizers & snacks

California Beef Crostini, 170

Garlic and Herb Beef Appetizers, 172

Individual Beef Wellingtons with Madeira Sauce, 10

Mini Beef and Provolone Crescents, 153

Roast Beef Rolls, 37

main dishes

Herb-Stuffed Flank Steak, 111

Pepper-Rubbed Steaks with Caramelized Onions, 115

Pot Roast with Sweet Potatoes and Parsnips, 95

Short Ribs in Red Wine, 106

salad

Grilled Caesar Steak and Potato Salad, 80

sandwiches

Cheese Steak Crescent Braids, 59

Cheesy Hot Beef Sandwiches, 171

Individual Pastrami Braids, 146

## beverages

Berry Sherbet Punch, 25

Blueberry-Pomegranate Smoothies, 15

Grapefruit Citrus Cooler, 33
Hot Spiced Cranberry Cider, 30
Mocha Mix, 308

### breads (also see coffee cakes)
Almond Scones, 55
Apple-Cream Cheese Muffins, 188
Artichoke-Cheese Braids, 45
Banana Peanut Butter Bread, 302
Banana-Strawberry Muffins, 60
Cheddar Twisters, 54
Cheese Crescent Triangles, 42
Cheese Steak Crescent Braids, 59
Chive Crescents, 46
Christmas Fruitcake Braid, 294
Cinnamon Twisties, 181
Crescent Bear Claws, 56
Giant Cinnamon-Cheese Danish, 43
Gingerbread Bran Muffins, 49
Gumdrop Spice Muffins, 60
Ham and Swiss Double Pinwheels, 144
Individual Pastrami Braids, 146
Maple Pecan Crescent Twists, 41
Meatball Bubble Biscuits, 51
Mexican Confetti Pinwheels, 159
Mini Soft Pretzels and Dip, 40
Peach Crescent Palmiers, 59
Pesto Cheese Bread, 50
Pizza Biscuit Wreath, 48
Poppin' Fresh® Citrus-Glazed Crullers, 177
Simply Super Crescent Cinnamon Rolls, 49
Strawberry-Orange Butterfly Biscuits, 57

### breakfast & brunch
Almond Scones, 55
Apple-Cream Cheese Muffins, 188
Apricot-Almond Coffee Cake, 44
Banana-Strawberry Muffins, 60
Banana-Walnut Brunch Squares, 176
Cheesy Apple Chunk Bagels, 197
Cherry Cream Cheese Coffee Cake, 52
Cinnamon Twisties, 181
Crescent Bear Claws, 56
Flaky Sausage Foldovers, 186
Fresh Fruit Orange Fizz, 185
Giant Cinnamon-Cheese Danish, 43
Gingerbread Bran Muffins, 49
Granola Fruit Kabobs, 189
Ham 'n Cheese Omelet Bake, 183
Ham Frittata, 190
Italian Dinner Frittata, 132
Italian Egg Bake, 181
Kiwi-Pineapple Yogurt Parfaits, 197
Leek Quiche, 178
Lemon-Almond Breakfast Pastry, 61
Lemon Surprise Coffee Cake, 46
Onion-Cheese Custard Tartlets, 178

Piglets in Blankets, 194
Pineapple-Orange Blossoms, 180
Poppin' Fresh® Citrus-Glazed Crullers, 177
Provolone and Pesto Quiche, 190
Sausage and Apple Bake, 182
Scrambled Egg-Parmesan Soft Crust
    Pizza, 187
Southwestern Brunch Eggs, 192
Spinach Sausage Brunch Casserole, 185
Spinach, Strawberry and Grapefruit
    Toss, 189
Spinach-Tomato Frittata, 194
Three-Pepper Galette, 193
Topped Mini Quiches, 195

### cakes & cupcakes
Banana-Chocolate-Caramel Cake, 261
Carousel Cupcakes, 274
Chocolate Candy Cupcakes, 287
Confetti Snowman Cake, 274
Cranberry Cornmeal Torte, 238
Cupcake Strawberries, 266
Family Tree Cake, 280
Layered Christmas Cake, 28
Lime Angel Food Cake Roll, 260

### candies & sweets
Candy Cane Cookie Box, 276
Cereal-Almond Brittle, 310
Charming Cheerios® Necklace, 308
Chocolate Swirl Almond Toffee, 294
Cookie Crumb Truffle Mice, 293
Marshmallow Melties, 299
Marshmallow Santas, 271
Marzipan Snow People, 281
Secret Santa Trees, 284
Star Puzzle Decorations, 280

### caramel
Banana-Chocolate-Caramel Cake, 261
Caramel and Nut Diamond Delights, 219
Chocolate-Caramel Oatmeal
    Thumbprints, 307
Double Chocolate-Caramel-Fudge
    Brownies, 212
Oh-So-Easy Chocolate-Peanut-Caramel
    Bars, 222

### casseroles
Chicken-Chile Casserole, 124
Country French Apple Crescent
    Casserole, 262
Crescent-Topped Burger Bake, 119
Mediterranean Chicken Bake, 132
Patchwork Pot Pie, 126
Sausage and Apple Bake, 182
Sausage Ravioli Casserole, 134
Spinach Sausage Brunch Casserole, 185

### cheese (also see cream cheese)
Artichoke-Cheese Braids, 45
Asparagus Melts with Horseradish
    Sauce, 29
Bacon-Cheddar Pinwheels, 167
Bacon-Cheeseburger Calzones, 8
Bagel Nachos, 167
Baja Pie, 108
Basil and Havarti Cheese Pinwheels, 169
Buffalo Chicken Pinwheels, 13
Cheddar Twisters, 54
Cheese Crescent Triangles, 42
Cheese Mini-wiches, 144
Cheese-Stuffed Pizza, 152
Cheesy Chicken and Artichoke Bites, 168
Cheesy Fish Stick Taco Dogs, 18
Cheesy Hot Beef Sandwiches, 171
Cheesy Potatoes, 75
Cheesy Sausage Calzones, 172
Chicken and Blue Cheese Bundles, 28
Chicken Cordon Bleu Lasagna, 99
Crescent-Wrapped Brie, 166
Easy Buffalo Chicken Stromboli, 149
Easy Chicken Chilaquiles Skillet, 120
Easy Crescent Dogs™, 9
Elegant Cheese and Fruit Platter, 155
Grilled Stuffed Pizza Burgers, 157
Ham and Cheese Crescent Sandwiches, 30
Ham 'n Cheese Omelet Bake, 183
Ham and Swiss Double Pinwheels, 144
Italian Cheese-Stuffed Meat Loaf, 119
Italian Vegetarian Lasagna, 118
Lasagna Roll-Ups, 113
Mascarpone-Filled Fresh Strawberries, 256
Mediterranean Chicken Bake, 132
Mexican Ham and Cheese, 171
Mini Beef and Provolone Crescents, 153
Onion-Cheese Custard Tartlets, 178
Parmesan Rounds with Lox, 147
Pesto Cheese Bread, 50
Pesto-Chicken Manicotti, 112
Pizza Crisps, 36
Pizza in a Crescent, 141
Polka Dot Meat Loaf, 135
Provolone and Pesto Quiche, 190
Scrambled Egg-Parmesan Soft Crust
    Pizza, 187
Seafood and Asparagus Manicotti, 120
Stuffed Chicken Breasts Cordon Bleu, 112
Tiramisu Bites, 255

### cherries
Brownie Sundae Pizza, 27
Cherry Chocolate Biscotti, 300
Cherry Chocolate Blossoms, 213
Cherry-Chocolate Chip Cookies, 218
Cherry Christmas Trifle, 250

**cherries** (continued)
Cherry Cream Cheese Coffee Cake, 52
Cherry-Macaroon Bars, 232

**chicken & poultry**
appetizers & snacks
Buffalo Chicken Pinwheels, 13
Cheesy Chicken and Artichoke Bites, 168
Chicken and Blue Cheese Bundles, 28
Chicken Crescent Pot Stickers, 16
Mini Buffalo Chicken Pastries, 160
Spicy Chicken Mini Burritos, 12
main dishes
Apricot-Glazed Chicken Breasts with
    Almond Couscous, 124
Baja Pie, 108
Chicken-Chile Casserole, 124
Chicken Cordon Bleu Lasagna, 99
Chicken Phyllo Bundles, 100
Chicken Saté with Spicy Peanut Sauce, 139
Chicken Waikiki, 125
Cornish Hens with Apple-Raisin
    Stuffing, 122
Easy Buffalo Chicken Stromboli, 149
Easy Chicken Chilaquiles Skillet, 120
Grilled Chicken-Asparagus Bundles, 117
Jerk-Seasoned Chicken and Pepper
    Saute, 131
Mediterranean Chicken Bake, 132
Mini Chicken Pot Pies, 161
Orange Chicken Stir-Fry, 96
Orange Soda Grilled Chicken, 131
Oven-Baked Chicken Nuggets and French
    Fries, 143
Pesto-Chicken Manicotti, 112
Roast Cornish Hen with Vegetables, 103
Sesame Asian Grilled Cornish Hen
    Halves, 104
Stuffed Chicken Breasts Cordon Bleu, 112
Taco Chicken Wraps, 143
Tomato-Basil Linguine with Chicken, 133
salads
Chicken Salad Cups, 78
Honey-Mustard Chicken Salad, 85
Party Chicken and Pasta Salad, 138
sandwiches
Chicken Caesar Sandwich Ring, 155
Chicken Cordon Bleu Sandwich Ring, 150
Greek Kabob Sandwiches, 156
Grilled Spicy Chicken Sandwiches, 163
Lettuce Wraps, 173
soups
Chicken Soup Italiano, 83
White Chicken Chili, 79

**chocolate**
Banana-Chocolate-Caramel Cake, 261

Brownie Sundae Pizza, 271
Candy Bar-Frosted Chippers, 205
Cherry Chocolate Biscotti, 300
Cherry Chocolate Blossoms, 213
Cherry-Chocolate Chip Cookies, 218
Chocolate-Almond Layered Hearts, 214
Chocolate Candy Cupcakes, 287
Chocolate-Caramel Oatmeal
    Thumbprints, 307
Chocolate Chip-Almond-Cherry Cups, 209
Chocolate Chip Cheesecake Bars, 258
Chocolate-Covered Cheesecake Trees, 279
Chocolate Mousse Cones, 249
Chocolate-Orange Shortbread Bites, 52
Chocolate Supreme Fondue, 265
Chocolate Swirl Almond Toffee, 294
Christmas Cookie Meringues, 277
Cream Cheese Brownie Cups, 258
Creamy Chocolate-Mint Pie, 254
Dipped Cream Cheese Strawberries, 242
Double Chocolate-Caramel-Fudge
    Brownies, 212
Hidden Marshmallow Chippers, 218
Mint-in-the-Middle Brownies, 233
Mint Meringue Parfaits, 282
No-Bake Cereal Bars, 210
Oh-So-Easy Chocolate-Peanut-Caramel
    Bars, 222
Peanut Butter Cookie Bark, 288
Peanut Butter Cup Cookies, 230
Peppermint-Fudge Pie, 264
Peppermint Mousse Cups, 248
Poppin' Fresh® Double-Decker
    Cookies, 223
Raspberry Mousse in Chocolate Cups, 257
Royal Marble Cheesecake, 244
Soft and Chewy Chocolate Chip
    Cookies, 304
Sweetheart Cookie Bouquet, 272
White Chocolate Bread Pudding with Red
    Berry Sauce, 236
White Chocolate Gingerbread Bears, 285

**coconut**
Confetti Snowman Cake, 274
Easy Baklava Bars, 222
Granola-Almond Macaroons, 226
Heavenly Layered Bars, 202
Macaroon-Topped Sugar Cookies, 201
Sweet 'n Salty Crunch Bars, 231

**coffee cakes**
Apricot-Almond Coffee Cake, 44
Cherry Cream Cheese Coffee Cake, 52
Lemon Surprise Coffee Cake, 46

**cookies**
Almond Holly Wreaths, 200

Candy Bar-Frosted Chippers, 205
Cherry Chocolate Biscotti, 300
Cherry Chocolate Blossoms, 213
Cherry-Chocolate Chip Cookies, 218
Chocolate-Almond Layered Hearts, 214
Chocolate-Caramel Oatmeal
    Thumbprints, 307
Chocolate Chip-Almond-Cherry Cups, 209
Chocolate-Orange Shortbread Bites, 52
Christmas Cookie Meringues, 277
Christmas Ornament Cookies, 226
Cinnamon-Toffee Pecan Cookies, 206
Coffee Shop Cookies, 233
Cookie Pizza, 221
Cranberry-Orange Biscotti, 299
Easy Gumdrop Whirligigs, 289
Flip-Flop Fun Cookies, 229
Festive Fruitcake Treats, 300
Fresh Orange Cookies, 230
Ginger Sandwich Cookies, 202
Gingerbread Pinwheels, 229
Gingerbread Teddies, 305
Glazed Peanut Butter Cups, 225
Granola-Almond Macaroons, 226
Happy Face Cookie Pops, 277
Hidden Marshmallow Chippers, 218
Lemon-Ginger Thumbprints, 211
Macaroon-Topped Sugar Cookies, 201
Marshmallow Peanut Blossoms, 214
Molasses Raisin Cookies, 309
Mrs. Claus' Mittens, 273
Nutty Little Mice, 272
Orange-Pecan Cookies, 296
Peanut Butter Cookie Bark, 288
Peanut Butter Cup Cookies, 230
Polvorones Cookies, 213
Poppin' Fresh® Double-Decker
    Cookies, 223
Quick Cashew Cookies with Brown Butter
    Icing, 216
Quick Snickerdoodles, 233
Soft and Chewy Chocolate Chip
    Cookies, 304
Sugar Cookie Shortcake, 207
Thumbprint Heart Sugar Cookies, 210
White Chocolate Gingerbread Bears, 285

**cranberries & cranberry juice**
Berry Sherbet Punch, 25
Cranberry Cornmeal Torte, 2
Cranberry-Glazed Apple Dumplings, 266
Cranberry-Orange Biscotti, 299
Hot Spiced Cranberry Cider, 30

**cream cheese**
Apple-Cream Cheese Muffins, 188
Bacon-Crab Dip, 35

Cheesy Apple Chunk Bagels, 197
Cherry Cream Cheese Coffee Cake, 52
Chocolate Chip Cheesecake Bars, 258
Chocolate-Covered Cheesecake Trees, 279
Cream Cheese Brownie Cups, 258
Dipped Cream Cheese Strawberries, 242
Giant Cinnamon-Cheese Danish, 43
Holly and Eggnog Pie, 241
Lemon Cheesecake Tarts, 240
Royal Marble Cheesecake, 244
Rudolph Nibblers with Cinnamon-Orange
    Dip, 25
Strawberry-Orange Fruit Dip, 33
Stuffed Cucumber Snacks, 14
Tropical Cheesecake Bars, 205
Turtle Cheesecake Tartlets, 247

**desserts** *(also see bars & brownies;*
*cakes & cupcakes; candies & sweets;*
*cookies; pies & tarts)*
Apple-Raspberry Cookie Cobbler, 253
Brownie Sundae Pizza, 271
Cherry Christmas Trifle, 250
Chocolate-Covered Cheesecake Trees, 279
Chocolate Mousse Cones, 249
Chocolate Supreme Fondue, 265
Cookie Dough Ice Cream Dessert, 246
Cookie Ice Cream-a-Rounds, 262
Country French Apple Crescent
    Casserole, 262
Cranberry-Glazed Apple Dumplings, 266
Cream Cheese Brownie Cups, 258
Dipped Cream Cheese Strawberries, 242
Easy-As-Peach-Pie Wedges, 249
Frozen Raspberry Dessert, 242
Grands® Strawberry Shortcakes, 237
Lemon-Pineapple Dessert Squares, 239
Lime-Kiwi Cloud with Strawberry
    Sauce, 253
Mascarpone-Filled Fresh Strawberries, 256
Mint Meringue Parfaits, 282
Peppermint Mousse Cups, 248
Pumpkin Pie Cream Cups, 245
Raspberry Mousse in Chocolate Cups, 257
Rhubarb and Strawberry Cornbread
    Cobbler, 246
Royal Marble Cheesecake, 244
Seaside Pudding Cups, 287
Strawberry-Rhubarb Meringue Clouds, 289
Tiramisu Bites, 255
White Chocolate Bread Pudding with Red
    Berry Sauce, 236

**eggs**
Ham 'n Cheese Omelet Bake, 183
Ham Frittata, 190
Italian Dinner Frittata, 132
Italian Egg Bake, 181

Leek Quiche, 178
Provolone and Pesto Quiche, 190
Ranch Deviled Eggs, 17
Scrambled Egg-Parmesan Soft Crust
    Pizza, 187
Southwestern Brunch Eggs, 192
Spinach Sausage Brunch Casserole, 185
Spinach-Tomato Frittata, 194
Three-Pepper Galette, 193
Topped Mini Quiches, 195

**fish & seafood**
appetizers
Bacon-Crab Dip, 35
Cheesy Fish Stick Taco Dogs, 18
Chile-Lime Shrimp with Creamy Chipotle
    Dip, 21
Elegant Cheese and Fruit Platter, 155
Festive Shrimp Pinwheels, 164
Parmesan Rounds with Lox, 147
Smoked Salmon Pinwheels, 162
main dishes
Fish Fillets Primavera, 114
Fish Fillets with Herbed Tartar Sauce, 127
Salmon with Lemon Butter and Pineapple
    Salsa, 99
Seafood and Asparagus Manicotti, 120
Southwestern Chili Shrimp, 105
salads
Mojito Shrimp Salad in Biscuit Bowls, 66
Southwestern Shrimp Taco Salad, 90
soups
Zesty Tomato-Crab Bisque, 75

**fruit** *(also see specific kinds)*
Blueberry-Pomegranate Smoothies, 15
Carved Watermelon Bowl, 69
Christmas Fruitcake Braid, 294
Cinnamon-Fruit Snack Mix, 186
Easy-As-Peach-Pie Wedges, 249
Festive Fruitcake Treats, 300
Fresh Fruit Orange Fizz, 185
Gingered Fresh Fruit Salad, 64
Granola Fruit Kabobs, 189
Mango-Mint Fruit Dip, 19
Peach Crescent Palmiers, 59
Rudolph Nibblers with Cinnamon-Orange
    Dip, 25
Speedy Honey-Lime Fruit Salad, 82
Tropical Fruit Salad with Poppy Seed
    Dressing, 70
Two-in-One Holiday Bars, 297

**gifts**
Banana Peanut Butter Bread, 302
Candy Cane Cookie Box, 276
Cereal-Almond Brittle, 310

Charming Cheerios® Necklace, 308
Cherry Chocolate Biscotti, 300
Chipotle Pico de Gallo, 311
Chocolate-Caramel Oatmeal
    Thumbprints, 307
Chocolate Swirl Almond Toffee, 294
Christmas Fruitcake Braid, 294
Cookie Crumb Truffle Mice, 293
Cranberry-Orange Biscotti, 299
Festive Fruitcake Treats, 300
Fire-It-Up Snack Mix, 301
Gingerbread Teddies, 305
Glazed Pecans, 307
Great Day Granola, 302
Marshmallow Melties, 299
Mocha Mix, 308
Molasses Raisin Cookies, 309
Orange-Pecan Cookies, 296
Puffy Pink Popcorn Hearts, 292
Soft and Chewy Chocolate Chip Cookies, 304
Star Puzzle Decorations, 280
Strawberry-Almond Crumble Bars, 305
Sugar and Spice Candied Walnuts, 308
Sweetheart Cookie Bouquet, 272
Two-in-One Holiday Bars, 297

**ground beef**
appetizers & snacks
Bacon-Cheeseburger Calzones, 8
Bourbon Cocktail Meatballs, 148
Crescent Sloppy Joes, 26
Picadillo Empanadas, 34
Pizza Crisps, 36
Slow Cooker Spicy Cheeseburger
    Nachos, 33
bread
Meatball Bubble Biscuits, 51
main dishes
Crescent-Topped Burger Bake, 119
Italian Cheese-Stuffed Meat Loaf, 119
Italian Square Meatballs, 148
Layered Italian Meat Loaf, 116
Polka Dot Meat Loaf, 135
Rolled Italian Meat Loaf, 129
Stuffed Cabbage Rolls, 128
Sweet-and-Sour Meat Loaf, 100
Tomato-Basil Meat Loaves, 111
sandwiches
Grilled Stuffed Pizza Burgers, 157
Sloppy Joe Biscuit Rounds, 156
side
Crispy-Topped Meatballs and Baked
    Beans, 86

**ham**
breads
Ham and Swiss Double Pinwheels, 144

## ham *(continued)*

breakfast & brunch
Ham 'n Cheese Omelet Bake, 183
Ham Frittata, 190
main dishes
Stuffed Chicken Breasts Cordon Bleu, 112
Tiny Ham and Pineapple Pot Pies, 98
sandwiches
Chicken Cordon Bleu Sandwich Ring, 150
Flaky Ham and Turkey Sandwich Slices, 151
Ham and Cheese Crescent Sandwiches, 30
Mexican Ham and Cheese, 171
soup
Ham and Asparagus Chowder, 79

## honey

Honey-Mustard Chicken Salad, 85
Honey-Mustard Sweet Onion Blossoms, 29
Honeyed Pumpkin Pie with Broiled Praline
   Topping, 251
Oats 'n Honey Granola Pie, 259
Speedy Honey-Lime Fruit Salad, 82

## lemons

Lemon-Almond Breakfast Pastry, 61
Lemon Cheesecake Tarts, 240
Lemon-Glazed Pistachio Bars, 217
Lemon Mini Tarts, 250
Lemon-Pineapple Dessert Squares, 239
Lemon Surprise Coffee Cake, 46
Poppin' Fresh® Citrus-Glazed Crullers, 177
So-Easy Lemon Bars, 228

## limes

Chile-Lime Shrimp with Creamy Chipotle
   Dip, 21
Citrus Gazpacho with Honey-Lime
   Cream, 27
Lime Angel Food Cake Roll, 260
Lime-Kiwi Cloud with Strawberry
   Sauce, 253
Speedy Honey-Lime Fruit Salad, 82

## marshmallows

Hidden Marshmallow Chippers, 218
Marshmallow Melties, 299
Marshmallow Peanut Blossoms, 214
Marshmallow Santas, 271
Monkey Cereal Bars, 204
Puffy Pink Popcorn Hearts, 292

## mint

Creamy Chocolate-Mint Pie, 254
Mango-Mint Fruit Dip, 19
Mint-in-the-Middle Brownies, 233
Mint Meringue Parfaits, 282
Peppermint-Fudge Pie, 264
Peppermint Mousse Cups, 248

## mushrooms

Individual Beef Wellingtons with Madeira
   Sauce, 10
Sausage Ravioli Casserole, 134
Squash and Mushroom Soup, 65

## nuts & peanut butter

Almond Scones, 55
Apricot-Almond Coffee Cake, 44
Banana Peanut Butter Bread, 302
Banana-Walnut Brunch Squares, 176
Caramel and Nut Diamond Delights, 219
Cereal-Almond Brittle, 310
Cherry-Macaroon Bars, 232
Chicken Saté with Spicy Peanut Sauce, 139
Chocolate-Almond Layered Hearts, 214
Chocolate Swirl Almond Toffee, 294
Cinnamon-Fruit Snack Mix, 186
Cinnamon-Toffee Pecan Cookies, 206
Easy Baklava Bars, 222
Fire-It-Up Snack Mix, 301
Glazed Peanut Butter Cups, 225
Glazed Pecans, 307
Great Day Granola, 302
Lemon-Glazed Pistachio Bars, 217
Maple Pecan Crescent Twists, 41
Maple-Walnut-Pumpkin Pie, 261
Marshmallow Peanut Blossoms, 214
No-Bake Cereal Bars, 210
Nutty Little Mice, 272
Oh-So-Easy Chocolate-Peanut-Caramel
   Bars, 222
Orange-Pecan Cookies, 296
Orangeburst Cookie Bars, 224
Peanut Butter Cookie Bark, 288
Peanut Butter Cup Cookies, 230
Peanutty Rice Cake Rounds, 23
Poppin' Fresh® Double-Decker
   Cookies, 223
Quick Cashew Cookies with Brown Butter
   Icing, 216
Strawberry-Almond Crumble Bars, 305
Sugar and Spice Candied Walnuts, 308
Sweet 'n Salty Crunch Bars, 231
Thai Appetizer Pizza, 164

## oats

Apple-Raspberry Cookie Cobbler, 253
Chocolate-Caramel Oatmeal
   Thumbprints, 307
Coffee Shop Cookies, 233
Easy Baklava Bars, 222
Oats 'n Honey Granola Pie, 259
Rhubarb and Strawberry Cornbread
   Cobbler, 246

## onions

Chive and Onion Mashed Potato
   Triangles, 6

Honey-Mustard Sweet Onion Blossoms, 29
Onion-Cheese Custard Tartlets, 178
Pepper-Rubbed Steaks with Caramelized
   Onions, 115

## oranges

Chipotle Pico de Gallo, 311
Chocolate-Orange Shortbread Bites, 52
Cranberry-Orange Biscotti, 299
Fresh Fruit Orange Fizz, 185
Fresh Orange Cookies, 230
Orange Chicken Stir-Fry, 96
Orange-Pecan Cookies, 296
Orangeburst Cookie Bars, 224
Poppin' Fresh® Citrus-Glazed Crullers, 177
Strawberry-Orange Butterfly Biscuits, 57

## pasta

Chicken Cordon Bleu Lasagna, 99
Herbed Alfredo Sauce over Linguine, 94
Italian Vegetarian Lasagna, 118
Lasagna Roll-Ups, 113
Mac 'n Cheese Soup, 88
Manicotti Al Forno, 109
Party Chicken and Pasta Salad, 138
Pesto-Chicken Manicotti, 112
Sausage Ravioli Casserole, 134
Seafood and Asparagus Manicotti, 120
Spinach Tortellini Soup, 73
Tomato-Basil Linguine with Chicken, 133

## peppers

Chicken Saté with Spicy Peanut Sauce, 139
Chicken Waikiki, 125
Chile-Lime Shrimp with Creamy Chipotle
   Dip, 21
Crescent Nacho Mini Cups, 158
Jerk-Seasoned Chicken and Pepper
   Saute, 131
Mexican Ham and Cheese, 171
Polenta Rounds with Caramelized
   Vegetables, 142
Spicy Chicken Mini Burritos, 12
Three-Pepper Galette, 193

## pies & tarts

Black-Bottom Banana Cream Pie, 267
Creamy Chocolate-Mint Pie, 254
Holly and Eggnog Pie, 241
Honeyed Pumpkin Pie with Broiled Praline
   Topping, 251
Lemon Cheesecake Tarts, 240
Lemon Mini Tarts, 250
Maple-Walnut-Pumpkin Pie, 261
Oats 'n Honey Granola Pie, 259
Peppermint-Fudge Pie, 264
Turtle Cheesecake Tartlets, 247

## pineapple

Kiwi-Pineapple Yogurt Parfaits, 19
Lemon-Pineapple Dessert Squares, 239
Pineapple-Orange Blossoms, 180
Salmon with Lemon Butter and Pineapple Salsa, 99
Sweet and Sour Pork, 104
Tiny Ham and Pineapple Pot Pies, 98

## pork (also see bacon & canadian bacon; ham; sausage & pepperoni)

Creamy Potatoes and Pork Chops, 107
Southwestern Pork and Vegetable Stew, 102
Spinach and Basil-Stuffed Pork Tenderloin, 9
Sweet-and-Sour Meat Loaf, 100
Sweet and Sour Pork, 104
Sweet Plum-Pork Stir-Fry, 123

## potatoes

California Beef Crostini, 170
Cheesy Potatoes, 75
Chive and Onion Mashed Potato Triangles, 69
Creamy Potatoes and Pork Chops, 107
Crescent-Topped Burger Bake, 119
Grilled Caesar Steak and Potato Salad, 80
Ham Frittata, 190
Italian Egg Bake, 181
Layered Picnic Potato Salad, 77
Lentil-Potato Stew, 135
Mini Chicken Pot Pies, 161
Oven-Baked Chicken Nuggets and French Fries, 143
Pot Roast with Sweet Potatoes and Parsnips, 95
Slow Cooker Two-Potato Vegetable Soup, 68
Southwestern Brunch Eggs, 192

## pumpkin

Honeyed Pumpkin Pie with Broiled Praline Topping, 251
Maple-Walnut-Pumpkin Pie, 261
Pumpkin Pie Cream Cups, 245

## raspberries

Apple-Raspberry Cookie Cobbler, 25
Frozen Raspberry Dessert, 242
Raspberry Mousse in Chocolate Cups, 257
White Chocolate Bread Pudding with Red Berry Sauce, 236

## rice

Chicken Waikiki, 125
Orange Chicken Stir-Fry, 96
Peanutty Rice Cake Rounds, 23

Smoked Turkey and Rice Soup, 80
Stuffed Cabbage Rolls, 128
Sweet and Sour Pork, 104
Sweet Plum-Pork Stir-Fry, 123

## salads

Chicken Salad Cups, 78
Cucumber and Tomato Salad Caprese, 89
Gingered Fresh Fruit Salad, 64
Grilled Caesar Steak and Potato Salad, 80
Honey-Mustard Chicken Salad, 85
Layered Picnic Potato Salad, 77
Mojito Shrimp Salad in Biscuit Bowls, 6
Party Chicken and Pasta Salad, 138
Southwestern Shrimp Taco Salad, 90
Speedy Honey-Lime Fruit Salad, 82
Spinach, Strawberry and Grapefruit Toss, 189
Tropical Fruit Salad with Poppy Seed Dressing, 70

## sandwiches

Cheese Mini-wiches, 14
Cheesy Hot Beef Sandwiches, 171
Cheesy Sausage Calzones, 172
Chicken Caesar Sandwich Ring, 155
Chicken Cordon Bleu Sandwich Ring, 150
Flaky Ham and Turkey Sandwich Slices, 151
Greek Kabob Sandwiches, 156
Grilled Spicy Chicken Sandwiches, 163
Grilled Stuffed Pizza Burgers, 157
Ham and Cheese Crescent Sandwiches, 30
Lettuce Wraps, 173
Mexican Ham and Cheese, 171
Pizzazzy Sausage Crescent Sandwiches, 152
Sloppy Joe Biscuit Rounds, 156
Terrific Turkey Burgers, 163
Warm Grilled Veggie Sandwiches, 72

## sausage & pepperoni

appetizers & snacks
Bratwurst Braids, 37
Easy Crescent Dogs™, 9
Layered Italian Dip with Crisp Wontons, 22
bread
Pizza Biscuit Wreath, 48
breakfast & brunch
Flaky Sausage Foldovers, 186
Piglets in Blankets, 194
Sausage and Apple Bake, 182
Spinach Sausage Brunch Casserole, 185
main dishes
Cheese-Stuffed Pizza, 152
Italian Square Meatballs, 148
Manicotti Al Forno, 109
Rolled Italian Meat Loaf, 129
Sausage Ravioli Casserole, 134

## sandwiches

Cheesy Sausage Calzones, 172
Pizza in a Crescent, 141
Pizzazzy Sausage Crescent Sandwiches, 152

## side dishes (also see salads; soups & chili)

Baked Tomatoes with Zucchini, 76
Carved Watermelon Bowl, 69
Cheesy Potatoes, 75
Chive and Onion Mashed Potato Triangles, 69
Crispy-Topped Meatballs and Baked Beans, 86
Fresh Sugar Snaps with Sesame, 85
Mexicorn®-Topped Tomatoes, 71
Orange-Caramelized Squash Rings, 72
Warm Grilled Veggie Sandwiches, 72

## snack mixes

Cinnamon-Fruit Snack Mix, 186
Fire-It-Up Snack Mix, 301
Great Day Granola, 302

## soups & chili

Bean and Barley Vegetable Soup, 66
Broccoli Alfredo Soup, 87
Chicken Soup Italiano, 83
Chili Con Crescent Snacks, 9
Citrus Gazpacho with Honey-Lime Cream, 27
Easy Chunky Tomato Soup, 91
Ham and Asparagus Chowder, 79
Hearty Multi-Bean Chili, 127
Mac 'n Cheese Soup, 88
Mixed Vegetable Clam Chowder, 88
Slow Cooker Two-Potato Vegetable Soup, 68
Smoked Turkey and Rice Soup, 80
Spinach Tortellini Soup, 73
Squash and Mushroom Soup, 65
White Chicken Chili, 79
Zesty Tomato-Crab Bisque, 75

## spinach

Festive Spinach Dip, 30
Layered Italian Meat Loaf, 116
Spinach and Basil-Stuffed Pork Tenderloin, 97
Spinach Sausage Brunch Casserole, 185
Spinach, Strawberry and Grapefruit Toss, 189
Spinach-Tomato Frittata, 194
Spinach Tortellini Soup, 73

## squash

Baked Tomatoes with Zucchini, 76

**squash** (continued)
Fresh Tomato-Basil Caprese Kabobs, 151
Orange-Caramelized Squash Rings, 72
Squash and Mushroom Soup, 65

**strawberries**
Banana-Strawberry Muffins, 60
Dipped Cream Cheese Strawberries, 242
Grands® Strawberry Shortcakes, 237
Lime-Kiwi Cloud with Strawberry
    Sauce, 253
Mascarpone-Filled Fresh Strawberries, 256
Rhubarb and Strawberry Cornbread
    Cobbler, 246
Spinach, Strawberry and Grapefruit
    Toss, 189
Strawberry-Almond Crumble Bars, 305
Strawberry-Orange Butterfly Biscuits, 57
Strawberry-Orange Fruit Dip, 33
Strawberry-Rhubarb Meringue Clouds, 289
Sugar Cookie Shortcake, 207

**tomatoes**
Baked Tomatoes with Zucchini, 76
Cucumber and Tomato Salad Caprese, 89
Easy Chunky Tomato Soup, 91
Fresh Tomato-Basil Caprese Kabobs, 151
Mexicorn®-Topped Tomatoes, 71
Spanish Salsa with Crispy French Bread, 32
Spinach-Tomato Frittata, 194
Tomato-Basil Linguine with Chicken, 133
Tomato-Basil Meat Loaves, 111
Zesty Tomato-Crab Bisque, 75

**turkey**
main dishes
Lasagna Roll-Ups, 113
Patchwork Pot Pie, 126
sandwiches
Flaky Ham and Turkey Sandwich Slices, 151
Terrific Turkey Burgers, 163
soup
Smoked Turkey and Rice Soup, 80

**vegetables** (also see specific kinds)
Bean and Barley Vegetable Soup, 66
Broccoli Alfredo Soup, 87
Chipotle Pico de Gallo, 311
Cucumber and Tomato Salad Caprese, 89
Cucumber-Hummus Stacks, 24
Fresh Sugar Snaps with Sesame, 85
Greek Kabob Sandwiches, 156
Italian Vegetarian Lasagna, 118
Lettuce Wraps, 173
Mixed Vegetable Clam Chowder, 88
Slow Cooker Two-Potato Vegetable
    Soup, 68
Southwestern Pork and Vegetable
    Stew, 102
Stuffed Cabbage Rolls, 128
Stuffed Cucumber Snacks, 14
Warm Grilled Veggie Sandwiches, 72

# alphabetical index

**a**
Almond Holly Wreaths, 200
Almond Scones, 55
Apple-Cream Cheese Muffins, 188
Apple-Raspberry Cookie Cobbler, 253
Apple Snack Stacks, 21
Apricot-Almond Coffee Cake, 44
Apricot-Glazed Chicken Breasts with
    Almond Couscous, 124
Artichoke-Cheese Braids, 45
Asparagus Melts with Horseradish
    Sauce, 29

**b**
Bacon-Cheddar Pinwheels, 167
Bacon-Cheeseburger Calzones, 8
Bacon-Crab Dip, 35
Bagel Nachos, 167
Baja Pie, 108
Baked Tomatoes with Zucchini, 76
Banana-Chocolate-Caramel Cake, 261
Banana Peanut Butter Bread, 302
Banana-Strawberry Muffins, 60
Banana-Walnut Brunch Squares, 176
Basil and Havarti Cheese Pinwheels, 169
Bean and Barley Vegetable Soup, 66
Berry Sherbet Punch, 25
Black-Bottom Banana Cream Pie, 267
Blueberry-Pomegranate Smoothies, 15
Bourbon Cocktail Meatballs, 148

Bratwurst Braids, 37
Brickle Bars, 209
Broccoli Alfredo Soup, 87
Brownie Sundae Pizza, 271
Buffalo Chicken Pinwheels, 13

**c**
California Beef Crostini, 170
Candy Bar-Frosted Chippers, 205
Candy Cane Cookie Box, 276
Caramel and Nut Diamond Delights, 219
Carousel Cupcakes, 274
Carved Watermelon Bowl, 69
Cereal-Almond Brittle, 310
Charming Cheerios® Necklace, 308
Cheddar Twisters, 54
Cheese Crescent Triangles, 42
Cheese Mini-wiches, 144
Cheese Steak Crescent Braids, 59
Cheese-Stuffed Pizza, 152
Cheesy Apple Chunk Bagels, 197
Cheesy Chicken and Artichoke Bites, 168
Cheesy Fish Stick Taco Dogs, 18
Cheesy Hot Beef Sandwiches, 171
Cheesy Potatoes, 75
Cheesy Sausage Calzones, 172
Cherry Chocolate Biscotti, 300
Cherry Chocolate Blossoms, 213
Cherry-Chocolate Chip Cookies, 218
Cherry Christmas Trifle, 250

Cherry Cream Cheese Coffee Cake, 52
Cherry-Macaroon Bars, 232
Chicken and Blue Cheese Bundles, 28
Chicken Caesar Sandwich Ring, 155
Chicken-Chile Casserole, 124
Chicken Cordon Bleu Lasagna, 99
Chicken Cordon Bleu Sandwich Ring, 150
Chicken Crescent Pot Stickers, 16
Chicken Phyllo Bundles, 100
Chicken Salad Cups, 78
Chicken Saté with Spicy Peanut Sauce, 139
Chicken Soup Italiano, 83
Chicken Waikiki, 125
Chile-Lime Shrimp with Creamy Chipotle
    Dip, 21
Chili con Crescent Snacks, 9
Chipotle Pico de Gallo, 311
Chive and Onion Mashed Potato
    Triangles, 69
Chive Crescents, 46
Chocolate-Almond Layered Hearts, 214
Chocolate Candy Cupcakes, 287
Chocolate-Caramel Oatmeal
    Thumbprints, 307
Chocolate Chip-Almond-Cherry Cups, 209
Chocolate Chip Cheesecake Bars, 258
Chocolate-Covered Cheesecake Trees, 279
Chocolate Mousse Cones, 249
Chocolate-Orange Shortbread Bites, 52
Chocolate Supreme Fondue, 265
Chocolate Swirl Almond Toffee, 294

Christmas Cookie Meringues, 277
Christmas Fruitcake Braid, 294
Christmas Ornament Cookies, 226
Cinnamon-Fruit Snack Mix, 186
Cinnamon-Toffee Pecan Cookies, 206
Cinnamon Twisties, 181
Citrus Gazpacho with Honey-Lime
    Cream, 27
Coffee Shop Cookies, 233
Confetti Snowman Cake, 274
Cookie Crumb Truffle Mice, 293
Cookie Dough Ice Cream Dessert, 246
Cookie Ice Cream-a-Rounds, 262
Cookie Pizza, 221
Cornish Hens with Apple-Raisin
    Stuffing, 122
Country French Apple Crescent
    Casserole, 262
Cranberry Cornmeal Torte, 238
Cranberry-Glazed Apple Dumplings, 266
Cranberry-Orange Biscotti, 299
Cream Cheese Brownie Cups, 258
Creamy Chocolate-Mint Pie, 254
Creamy Potatoes and Pork Chops, 107
Crescent Bear Claws, 56
Crescent Nacho Mini Cups, 158
Crescent Sloppy Joes, 26
Crescent-Topped Burger Bake, 119
Crescent-Wrapped Brie, 166
Crispy-Topped Meatballs and Baked
    Beans, 86
Cucumber and Tomato Salad Caprese, 89
Cucumber-Hummus Stacks, 24
Cupcake Strawberries, 266

d
Dipped Cream Cheese Strawberries, 242
Double Chocolate-Caramel-Fudge
    Brownies, 212

e
Easy-As-Peach-Pie Wedges, 249
Easy Baklava Bars, 222
Easy Buffalo Chicken Stromboli, 149
Easy Chicken Chilaquiles Skillet, 120
Easy Chunky Tomato Soup, 91
Easy Crescent Dogs™, 9
Easy Gumdrop Whirligigs, 289
Elegant Cheese and Fruit Platter, 155

f
Family Tree Cake, 280
Festive Fruitcake Treats, 300
Festive Shrimp Pinwheels, 164
Festive Spinach Dip, 30
Fire-It-Up Snack Mix, 301

Fish Fillets Primavera, 114
Fish Fillets with Herbed Tartar Sauce, 127
Flaky Ham and Turkey Sandwich Slices, 151
Flaky Sausage Foldovers, 186
Flip-Flop Fun Cookies, 229
Fresh Fruit Orange Fizz, 185
Fresh Orange Cookies, 230
Fresh Sugar Snaps with Sesame, 85
Fresh Tomato-Basil Caprese Kabobs, 151
Frozen Raspberry Dessert, 242

g
Garlic and Herb Beef Appetizers, 172
Giant Cinnamon-Cheese Danish, 43
Ginger Sandwich Cookies, 202
Gingerbread Bran Muffins, 49
Gingerbread Pinwheels, 229
Gingerbread Teddies, 305
Gingered Fresh Fruit Salad, 64
Glazed Peanut Butter Cups, 225
Glazed Pecans, 307
Grands® Strawberry Shortcakes, 237
Granola-Almond Macaroons, 226
Granola Fruit Kabobs, 189
Grapefruit Citrus Cooler, 33
Great Day Granola, 302
Greek Kabob Sandwiches, 156
Grilled Caesar Steak and Potato Salad, 80
Grilled Chicken-Asparagus Bundles, 117
Grilled Spicy Chicken Sandwiches, 163
Grilled Stuffed Pizza Burgers, 157
Gumdrop Spice Muffins, 60

h
Ham and Asparagus Chowder, 79
Ham and Cheese Crescent Sandwiches, 30
Ham 'n Cheese Omelet Bake, 183
Ham and Swiss Double Pinwheels, 144
Ham Frittata, 190
Happy Face Cookie Pops, 277
Hearty Multi-Bean Chili, 127
Heavenly Layered Bars, 202
Herb-Stuffed Flank Steak, 111
Herbed Alfredo Sauce Over Linguine, 94
Hidden Marshmallow Chippers, 218
Holly and Eggnog Pie, 241
Honey-Mustard Chicken Salad, 85
Honey-Mustard Sweet Onion Blossoms, 29
Honeyed Pumpkin Pie with Broiled Praline
    Topping, 251
Hot Spiced Cranberry Cider, 30

i
Individual Beef Wellingtons with Madeira
    Sauce, 10
Individual Pastrami Braids, 146

Italian Cheese-Stuffed Meat Loaf, 119
Italian Dinner Frittata, 132
Italian Egg Bake, 181
Italian Square Meatballs, 148
Italian Vegetarian Lasagna, 118

j
Jerk-Seasoned Chicken and Pepper Saute,
    131

k
Kiwi-Pineapple Yogurt Parfaits, 197

l
Lasagna Roll-Ups, 113
Layered Christmas Cake, 282
Layered Italian Dip with Crisp Wontons, 22
Layered Italian Meat Loaf, 116
Layered Picnic Potato Salad, 77
Leek Quiche, 178
Lemon-Almond Breakfast Pastry, 61
Lemon Cheesecake Tarts, 240
Lemon-Ginger Thumbprints, 211
Lemon-Glazed Pistachio Bars, 217
Lemon Mini Tarts, 250
Lemon-Pineapple Dessert Squares, 239
Lemon Surprise Coffee Cake, 46
Lentil-Potato Stew, 135
Lettuce Wraps, 173
Lime Angel Food Cake Roll, 260
Lime-Kiwi Cloud with Strawberry
    Sauce, 253

m
Mac 'n Cheese Soup, 88
Macaroon-Topped Sugar Cookies, 201
Mango-Mint Fruit Dip, 19
Manicotti Al Forno, 109
Maple Pecan Crescent Twists, 41
Maple-Walnut-Pumpkin Pie, 261
Marshmallow Melties, 299
Marshmallow Peanut Blossoms, 214
Marshmallow Santas, 271
Marzipan Snow People, 281
Mascarpone-Filled Fresh Strawberries, 256
Meatball Bubble Biscuits, 51
Mediterranean Chicken Bake, 132
Mexican Confetti Pinwheels, 159
Mexican Ham and Cheese, 171
Mexicorn®-Topped Tomatoes, 71
Mini Beef and Provolone Crescents, 153
Mini Buffalo Chicken Pastries, 160
Mini Chicken Pot Pies, 161
Mini Soft Pretzels and Dip, 40
Mint-in-the-Middle Brownies, 233
Mint Meringue Parfaits, 282

**m** *(continued)*

Mixed Vegetable Clam Chowder, 88
Mocha Mix, 308
Mojito Shrimp Salad in Biscuit Bowls, 66
Molasses Raisin Cookies, 309
Monkey Cereal Bars, 204
Mrs. Claus' Mittens, 273

**n**

No-Bake Cereal Bars, 210
Nutty Little Mice, 272

**o**

Oats 'n Honey Granola Pie, 259
Oh-So-Easy Chocolate-Peanut-Caramel Bars, 222
Onion-Cheese Custard Tartlets, 178
Orange-Caramelized Squash Rings, 72
Orange Chicken Stir-Fry, 96
Orange-Pecan Cookies, 296
Orange Soda Grilled Chicken, 131
Orangeburst Cookie Bars, 224
Oven-Baked Chicken Nuggets and French Fries, 143

**p**

Parmesan Rounds with Lox, 147
Party Chicken and Pasta Salad, 138
Patchwork Pot Pie, 126
Peach Crescent Palmiers, 59
Peanut Butter Cookie Bark, 288
Peanut Butter Cup Cookies, 230
Peanutty Rice Cake Rounds, 23
Pepper-Rubbed Steaks with Caramelized Onions, 115
Peppermint-Fudge Pie, 264
Peppermint Mousse Cups, 248
Pesto Cheese Bread, 50
Pesto-Chicken Manicotti, 112
Picadillo Empanadas, 34
Piglets in Blankets, 194
Pineapple-Orange Blossoms, 180
Pita Triangles with Olive Relish, 140
Pizza Biscuit Wreath, 48
Pizza Crisps, 36
Pizza in a Crescent, 141
Pizzazzy Sausage Crescent Sandwiches, 152
Polenta Rounds with Caramelized Vegetables, 142
Polka Dot Meat Loaf, 135
Polvorones Cookies, 213
Poppin' Fresh® Citrus-Glazed Crullers, 177
Poppin' Fresh® Double-Decker Cookies, 223

Pot Roast with Sweet Potatoes and Parsnips, 95
Pretzel Butterflies, 25
Provolone and Pesto Quiche, 190
Puffy Pink Popcorn Hearts, 292
Pumpkin Pie Cream Cups, 245

**q**

Quick Cashew Cookies with Brown Butter Icing, 216
Quick Cookie Bars, 221
Quick Snickerdoodles, 233

**r**

Ranch Deviled Eggs, 17
Raspberry Mousse in Chocolate Cups, 257
Rhubarb and Strawberry Cornbread Cobbler, 246
Roast Beef Rolls, 37
Roast Cornish Hen with Vegetables, 103
Rolled Italian Meat Loaf, 129
Royal Marble Cheesecake, 244
Rudolph Nibblers with Cinnamon-Orange Dip, 25

**s**

Salmon with Lemon Butter and Pineapple Salsa, 99
Sausage and Apple Bake, 182
Sausage Ravioli Casserole, 134
Scrambled Egg-Parmesan Soft Crust Pizza, 187
Seafood and Asparagus Manicotti, 120
Seaside Pudding Cups, 287
Secret Santa Trees, 284
Sesame Asian Grilled Cornish Hen Halves, 104
Short Ribs in Red Wine, 106
Simply Super Crescent Cinnamon Rolls, 49
Sloppy Joe Biscuit Rounds, 156
Slow Cooker Spicy Cheeseburger Nachos, 33
Slow Cooker Two-Potato Vegetable Soup, 68
Smoked Salmon Pinwheels, 162
Smoked Turkey and Rice Soup, 80
So-Easy Lemon Bars, 228
Soft and Chewy Chocolate Chip Cookies, 304
Southwestern Brunch Eggs, 192
Southwestern Chili Shrimp, 105
Southwestern Pork and Vegetable Stew, 102
Southwestern Shrimp Taco Salad, 90
Spanish Salsa with Crispy French Bread, 32
Speedy Honey-Lime Fruit Salad, 82

Spicy Chicken Mini Burritos, 12
Spinach and Basil-Stuffed Pork Tenderloin, 97
Spinach Sausage Brunch Casserole, 185
Spinach, Strawberry and Grapefruit Toss, 189
Spinach-Tomato Frittata, 194
Spinach Tortellini Soup, 73
Squash and Mushroom Soup, 65
Star Puzzle Decorations, 280
Strawberry-Almond Crumble Bars, 305
Strawberry-Orange Butterfly Biscuits, 57
Strawberry-Orange Fruit Dip, 33
Strawberry-Rhubarb Meringue Clouds, 289
Stuffed Cabbage Rolls, 128
Stuffed Chicken Breasts Cordon Bleu, 112
Stuffed Cucumber Snacks, 14
Sugar and Spice Candied Walnuts, 308
Sugar Cookie Shortcake, 207
Sweet 'n Salty Crunch Bars, 231
Sweet-and-Sour Meat Loaf, 100
Sweet and Sour Pork, 104
Sweet Plum-Pork Stir-Fry, 123
Sweetheart Cookie Bouquet, 272

**t**

Taco Chicken Wraps, 143
Terrific Turkey Burgers, 163
Thai Appetizer Pizza, 164
Three-Pepper Galette, 193
Thumbprint Heart Sugar Cookies, 210
Tiny Ham and Pineapple Pot Pies, 98
Tiramisu Bites, 255
Tomato-Basil Linguine with Chicken, 133
Tomato-Basil Meat Loaves, 111
Topped Mini Quiches, 195
Tropical Cheesecake Bars, 205
Tropical Fruit Salad with Poppy Seed Dressing, 70
Turtle Cheesecake Tartlets, 247
Two-in-One Holiday Bars, 297

**w**

Warm Grilled Veggie Sandwiches, 72
White Chicken Chili, 79
White Chocolate Bread Pudding with Red Berry Sauce, 236
White Chocolate Gingerbread Bears, 285

**z**

Zesty Tomato-Crab Bisque, 75